Burn It Down!

Burn It Down!

Feminist Manifestos
for the Revolution

Edited by
Breanne Fahs

VERSO
London • New York

First published by Verso 2020
The collection © Breanne Fahs 2020
The contributions © The contributors 2020
Introduction © Breanne Fahs 2020

Verso
UK: 6 Meard Street, London W1F 0EG
US: 20 Jay Street, Suite 1010, Brooklyn, NY 11201
versobooks.com

Verso is the imprint of New Left Books

ISBN-13: 978-1-78873-538-4
ISBN-13: 978-1-78873-541-4 (US EBK)
ISBN-13: 978-1-78873-540-7 (UK EBK)

British Library Cataloguing in Publication Data
A catalogue record for this book is available from the British Library

Library of Congress Cataloging-in-Publication Data
A catalog record for this book is available from the Library of Congress

Typeset in Minion by MJ&N Gavan, Truro, Cornwall
Printed and bound by CPI Group (UK) Ltd, Croydon CR0 4YY

For Sarah Stage

It is not the anger of other women that will destroy us but our refusals to stand still, to listen to its rhythms, to learn within it, to move beyond the manner of presentation to the substance, to tap that anger as an important source of empowerment.

—Audre Lorde, *Sister Outsider*

Someone will pull you from the fire, someone else wrap you in flames.

—Kim Addonizio, *Mortal Trash*

NOW THAT YOU HAVE TOUCHED THE WOMEN,
YOU HAVE STRUCK A ROCK;
YOU HAVE DISLODGED A BOULDER;
YOU WILL BE CRUSHED.

—Anti-Apartheid Song, South Africa
Women's Day, August 9, 1956

Contents

II. ANTICAPITALIST/ANARCHIST

III. ANGRY/VIOLENT

IV. INDIGENOUS/WOMEN OF COLOR

Introduction. The Bleeding Edge: On the Necessity of Feminist Manifestos

Breanne Fahs

> Life in this society being, at best, an utter bore and no aspect of society being at all relevant to women, there remains to civic-minded, responsible, thrill-seeking females only to overthrow the government, eliminate the money system, institute complete automation and destroy the male sex.

So begins Valerie Solanas's 1967 *SCUM Manifesto*, with one of the all-time great declarations of war against the patriarchal status quo. Solanas imagined not only an entirely new world—where men no longer defined Great Art, Money, Government, and Culture—but also one populated by thrill-seeking females: "dominant, secure, self-confident, nasty, violent, selfish, independent, proud, thrill-seeking, free-wheeling, arrogant females, who consider themselves fit to rule the universe, who have freewheeled to the limits of this 'society,' and are ready to wheel on to something far beyond what it has to offer."[1]

She wrote the manifesto for those in the gutter—"whores, dykes, criminals, and homicidal maniacs"—wholly refusing to pander to "nice, passive, accepting, 'cultivated,' polite, dignified, subdued, dependent, scared, mindless, insecure, approval-seeking Daddy's Girls."[2]

---

1 Valerie Solanas, *SCUM Manifesto*, San Francisco: AK Press, 1996, 37. The text was originally self-published in 1967.
2 Ibid.

Feminist manifestos exploded onto the scene from 1967 to 1971, a period marked by rampant sexism, emerging feminist resistance, consciousness-raising, and collective organizing. Building on the momentum of the civil rights movement, the feminist revolts of the late 1960s paved the way for decades of feminist activism that followed. The validation of women's anger in the late 1960s—a cultural zeitgeist moment that recognized women as, finally, fed up and truly *enraged*— made it possible for women to push back against cultural pressures for politeness and respectability. Instead, they fumed and ranted, scuffled and shouted, locked arms and marched. The sort of feminism found in early manifestos featured a starkly different brand of feminism from the more likeable, friendly, and benign one we have come to know today in institutions like education, government, and corporate leadership. Second-wave feminist manifestos honored a sweaty, frothing, high-stakes feminist anger that swept through the writing. Their words burn and simmer even today, giving them an unexpected freshness.

And so feminism and its explosive anger have borne many fruits, owed in large part to feminism's politics of disruption.[3] Women today have access to domestic violence shelters and federally supported (albeit often unpaid) family leave time. Women have far more financial rights than previous generations, particularly with regard to loans, inheritances, and owning businesses. Women's studies programs, though dwindling in numbers, offer an abundance of courses on a wide range of topics such as gender, race, class, sexuality, identity, politics, bodies, technology, communication, and human rights. As of this writing (Fall 2019), abortion is still legal (though in jeopardy) in the United States, and abortion rights have expanded throughout the world. Women have more control than previous generations over their reproductive decisions and parenting options. A huge shift toward gender equality for domestic work and parenting labor has begun. Increasing numbers of museum exhibitions and cultural events feature feminist politics and ideologies. Sexual freedoms have expanded, even as new challenges present themselves. Record numbers of women now represent us in both state-level and federal-level governmental offices.

---

3 Holly J. McCammon, Erin M. Bergner, and Sandra C. Arch, "Are You One of Those Women? Within-Movement Conflict, Radical Flank Effects, and Social Movement Political Outcomes," *Mobilization: An International Quarterly* 20: 2, 2015, 157–78.

The percentage of women in the workforce and in higher education consistently has increased.

And yet, as if living out in real time Jeanette Winterson's claim that "I seem to have run in a great circle, and met myself again on the starting line," we have returned again to a period of cultural reckoning.[4] On the one hand, we better understand the necessity of collective movements and intermovement solidarity; people march side by side with those who have different stakes in the game and have vastly different perspectives and reasons for anger. Within universities, we now study all sorts of social identities and bodies in academic fields—queer studies, ethnic studies, women and gender studies, American studies, disability studies, and fat studies are becoming more firmly entrenched within the academy. People who once stood on the sidelines are jumping into the fray, escorting women into Planned Parenthood clinics, organizing with their neighbors against police brutality, reading anarchist and anticapitalist books, fighting back against transphobic policies and politics, seeking political office or new positions of power, and making revolutionary art in their basements. Many of the oppressive conditions faced by second-wave feminist activists now seem laughably outdated and happily "in the past." On the other hand, the reinvigoration of misogyny and racism as institutionalized practices has sounded new alarm bells. An eerily familiar set of conditions has now presented itself, dominated by financial precarity, tense gender relations, racialized violence, rampant homophobia, public and unapologetic victim blaming, and ever-worsening class inequalities. We have met ourselves again on the starting line, once again up against the behemoths of greedy capitalism, selfish conservativism, anti-intellectual masculinity, and increasingly dire conditions for nearly all oppressed people.

In many ways, I assembled this book not to entertain or to amuse, but because we *need* this kind of work in our lives. Feminist manifestos are a necessity in times of great social stress. How else are we to make sense of our own anger, our sense of confusion and implosion, our imminent feelings of doom and stifled possibilities? The urgency of manifestos—that clear sense that they sit right on the cutting edge—leaves a palpable feeling that the ink has yet to dry, that we are, as Julian

---

4 Jeanette Winterson, *Oranges Are Not the Only Fruit*, New York: Grove Press, 1985, 173.

Hanna writes, on the "bleeding edge" of things.[5] Regardless of when they were written, manifestos pulsate with newness and freshness. They pry open the eyes we would rather shut, forcing us to reckon with the scummy, dirty, awful truths we would rather not face. And if ever there was a time for a collection of feminist manifestos, if ever it felt *necessary* to compile documents that celebrate women's rage, *now* is that time.

The Manifesto

Full of contradictions, ironies, and clashes, manifestos operate on unsteady ground. The genre combines the romantic quality of dreamers and artists imagining something new and whimsical together with the crushing power of a Mack truck bulldozing over established traditions, trashing accepted modes of thought, and eradicating the past. Manifestos do the transformative work of hoping *and* destroying, reflecting *and* violently ending things. As Hanna wrote, "Part of the attraction of the manifesto is that it remains a surprisingly complex and often paradoxical genre: flippant and sincere, prickly and smooth, logical and absurd, material and immaterial, shallow and profound."[6] This complexity arises in part because manifestos have no reverence for the past, no homage to what has come before. They want only what is *new*, of the *now*, in the *present tense*, and they want it immediately.

This urgency of manifestos often veers into outright nihilism: In 1909, the Futurists expected the next generation to overthrow them: "Younger and stronger men will throw us in the wastebasket like useless manuscripts. We want it to happen!"[7] As many good manifestos do, the Futurists imagined their own demise and expected to be railroaded over by the next generation of writers and thinkers. Good manifestos know that others in the future will annihilate them, too. They do not claim to know things *for all time*; they only claim to know things *for this moment*. They trash and will be trashed.

Manifestos have constituted a notable part of Left History in this way, making room for something new through hot-headed, urgent,

---

5 Julian Hanna, "Manifestos: A Manifesto," *Atlantic*, June 24, 2014, theatlantic.com.
6 Ibid.
7 The Futurists, as quoted in Ibid.

sweeping, radical, revolutionary thinking that marked major breaks with traditionalism and incremental, slow, steady change. Instead, manifestos inject forceful, dramatic claims that could feel strictly performative to the audience if not for the unabashed sincerity of the author's worldview. Manifestos are not merely performance art; the authors mean what they say. And, more importantly, who gets to say things also shifts and changes with manifestos. Manifestos are more often "found" than they are officially published, giving them an ephemeral, unedited, and immediate feel. Once mostly the domain of the art world, manifestos at their core want to radically upend and subvert public consciousness around disempowerment, giving voice to those stripped of social and political power.

Reading manifestos can feel like being on fire. We light up aflame and then are left raw and exposed. Manifestos operate as an infectious, contagious kind of document, one that purposefully ignites readers or listeners with its messages, making little room for disagreement or rational back-and-forth discourse. The manifesto author tells us how to think, assumes we agree with them, and imagines no possibility for refusal or resistance. They do not invite us to carefully piece apart the claims; rather, they want an emotional response. We should laugh, shout, or feel fear. We should imagine the world as the manifesto constructs it. As Charles Jencks wrote, "The genre demands blood."[8] It is not unusual to read manifestos and imagine the imminent importance of one's own annihilation.

History of the Manifesto

Manifestos have, somewhat remarkably, avoided having much of a written history.[9] Corralling them into a collection—this book or any other—feels a bit like rounding up wild, bucking, temperamental horses. Manifestos dislike clean and distant intellectual framing

---

8 Charles Jencks, Preface to *Theories and Manifestos of Contemporary Architecture*, eds. Charles Jencks and Karl Kropf, Chichester, West Sussex: Academy Editions, 1997, xxiii.

9 See Galia Yanoshevsky, "Three Decades of Writing on Manifesto: The Making of a Genre," *Poetics Today* 30: 2, Summer 2009, 257–86, and Janet Lyon, *Manifestoes: Provocations of the Modern*, Ithaca, NY: Cornell University Press, 1999. Yanoshevsky believes manifestos have been overstudied, while Lyon convincingly argues the opposite.

and predigestion, careful editing and savvy marketing. After all, manifestos were "ephemeral, hurled off balconies and out of speeding automobiles,"[10] perhaps never meant for study or careful curation. The history of what manifestos are, what they typically do, and how they travel in time and space presents a curious question: How do we make coherent narratives about documents that are *of the now*, disinterested in canonical categorization, lacking scholarly pedigree (for the most part), and bad-tempered? Manifestos are wonderfully cranky about such questions.

The word *manifesto* seems relatively ubiquitous today, proliferating in all the wrong places: subway advertisements and billboards, fancy perfumes, corporate branding on Pinterest, t-shirts, waiting room magazines, startup company slogans, self-help books, and even bottles of wine.[11] Corporate appropriation of the word *manifesto* has seriously undermined and diluted the potential political impact and significance of the manifesto as a highly charged genre of thinking and writing. Manifestos fit nicely into that corporate model of faux rebellion, so-called good taste, and an imagined lack of mediocrity. Here the radical intention of the manifesto—to break with old and outdated modes of thinking and living—becomes instead a highly corporatized version of resistance, innovation, and enjoyment. Actual manifestos often rail against capitalism and neoliberalism, pushing their own obsolescence, ending the practice of selling anything but the juggernaut force of freedom.

These contradictions—between the genre's purpose and its corporate and popular usurpation—underscore the jagged history of the manifesto and the ease of *mis*understanding manifestos. The manifesto genre is much misunderstood and misrepresented in part because scholars outside of art and art history rarely study or examine manifestos. Further, manifestos are intentionally ephemeral, allowing them to evade the grasp of historians. They invite disorientation and distort time. As Peter Stansill and David Zane Mairowitz wrote, manifestos are often not designed for remembering:

---

10 Hanna, "Manifestos."

11 See Vodafone Advertisement (adforum.com); Yves St. Laurent perfume advertisement (yslbeauty.ca); Pinterest advertising manifestos (pinterest.com); Brands on Fire manifesto (i.pinimg.com); Holly Bourne, *The Manifesto on How to be Interesting*, London: Usborne, 2014. See also Manifesto Wines, manifestowines.com.

perhaps it caught your eye as a flyposter, nailed to a tree, published in a "now-you-see-it-now-you-don't" magazine or news-sheet. It could have been incanted at a wedding service, passed round as trading cards, posted as a chain letter, read on a menu. It may even have whizzed past your head while wrapped round a brick or thrown through an established window.[12]

Given this intentional slipperiness, how, then, do we find manifestos, or know how to historicize them?

We do know that manifestos have made a rather fascinating left-turn in their relatively short history, moving from documents used by kings and rulers to documents used to *overthrow* kings and rulers. Historians note that manifestos have moved from quite conservative (reverent of authority) to revolutionary (refusing any sort of authority) in the last two centuries. For example, the earliest uses of the word *manifesto* appeared in 1775 with conservative intentions. Back then, the manifesto did not advocate for a "collective, revolutionary, and subversive voice"[13] but instead for a "declaration of the will of a sovereign. It is a communication, authored by those in authority, by the state, the military, or the church, to let their subjects know their sovereign intentions and laws."[14] The earliest manifestos starkly contrasted with contemporary manifestos, as the early examples sought to preserve and extend dominant institutions while creating, maintaining, and enacting power over the masses. Far from a lefty genre of disobedience and unruly outrage, early manifestos consolidated state power.

Contemporary manifestos, by contrast, argue against any sort of ruler or authority or boss, using words to explosively resist. They are documents of overthrow and revolution. As Tristan Tzara wrote, "Every page should explode, either because of its staggering absurdity, the enthusiasm of its principles, or its typography."[15] Manifestos rely on words to "do the work of bombs," to use the phrase of scholar Kyra

---

12 Peter Stansill and David Zane Mairowitz, "Foreword," *BAMN (By Any Means Necessary): Outlaw Manifestos and Ephemera, 1965–1970*, New York: Autonomedia, 1999, 13.

13 Martin Puchner, *Poetry of the Revolution; Marx, Manifestos, and the Avant-Gardes*, New Brunswick, NJ: Princeton University Press, 2005, 12.

14 Ibid.

15 Tristan Tzara, Ornella Volta, and Pablo Volta, *Manifesti del Dadaismo e Lapisterie*, Torino: Einaudi, 1964.

Pearson.[16] They explode and implode. The modern manifesto loathes authority altogether and radically asserts its own sense of authority with regard to whether the author has "earned" such authority. In this sense, manifestos from the nineteenth and twentieth centuries—the period when manifestos were taking off politically—fit in with mass cultural and revolutionary moments of working to break old forms and create new ones.

Manifestos came onto the scene as impatient, scrappy, demanding, radical, and impolite. Manifestos as a genre sought something new, something better, even if it meant destroying and smashing the existing social order. They took a repressive, ruling class mode of communication and flipped it on its head. In this way, the manifesto genre seems prone to constant re-evaluation and revamping; it can *become* something else, something new, quite easily and adeptly. Many of the key early manifestos—*The Communist Manifesto* (1848), *The Cartagena Manifesto* (1812), and the *Port Huron Statement* (1962) all served as revolutionary documents reacting to their time and context, drawing from and building on the unsettling times in which they were written.[17] Over time, though, they mean something different at different cultural moments, yet always feel fresh, angry, and newer than they actually are.

To accomplish such a feat requires a certain degree of madness. Mary Ann Caws described manifestos as necessarily mad: "At its most endearing, a manifesto has madness about it. It is peculiar and angry, quirky, or downright crazed. Always opposed to something, particular or general, it has not only to be striking but to stand up straight."[18] I would add that, like madness itself, manifestos straddle the line between completely unreasonable and entirely judicious. No matter how outrageous, they also tell the truth. Manifestos reward the author who embraces her or his own madness: "It takes itself and its own spoof

---

16 Kyra Pearson, "'Words Should do the Work of Bombs': Margaret Cho as Symbolic Assassin," *Women and Language* 32: 1, 2009, 36–43.

17 See Karl Marx and Frederick Engels, *The Communist Manifesto*, Chicago: Charles H. Herr Co., 1906 (Originally published in 1848 as *Manifesto of the Communist Party*). See also Simón Bolívar, *The Cartagena Manifesto* (El Manifiesto de Cartagena), 1812. See also Students for a Democratic Society (SDS), *Port Huron Statement*, 1962.

18 Mary Ann Caws, *Manifesto: A Century of Isms*, Lincoln: University of Nebraska Press, 2000, xxi.

seriously."[19] Real manifestos rely on the style itself to communicate the urgency of the ideas and to performatively engage an audience; in other words, in both style and content, manifestos embody resistance. Caws writes, "[A manifesto] calls for capital letters, loves bigness, demands attention ... going past what is thought of as proper, sane, and literary. Its outreach demands an extravagant self-assurance. *At its peak of performance, its form creates its meaning.*"[20] The manifesto brings forth something new, ushers it into being through sheer willpower and gutsy language. It makes things while shattering the old way of doing things. It radically destroys and rebuilds from the ground up.

In this sense, for feminists, the manifesto became an ideal mode of communication, as women usurped power typically reserved for men, expressed rage and anger typically denied to them, and sought revolutionary goals and principles. Within the manifesto genre, they *could be mad* (both emotionally and psychologically). As such, manifestos require mania and are intentionally and consistently extreme, creating yet another avenue for feminists to both break down and embody notions of the "monstrous feminine." They allow no possibility for equivocation, refutation, or disagreement, shattering possibilities for other ways of seeing. Enamored with the sweeping "we" pronoun, manifestos imagine *everyone* as a member of their audience. *We need ... We are ... We must ... We require ... We feel.* With nothing in moderation, manifestos have contempt for incremental change or measured, careful allowances for disagreement. Instead, the tone becomes "hortatory, contrarian, bullying, rapid-paced"[21] and works by eliminating

> all adjectives or useless words that would slow down the others...
> Stripped to its bare bones, clean as a whistle and as piercing, the
> manifesto is immodest and forceful, exuberant and vivid, attention-
> grabbing. Immediate and urgent, it never mumbles, is always in
> overdose and overdrive.[22]

Operating as a way for women to take power, the genre also insists on its own authority even when it frankly lacks such authority in the most traditional sense (e.g., professionalism, credentialing). Manifesto

---

19 Ibid.
20 Ibid., xx, my emphasis.
21 Ibid., xxi.
22 Ibid.

writers *perform* authority—establishing themselves as speakers, insisting (often through shouting) that their voice has an audience. Manifestos belong to the people. They do not need gatekeeping to allow room for their authority. As such, manifestos emphasize the political qualities of both reading and writing, as the writer (who often lacks social and institutional power but insists on taking it anyway) demands to be heard, and the reader (who often feels at once seduced or perhaps assaulted by the text) is absorbed into the writer's urgent and impatient language. This play on marginality allows people typically without voice to assert and emotionally cry out for radical social change. Manifestos encourage audiences to take (dead) seriously the writer, no matter how marginal. For women, manifestos open a door to authority, rage, and audience—all of which were typically denied to them over the last 200+ years.

The opening of these doors, however, relied on the embrace of total marginality. As radical feminist Ti-Grace Atkinson said, the manifesto is perhaps a "schizophrenic scream,"[23] a call from the extreme edges of society, attention-grabbing of both writer and reader. Its marginality is such that it even literally and materially embodies the margins, as in the case of marginalia (notes on the side of texts) or manifestos written on scraps of paper, pamphlets (seventeenth-century England), in the margins of liner notes (in Refused's *The Shape of Punk to Come*), or on public graffiti.[24] Manifestos make new knowledge possible, knowledge gleaned from "improper" and impolite places, using language deemed obscene or impolite. As Teresa Ebert wrote:

> The manifesto is writing in struggle. It is writing on the edge where textuality is dragged into the streets and language is carried to the barricades. It is writing confronting established practices in order to open up new spaces for oppositional praxis.[25]

---

23 Ti-Grace Atkinson, as quoted in Breanne Fahs, *Valerie Solanas: The Defiant Life of the Woman Who Wrote SCUM (and Shot Andy Warhol)*, New York: Feminist Press, 2014, 312.

24 Craig Castleman, "The Politics of Graffiti," in *That's the Joint! The Hip-Hop Studies Reader*, eds. Murray Forman and Mark Anthony Neal, New York: Psychology Press, 2004, 21–29; Brian Fateau, "'New Noise' Versus the Old Sound: Manifestos and the Shape of Punk to Come," *Popular Music and Society* 35: 4, 2012, 465–82; Lyon, *Manifestoes.*

25 Teresa Ebert, "Manifesto as Theory and Theory as Material Force: Toward a Red Polemic," *JAC* 23: 3, 2003, 553.

Historically, this debunking of ruling ideas, the making of new visions and dreams, gives manifestos a sense of perpetual freshness that has had long-lasting impacts on different historical periods. Consider the case of the *Communist Manifesto*, one of the great nineteenth century historical documents still referenced commonly today. According to Puchner:

> The *Communist Manifesto* influenced the course of history more directly and lastingly than almost any other text. The Paris Commune, the Russian Revolution, and the independence movements in the colonial world are only some of the historical events that were inspired and shaped by this document.[26]

The genre itself allowed for its historical impact; it stripped away the requirements for stuffy and formal ways of communicating in favor of urgent, angry, and revolutionary writing:

> How could a single text achieve such a feat? To be sure, none of these events were thinkable without the histories of capitalism and colonialism or the effects of the two world wars. And yet, these broad historical forces do not explain why it was the *Manifesto*, and not one of its many rival documents, that acquired such central importance. The answer to this question must be sought not so much in the history of revolutions but in the *Manifesto* itself, and it must be sought not only in its content but also in its form.[27]

Manifestos are mighty, pushing forth the dual goals of undermining reality and making a new reality. The manifesto took concrete social problems and infused them with the emotional and *affective* qualities of resistance and revolution. The manifesto did this by uniting previously incompatible fields and practices: "This new genre brought into a novel and startling juncture philosophy and politics, analysis and action, historiography and intervention."[28] Janet Lyon also argued for this strange bringing together of seemingly incompatible goals: "The formal membrane of the manifesto must hold together an unlikely

---

26 Puchner, *Poetry of the Revolution*, 11.
27 Ibid.
28 Ibid.

dyad of idiosyncratic rage and Utopian social scripture, for it aims to programmatize anger as it creates audiences."[29] Further, manifesto authors used hyperbolic rhetoric as the lynchpin for recruiting readers to join a new collective movement and were not particularly interested in aesthetics beyond that.[30] Manifestos were not for the faint of heart; they were not "pretty."

Tracing the history of manifestos has, for all of the reasons outlined above, proven difficult. Even deciding what "counts" as a manifesto brings to light contentious ideas about the manifesto genre and its impact. For example, historians can identify threads and splices of texts that would eventually come to be recognized as "manifesto" in nature—texts that put forth a rambunctious, rebellious, culturally relevant critique, or texts that incited violence or social change, or texts that felt angry or generally intent on urging revolution—but these remnants still render the history of the manifesto as permanently slippery. Scholarly work on manifestos continues to be scarce, suggesting that manifestos have a permanent status as outlaw texts. Often, manifestos are buried in broader inquiries about social movements,[31] and the majority of scholarly work that examines manifestos in any sustained way hides away in doctoral dissertations that never became books or articles.[32]

What counts as the "key manifestos" of the genre's history also brings up difficult questions. Do we call something a manifesto that does not self-identify as a manifesto? Can we retrospectively identify manifestos or manifesto-like documents, and how might this impact the entire study of the manifesto genre? How do we decide which manifestos matter more, or which manifestos will have the most lasting impact? As Ebert writes:

---

29 Janet Lyon, "Transforming Manifestoes: A Second-Wave Problematic," *The Yale Journal of Criticism* 5, 1991, 101.

30 Thomas Reynolds, "'Peculiar, Angry, and Downright Crazed': Exploring Rhetoric in Manifestos," unpublished dissertation, Austin State University, 2010.

31 Ian Summers, "Generic Criticism of Extraordinary Documents: An Inquiry into Manifesto Texts and Genre Scholarship," unpublished master's thesis, University of Alabama, 2013.

32 Elliott C. Adams, "American Feminist Manifestos and the Rhetoric of Whiteness," unpublished dissertation, Bowling Green University, 2006; Jeffrey M. Encke, "Manifestos: A Social History of Proclamation," unpublished dissertation, Columbia University, 2002; Reynolds, "Peculiar, Angry, and Downright Crazed," and Summers, "Generic Criticism of Extraordinary Documents."

The mainstream resistance to these manifestos is no more a matter of authorial insight than is the canonical absorption of more favored manifestos—rather, the cultural incorporation or resistance to specific manifestos is an effort of the historical conditions with which they engage.[33]

What seems relevant today might soon fade away, and what is now hiding in plain sight may suddenly strike us as necessary and all-important in the future.

The Feminism of Againstness

If the manifesto has a particularly obscure history, what then of the feminist manifesto? Until recently, almost nothing had been written about feminist manifestos at all.[34] Perhaps the feminist manifesto poses a different set of questions to us as readers: How can we imagine a place for a new vision of feminism that poses itself as oppositional and defiant, with *againstness* as its key goal? To imagine the essential role of feminist manifestos is to situate an angry, manic, authority-grabbing, insubordinate voice at the center of feminism rather than at its margins. A feminism of againstness values complaint, rage, tension, new forms of solidarity, and radical social change. This reconfiguration also allows us to better consider the very painful ways in which feminist writing and thinking is often dismissed as trivial, overly emotional, and unsophisticated.

In this collection, I argue that we need a feminism full of outbursts and ill-temper, full of "Pussy Grabs Back" and fire in its belly.[35] We

---

33 Ebert, "Manifesto as Theory and Theory as Material Force," 555.

34 Two notable exceptions are Kimber Charles Pearce, "The Radical Feminist Manifesto as Generic Appropriation: Gender, Genre, and Second Wave Resistance," *Southern Communication Journal* 64: 4, 1999, 307–15, and Penny A. Weiss, ed., *Feminist Manifestos: A Global Documentary Reader*, New York: New York University Press, 2018. Weiss focuses mostly on charter documents for women's organizations throughout the world and includes very few documents that are actual manifestos.

35 After a recording of Donald Trump bragging about grabbing women "by the pussy" was widely released in the press, the viral campaign, "Pussy Grabs Back," both in visual form and in music video form, allowed for a collective response of rebellious and angry outrage, something too often squashed by the polite impulses of mainstream feminism. (One especially poignant line of the song said, "The man's been racist as Fuck/But now he's out of luck?/If pussy is his downfall/We'll take it.")

need a feminism of *againstness*, for which the manifesto perfectly fits the bill. As Caws writes, "The manifesto generally proclaims what it wants to oppose, to leave, to defend, to change. Its oppositional tone is constructed of *againstness* and generally in a spirit of a one time only moment."[36] The feminist manifesto invests itself with authority; "the manifesto stands alone, does not need to lean on anything else, demands no other text than itself. Its rules are self-contained, included in its own body."[37] At its best, the feminist manifesto is not only a weapon against patriarchy but a weapon against the worst aspects of feminist politics—it refutes liberal tendencies of moderation and incremental, slow, "wait and be patient" modes of reform. It is a rebuttal to institutional practices of silencing women's voices, and it refuses to ignore anger. It rips down the principles that underlie institutional politeness, women's complicity in their own oppression, and authorial passivity. With renewed attention to the feminist manifesto as full of contradictions and new ways to find voice,[38] the feminist manifesto could inform a feminist politics we can take pride in, one that is rambunctious, impolite, uncompromising, unapologetic, brave, and loud-mouthed.

Many feminist manifestos and their authors have been criticized for attempting to be any of these things and have consequently been discarded as mad, shocking, outrageous, difficult, hateful, and man-hating. Feminist writers have been trashed for criticizing the contemporary patterns of feminist politics that have "rebranded into banality" the goals of feminism.[39] Any efforts to argue against a "feminism is for everybody" lens have typically been swiftly squashed. Feminists constantly deride and degrade each other's work, even as they are derided and degraded by anti-feminist forces with even more vitriol. The growing piles of hate mail and internet trolling of radical feminist writings—particularly manifestos—reveals something of the threat that this work poses to the status quo. Feminist manifestos do not hide behind rarified and obscure language; they pulsate with reality, breaking things.

---

36 Caws, *Manifesto*, xxiii–xxvii.

37 Ibid., xxv.

38 Felicity Colman, "Notes on the Feminist Manifesto: The Strategic Use of Hope," *Journal for Cultural Research* 14: 4, 2010, 375–92; Emily Nussbaum, "The Rebirth of the Feminist Manifesto," *New York Magazine*, October 30, 2011.

39 Suzanne Moore, "It's Time to Get Radical," review of *Why I Am Not a Feminist: A Feminist Manifesto*, Jessa Crispin, *Guardian*, February 17, 2017.

Feminist manifestos level the playing field of knowledge-making, in ways far beyond the inadequate contemporary practices of mere inclusion of intersectional work by diverse scholars. I like to imagine feminist manifestos most basically as a genre of class-based rage, a fight against the ruling class, against unbridled wealth, against the policing of language and text, against the practices that exclude certain kinds of voices and certain kinds of thinking under the guise of respectability and politeness. As Penny Weiss writes:

> manifestos allow us to hear from the professional and the educated, the more privileged and the politically experienced, and also from the battered, the prostituted, and the illiterate, and from the poor, the peasant, the indigenous, and the "untouchable," often while attending the same meeting.[40]

I would add to this that manifestos allow for a real politics of the gutter to emerge—from, as Valerie Solanas writes, "the garbage pail that men have made of the world"—where a trashy, scrappy, fed up, angry vision of tomorrow emerges.[41] As Solanas argues, we need a "fuck-up force."[42]

After all, the feminist manifesto represents a taking of ruling-class, masculinized, and patriarchal power, a usurping of authoritative speech typically ascribed only to wealthy and powerful men.[43] The feminist manifesto is impolite by nature, refusing the very qualities—politeness and deference in particular—that women are socialized to cultivate in themselves; it is frankly impatient, unmotherly, irritated, revolutionary, nasty, ambitious, bossy, and at times violent—all of which constitute traditionally "unfeminine" qualities. (Whether this usurpation has its own hazards is an ongoing point of contention among feminist scholars.)[44] The feminist manifesto takes direct aim at the implicit goals of liberal feminism as necessarily welcoming, polite, and inclusive, instead advocating for a vision of feminism that

---

40 Weiss, *Feminist Manifestos*, 2.
41 Valerie Solanas, "SCUM Ad," *Village Voice*, March 30, 1967.
42 Solanas, *SCUM Manifesto*, 38.
43 Pearce, "The Radical Feminist Manifesto."
44 Natalya Lusty, "Valerie Solanas and the Limits of Speech," *Australian Literary Studies* 24: 3-4, 2009, 144–54; Pearce, "The Radical Feminist Manifesto"; Laura Winkiel, "The 'Sweet Assassin' and the Performative Politics of *SCUM Manifesto*," in *The Queer Sixties*, ed. Patricia J. Smith, New York: Routledge, 1999, 62–85.

is difficult, contentious and unruly. This kind of pushing back against moderate, incremental impulses of liberal feminism is crucial to the continued growth of feminism's edges.[45] In fact, many scholars have argued that having a radical flank of a movement is crucially important for innovating thinking within feminism and for creating a sense of fear among the targets of feminist activism.[46]

Feminist manifestos also reimagine notions of collectivity and solidarity between and among women. As Weiss points out, though feminism itself has been valued as a collective political movement, little attention has been directed toward documents written and ratified collectively. The feminist manifesto—as evident throughout this collection—often has collective authorship by groups of people working together to imagine a new future. As Weiss writes:

> Perhaps we remain convinced that great ideas come from individual geniuses laboring alone in dimly lit libraries... The common representation of collectively authored manifestos as "applied" or "activist" pieces, rather than more highly esteemed "theoretical" pieces, also contributes to our neglect of them.[47]

Feminist manifestos often advance the cause of collective work and collective writing. That said, this collection does not intend to legitimize or formalize the importance of feminist manifestos—that would go against the very nature of them, in fact—but rather to showcase the collective power of reading, absorbing, and engaging with them in groups and clusters. My pitch here is not to ask readers to see feminist manifestos as academically legitimate, but rather, to delegitimize the way that knowledge practices work, particularly those that sideline and trivialize radical feminist writings.

Feminist manifestos argue for a new vision of gender, new roles for women, new identities and postures and stances for people to take on.

---

45 Jennifer Baumgardner and Amy Richard, *Manifesta: Young Women, Feminism, and the Future*, New York: Farrar, Straus, and Giroux, 2000; Anne Sinkey, "The Rhetoric of the Manifesto," unpublished dissertation, Emory University, 2009.

46 McCammon, Bergner, and Arch, "'Are You One of Those Women?'": 157–78; Lorna Weir, "Left Popular Politics in Canadian Feminist Abortion Organizing, 1982–1991," *Feminist Studies* 20: 2, 1994, 249–74.

47 Weiss, *Feminist Manifestos*, 1.

Joreen's *Bitch Manifesto*, for example, argues for the embrace of the word *bitch*:

> Bitches are aggressive, assertive, domineering, overbearing, strong-minded, spiteful, hostile, direct, blunt, candid, obnoxious, thick-skinned, hard-headed, vicious, dogmatic, competent, competitive, pushy, loud-mouthed, independent, stubborn, demanding, manipulative, egoistic, driven, achieving, overwhelming, threatening, scary, ambitious, tough, brassy, masculine, boisterous, and turbulent. Among other things. A Bitch occupies a lot of psychological space. You always know she is around. A Bitch takes shit from no one. You may not like her, but you cannot ignore her.[48]

The feminist manifesto reclaims language, takes back power, decides for itself what words can and cannot injure. There is a sense of self-constructing in feminist manifestos, bending the world to their will. Said more cerebrally, Donna Haraway's *A Cyborg Manifesto* argues that "Liberation rests on the construction of the consciousness, the imaginative apprehension, of oppression and so of possibility."[49]

In this collection, we find possibilities for all kinds of ways out of our current predicaments. We find new ways to imagine bodies and sexualities, queer politics and trans bodies, borders and badlands, emotions and memories. We hear the forceful collective rage of brown and black women making space for a new postcolonial politics. We hear from poor women, trashy women, sex workers, and unapologetically angry women. We veer between the ethics of feminist hacking, the celebration of not having kids, a critique of contemporary "wokeness," and the lesbian mafia. We even return to 1970s-style witches and bitches—or more accurately, witchiness and bitchiness—and its wonderfully defiant way of turning supposedly negative stereotypes about women back onto the oppressor. This collection presents an imperfect and jagged path full of edges and abrupt turns, but it also serves other multiple roles—perhaps as an exit strategy, a call to arms,

---

48 Joreen (aka Jo Freeman), *Bitch Manifesto*, 1968, jofreeman.com/joreen/bitch
.htm.
49 Donna Haraway, "A Manifesto for Cyborgs: Science, Technology, and Socialist Feminism in the 1980s," *Socialist Review,* no. 80, 1985, 65–108.

or a comforting note of solidarity in times where people on the radical fringe often feel deeply and profoundly alone.

Traveling Through

Burn It Down! focuses on a wide range of sources that span first, second, and third-wave feminisms (and beyond) that have shaped, moved, inspired, repelled, and forged new ground for feminism and US feminist politics in particular. Drawing from sources often discarded as "crazy," "unpleasant," "out there," difficult, or contentious, the book embraces both well-known and obscure feminist manifestos, many of which have not been formally published before. The collection draws from a range of sources and subjects—postcolonial studies, radical youth movements, indigenous rights, women of color activisms, anarchism, unpublished and unknown authors publishing manifestos under pseudonyms, trans feminisms, radical psychiatry, folk music, fat studies, radical feminism, art history, technology studies, and long forgotten missives resuscitated from the early women's movement, among others. Not all of these documents are manifestos in the strictest sense, but they come from the radical tradition of feminist writing that is meant to provoke, unnerve, and break new ground. This assortment is meant to rekindle radical prescriptions from the past (distant and not-so-distant) and present in order to shape a vision for the future of feminisms on the margin.

Most existing collections focus heavily on art manifestos (primarily written by men) and revolutionary manifestos (also primarily written by men). (Some people seem to imagine *The Communist Manifesto* as the only manifesto ever written.) This collection, by contrast, foregrounds the voices of activists and agitators, troublemakers and complainers, most of whom are women. It is designed as a text that works against the highly gendered norms of respectability and, consequently, works both within and outside of the academy. Inside the academy it might serve as a documentary reader in feminist/women's/ gender studies courses or in women's history courses, while outside of the academy, it might work more as a cathartic text of resistance possibilities. In both cases, the collection works as a permanently and intentionally marginalized body of work. It exists to inspire rage and nurture activists, to remind fellow academics of who and what we too often forget, and it unites seemingly disparate bodies of knowledge into one collective body. If you're angry and fed up and need some company in the struggle, this book is for you. If you're wondering if you are enough of an activist, rebel, countercultural punk, radical, and so on to enjoy this book, my emphatic answer is: Yes.

Burn It Down! approaches its content as sites of eruption, where knowledge is not assembled as a collection of facts but as a diverse set of affects, histories, styles, and ideologies that circulate through complex networks of oppression and dissent. These manifestos represent the patterns and paradoxes that have emerged—and continue to emerge—in the wake of radical social upheavals. Some of these texts will feel especially relevant and alive in this cultural moment, while others might feel out of place or even dated. Some will feel fresh while others won't; some speak directly to you while others invite you to consider new modes of feminist solidarity you had not previously considered. Some you might hate. The collection is designed to present bodies of work—individually and together—to think about radical social thought and its expression. It should, in one way or another, hit a nerve.

As such, I have chosen to organize the book thematically rather than chronologically, geographically, or disciplinarily. This thematic orientation invites readers to look at some of the most highly charged critical, aesthetic, political, and social topics that feminist manifestos take on, particularly as tensions and contradictions are highlighted. For example, we read Andrea Dworkin and pro-sex-work manifestos in tandem with one another; we look at anti-violence and pro-violence work in unison. The story is not clean or unified, and it is not designed to make you as the reader feel comfortable or calm. These pieces highlight the edges of feminism.

By juxtaposing manifestos from different time periods, authors, perspectives, and tones, the following eight sections leap across time periods and movements and move wildly through ideas that inspire, startle, and energize. Further, by incorporating manifestos that are short and long, visual and written, traditional and nontraditional, easy to understand and quite obscure, famous and absolutely brand new, the collection challenges and upends knowledge-making practices that overvalue academic and nonemotional documents over those pulsating with fiery feelings. And while I have made some controversial choices—for example, keeping a sizeable amount of the women of color and indigenous work in one section—I have made these decisions to maximize the impact of reading a body of work together. The indigenous/women of color section is meant to allow readers to see the kinds of visionary solidarities that emerge between Chicana, Black, and indigenous feminist writings, with whiteness as a common target for anger and rage. The queer/trans section similarly allows for a collective body of work to emerge around queerness, envisioned from a wide range of voices across time, location, and identities. I believe this has a greater impact than presenting the work scattershot. Some readers may feel dismayed by my choice to include chunks of early second-wave radical feminist writing despite its notable blind spots, or they might find my embrace of totally unknown writers as problematic—to this I argue that a book of feminist manifestos is likely to be upsetting for many reasons and that it can and should provoke new thinking about the borders and boundaries for feminist politics. And while I welcome such critiques of my choices here of what to include, I do strongly encourage readers to sit with the work and let it draw you in.

The book's organization focuses on eight themes: Queer/Trans, Anticapitalist/Anarchist, Angry/Violent, Indigenous/Women of Color, Sex/Body, Hacker/Cyborg, Trashy/Punk, and Witchy/Bitchy. Each of these sections includes a diverse range of manifestos and encompasses both historical and contemporary manifestos (and some right in the middle). This design invites readers to see themselves reflected in this collection, often in surprising ways. As Audre Lorde argues:

> So we are working in a context of opposition and threat, the cause of which is certainly not the angers which lie between us, but rather that virulent hatred leveled against all women, people of color, lesbians and gay men, poor people—against all of us who are seeking to examine the particulars of our lives as we resist our oppressions, moving toward coalition and effective action.[50]

---

50 Audre Lorde, "The Uses of Anger," *Women's Studies Quarterly* 9: 3, 1981, 8.

The ultimate goal of this collection of feminist manifestos is to direct our energies to the wide range of targets for our oppression, to shamelessly operate as both individuals and a collective body, to welcome into the fold new and forgotten voices of feminist resistance, and to express righteous anger loudly and forcefully, even with the weight of the world on our shoulders. Let's burn it down.

A Note on Source Material

In order to preserve the idiosyncrasies and uniqueness of each text, the spelling, punctuation, format, capitalization, and grammar have been meticulously reproduced from the original published version of each document. Apparent errors are likely to reflect a choice of the author's or to recapture something of the manner of the original document's publication. By reproducing the texts in this way, something of the rawness and immediacy of the manifestos as they were originally conceived is maintained. All footnotes date to the original publication.

The texts have been sourced from the first publication or the publication the author or authors deemed closest to their intentions. Further information on sources is provided in the back matter. In the case of Sojourner Truth, the text "I Am as Strong as Any Man" is drawn from Marius Robinson's 1851 transcription for the *Anti-Slavery Bugle*, rather than the more commonly known, but less accurate, constructions by Frances Dana Gage that first appeared in 1863 as "Ain't I a Woman." In the case of Valeries Solanas's *SCUM Manifesto*, the text reproduced is from the 1977 self-published and self-edited publication Solanas circulated herself and that she dubbed the "CORRECT" version of *SCUM Manifesto*.

PART I

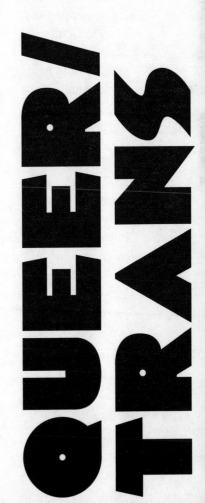

QUEER/
TRANS

Introduction to Queer/Trans

It's raining dykes! Situating unabashed queer feminist voices as a persistent force of resistance, not just at the peak of queer rights in the early 1970s but throughout the last fifty years, *Queer/Trans* showcases queer and trans rage. In this section we consider three major clusters of queer and trans manifestos, moving from the earlier days of queer resistance (1970–71), fast-forwarding to the early 1990s, and ending with the 2000s (2002–9). Rather than presenting these in a temporal and linear fashion, the section moves back and forth between ideas that embrace shamelessness, anger, and new queer futures.

No one is off the hook here; no subject is off limits. We move between early texts of gay liberation that warn of the mainstreaming of queer culture (Queer Nation Manifesto, Gay Liberation Front Manifesto) to a call to action for contemporary lesbian politics to forge new ground (Eskalera Karakola, Katie Tastrom, and Lesbian Avengers). We see lesbians avenging and we read some of the more in-your-face queer work that smashes boundaries, distorts edges, and tells the wimpier side of identity politics to "eat some dicks."

We work both within and outside the notions of borders, with lesbians at the fore—as president of the US (Zoe Leonard) and as gangs of troublemakers (ACT UP, Lesbian Mafia). We also transgress borders and look at work that insists on lesbianism as both idealized and wholly natural (Jill Johnston, Radicalesbians), working in tandem with an unapologetic gay rebel (Boyfunk), men who insist on feminist politics (Steven F. Dansky, John Knoebel, and Kenneth Pitchford), and a shameless voice of trans rights (Emi Koyama). In the words of the famous protest slogan, "Gays Bash Back."

1 I Want a President

1992

Zoe Leonard

I want a dyke for president. I want a person
with aids for president and I want a fag for
vice president and I want someone with no
health insurance and I want someone who grew
up in a place where the earth is so saturated
with toxic waste that they didn't have a
choice about getting leukemia. I want a
president that had an abortion at sixteen and
I want a candidate who isn't the lesser of two
evils and I want a president who lost their
last lover to aids, who still sees that in
their eyes every time they lay down torest,
who held their lover in their arms and knew
they were dying. I want a president with no
airconditioning, a president who has stood on
line at the clinic, at the dmv, at the welfare
office and has been unemployed and layed off and
sexually harrassed and gaybashed and deported.
I want someone who has spent the night in the
tombs and had a cross burned on their lawn and
survived rape. I want someone who has been in
love and been hurt, who respects sex, who has
made mistakes and learned from them. I want a
Black woman for president. I want someone with
bad teeth and an attitude, someone who has
eaten that nasty hospital food, someone who
crossdresses and has done drugs and been in
therapy. I want someone who has committed
civil disobedience. And I want to know why this
isn't possible. I want to know why we started
learning somewhere down the line that a president
is always a clown: always a john and never
a hooker. Always a boss and never a worker,
always a liar, always a thief and never caught.

Queer Nation Manifesto:
Queers Read This

1990

ACT UP

How can I tell you. How can I convince you, brother, sister that your
life is in danger: That everyday you wake up alive, relatively happy, and
a functioning human being, you are committing a rebellious act. You
as an alive and functioning queer are a revolutionary. There is nothing
on this planet that validates, protects or encourages your existence. It
is a miracle you are standing here reading these words. You should by
all rights be dead. Don't be fooled, straight people own the world and
the only reason you have been spared is you're smart, lucky or a fighter.
Straight people have a privilege that allows them to do whatever they
please and fuck without fear. But not only do they live a life free of fear;
they flaunt their freedom in my face. Their images are on my TV, in
the magazine I bought, in the restaurant I want to eat in, and on the
street where I live. I want there to be a moratorium on straight marriage, on babies, on public displays of affection among the opposite sex
and media images that promote heterosexuality. Until I can enjoy the
same freedom of movement and sexuality, as straights, their privilege
must stop and it must be given over to me and my queer sisters and
brothers. Straight people will not do this voluntarily and so they must
be forced into it. Straights must be frightened into it. Terrorized into
it. Fear is the most powerful motivation. No one will give us what we
deserve. Rights are not given they are taken, by force if necessary. It is
easier to fight when you know who your enemy is. Straight people are
your enemy. They are your enemy when they don't acknowledge your
invisibility and continue to live in and contribute to a culture that kills

you. Every day one of us is taken by the enemy. Whether it's an AIDS death due to homophobic government inaction or a lesbian bashing in an all-night diner (in a supposedly lesbian neighborhood).

AN ARMY OF LOVERS CANNOT LOSE

Being queer is not about a right to privacy; it is about the freedom to be public, to just be who we are. It means everyday fighting oppression; homophobia, racism, misogyny, the bigotry of religious hypocrites and our own self-hatred. (We have been carefully taught to hate ourselves.) And now of course it means fighting a virus as well, and all those homo-haters who are using AIDS to wipe us off the face of the earth. Being queer means leading a different sort of life. It's not about the mainstream, profit-margins, patriotism, patriarchy or being assimilated. It's not about executive directors, privilege and elitism. It's about being on the margins, defining ourselves; it's about gender-fuck and secrets, what's beneath the belt and deep inside the heart; it's about the night. Being queer is "grass roots" because we know that everyone of us, every body, every cunt, every heart and ass and dick is a world of pleasure waiting to be explored. Everyone of us is a world of infinite possibility. We are an army because we have to be. We are an army because we are so powerful. (We have so much to fight for; we are the most precious of endangered species.) And we are an army of lovers because it is we who know what love is. Desire and lust, too. We invented them. We come out of the closet, face the rejection of society, face firing squads, just to love each other! Every time we fuck, we win. We must fight for ourselves (no one else is going to do it) and if in that process we bring greater freedom to the world at large then great. (We've given so much to that world: democracy, all the arts, the concepts of love, philosophy and the soul, to name just a few gifts from our ancient Greek Dykes, Fags.) Let's make every space a Lesbian and Gay space. Every street a part of our sexual geography. A city of yearning and then total satisfaction. A city and a country where we can be safe and free and more. We must look at our lives and see what's best in them, see what is queer and what is straight and let that straight chaff fall away! Remember there is so, so little time. And I want to be a lover of each and every one of you. Next year, we march naked.

Anger

"The strong sisters told the brothers that there were two important things to remember about the coming revolutions. The first is that we will get our asses kicked. The second is that we will win." I'm angry. I'm angry for being condemned to death by strangers saying, "You deserve to die" and "AIDS is the cure." Fury erupts when a Republican woman wearing thousands of dollars of garments and jewelry minces by the police lines shaking her head, chuckling and wagging her finger at us like we are recalcitrant children making absurd demands and throwing temper tantrum when they aren't met. Angry while Joseph agonizes over $8,000 a year for AZT which might keep him alive a little longer and which makes him sicker than the disease he is diagnosed with. Angry as I listen to a man tell me that after changing his will five times he's running out of people to leave things to. All of his best friends are dead. Angry when I stand in a sea of quilt panels, or go to a candlelight march or attend yet another memorial service. I will not march silently with a fucking candle and I want to take that god-damned quilt and wrap myself in it and furiously rend it and my hair and curse every god religion ever created. I refuse to accept a creation that cuts people down in the third decade of their life.

It is cruel and vile and meaningless and everything I have in me rails against the absurdity and I raise my face to the clouds and a ragged laugh that sounds more demonic than joyous erupts from my throat and tears stream down my face and if this disease doesn't kill me, I may just die of frustration. My feet pound the streets and Peter's hands are chained to a pharmaceutical company's reception desk while the receptionist looks on in horror and Eric's body lies rotting in a Brooklyn cemetery and I'll never hear his flute resounding off the walls of the meeting house again. And I see the old people in Tompkins Square Park huddled in their long wool coats in June to keep out the cold they perceive is there and to cling to whatever little life has left to offer them. I'm reminded of the people who strip and stand before a mirror each night before they go to bed and search their bodies for any mark that might not have been there yesterday. A mark that this scourge has visited them.

And I'm angry when the newspapers call us "victims" and sound alarms that "it" might soon spread to the "general population." And I want to scream "Who the fuck am I?" And I want to scream at New

York Hospital with its yellow plastic bags marked "isolation linen," "ropa infecciosa" and its orderlies in latex gloves and surgical masks skirting the bed as if its occupant will suddenly leap out and douse them with blood and semen giving them too the plague.

And I'm angry at straight people who sit smugly wrapped in their self-protective coat of monogamy and heterosexuality confident that this disease has nothing to do with them because "it" only happens to "them." And the teenage boys who upon spotting my Silence=Death button begin chanting "Faggot's gonna die" and I wonder, who taught them this? Enveloped in fury and fear, I remain silent while my button mocks me every step of the way. And the anger I feel when a television program on the quilt gives profiles of the dead and the list begins with a baby, a teenage girl who got a blood transfusion, an elderly baptist minister and his wife and when they finally show a gay man, he's described as someone who knowingly infected teenage male prostitutes with the virus. What else can you expect from a faggot?

I'm angry.

Queer Artists

Since time began, the world has been inspired by the work of queer artists. In exchange, there has been suffering, there has been pain, there has been violence. Throughout history, society has struck a bargain with its queer citizens: they may pursue creative careers, if they do it discreetly. Through the arts queers are productive, lucrative, entertaining and even uplifting. These are the clear-cut and useful by-products of what is otherwise considered antisocial behavior. In cultured circles, queers may quietly coexist with an otherwise disapproving power elite.

At the forefront of the most recent campaign to bash queer artists is Jesse Helms, arbiter of all that is decent, moral, christian and amerikan. For Helms, queer art is quite simply a threat to the world. In his imaginings, heterosexual culture is too fragile to bear up to the admission of human or sexual diversity. Quite simply, the structure of power in the Judeo-Christian world has made procreation its cornerstone. Families having children assures consumers for the nation's products and a work force to produce them, as well as a built-in family system to care for its ill, reducing the expense of public healthcare systems.

ALL NON-PROCREATIVE BEHAVIOR IS CONSIDERED A THREAT, from homosexuality to birth control to abortion as an option. It is not enough, according to the religious right, to consistently advertise procreation and heterosexuality ... it is also necessary to destroy any alternatives. It is not art Helms is after ... IT IS OUR LIVES! Art is the last safe place for lesbians and gay men to thrive. Helms knows this, and has developed a program to purge queers from the one arena they have been permitted to contribute to our shared culture.

Helms is advocating a world free from diversity or dissent. It is easy to imagine why that might feel more comfortable to those in charge of such a world. It is also easy to envision an amerikan landscape flattened by such power. Helms should just ask for what he is hinting at: State sponsored art, art of totalitarianism, art that speaks only in christian terms, art which supports the goals of those in power, art that matches the sofas in the Oval Office. Ask for what you want, Jesse, so that men and women of conscience can mobilize against it, as we do against the human rights violations of other countries, and fight to free our own country's dissidents.

IF YOU'RE QUEER,

Queers are under siege.

Queers are being attacked on all fronts and I'm afraid it's ok with us.

In 1969, there were 50 "Queer Bashings" in the month of May alone. Violent attacks, 3,720 men, women and children died of AIDS in the same month, caused by a more violent attack—government inaction, rooted in society's growing homophobia. This is institutionalized violence, perhaps more dangerous to the existence of queers because the attackers are faceless. We allow these attacks by our own continued lack of action against them. AIDS has affected the straight world and now they're blaming us for AIDS and using it as a way to justify their violence against us. They don't want us anymore. They will beat us, rape us and kill us before they will continue to live with us. What will it take for this not to be ok? Feel some rage. If rage doesn't empower you, try fear. If that doesn't work, try panic.

SHOUT IT!

Be proud. Do whatever you need to do to tear yourself away from your customary state of acceptance. Be free. Shout.

In 1969, Queers fought back. In 1990, Queers say ok. Next year, will we be here?

I HATE …

I hate Jesse Helms. I hate Jesse Helms so much I'd rejoice if he dropped down dead. If someone killed him I'd consider it his own fault.

I hate Ronald Reagan, too, because he mass-murdered my people for eight years. But to be honest, I hate him even more for eulogizing Ryan White without first admitting his guilt, without begging forgiveness for Ryan's death and for the deaths of tens of thousands of other PWA's—most of them queer. I hate him for making a mockery of our grief.

I hate the fucking Pope, and I hate John fucking Cardinal fucking O'Connor, and I hate the whole fucking Catholic Church. The same goes for the Military, and especially for Amerika's Law Enforcement Officials—the cops—state sanctioned sadists who brutalize street transvestites, prostitutes and queer prisoners. I also hate the medical and mental health establishments, particularly the psychiatrist who convinced me not to have sex with men for three years until we (meaning he) could make me bisexual rather than queer. I also hate the education profession, for its share in driving thousands of queer teens to suicide every year. I hate the "respectable" art world; and the entertainment industry, and the mainstream media, especially The New York Times. In fact, I hate every sector of the straight establishment in this country—the worst of whom actively want all queers dead, the best of whom never stick their necks out to keep us alive.

I hate straight people who think they have anything intelligent to say about "outing." I hate straight people who think stories about themselves are "universal" but stories about us are only about homosexuality. I hate straight recording artists who make their careers off of queer people, then attack us, then act hurt when we get angry and then deny having wronged us rather than apologize for it. I hate straight people who say, "I don't see why you feel the need to wear those buttons and t-shirts. I don't go around telling the whole world I'm straight."

I hate that in twelve years of public education I was never taught about queer people. I hate that I grew up thinking I was the only queer in the world, and I hate even more that most queer kids still grow up the same way. I hate that I was tormented by other kids for being a faggot, but more that I was taught to feel ashamed for being the object of their cruelty, taught to feel it was my fault. I hate that the Supreme Court of this country says it's okay to criminalize me because of how I make love. I hate that so many straight people are so concerned about my goddamned sex life. I hate that so many twisted straight people become parents, while I have to fight like hell to be allowed to be a father. I hate straights.

WHERE ARE YOU SISTERS?

I wear my pink triangle everywhere. I do not lower my voice in public when talking about lesbian love or sex. I always tell people I'm a lesbian. I don't wait to be asked about my "boyfriend." I don't say it's "no one's business."

I don't do this for straight people. Most of them don't know what the pink triangle even means. Most of them couldn't care less that my girlfriend and I are totally in love or having a fight on the street. Most of them don't notice us no matter what we do. I do what I do to reach other lesbians. I do what I do because I don't want lesbians to assume I'm a straight girl. I am out all the time, everywhere, because I WANT TO REACH YOU. Maybe you'll notice me, maybe we'll start talking, maybe we'll exchange numbers, maybe we'll become friends. Maybe we won't say a word but our eyes will meet and I will imagine you naked, sweating, openmouthed, your back arched as I am fucking you. And we'll be happy to know we aren't the only ones in the world. We'll be happy because we found each other, without saying a word, maybe just for a moment. But no. You won't wear a pink triangle on that linen lapel. You won't meet my eyes if I flirt with you on the street. You avoid me on the job because I'm "too" out. You chastise me in bars because I'm "too political." You ignore me in public because I bring "too much" attention to "my" lesbianism. But then you want me to be your lover, you want me to be your friend, you want me to love you, support, you, fight for "OUR" right to exist.

WHERE ARE YOU?

You talk, talk, talk about invisibility and then retreat to your homes to nest with your lovers or carouse in a bar with pals and stumble home in a cab or sit silently and politely by while your family, your boss, your neighbors, your public servants distort and disfigure us, deride us and punish us. Then home again and you feel like screaming. Then you pad your anger with a relationship or a career or a party with other dykes like you and still you wonder why we can't find each other, why you feel lonely, angry, alienated.

GET UP, WAKE UP SISTERS!!

Your life is in your hands.

When I risk it all to be out, I risk it for both of us. When I risk it all and it works (which it often does if you would try it), I benefit and so do you. When it doesn't work, I suffer and you do not.

But girl you can't wait for other dykes to make the world safe for you. STOP waiting for a better more lesbian future! The revolution could be here if we started it. Where are you sisters? I'm trying to find you, I'm trying to find you. How come I only see you on Gay Pride Day? We're OUT, Where the fuck are YOU?

WHEN ANYONE ASSAULTS YOU FOR BEING QUEER, IT IS QUEER BASHING. Right?

A crowd of 50 people exit a gay bar as it closes. Across the street, some straight boys are shouting "Faggots" and throwing beer bottles at the gathering, which outnumbers them by 10 to 1. Three queers make a move to respond, getting no support from the group. Why did a group this size allow themselves to be sitting ducks? Tompkins Square Park, Labor Day. At an annual outdoor concert/drag show, a group of gay men were harassed by teens carrying sticks. In the midst of thousands of gay men and lesbians, these straight boys beat two gay men to the ground, then stood around triumphantly laughing amongst themselves. The emcee was alerted and warned the crowd from the stage, "You girls be careful. When you dress up it drives the boys crazy," as if it were a practical joke inspired by what the victims were wearing rather than a pointed attack on anyone and everyone at that event.

What would it have taken for that crowd to stand up to its attackers?

After James Zappalorti, an openly gay man, was murdered in cold blood on Staten Island this winter, a single demonstration was held in protest. Only one hundred people came. When Yuseuf Hawkins, a black youth, was shot to death for being on "white turf" in Bensonhurst, African Americans marched through that neighborhood in large numbers again and again. A black person was killed BECAUSE HE WAS BLACK, and people of color throughout the city recognized it and acted on it. The bullet that hit Hawkins was meant for a black man, ANY black man. Do most gays and lesbians think that the knife that punctured Zappalorti's heart was meant only for him?

The straight world has us so convinced that we are helpless and deserving victims of the violence against us, that queers are immobilized when faced with a threat. BE OUTRAGED! These attacks must not be tolerated. DO SOMETHING. Recognize that any act of aggression against any member of our community is an attack on every member of the community. The more we allow homophobes to inflict violence, terror and fear on our lives, the more frequently and ferociously we will be the object of their hatred. You're immeasurably valuable, because unless you start believing that, it can easily be taken from you. If you know how to gently and efficiently immobilize your attacker, then by all means, do it. If you lack those skills, then think about gouging out his fucking eyes, slamming his nose back into his brain, slashing his throat with a broken bottle—do whatever you can, whatever you have to, to save your life!

reeuQ yhW

Ah, do we really have to use that word? It's trouble. Every gay person has his or her own take on it. For some it means strange and eccentric and kind of mysterious. That's okay, we like that. But some gay girls and boys don't. They think they're more normal than strange. And for others "queer" conjures up those awful memories of adolescent suffering. Queer. It's forcibly bittersweet and quaint at best—weakening and painful at worst. Couldn't we just use "gay" instead? It's a much brighter word and isn't it synonymous with "happy?" When will you militants grow up and get over the novelty of being different?

Why Queer

Well, yes, "gay" is great. It has its place. But when a lot of lesbians and gay men wake up in the morning we feel angry and disgusted, not gay. So we've chosen to call ourselves queer. Using "queer" is a way of reminding us how we are perceived by the rest of the world. It's a way of telling ourselves we don't have to be witty and charming people who keep our lives discreet and marginalized in the straight world. We use queer as gay men loving lesbians and lesbians loving being queer.

Queer, unlike GAY, doesn't mean MALE.

And when spoken to other gays and lesbians it's a way of suggesting we close ranks, and forget (temporarily) our individual differences because we face a more insidious common enemy. Yeah, QUEER can be a rough word but it is also a sly and ironic weapon we can steal from the homophobe's hands and use against him.

NO SEX POLICE

For anyone to say that coming out is not part of the revolution is missing the point. Positive sexual images and what they manifest saves lives because they affirm those lives and make it possible for people to attempt to live as self-loving instead of self-loathing. As the famous "Black is beautiful" slogan changed many lives, so does "Read my lips" affirm queerness in the face of hatred and invisibility as displayed in a recent governmental study of suicides that states at least one third of all teen suicides are Queer kids. This is further exemplified by the rise in HIV transmission among those under 21.

We are most hated as queers for our sexualness, that is, our physical contact with the same sex. Our sexuality and sexual expression are what makes us most susceptible to physical violence. Our difference, our otherness, our uniqueness can either paralyze us or politicize us. Hopefully, the majority of us will not let it kill us.

QUEER SPACE

Why in the world do we let heteros into queer clubs? Who gives a fuck if they like us because we "really know how to party?" WE HAVE TO IN ORDER TO BLOW OFF THE STEAM THEY MAKE US FEEL ALL THE TIME! They make out wherever they please, and take up too much room on the dance floor doing ostentatious couples dances. They wear their heterosexuality like a "Keep Out" sign, or like a deed of ownership.

Why the fuck do we tolerate them when they invade our space like it's their right? Why do we let them shove heterosexuality—a weapon their world wields against us—right in our faces in the few public spots where we can be sexy with each other and not fear attack?

It's time to stop letting the straight people make all the rules. Let's start by posting this sign outside every queer club and bar:

RULES OF CONDUCT FOR STRAIGHT PEOPLE

1. Keep your display of affection (kissing, handholding, embracing) to a minimum. Your sexuality is unwanted and offensive to many here.
2. If you must slow dance, be as inconspicuous as possible.
3. Do not gawk or stare at lesbians or gay men, especially bull dykes or drag queens. We are not your entertainment.
4. If you cannot comfortably deal with someone of the same sex making a pass at you, get out.
5. Do not flaunt your heterosexuality. Be Discreet. Risk being mistaken for a lezzie or a homo.
6. If you feel these rules are unfair, go fight homophobia in straight clubs, or:
7. Go Fuck Yourself.

I HATE STRAIGHTS

I have friends. Some of them are straight.

Year after year, I see my straight friends. I want to see them, to see how they are doing, to add newness to our long and complicated histories, to experience some continuity. Year after year I continue to realize that the facts of my life are irrelevant to them and that I am only half listened to, that I am an appendage to the doings of a greater world, a world of power and privilege, of the laws of installation, a world of exclusion. "That's not true," argue my straight friends. There is the one certainty in the politics of power: those left out of it beg for inclusion, while the insiders claim that they already are. Men do it to women, whites do it to blacks, and everyone does it to queers. The main dividing line, both conscious and unconscious, is procreation ... and that magic word—Family. Frequently, the ones we are born into disown us when they find out who we really are, and to make matters worse, we are prevented from having our own. We are punished, insulted, cut off, and treated like seditionaries in terms of child rearing, both damned if we try and damned if we abstain. It's as if the propagation of the species is such a fragile directive that without enforcing it as if it were an agenda, humankind would melt back into the primeval ooze.

I hate having to convince straight people that lesbians and gays live in a war zone, that we're surrounded by bomb blasts only we seem to hear, that our bodies and souls are heaped high, dead from fright or bashed or raped, dying of grief or disease, stripped of our personhood.

I hate straight people who can't listen to queer anger without saying "hey, all straight people aren't like that. I'm straight too, you know," as if their egos don't get enough stroking or protection in this arrogant, heterosexist world. Why must we take care of them, in the midst of our just anger brought on by their fucked up society?! Why add the reassurance of "Of course, I don't mean you. You don't act that way." Let them figure out for themselves whether they deserve to be included in our anger.

But of course that would mean listening to our anger, which they almost never do. They deflect it, by saying "I'm not like that" or "Now look who's generalizing" or "You'll catch more flies with honey ..." or "If you focus on the negative you just give out more power" or "you're not the only one in the world who's suffering." They say "Don't yell

at me, I'm on your side" or "I think you're overreacting" or "BOY,
YOU'RE BITTER."

They've taught us that good queers don't get mad. They've taught
us so well that we not only hide our anger from them, we hide it from
each other. WE EVEN HIDE IT FROM OURSELVES. We hide it with
substance abuse and suicide and overachieving in the hope of proving
our worth. They bash us and stab us and shoot us and bomb us in ever
increasing numbers and still we freak out when angry queers carry
banners or signs that say BASH BACK. For the last decade they let us
die in droves and still we thank President Bush for planting a fucking
tree, applaud him for likening PWAs to car accident victims who
refuse to wear seatbelts. LET YOURSELF BE ANGRY. Let yourself be
angry that the price of our visibility is the constant threat of violence,
anti- queer violence to which practically every segment of this society
contributes. Let yourself feel angry that THERE IS NO PLACE IN
THIS COUNTRY WHERE WE ARE SAFE, no place where we are
not targeted for hatred and attack, the self-hatred, the suicide—of the
closet. The next time some straight person comes down on you for
being angry, tell them that until things change, you don't need any
more evidence that the world turns at your expense. You don't need
to see only hetero couple grocery shopping on your TV ... You don't
want any more baby pictures shoved in your face until you can have
or keep your own. No more weddings, showers, anniversaries, please,
unless they are our own brothers and sisters celebrating. And tell them
not to dismiss you by saying "You have rights," "You have privileges,"
"You're overreacting," or "You have a victim's mentality." Tell them
"GO AWAY FROM ME, until YOU can change." Go away and try on
a world without the brave, strong queers that are its backbone, that
are its guts and brains and souls. Go tell them go away until they have
spent a month walking hand in hand in public with someone of the
same sex. After they survive that, then you'll hear what they have to
say about queer anger.

Otherwise, tell them to shut up and listen.

3 The Woman Identified Woman

1970

Radicalesbians

What is a lesbian? A lesbian is the rage of all women condensed to the point of explosion. She is the woman who, often beginning at an extremely early age, acts in accordance with her inner compulsion to be a more complete and freer human being than her society—perhaps then, but certainly later—cares to allow her. These needs and actions, over a period of years, bring her into painful conflict with people, situations, the accepted ways of thinking, feeling and behaving, until she is in a state of continual war with everything around her, and usually with herself. She may not be fully conscious of the political implications of what for her began as personal necessity, but on some level she has not been able to accept the limitations and oppression laid on her by the most basic role of her society—the female role. The turmoil she experiences tends to induce guilt proportional to the degree to which she feels she is not meeting social expectations, and/or eventually drives her to question and analyze what the rest of her society more or less accepts. She is forced to evolve her own life pattern, often living much of her life alone, learning usually much earlier than her "straight" (heterosexual) sisters about the essential aloneness of life (which the myth of marriage obscures) and about the reality of illusions. To the extent that she cannot expel the heavy socialization that goes with being female, she can never truly find peace with herself. For she is caught somewhere between accepting society's view of her—in which case she cannot accept herself—and coming to understand what this sexist society has done to her and why it is functional and necessary for it to do so. Those of us who work that through find ourselves on the other side of a tortuous journey through a night that may have been decades long. The perspective gained from that journey, the liberation of self, the inner peace, the real love of self and of all women, is something to be shared with all women—because we are all women.

It should first be understood that lesbianism, like male homosexuality, is a category of behavior possible only in a sexist society characterized by rigid sex roles and dominated by male supremacy. Those sex roles dehumanize women by defining us as a supportive/serving caste <u>in relation to</u> the master caste of men, and emotionally cripple men by demanding that they be alienated from their own bodies and emotions in order to perform their economic/political/military functions effectively. Homosexuality is a by-product of a particular way of setting up roles (or approved patterns of behavior) on the basis of sex; as such it is an inauthentic (not consonant with "reality") category. In a society in which men do not oppress women, and sexual expression is allowed to follow feelings, the categories of homosexuality and heterosexuality would disappear.

But lesbianism is also different from male homosexuality, and serves a different function in the society. "Dyke" is a different kind of put-down from "faggot", although both imply you are not playing your socially assigned sex role ... are not therefore a "real woman" or a "real man." The grudging admiration felt for the tomboy, and the queasiness felt around a sissy boy point to the same thing: the contempt in which women—or those who play a female role—are held. And the investment in keeping women in that contemptuous role is very great. Lesbian is a word, the label, the condition that holds women in line. When a woman hears this word tossed her way, she knows she is stepping out of line. She knows that she has crossed the terrible boundary of her sex role. She recoils, she protests, she reshapes her actions to gain approval. Lesbian is a label invented by the Man to throw at any woman who dares to be his equal, who dares to challenge his prerogatives (including that of all women as part of the exchange medium among men), who dares to assert the primacy of her own needs. To have the label applied to people active in women's liberation is just the most recent instance of a long history; older women will recall that not so long ago, any woman who was successful, independent, not orienting her whole life about a man, would hear this word. For in this sexist society, for a woman to be independent means she <u>can't be</u> a woman—she must be a dyke. That in itself should tell us where women are at. It says as clearly as can be said: women and person are contra-dictory terms. For a lesbian is not considered a "real woman." And yet, in popular thinking, there is really only one essential difference between a lesbian and other women: that of sexual orientation—which is to say, when you strip off all the packaging, you must finally realize that the essence of being a "woman" is to get fucked by men.

"Lesbian" is one of the sexual categories by which men have divided up humanity. While all women are dehumanized as sex objects, as the objects of men they are given certain compensations: identification with his power, his ego, his status, his protection (from other males), feeling like a "real woman," finding social acceptance by adhering to her role, etc. Should a woman confront herself by confronting another woman, there are fewer rationalizations, fewer buffers by which to avoid the stark horror of her dehumanized condition. Herein we find the overriding fear of many women toward being used as a sexual object by a woman, which not only will bring her no male-connected compensations, but also will reveal the void which is woman's real situ-ation. This dehumanization is expressed when a straight woman learns that a sister is a lesbian; she begins to relate to her lesbian sister as her potential sex object, laying a surrogate male role on the lesbian. This reveals her heterosexual conditioning to make herself into an object when sex is potentially involved in a relationship, and it denies the lesbian her full humanity. For women, especially those in the move-ment, to perceive their lesbian sisters through this male grid of role definitions is to accept this male cultural conditioning and to oppress their sisters much as they themselves have been oppressed by men. Are we going to continue the male classification system of defining all females in sexual relation to some other category of people? Affixing the label lesbian not only to a woman who aspires to be a person, but also to any situation of real love, real solidarity, real primacy among women, is a primary form of divisiveness among women: it is the con-dition which keeps women within the confines of the feminine role, and it is the debunking/scare term that keeps women from forming any primary attachments, groups, or associations among ourselves.

Women in the movement have in most cases gone to great lengths to avoid discussion and confrontation with the issue of lesbianism. It puts people up-tight. They are hostile, evasive, or try to incorporate it into some "broader issue." They would rather not talk about it. If they have to, they try to dismiss it as a "lavender herring." But it is no side issue. It is absolutely essential to the success and fulfillment of the women's liberation movement that this issue be dealt with. As long as the label "dyke" can be used to frighten women into a less militant stand, keep her separate from her sisters, keep her from giving primacy to anything other than men and family—then to that extent she is controlled by the male culture. Until women see in each other the possibility of a primal commitment which includes sexual love, they will be denying themselves the love and value they readily accord to men, thus affirming their second-class status. As long as male acceptability is primary—both to individual women and to the movement as a whole—the term lesbian will be used effectively against women. Insofar as women want only more privileges within the system, they do not want to antagonize male power. They instead seek acceptability for women's liberation, and the most crucial aspect of the acceptability is to deny lesbianism—i.e., to deny any fundamental challenge to the basis of the female. It should also be said that some younger, more radical women have honestly begun to discuss lesbianism, but so far it has been primarily as a sexual "alternative" to men. This, however, is still giving primacy to men, both because the idea of relating more completely to women occurs as a negative reaction to men, and because the lesbian relationship is being characterized simply by sex, which is divisive and sexist. On one level, which is both personal and political, women may withdraw emotional and sexual energies from men, and work out various alternatives for those energies in their own lives. On a different political/psychological level, it must be understood that what is crucial is that women begin disengaging from male-defined response patterns. In the privacy of our own psyches, we must cut those cords to the core. For irrespective of where our love and sexual energies flow, if we are male-identified in our heads, we cannot realize our autonomy as human beings.

But why is it that women have related to and through men? By virtue of having been brought up in a male society, we have internalized the male culture's definition of ourselves. That definition consigns us to sexual and family functions, and excludes us from defining and shaping the terms of our lives. In exchange for our psychic servicing and for performing society's non-profit-making functions, the man confers on us just one thing: the slave status which makes us legitimate in the eyes of the society in which we live. This is called "femininity" or "being a real woman" in our cultural lingo. We are authentic, legitimate, real to the extent that we are the property of some man whose name we bear. To be a woman who belongs to no man is to be invisible, pathetic, inauthentic, unreal. He confirms his image of us—of what we have to be in order to be acceptable by him—but not our real selves; he confirms our womanhood—as he defines it, in relation to him—but cannot confirm our personhood, our own selves as absolutes. As long as we are dependent on the male culture for this definition, for this approval, we cannot be free.

The consequence of internalizing this role is an enormous reservoir of self-hate. This is not to say the self-hate is recognized or accepted as such; indeed most women would deny it. It may be experienced as discomfort with her role, as feeling empty, as numbness, as restlessness, as a paralyzing anxiety at the center. Alternatively, it may be expressed in shrill defensiveness of the glory and destiny of her role. But it does exist, often beneath the edge of her consciousness, poisoning her existence, keeping her alienated from herself, her own needs, and rendering her a stranger to other women. They try to escape by identifying with the oppressor, living through him, gaining status and identity from his ego, his power, his accomplishments. And by not identifying with other "empty vessels" like themselves. Women resist relating on all levels to other women who will reflect their own oppression, their own secondary status, their own self-hate. For to confront another woman is finally to confront one's self—the self we have gone to such lengths to avoid. And in that mirror we know we cannot really respect and love that which we have been made to be.

As the source of self-hate and the lack of real self are rooted in our male-given identity, we must create a new sense of self. As long as we cling to the idea of "being a woman," we will sense some conflict with that incipient self, that sense of I, that sense of a whole person. It is very difficult to realize and accept that being "feminine" and being a whole person are irreconcilable. Only women can give to each other a new sense of self. That identity we have to develop with reference to ourselves, and not in relation to men. This consciousness is the revolutionary force from which all else will follow, for ours is an organic revolution. For this we must be available and supportive to one another, give our commitment and our love, give the emotional support necessary to sustain this movement. Our energies must flow toward our sisters, not backward toward our oppressors. As long as woman's liberation tries to free women without facing the basic heterosexual structure that binds us in one-to-one relationship with our oppressors, tremendous energies will continue to flow into trying to straighten up each particular relationship with a man, into finding how to get better sex, how to turn his head around—into trying to make the "new man" out of him, in the delusion that this will allow us to be the "new woman." This obviously splits our energies and commitments, leaving us unable to be committed to the construction of the new patterns which will liberate us.

It is the primacy of women relating to women, of women creating a new consciousness of and with each other, which is at the heart of women's liberation, and the basis for the cultural revolution. Together we must find, reinforce, and validate our authentic selves. As we do this, we confirm in each other that struggling, incipient sense of pride and strength, the divisive barriers begin to melt, we feel this growing solidarity with our sisters. We see ourselves as prime, find our centers inside of ourselves. We find receding the sense of alienation, of being cut off, of being behind a locked window, of being unable to get out what we know is inside. We feel a realness, feel at last we are coinciding with ourselves. With that real self, with that consciousness, we begin a revolution to end the imposition of all coercive identifications, and to achieve maximum autonomy in human expression.

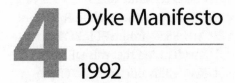

Dyke Manifesto

1992

Lesbian Avengers

lesbian avengers **DYKE MANIFESTO** lesbian avengers

CALLING ALL LESBIANS
WAKE UP! WAKE UP! WAKE UP!

IT'S TIME TO GET OUT OF THE BEDS, OUT OF THE BARS
AND INTO THE STREETS
TIME TO SEIZE THE POWER OF DYKE LOVE, DYKE VISION,
DYKE ANGER, DYKE INTELLIGENCE, DYKE STRATEGY.
TIME TO ORGANIZE AND IGNITE. TIME TO GET
TOGETHER AND FIGHT
WE'RE INVISIBLE AND IT'S NOT SAFE—NOT AT HOME, ON
THE JOB, IN THE STREETS OR IN THE COURTS
WHERE ARE OUR LESBIAN LEADERS?
WE NEED YOU
WE'RE NOT WAITING FOR THE RAPTURE. WE ARE THE
APOCALYPSE.
WE'LL BE YOUR DREAM AND THEIR NIGHTMARE.
LESBIAN POWER
BELIEVE IN CREATIVE ACTIVISM: LOUD, BOLD, SEXY,
SILLY, FIERCE, TASTY AND DRAMATIC. ARREST OPTIONAL.
THINK DEMONSTRATIONS ARE A GOOD TIME AND
A GREAT PLACE TO CRUISE WOMEN. DON'T HAVE
PATIENCE FOR POLITE POLITICS. ARE BORED WITH THE
BOYS. BELIEVE CONFRONTATION FOSTERS GROWTH AND

STRONG BONES. BELIEVE IN RECRUITMENT. NOT BY THE
ARMY; NOT OF STRAIGHT WOMEN. ARE NOT CONTENT
WITH GHETTOS: WE WANT YOUR HOUSE, YOUR JOB,
YOUR FREQUENT FLYER MILES. WE'LL SELL YOUR
JEWELRY TO SUBSIDIZE OUR MOVEMENT. WE DEMAND
UNIVERSAL HEALTH INSURANCE AND HOUSING. WE
DEMAND FOOD AND SHELTER. FOR ALL HOMELESS
LESBIANS. WE ARE THE 13TH STEP. THINK GIRL GANGS
ARE THE WAVE OF THE FUTURE
LESBIAN SEX
THINK SEX IS A DAILY LIBATION. GOOD ENERGY FOR
ACTIONS. CRAVE, ENJOY, EXPLORE, SUFFFR FROM NEW
IDEAS ABOUT RELATIONSHIPS: SLUMBER PARTIES,
POLYGAMY, PERSONAL ADS, AFFINITY GROUPS.
USE LIVE ACTION WORDS: lick, waltz, eat, fuck, kiss, bite, give
it up, hit the dirt
LESBIAN ACTIVISM
THINK ACTIONS MUST BE LOCAL, REGIONAL, NATIONAL,
GLOBAL, COSMIC.
THINK CLOSETED LESBIANS, QUEER BOYS AND
SYMPATHETIC STRAIGHTS SHOULD SEND US MONEY.

PLAN TO TARGET HOMOPHOBES OF EVERY STRIPE AND
INFILTRATE THE CHRISTIAN RIGHT.
SCHEME AND SCREAM AND FIGHT REAL MEAN
THE LESBIAN AVENGERS: WE RECRUIT

WELCOME AVENGER!

WHO ARE THE LESBIAN AVENGERS?

The Lesbian Avengers is a **direct action** group focused on issues vital
to **lesbian survival and visibility.** There are many ideas in the lesbian
community about what kind of strategies to employ—electoral and
legal reform, therapy groups, social services, theoretical development. These are all valid strategies, but they are not the strategies of
the Avengers. Direct action is what the Lesbian Avengers do. It is the
reason for our existence.

WHAT IS DIRECT ACTION?

The real question is "Do we have to spray paint billboards to be a Lesbian Avenger?" Direct Action is a **public intervention** ranging in creative form from marches to street theatre to speakouts to cathartic spray painting of anti-hate slogans. Direct action is about getting attention, and that means media coverage. The purpose of direct action is **visibility**, so we can't be shy. As a direct action group, the Lesbian Avengers is for women who want to be activists, want to take responsibility for making things happen, want to do the shit work, have their minds blown, change their opinions, share organizing skills, and work in community. You don't have to spray paint billboards (although it's really fun)! You have to be willing to act-out publicly. We want to empower **lesbians** as leaders!

WHY NO ABSTRACT THEORETICAL DISCUSSION?

How many of us have sat in meetings arguing political theory to the point of mental and physical exhaustion, to the point where we run screaming to the nearest dance floor for release from the frustration?! To keep our work pro-active and fulfilling and successful, we focus our political discussions on the creation and purpose of an **action**. We agree to disagree on political ideology—it is too easy to create false polarities. We also encourage women to **take responsibility** for their own suggestions—be willing to make them happen. Instead of saying "Someone should ... " try saying "I will ..." or "Who will do this with me?" In our meetings, if you disagree with a proposal on the floor, instead of tearing it apart, propose another way of realizing the goal. The Avengers is a place where ideas are realized, where lesbians can have an impact. A crucial part of that is learning how to **propose alternatives** instead of just offering critiques. Be willing to put your body where your brain is—matter over mind!

A BRIEF HISTORY OF THE LESBIAN AVENGERS

The first Lesbian Avenger group was founded in New York City in June 1992 by a group of experienced activists who were frustrated with their participation in W.H.A.M. and ACT UP where they felt overshadowed and undervalued as lesbians. They called a first meeting by handing out fluorescent green club cards reading "Lesbians! Dykes! Gay Women! We want revenge and we want it now." The idea took off and the group has created many successful actions, including: arriving at public schools on the first day of school to give out balloons inscribe "Ask about Lesbian Lives"—this was surrounding the attempt to include teaching about gay and lesbian lives in the public school curriculum; an anti-violence march and fire eating ceremony in response to the murders of gays and lesbians in Oregon; following Mayor Webb of Colorado (on his visit to New York City to promote tourism) to make sure the media focus was on Amendment 2; a Valentine's Day celebration of romantic love, butch genius and forgotten femmes, featuring the erection of a statue of Alice B. Toklas next to the statue of Gertrude Stein in Bryant Park (poetry and waltzing galore!); and organizing the Dyke March preceding the March on Washington 1993.

The Minneapolis Chapter started on International Women's Day, 1993, when a bunch of dykes got together to potluck and discuss forming a direct action group. Lesbian direct action groups have existed in the Twin Cities before—Tornado Warning, Lesbians Against Imperialism, and other informal and individual efforts. From the first meeting, we discovered the common goals of: action not theory, proactive not reactive, and fun, fun, fun! Everything that we wanted to do as a group fit with what the Lesbian Avengers were doing. Thus the Minneapolis Chapter was born! To announce our birth, we went out that night and appropriated a Navy billboard: ta da!

ACTIONS IN THE WORKS

Minneapolis Pride March; creating lesbian bar/dance space; radio and video projects; interfering with the Operation Rescue boot camp activities; continued watch-dogging of media to combat homophobic and sexist imagery; a summer celebration of dyke love; fundraising for hellraising! We welcome your ornery ideas for frisky antics and hotheaded capers!

TOP TEN AVENGER QUALITIES
10. COMPASSION
9. LEADERSHIP
8. NO BIG EGO
7. INFORMED
6. FEARLESSNESS
5. RIGHTEOUS ANGER
4. FIGHTING SPIRIT
3. PRO SEX
2. GOOD DANCER
1. ACCESS TO RESOURCES (XEROX MACHINES)

5 Do Approach (excerpt)

1971

Jill Johnston

All women are lesbians except those who don't know it naturally, they are but don't know it yet. I am a woman and therefore a lesbian. I am a woman who is a lesbian because I am a woman, and a woman who loves herself naturally, who is other women, is a lesbian. A woman who loves women loves herself naturally, this is the case. A woman is herself is all woman is a natural born lesbian, so we don't mind using the name like any name it is quite meaningless, it means, naturally, I am a woman, and whatever I am we are, we affirm being what we are, the way of course all men are homosexuals. Being, having a more sense of their homo, their homo-ness, their ecce homo-ness, their ecce prince and lord and master-ness.

Until all women are lesbians, there will be no true political revolution. I suppose I should be leaning on my sword describing my defeat. Some women want to have their cock and eat it too. And lesbian is a label, a label invented by anybody to throw it at any woman who dares to be a man's equal. And lesbian is a good name, it means nothing of course, or everything, so we don't mind using the name, in fact we like it for we can be proud to claim allusion to the island made famous by Sappho… He said, "I want your body" and she said, "You can have it when I'm through with it."

Gay Liberation Front Manifesto (excerpt)

1971

Gay Liberation Front

Introduction

Throughout recorded history, oppressed groups have organised to claim their rights and obtain their needs. Homosexuals, who have been oppressed by physical violence and by ideological and psychological attacks at every level of social interaction, are at last becoming angry.

To you, our gay sisters and brothers, we say that you are oppressed; we intend to show you examples of the hatred and fear with which straight society relegates us to the position and treatment of sub-humans, and to explain their basis. We will show you how we can use our righteous anger to uproot the present oppressive system with its decaying and constricting ideology, and how we, together with other oppressed groups, can start to form a new order, and a liberated life-style, from the alternatives which we offer.

HOW We Are Oppressed

FAMILY

The oppression of gay people starts in the most basic unit of society, the family. Consisting of the man in charge, a slave as his wife, and their children on whom they force themselves as the ideal models. The very form of the family works against homosexuality.

At some point nearly all gay people have found it difficult to cope with having the restricting images of man or woman pushed on them by their parents. It may have been from very early on, when the pressures to play with the "right" toys, and thus prove boyishness or girlishness, drove against the child's inclinations. But for all of us this is certainly a problem by the time of adolescence, when we are expected to prove ourselves socially to our parents as members of the right sex (to bring home a boy/girl friend) and to start being a "real" (oppressive) young man or a "real" (oppressed) young woman. The tensions can be very destructive.

The fact that gay people notice they are different from other men and women in the family situation, causes them to feel ashamed, guilty and failures. How many of us have really dared be honest with our parents? How many of us have been thrown out of home? How many of us have been pressured into marriage, sent to psychiatrists, frightened into sexual inertia, ostracised, banned, emotionally destroyed—all by our parents?

SCHOOL

Family experiences may differ widely, but in their education all children confront a common situation. Schools reflect the values of society in their formal academic curriculum, and reinforce them in their morality and discipline. Boys learn competitive ego-building sports, and have more opportunity in science, whereas girls are given emphasis on domestic subjects, needlework etc. Again, we gays were all forced into a rigid sex role which we did not want or need. It is quite common to discipline children for behaving in any way like the opposite sex; degrading titles like "sissy" and "tomboy" are widely used.

In the context of education, homosexuality is generally ignored, even where we know it exists, as in history and literature. Even sex education, which has been considered a new liberal dynamic of secondary schooling, proves to be little more than an extension of Christian morality. Homosexuality is again either ignored, or attacked with moralistic warnings and condemnations. The adolescent recognising his or her homosexuality might feel totally alone in the world, or a pathologically sick wreck.

CHURCH

Formal religious education is still part of everyone's schooling, and our whole legal structure is supposedly based on Christianity whose archaic and irrational teachings support the family and marriage as the only permitted condition for sex. Gay people have been attacked as abominable and sinful since the beginning of both Judaism and Christianity, and even if today the Church is playing down these strictures on homosexuality, its new ideology is that gay people are pathetic objects for sympathy.

THE MEDIA

The press, radio, television and advertising are used as reinforcements against us, and make possible the control of people's thoughts on an unprecedented scale. Entering everyone's home, affecting everyone's life, the media controllers, all representatives of the rich, male-controlled world, can exaggerate or suppress whatever information suits them.

Under different circumstances, the media might not be the weapon of a small minority. The present controllers are therefore dedicated defenders of things as they stand. Accordingly, the images of people which they transmit in their pictures and words do not subvert, but support society's image of "normal" man and woman. It follows that we are characterised as scandalous, obscene perverts; as rampant, wild sex-monsters; as pathetic, doomed and compulsive degenerates; while the truth is blanketed under a conspiracy of silence.

WORDS

Anti-homosexual morality and ideology, at every level of society, manifest themselves in a special vocabulary for denigrating gay people. There is abuse like "pansy," "fairy," "lesbo" to hurl at men and women who can't or won't fit stereotyped preconceptions. There are words like "sick," "bent" and "neurotic" for destroying the credence of gay people. But there are no positive words. The ideological intent of our language makes it very clear that the generation of words and meanings is, at the moment, in the hands of the enemy. And that so many gay people pretend to be straight, and call each other "butch dykes" or "screaming queens" only makes that fact the more real.

The verbal attack on men and women who do not behave as they are supposed to, reflects the ideology of masculine superiority. A man who behaves like a woman is seen as losing something, and a woman who behaves like a man is put down for threatening men's environment of their privileges.

EMPLOYMENT

If our upbringing so often produces guilt and shame, the experience of an adult gay person is oppressive in every aspect. In their work situation, gay people face the ordeal of spending up to fifty years of their lives confronted with the anti-homosexual hostility of their fellow employees.

A direct consequence of the fact that virtually all employers are highly privileged heterosexual men, is that there are some fields of work which are closed to gay people, and others which they feel some compulsion to enter. A result of this control for gay women is that they are perceived as a threat in the man's world. They have none of the sexual ties of dependence to men which make most women accept men as their "superiors." They are less likely to have the bind of children, and so there is nothing to stop them showing that they are as capable as any man, and thus deflating the man's ego, and exposing the myth that only men can cope with important jobs.

We are excluded from many jobs in high places where being married is the respectable guarantee, but being homosexual apparently makes us unstable, unreliable security risks. Neither, for example, are we allowed the job of teaching children, because we are all reckoned to be compulsive, child molesting maniacs.

There are thousands of examples of people having lost their jobs due to it becoming known that they were gay, though employers usually contrive all manner of spurious reasons.

There occurs, on the other hand, in certain jobs, such a concentration of gay people as to make an occupational ghetto. This happens, for women, in the forces, ambulance driving, and other uniformed occupations: and for men, in the fashion, entertainment and theatrical professions, all cases where the roles of "man" and "woman" can perhaps be undermined or overlooked.

THE LAW

If you live in Scotland or Ireland; if you are under 21, or over 21 but having sex with someone under 21; if you are in the armed forces or the merchant navy; if you have sex with more than one other person at the same time—and you are a gay male, you are breaking the law.

The 1967 Sexual Offences Act gave a limited license to adult gay men. Common law however can restrict us from talking about and publicising both male and female homosexuality by classing it as "immoral." Beyond this there are a whole series of specific minor offences. Although "the act" is not illegal, asking someone to go to bed with you can be classed as "importuning for an immoral act," and kissing in public is classed as "public indecency."

Even if you do not get into trouble, you will find yourself hampered by the application of the law in your efforts to set up home together, to raise children, and to express your love as freely as straight people may do.

The practice of the police in "enforcing" the law makes sure that cottagers and cruisers will be zealously hunted, while queer-bashers may be apprehended, half-heartedly after the event.

PHYSICAL VIOLENCE

On 25 September 1969 a man walked onto Wimbledon Common. We know the common to be a popular cruising ground, and believe the man to have been one of our gay brothers. Whether or not this is the case, the man was set upon by a group of youths from a nearby housing estate, and literally battered to death with clubs and boots. Afterwards, a boy from the same estate said: "When you're hitting a queer, you don't think you're doing wrong. You think you're doing good. If you want money off a queer, you can get it off him—there's nothing to be scared of from the law, cause you know they won't go to the law." (Sunday Times, 7/21/1971).

Since that time, another man has been similarly murdered on Hampstead Heath. But murder is only the most extreme form of violence to which we are exposed, not having the effective rights of protection. Most frequently we are "rolled" for our money, or just beaten up: and this happens to butch looking women in some districts.

PSYCHIATRY

One way of oppressing people and preventing them getting too angry about it, is to convince them, and everyone else, that they are sick. There has hence arisen a body of psychiatric "theory" and "therapy" to deal with the "problems" and "treatment" of homosexuality.

Bearing in mind what we have so far described, it is quite understandable that gay people get depressed and paranoid; but it is also, of course, part of the scheme that gay people should retreat to psychiatrists in times of troubles.

Operating as they do on the basis of social convention and prejudice, NOT scientific truth, mainstream psychiatrists accept society's prevailing view that the male and female sex roles are "good" and "normal," and try to adjust people to them. If that fails, patients are told to "accept themselves" as "deviant." For the psychiatrist to state that homosexuality was perfectly valid and satisfying, and that the hang-up was society's inability to accept that fact, would result in the loss of a large proportion of his patients.

Psychiatric "treatment" can take the form either of mindbending "psychotherapy," or of aversion therapy which operates on the crude conditioning theory that if you hit a person hard enough, he'll do what you want. Another form of "therapy" is chemically induced castration, and there is a further form of "treatment" which consists in erasing part of the brain, with the intent (usually successful) of making the subject an asexual vegetable.

This "therapy" is not the source of the psychiatrist's power, however. Their social power stems from the facile and dangerous arguments by which they contrive to justify the prejudice that homosexuality is bad or unfortunate, and to mount this fundamental attack upon our right to do as we think best. In this respect, there is little difference between the psychiatrist who says: "From statistics we can show that homosexuality is connected with madness," and the one who says: "Homosexuality is unfortunate because it is socially rejected." The former is a dangerous idiot—he cannot see that it is society which drives gay people mad. The second is a pig because he does see this, but sides consciously with the oppressors.

That psychiatrists command such credence and such income is surprising if we remember the hysterical disagreements of theory and practice in their field, and the fact that in formulating their opinions, they rarely consult gay people. In fact, so far as is possible, they avoid talking to them at all, because they know that such confrontation would wreck their theories.

SELF-OPPRESSION

The ultimate success of all forms of oppression is our self-oppression. Self-oppression is achieved when the gay person has adopted and internalised straight people's definition of what is good and bad. Self-oppression is saying: "When you come down to it, we are abnormal." Or doing what you most need and want to do, but with a sense of shame and loathing, or in a state of disassociation, pretending it isn't happening; cruising or cottaging not because you enjoy it, but because you're afraid of anything less anonymous. Self-oppression is saying: "I accept what I am," and meaning: "I accept that what I am is second-best and rather pathetic." Self-oppression is any other kind of apology: "We've been living together for ten years and all our married friends know about us and think we're just the same as them." Why? You're not.

Self-oppression is the dolly lesbian who says: "I can't stand those butch types who look like truck drivers"; the virile gay man who shakes his head at the thought of "those pathetic queens." This is self-oppression because it's just another way of saying: "I'm a nice normal gay. just like an attractive heterosexual."

The ultimate in self-oppression is to avoid confronting straight society, and thereby provoking further hostility: Self-oppression is saying, and believing: "I am not oppressed."

WHY we're oppressed

Gay people are oppressed. As we've just shown, we face the prejudice, hostility and violence of straight society, and the opportunities open to us in work and leisure are restricted, compared with those of straight people. Shouldn't we demand reforms that will give us tolerance and equality? Certainly we should—in a liberal-democratic society, legal equality and protection from attack are the very least we should ask for. They are our civil rights.

But gay liberation does not just mean reforms. It means a revolutionary change in our whole society. Is this really necessary? Isn't it hard enough for us to win reforms within the present society, and how will we engage the support of straight people if we get ourselves branded as revolutionaries?

Reforms may make things better for a while; changes in the law can make straight people a little less hostile, a little more tolerant—but reform cannot change the deep-down attitude of straight people that homosexuality is at best inferior to their own way of life, at worst a sickening perversion. It will take more than reforms to change this attitude, because it is rooted in our society's most basic institutions— the Patriarchal Family.

We've all been brought up to believe that the family is the source of our happiness and comfort. But look at the family more closely. Within the small family unit, in which the dominant man and submissive woman bring up their children in their own image, all our attitudes towards sexuality are learned at a very early age. Almost before we can talk, certainly before we can think for ourselves, we are taught that there are certain attributes that are "feminine" and other that are "masculine," and that they are God-given and unchangeable. Beliefs learned so young are very hard to change; but in fact these are false beliefs. What we are taught about the differences between man and woman is propaganda, not truth.

The truth is that there are no proven systematic differences between male and female, apart from the obvious biological ones. Male and female genitals and reproductive systems are different, and so are certain other physical characteristics, but all differences of temperament, aptitudes and so on, are the result of upbringing and social pressures. They are not inborn.

Human beings could be much more various than our constricted patterns of "masculine" and "feminine" permit—we should be free to develop with greater individuality. But as things are at present, there are only these two stereotyped roles into which everyone is supposed to fit, and most people—including gay people too—are apt to be alarmed when they hear these stereotypes or gender roles attacked, fearing that children "won't know how to grow up if they have no one to identify with," or that "everyone will be the same," i.e. that there will be either utter chaos or total conformity. There would in fact be a greater variety of models and more freedom for experimentation, but there is no reason to suppose this will lead to chaos.

By our very existence as gay people, we challenge these roles. It can easily be seen that homosexuals don't fit into the stereotypes of masculine and feminine, and this is one of the main reasons why we become the object of suspicion, since everyone is taught that these and only these two roles are appropriate.

Our entire society is built around the patriarchal family and its enshrinement of these masculine and feminine roles. Religion, popular morality art, literature and sport all reinforce these stereotypes. In other words, this society is a sexist society, in which one's biological sex determines almost all of what one does and how one does it; a situation in which men are privileged, and women are mere adjuncts of men and objects for their use, both sexually and otherwise.

Since all children are taught so young that boys should be aggressive and adventurous, girls passive and pliant, most children do tend to behave in these ways as they get older, and to believe that other people should do so too.

So sexism does not just oppose gay people, but all women as well. It is assumed that because women bear children they should and must rear them, and be simultaneously excluded from all other spheres of achievement.

However, as the indoctrination of the small child with these attitudes is not always entirely successful (if it were, there would be no gay people for a start), the ideas taken in by the young child almost unconsciously must be reinforced in the older child and teenager by a consciously expressed male chauvinism: the ideological expression of masculine superiority. Male chauvinism is not hatred of women, but male chauvinists accept women only on the basis that they are in fact lesser beings. It is an expression of male power and male privilege, and while it's quite possible for a gay man to be a male chauvinist, his very existence does also challenge male chauvinism in so far as he rejects his male supremacist role over women, and perhaps particularly if he rejects "masculine" qualities.

It is because of the patriarchal family that reforms are not enough. Freedom for gay people will never be permanently won until everyone is freed from sexist role-playing and the straightjacket of sexist rules about our sexuality. And we will not be freed from these so long as each succeeding generation is brought up in the same old sexist way in the Patriarchal family.

But why can't we just change the way in which children are brought up without attempting to transform the whole fabric of society?

Because sexism is not just an accident—it is an essential part of our present society, and cannot be changed without the whole society changing with it. In the first place, our society is dominated at every level by men, who have an interest in preserving the status quo; secondly, the present system of work and production depends on the existence of the patriarchal family. Conservative sociologists have pointed out that the small family unit of two parents and their children is essential in our contemporary advanced industrial family where work is minutely subdivided and highly regulated—in other words, for the majority very boring. A man would not work at the assembly line if he had no wife and family to support; he would not give himself fully to his work without the supportive and reassuring little group ready to follow him about and gear itself to his needs, to put up with his ill temper when he is frustrated or put down by the boss at work.

Were it not also for the captive wife, educated by advertising and everything she reads into believing that she needs ever more new goodies for the home, for her own beautification and for the children's well-being, our economic system could not function properly, depending as it does on people buying far more manufactured goods than they need. The housewife, obsessed with the ownership of as many material goods as possible, is the agent of this high level of spending. None of these goods will ever satisfy her, since there is always something better to be had, and the surplus of these pseudo "necessities" goes hand in hand with the absence of genuinely necessary goods and services, such as adequate housing and schools.

The ethic and ideology of our culture has been conveniently summed up by the enemy. Here is a quotation, intended quite seriously, from an American psychiatric primer. The author, Dr. Fred Brown, states:

> Our values in Western civilisation are founded upon the sanctity of the family, the right to property, and the worthwhileness of 'getting ahead ' The family can be established on/y through heterosexual intercourse, and this gives the woman a high value. (Note the way in which woman is appraised as a form of property.) Property acquisition and worldly success are viewed as distinctly masculine aims. The individual who is outwardly masculine but appears to fall into the feminine class by reason ... of his preference for other men denies these values of our civilisation. In denying them he belittles those goals which carry weight and much emotional colouring in our society and thereby earns the hostility of those to whom these values are of great importance.

We agree with his description of our society and its values—but we reach a different conclusion. We gay men and women do deny these values of our civilisation. We believe that the society Dr. Brown describes is an evil society. We believe that work in an advanced industrial society could be organised on more humane lines, with each job more varied and more pleasurable, and that the way society is at present organised operates in the interests of a small ruling group of straight men who claim most of the status and money, and not in the interests of the people as a whole. We also believe that our economic resources could be used in a much more valuable and constructive way than they are at the moment—but that will not happen until the present pattern of male dominance in our society changes too.

That is why any reforms we might painfully exact from our rulers would only be fragile and vulnerable; that is why we, along with the women's movement, must fight for something more than reform. We must aim at the abolition of the family, so that the sexist, male supremacist system can no longer be nurtured there.

WE CAN DO IT

Yet although this struggle will be hard, and our victories not easily won, we are not in fact being idealistic to aim at abolishing the family and the cultural distinctions between men and women. True, these have been with us throughout history, yet humanity is at last in a position where we can progress beyond this.

Only reactionaries and conservatives believe in the idea of "natural man." Just what is so different in human beings from the rest of the animal kingdom is their "unnaturalness." Civilisation is in fact our evolution away from the limitations of the natural environment and towards its ever more complex control. It is not "natural" to travel in planes. It is not "natural" to take medicines and perform operations. Clothing and shoes do not grow on trees. Animals do not cook their food. This evolution is made possible by the development of technology—i.e. all those tools and skills which help us to control the natural environment.

We have now reached a stage at which the human body itself, and even the reproduction of the species, is being "unnaturally" interfered with (i.e. improved) by technology. Reproduction used to be left completely to the uncontrolled biological processes inherited from our animal ancestors, but modern science, by drastically lowering infant mortality, has made it unnecessary for women to have more than two or three babies, while contraceptives have made possible the conscious control of pregnancy and the freeing of sexuality from reproduction. Today, further advances are on the point of making it possible for women to be completely liberated from their biology by means of the development of artificial wombs. Women need no longer be burdened with the production of children at their main task in life, and need be still less in the future.

The present gender-role system of "masculine" and "feminine" is based on the way that reproduction was originally organised. Men's freedom from the prolonged physical burden of bearing children gave them a privileged position which was then reinforced by an ideology of male superiority. But technology has now advanced to a stage at which the gender-role system is no longer necessary.

However, social evolution does not automatically take place with the steady advance of technology. The gender-role system and the family unit built around it will not disappear just because they have ceased to be necessary. The sexist culture gives straight men privileges which, like those of any privileged class, will not be surrendered without a struggle, so that all of us who are oppressed by this culture (women and gay people), must band together to fight it. The end of the sexist culture and of the family will benefit all women, and gay people. We must work together with women, since their oppression is our oppression, and by working together we can advance the day of our common liberation.

A NEW LIFE-STYLE

In the final section we shall outline some of the practical steps gay liberation will take to make this revolution. But linked with this struggle to change society there is an important aspect of gay liberation that we can begin to build here and now—a NEW, LIBERATED LIFE-STYLE which will anticipate, as far as possible, the free society of the future.

Gay shows the way. In some ways we are already more advanced than straight people. We are already outside the family and we have already, in part at least, rejected the "masculine" or "feminine" roles society has designed for us. In a society dominated by the sexist culture it is very difficult, if not impossible, for heterosexual men and women to escape their rigid gender-role structuring and the roles of oppressor and oppressed. But gay men don't need to oppress women in order to fulfill their own psycho-sexual needs, and gay women don't have to relate sexually to the male oppressor, so that at this moment in time, the freest and most equal relationships are most likely to be between homosexuals.

But because the sexist culture has oppressed us and distorted our lives too, this is not always achieved. In our mistaken, placating efforts to be accepted and tolerated, we've too often submitted to the pressures to conform to the straightjacket of society's rules and hang ups about sex.

Particularly oppressive aspects of gay society are the Youth Cult, Butch and Femme role-playing, and Compulsive Monogamy.

THE YOUTH CULT. Straight women are the most exposed in our society to the commercially manipulated (because very profitable) cult of youth and "beauty"—i.e. the conformity to an ideal of "sexiness" and "femininity" imposed from without, not chosen by women themselves. Women are encouraged to look into the mirror and love themselves because an obsession with clothes and cosmetics dulls their appreciation of where they're really at … until it's too late. The sight of an old woman bedizened with layers of make-up, her hair tortured into artificial turrets, provokes ridicule on all sides. Yet this grotesque denial of physical aging is merely the logical conclusion to the life of a woman who has been taught that her value lies primarily in her degree of sexual attractiveness.

Gay women, like straight men, are rather less into the compulsive search for youth, perhaps because part of their rebellion has been the rejection of themselves as sex objects—like men they see themselves as people; as subjects rather than objects. But gay men are very apt to fall victim to the cult of youth—those sexual parades in the "glamorous" meat-rack bars of London and New York, those gay beaches of the South of France and Los Angeles haven't anything to do with liberation. Those are the hang-outs of the plastic gays who are obsessed with image and appearance. In love with their own bodies, these gay men dread the approach of age, because to be old is to be "ugly," and with their youth they lose also the right to love and be loved, and are valued only if they can pay. This obsession with youth is destructive. We must all get away from the false commercial standards of "beauty" imposed on us by movie moguls and advertising firms, because the youth/beauty hang-up sets us against one another in a frenzied competition for attention, and leads in the end to an obsession with self which is death to real affection or real sensual love. Some gay men have spent so much time staring at themselves in the mirror that they've become hypnotised by their own magnificence and have ended up by being made unable to see anyone else.

BUTCH AND FEMME. Many gay men and women needlessly restrict their lives by compulsive role playing. They may restrict their own sexual behaviour by feeling that they must always take either a butch or a femme role, and worse, these roles are transposed to make even more distorting patterns in general social relationships. We gay men and women are outside the gender-role system anyway, and therefore it isn't surprising if some of us—of either six—are more "masculine" and others more "feminine." There is nothing wrong with this. What is bad is when gay people try to impose on themselves and on one another the masculine and feminine stereotypes of straight society, the butch seeking to expand his ego by dominating his/her partner's life and freedom, and the femme seeking protection by submitting to the butch. Butch really is bad—the oppression of others is an essential part of the masculine gender role. We must make gay men and women who lay claim to the privileges of straight males understand what they are doing; and those gay men and women who are caught up in the femme role must realise, as straight women increasingly do, that any security this brings is more than offset by their loss of freedom.

COMPULSIVE MONOGAMY. We do not deny that it is as possible for gay couples as for some straight couples to live happily and constructively together. We question however as an ideal, the finding and settling down eternally with one "right" partner. This is the blueprint of the straight world which gay people have taken over. It is inevitably a parody, since they haven't even the justification of straight couples— the need to provide a stable environment for their children (though in any case we believe that the suffocating small family unit is by no means the best atmosphere for bringing up children).

Monogamy is usually based on ownership—the woman sells her services to the man in return for security for herself and her children— and is entirely bound up in the man's idea of property. Furthermore in our society the monogamous couple, with or without children, is an isolated, shut-in, up-tight unit, suspicious of and hostile to outsiders. And though we don't lay down rules or tell gay people how they should behave in bed or in their relationships, we do want them to question society's blueprint for the couple. The blueprint says "we two against the world," and that can be protective and comforting. But it can also be suffocating, leading to neurotic dependence and underlying hostility, the emotional dishonesty of staying in the comfy safety of the home and garden, the security and narrowness of the life built for two, with the secret guilt of fancying someone else while remaining in thrall to the idea that true love lasts a lifetime—as though there were a ration of relationships, and to want more than one were greedy. Not that sexual fidelity is necessarily wrong; what is wrong is the inturned emotional exclusiveness of the couple which students the partners so they can no longer operate at all as independent beings in society. People need a variety of relationships in order to develop and grow, and to learn about other human beings.

It is especially important for gay people to stop copying straight— we are the ones who have the best opportunities to create a new lifestyle and if we don't, no one else will. Also, we need one another more than straight people do, because we are equals suffering under an insidious oppression from a society too primitive to come to terms with the freedom we represent. Singly, or isolated in couples, we are weak—the way society wants us to be. Society cannot put us down so easily if we fuse together. *We have to get together, understand one another, live together.*

Two ways we can do this are by developing consciousness-raising groups and gay communes.

Our gay communes and collectives must not be mere convenient living arrangements or worse, just extensions of the gay ghetto. They must be a focus of consciousness-raising lie. Raising or increasing our awareness of our real oppression and of gay liberation activity, a new focal point for members of the gay community. It won't be easy, because this society is hostile to communal living. And besides the practical hang-ups of finding money and a place large enough for a collective to live in, there are our own personal hang-ups: we have to change our attitudes to our personal property, to our lovers, to our day-to day priorities in work and leisure, even to our need for privacy.

But victory will come. If we're convinced of the importance of the new life-style, we can be strong and we can win through.

AIMS

The long-term goal of Gay Liberation, which inevitably brings us into conflict with the institutionalised sexism of this society, is to rid society of the gender-role system which is at the root of our oppression. This can only be achieved by eliminating the social pressures on men and women to conform to narrowly defined gender roles. It is particularly important that children and young people be encouraged to develop their own talents and interests and to express their own individuality rather than act out stereotyped parts alien to their nature.

As we cannot carry out this revolutionary change alone, and as the abolition of gender roles is also a necessary condition of women's liberation, we will work to form a strategic alliance with the women's liberation movement, aiming to develop our ideas and our practice in close inter-relation. In order to build this alliance, the brothers in gay liberation will have to be prepared to sacrifice that degree of male chauvinism and male privilege that they still all possess.

To achieve our long term goal will take many years, perhaps decades. But attitudes to the appropriate place of men and women in our society are changing rapidly, particularly the belief in the subordinate place for women. Modern conditions are placing increasing strain on the small nuclear family containing one adult male and one adult female with narrowly defined roles and bound together for life.

The way forward

FREE OUR HEADS

The starting point of our liberation must be to rid ourselves of the oppression which lies in the head of every one of us. This means freeing our heads from self oppression and male chauvinism, and no longer organising our lives according to the patterns with which we are indoctrinated by straight society. It means that we must root out the idea that homosexuality is bad, sick or immoral, and develop a gay pride. In order to survive, most of us have either knuckled under to pretended that no oppression exists, and the result of this has been further to distort our heads. Within gay liberation, a number of consciousness-raising groups have already developed, in which we try to understand our oppression and learn new ways of thinking and behaving. The aim is to step outside the experience permitted by straight society, and to learn to love and trust one another. This is the precondition for acting and struggling together.

By freeing our heads we get the confidence to come out publicly and proudly as gay people, and to win over our gay brothers and sisters to the ideas of gay liberation.

CAMPAIGN Before we can create the new society of the future, we have to defend our interests as gay people here and now against all forms of oppression and victimisation. We have therefore drawn up the following list of immediate demands:

- that all discrimination against gay people, male and female, by the law, by employers, and by society at large, should end.
- that all people who feel attracted to a member of their own sex be taught that such feeling are perfectly valid.
- that sex education in schools stop being exclusively heterosexual.

- that psychiatrists stop treating homosexuality as though it were a sickness, thereby giving gay people senseless guilt complexes.
- that gay people be as legally free to contact other gay people, though newspaper ads, on the streets and by any other means they may want as are heterosexuals, and that police harassment should cease right now.
- that employers should no longer be allowed to discriminate against anyone on account of their sexual preferences.
- that the age of consent for gay males be reduced to the same as for straight.
- that gay people be free to hold hands and kiss in public, as are heterosexuals.

Those who believe in gay liberation need to support actively their local gay group. With the rapid spread of the ideas of gay liberation, it is inevitable that many members of such groups have only partially come to terms with their homosexuality. The degree of self-oppression is often such that it is difficult to respect individuals in the group, and activists frequently feel tempted to despair. But if we are to succeed in transforming our society we must persuade others of the merits of our ideas, and there is no way we can achieve this if we cannot even persuade those most affected by our oppression to join us in fighting for justice.

We do not intend to ask for anything. We intend to stand firm and assert our basic rights. If this involves violence, it will not be we who initiate this, but those who attempt to stand in our way to freedom.

7 The Effeminist Manifesto

1973

Steven F. Dansky, John Knoebel, and Kenneth Pitchford

We, the undersigned Effeminists of Double-F hereby invite all like-minded men to join with us in making our declaration of independence from Gay Liberation and all other Male-Ideologies by unalterably asserting our stand of revolutionary commitment to the following Thirteen Principles that form the quintessential substance of our politics:

On the oppression of women.

1. SEXISM. All women are oppressed by all men, including ourselves. This systematic oppression is called sexism.

2. MALE SUPREMACY. Sexism itself is the product of male supremacy, which produces all other forms of oppression that patriarchal societies exhibit: racism, classism, ageism, economic exploitation, ecological imbalance.

3. GYNARCHISM. Only that revolution which strikes at the root of all oppression can end any and all of its forms. That is why we are gynarchists; that is, we are among those who believe that women will seize power from the patriarchy and, thereby, totally change life on this planet as we know it.

4. WOMEN'S LEADERSHIP. Exactly how women will go about seizing power is no business of ours, being men. But as effeminate men oppressed by masculinist standards, we ourselves have a stake in

the destruction of the patriarchy, and thus we must struggle with the dilemma of being partisans—as effeminists—of a revolution opposed to us—as men. To conceal our partisanship and remain inactive for fear of women's leadership or to tamper with questions which women will decide would be no less despicable. Therefore, we have a duty to take sides, to struggle to change ourselves, to act.

On the oppression of effeminate men.

5. MASCULINISM. Faggots and all effeminate men are oppressed by the patriarchy's systematic enforcement of masculinist standards, whether these standards are expressed as physical, mental, emotional, or sexual stereotypes of what is desirable in a man.

6. EFFEMINISM. Our purpose is to urge all such men as ourselves (whether celibate, homosexual, or heterosexual) to become traitors to the class of men by uniting in a movement of Revolutionary Effeminism so that collectively we can struggle to change ourselves from non-masculinists into anti-masculinists and begin attacking those aspects of the patriarchal system that most directly oppress us.

7. PREVIOUS MALE-IDEOLOGIES. Three previous attempts by men to create a politics of fighting oppression have failed because of their incomplete analysis: the Male Left, Male Liberation, and Gay Liberation. These and other formations, such as sexual libertarianism and the counter-culture, are all tactics for preserving power in men's hands by pretending to struggle for change. We specifically reject a hands by pretending to struggle for change. We specifically reject a carry-over from one or more of these earlier ideologies—the damaging combination of ultra-egalitarianism, anti-leadership, anti-technology, and downward mobility. All are based on a politics of guilt and a hypocritical attitude towards power which prevents us from developing skills urgently needed in our struggle and which confuses the competence needed for revolutionary work with the careerism of those who seek personal accommodation within the patriarchal system.

8. COLLABORATORS AND CAMP FOLLOWERS. Even we effeminate men are given an option by the patriarchy: to become collaborators in the task of keeping women in their place. Faggots, especially, are

offered a subculture by the patriarchy which is designed to keep us oppressed and also increase the oppression of women. This subculture includes a combination of anti-women mimicry and self-mockery known as camp which, to its trivializing effect, would deny us any chance of awakening to our own suffering, the expression of which can be recognized as revolutionary sanity by the oppressed.

9. SADO-MASCULINITY: ROLE PLAYING AND OBJECTIFICATION. The Male Principle, as exhibited in the last ten thousand years, is chiefly characterized by an appetite for objectification, role-playing, and sadism. First, the masculine preference for thinking as opposed to feeling encourages men to regard other people as things, and to use them accordingly. Second, inflicting pain upon people and animals has come to be deemed a mark of manhood, thereby explaining the well-known proclivity for rape and torture. Finally, a lust for power-dominance is rewarded in the playing out of that ultimate role, The Man, whose rapacity is amply displayed in witch-hunts, lynchings, pogroms, and episodes of genocide, not to mention the day-to-day (often life-long) subservience that he exacts from those closest to him.

Masculine bias, thus, appears in our behavior whenever we act out the following categories, regardless of which element in each pair we are most drawn to at any moment: subject/object; dominant/submissive; master/slave; butch/femme. All of these false dichotomies are inherently sexist, since they express the desire to be masculine or to possess the masculine in someone else. The racism of white faggots often reveals the same set of polarities, regardless of whether they choose to act out the dominant or submissive role with black or third-world men. In all cases, only by rejecting the very terms of these categories can we become effeminists. This means explicitly rejecting, as well, the objectification of people based on such things as age; body; build; color; size or shape of facial features, eyes, hair, genitals; ethnicity or race; physical and mental handicap; life-style; sex. We must therefore strive to detect and expose every embodiment of The Male Principle, no matter how and where it may be enshrined and glorified, including those arenas of faggot objectification (baths, bars, docks, parks) where power-dominance, as it operates in the selecting of roles and objects, is known as "cruising."

10. MASOCH-EONISM. Among those aspects of our oppression which The Man has foisted upon us, two male heterosexual perversions, in particular, are popularly thought of as being "acceptable" behavior for effeminate men: eonism (that is, male transvestitism) and masochism. Just as sadism and masculinism, by merging into one identity, tend to become indistinguishable one from the other, so masochism and eonism are born of an identical impulse to mock subservience in men, as a way to project intense anti-women feelings and also to pressure women into conformity by providing those degrading stereotypes most appealing to the sado-masculinist. Certainly, sado-masoch-eonism is in all its forms the very anti-thesis of effeminism. Both the masochist and the eonist are particularly an insult to women since they overtly parody female oppression and pose as object lessons in servility.

11. LIFE-STYLE: APPEARANCE AND REALITY. We must learn to discover and value The Female Principle in men as something inherent, beyond roles or superficial decoration, and thus beyond definition by any one particular life-style (such as the recent androgyny fad, transsexuality, or other purely personal solutions). Therefore, we do not automatically support or condemn faggots or effeminists who live alone, who live together in couples, who live together in all-male collectives, who live with women, or who live in any other way—since all these modes of living in and of themselves can be sexist but also can conceivably come to function as bases for anti-sexist struggle. Even as we learn to affirm in ourselves the cooperative impulse and to admire in each other what is tender and gentle, what is aesthetic, considerate, affectionate, lyrical, sweet, we should not confuse our own time with that post-revolutionary world when our effeminist natures will be free to express themselves openly without fear or punishment or danger of oppressing others. Above all, we must remember that it is not merely a change of appearance that we seek, but a change in reality.

12. TACTICS. We mean to support, defend and promote effeminism in all men everywhere by any means except those inherently male supremacist or those in conflict with the goals of feminists intent on seizing power. We hope to find militant ways for fighting our oppression that will meet these requirements. Obviously, we do not seek the legalization of faggotry, quotas, or civil-rights for faggots or other

measures designed to reform the patriarchy. Practically, we see three phases of activity: naming our enemies to start with, next confronting them, and ultimately divesting them of their power. This means both the Cock Rocker and the Drag Rocker among counter-cultist heroes, both the Radical Therapist and the Faggot-Torturer among effemiphobic psychiatrists, both the creators of beefcake pornography and of eonistic travesties. It also means all branches of the patriarchy that institutionalize the persecution of faggots (schools, church, army, prison, asylum, old-age home).

But whatever the immediate target, we would be wise to prepare for all forms of sabotage and rebellion which women might ask of us, since it is not as pacifists that we can expect to serve in the emerging world-wide anti-gender revolution. We must also constantly ask ourselves and each other for a greater measure of risk and commitment than we may have dreamt was possible yesterday. Above all, our joining in this struggle must discover in us a new respect for women, a new ability to love each other as effeminists, both of which have previously been denied us by our misogyny and effemiphobia, so that our bonding until now has been the traditional male solidarity that is always inimical to the interests of women and pernicious of our own sense of effeminist self-hood.

13. DRUDGERY AND CHILDCARE: RE-DEFINING GENDER. Our first and most important step, however, must be to take upon ourselves at least our own share of the day-to-day life-sustaining drudgery that is usually consigned to women alone. To be useful in this way can release women to do other work of their choosing and can also begin to re-define gender for the next generation. Of paramount concern here, we ask to be included in the time-consuming work of raising and caring for children, as a duty, right and privilege.

Attested to this twenty-seventh day of Teves and first day of January, in the year of our falthering Judeo-Christian Patriarchy, 5733 and 1973, by Steven Dansky, John Knoebel, and Kenneth Pitchford.

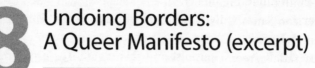

8 Undoing Borders: A Queer Manifesto (excerpt)

2007

HAVOQ

Structural, Institutional, Historical Context

Caminante, no hay puentes, se hace puentes al andar. (Voyager, there are no bridges, one builds them as one walks).
—Gloria E. Anzaldúa

As a group, we have focused primarily on the US/Mexico border—on the line itself as well as on how border-enforcement systems stretch much farther north and south. While much of what we say here can be extended to other borders worldwide, we believe it is important to consider the specific histories of the US/Mexican border and how that impacts what it is today. We also know that the history of the border describes ongoing structural and institutional oppressions that maintain the violence of that line deep into the interior of our country and to the south as well.

So, as a skeleton of a skeleton, a scratch at the surface of history, here are some reminders of what came before, with, and through the border:

- The United States was built on broken treaties with, robbery from, and genocide of indigenous people across the continent.
- It was built through slave labor and the labor of under- (and often un-) paid immigrants.
- It grew through the violent acquisition of even more lands,

from the Southwestern U.S. to Hawaii to Puerto Rico as well as the Philippines, Guantanamo Bay, the Panama Canal, Guam, American Samoa, the Northern Mariana Islands and the U.S. Virgin Islands.

- "Free trade" agreements that seek to break down some economic barriers to international trade have always been directly linked to militarization of the border region. For example, NAFTA's passage was followed by Operation Gatekeeper, which began the current tactic of sealing off popular border-crossing points by building more walls and fences and increasing border personnel, surveillance and other military technology.
- The more militarized the border becomes, the more people die trying to cross it. Since 1994, over 5,000 people have died at the border. U.S. policy makers call this "deterrence by death."
- This militarization is tied to free trade agreements because it works to trap vulnerable workforces on both sides of the border while granting freedom of movement to capital.

Through this history, we can see that the border is part of a larger cycle of violence. It is rooted in the ongoing colonization, imperialism, and global economic structures that continue to dominate our world. Any conversation about im/migration is not just about people moving across borders or from one country to another. It is inherently rooted in deep-seated racism, classism, xenophobia, sexism, homophobia, ableism and any other institutional or societal forms of dominance.

Therefore, we try to root our work in the historical struggle within the greater movement (we don't want to always be reinventing the wheel and we have a lot to learn from what came before us). We want to continue to question all forms of power and authority including but not limited to the law, the state, social norms and social relationships.

Guiding Principles

How We Will Organize with One Another: AKA, FABULOSITY

When we focus on organizing as part of everyday life, the process becomes as important as the final product.
—Paula X. Rojas, Are the Cops in our Heads and Hearts?

As we come together to organize around the demands we lay out in this document, we also want to keep in mind the culture we create with one another. Why? Because the same forces that make borders, racism and militarism have seeped into our relationships, our communities and ourselves. It's up to us to define, build and practice how we will treat each other and work together. We've heard some people call this praxis: putting our ideas into action, but we want to suggest another word for how we try to translate our queer perspectives on the oppressive forces around us into empowering action: FABULOSITY.

FABULOSITY means that we will strive for open and inclusive language and culture. We will try to recognize each of our different and overlapping experiences. We have a lot to learn from and offer one another even knowing that we won't always agree.

FABULOSITY means that we will also try to be open with one another, to new people and ideas. We will constantly try to expand or deepen our base of ideas, skills and energy. We respect and will use a diversity of tactics to achieve our goals.

FABULOSITY means that we will make time to do the work of building ways of being with one another that do not replicate the hierarchies that marginalize us in the first place. We believe that we can build coalitions and movements without relying on non-profits and professional activism. We want to create and maintain liberating and borderless spaces within which to meet and do work.

FABULOSITY means that we will work together not just to meet specific demands, but also to build a movement and a community.

This means that we will consider the sustainability of our projects, trying to find a balance between our immediate goals and needs and our longer-term vision or collective health. And it means that the community we make isn't confined to meetings and actions. We like to eat together, play together and spend unstructured time with one another.

FABULOSITY means that we will ask for what we want, not just what we think we can get. We know that compromise is part of working in coalition, but we will strive to keep in mind our larger vision of what kind of world we ultimately want to see. We know this is hard. We will probably mess up sometimes, but we will do our best.

So, What is "Queer Organizing?"

Are you afraid of the homosexualization of life? / And I'm not talking about sticking it in and pulling it out / I'm talking about tenderness "compañero"...
        —Pedro Lemebel, from the poem "Punto de Vista Diferente"

Some folks might look at this document or come to one of our meetings and ask what any of this has to do with being queer. We're not working primarily on the im/migration issues traditionally understood to be The Gay Ones (asylum, bi-national marriage, etc.), so what do our sexualities and our gender identities have to do with what we think about borders?

Is it just that we're a bunch of people organizing together who mostly happen to identify as queer? Not really, even though it's nice to get to use words like Fabulosity when we work on projects like this. Is this just another border-creating effort to define who's in and who's out? We hope not. Rather than viewing Queer as a who or a what, we see Queer as the how: the culture we create with one another, the platform from which we organize together. We want to focus on two things queers have historically been really excellent at building into our communities (and building our communities out of): one is an uncommon comfort with/love of gray areas, and another is a radical redefinition of family.

Gray Areas:
It's about breaking down binaries (like black/white, woman/man) and recognizing how complex we all are—how our identities and communities overlap, merge and intersect. These lines that separate us can be understood as borders. Sometimes they're literal or physical and sometimes they are cultural and social. Sometimes they are all of those things at once, but in any form, we're not into them.

In regards to the parts of movement focused on migrant justice, it's often about breaking down the rhetoric that separates us from one another: naming some immigrants (workers, members of nuclear family units) "good" and others "bad." It means looking at the diversity in im/migrant groups' relationships to the United States, and creating spaces for differences within the movement. It is from this platform that we recognize the power of vibrant, diverse spaces to be revolutionary sites to build collective liberation.

Radical & Chosen Families:

Excluded from the traditional nuclear family unit for a long time, queers have made their own families. There are many forms—from drag houses to communes—but again and again, these chosen families look like a complex network of people that take care of, care about, nurture and mentor us. Through this new imagining of family, we expand our understanding of who we are responsible to and whose struggles are intertwined with our own.

As we organize together against the racist, sexist, classist and otherwise oppressive impacts of borders and immigration policies, we take this redefinition of family as a model for deep solidarity, enabling us to develop networks and connections based on mutual support. It means we will recognize the needs and voices not prioritized in mainstream movements. And it means we will work to continually expand the boundaries of who we are and those we are responsible to, breaking down walls and building bridges as we imagine what collective liberation can look like.

POINTS OF UNITY/INTENTIONS

While many forces erect and sustain borders, we will work to dismantle them on all levels.

Freedom of Movement

We believe that freedom of movement is a fundamental human right. The right to mobility is more than the right to cross a national boundary. It is the right to live and work where we please, including the right to stay home. It means dismantling detention centers along with the larger

Prison Industrial Complex. It also means the right to full participation in our community without fear: without the threat of raids and deportation and without racist policies that seek to limit our access to community resources and spaces.

- We actively support the actions of individuals or groups (and the communities that support them) to stay or move where they choose. Often this is tied to the ways we seek to survive (and hopefully thrive) amidst the current extreme levels of economic and state imperialism.
- We oppose coercive forces like NAFTA, CAFTA, and other "free trade" agreements that, through job loss and land privatization, have forced people to urban areas and to the north, effectively denying individuals of their right to stay; their right to live in the community of their choosing.
- We oppose efforts to criminalize mutual aid, such as harboring provisions which penalize those who assist undocumented immigrants, their families and loved ones.
- We oppose the continued construction of a wall spanning the entire US-Mexico border and the increased policing in the border regions, which has only raised the death toll on the border. We recognize that increased enforcement has not decreased the number of people traveling north; it has just funneled them into more remote and dangerous areas.
- We oppose all state efforts to continue the splitting of the lands currently held by indigenous people, specifically the imposition of border policies on reservations that span both sides of the line. We support the indigenous people who continue to struggle to maintain the right to move through their own sovereign lands.

Resisting Militarization and Criminalization

We share in our common need to experience safety for ourselves and our communities, but do not believe in the use of punitive force to achieve this goal. Additionally, we find that the militarization of the border of the United States serves to prop up the illusion of separate communities, which in turn foster feelings of hate, xenophobia, and violence, rather than achieving safety.

*We assert our inherent interconnectedness and strive to cultivate
systems, strategies and tactics that create safe communities without the
use of militarization by the police, ICE or other forces. We challenge
the criminalization of people's survival behavior to create safe communities for themselves, such as crossing borders without documentation,
sex work, gang involvement and drug dealing. We will continue to push
to expand the choices we can make to not only survive, but to thrive in
freedom.*

In the short term this means that we call for a shift of resources
away from militarization, policing and criminalization toward our
shared need for education, health and economic sustainability.

Specifically,

- End Operation Streamline, 287g and the "Secure Communities" program as well as ICE raids, deportations, detentions, and
  any policies that grant local police the right to act as immigration enforcement. We support calls for local municipalities to
  opt out of such forced collaboration with federal immigration
  enforcement as well as refusing any allocation of local resources
  for enforcement of federal anti-immigrant policies.
- We reject any actions, policy or legislation that deny access to
  any public services or legal protections based on migratory
  status. This means that we support education as an option for
  all people.[1]
- We support and participate in mutual aid projects that share
  community resources with all people regardless of any societal
  status.
- We will strive to create sanctuary where we live and support
  others in similar steps towards removing ICE and all federal
  immigration enforcement from our communities entirely. We
  want a halt to the building and further enforcement of border
  walls and to see current fences torn down. We want an end to
  all private contracts that further the technological militarization

---

1 We feel the need to say, in light of the recent failure of the Dream Act, that while
we believe in access to education for all, we do not believe that higher education or
military service should be the only way for undocumented youth to gain residency/
path to citizenship. We also do not believe that we should have to concede to increased
militarization to gain access to educational resources.

of the border and create a new "Border-Military Industrial Complex."

- While we reject the false dichotomy of "citizen/non-citizen," we support the immediate and unconditional citizenship of all people living within the bounds of the United States as an initial step towards living without criminalization and fear from ICE. In addition, we support steps in that direction, such as ending the 1 year deadline for applying for asylum[2] and 3 and 10 year bars for "unlawful presence."

WORKING Against Borders

We will stand to root out racism and homophobia within the labor movement and work to break down all programs, laws and agreements that exist to divide workers. "An injury to one is an injury to all" does not stop at the border.

We will work to dismantle the tools of an economic system meant to separate us from one another. This includes opposing:

- Free trade agreements like NAFTA, CAFTA, etc.
- Workplace raids
- Labor laws that target workers who are trying to organize, regardless of documentation
- English-only workplace requirements and legislation that makes learning English and undergoing background checks a prerequisite for work or citizenship.
- Guest worker programs, H1 visas and other classist, racist, and sexist programs which establish hierarchies among migrants and ensure that individuals' stay in the country is dependent on their employers.
- Laws that threaten people who report exploitative labor conditions with deportation and other sanctions

---

2 While we acknowledge that the US is not inherently any safer for queer and transgender people than the rest of the world, we the support the expansion of accessibility to asylum. The current 1 year deadline is particularly challenging for queer and trans people who often experience high levels of isolation and as a result do not learn about asylum options until the deadline has passed.

- We support a version of the Employment Non Discrimination Act (ENDA) that includes protections for queer and trans immigrant workers.
- We call for a repeal of the Real ID Act, which creates a national database and makes it more difficult for immigrants and transgendered people to obtain legal identification. (This is especially troubling for transgender immigrants who could face deportation for having different genders listed on different documents). Further, we call for an end to penalties imposed on states and municipalities that choose to opt out of the Real ID Act.
- We oppose laws that criminalize people who are trafficked into the U.S. and forced to work in exploitative, dangerous, or coercive conditions. Unlike many anti-trafficking advocates who see sex work as inherently exploitative, we believe that all people should be able to engage in the work they choose (including sex work) in order to survive and provide for themselves and their loved ones.

Policing OurSelves

We see a connection between the policing of people's genders and sexualities with the policing of borders and seek to build a world where everyone may assert their right to self-determination. We reject the regulation of ourselves and our relationships through socially-created borders, such as those used to define traditional families, acceptable sex practices, ideal bodies and gender presentations, and love.

- We work to expand the definitions of "family" to include queer and other self-defined relationships. Rather than fight to extend marriage to queers, we strive to create free and inclusive communities where we do not place legal borders between coupled families and those who enjoy single, asexual or polyamorous lifestyles. We believe that freedom of movement, access to services and other benefits should be available to all of us regardless of our marital or immigration status.
- We believe in the right to access documentation regardless of our federal immigration status and documentation that reflects our self-identified genders or does not list our genders at all.

Further, we seek to build a world where government does not hold the power to legitimize our identities through access to documentation such as IDs and that government control over access to these documents no longer impacts our abilities to lead the lives we want to live.

- We support the dismantling of medical guidelines that are used as political borders to limit freedom of movement. Recent changes to medical requirements for im/migration, including the lift of the HIV ban and of mandatory HPV and herpes vaccinations are examples of steps in this direction. We believe that requirements such as these violate the health, sexual and reproductive rights of migrants. We want an end to all medical screenings as a prerequisite for immigration, which are developed and enforced in sexist, homophobic, transphobic, and racist ways.

The Transfeminist Manifesto (excerpt)

2001

Emi Koyama

Primary Principles

Primary principles of *transfeminism* are simple. First, it is our belief that each individual has the right to define her or his own identities and to expect society to respect them. This also includes the right to express our gender without fear of discrimination or violence. Second, we hold that we have the sole right to make decisions regarding our own bodies, and that no political, medical or religious authority shall violate the integrity of our bodies against our will or impede our decisions regarding what we do with them.

However, no one is completely free from the existing social and cultural dynamics of the institutionalized gender system. When we make any decisions regarding our gender identity or expression, we cannot escape the fact that we do so in the context of the patriarchal binary gender system. Trans women in particular are encouraged and sometimes required to adopt the traditional definition of femininity in order to be accepted and legitimatized by the medical community, which has appointed itself as the arbiter of who is genuinely woman enough and who is not. Trans women often find themselves having to "prove" their womanhood by internalizing gender stereotypes in order to be acknowledged as women or to receive hormonal and surgical interventions. This practice is oppressive to trans and non-trans women alike, as it denies uniqueness of each woman.

Transfeminism holds that nobody shall be coerced into or out of personal decisions regarding her or his gender identity or expression in order to be a "real" woman or a "real" man. We also believe that nobody should be coerced into or out of these personal decisions in order to qualify as a "real" feminist.

As trans women, we have learned that our safety is often dependent on how well we can "pass" as "normal" women; as transfeminists, we find ourselves constantly having to negotiate our need for safety and comfort against our feminist principles. *Transfeminism* challenges all women, including trans women, to examine how we all internalize heterosexist and patriarchal mandates of genders and what global implications our actions entail; at the same time, we make it clear that it is not the responsibility of a feminist to rid herself of every resemblance to the patriarchal definition of femininity. Women should not be accused of reinforcing gender stereotypes for making personal decisions, even if these decisions appear to comply with certain gender roles; such a purity test is disempowering to women because it denies our agency, and it will only alienate a majority of women, trans or not, from taking part in the feminist movement.

Transfeminism believes in the notion that there are as many ways of being a woman as there are women, that we should be free to make our own decisions without guilt. To this end, *transfeminism* confronts social and political institutions that inhibit or narrow our individual choices, while refusing to blame individual women for making whatever personal decisions. It is unnecessary—in fact *oppressive*—to require women to abandon their freedom to make personal choices to be considered a true feminist, for it will only replace the rigid patriarchal construct of ideal femininity with a slightly modified feminist version that is just as rigid. *Transfeminism* believes in fostering an environment where women's individual choices are honored, while scrutinizing and challenging institutions that limit the range of choices available to them.

The Question of Male Privilege

Some feminists, particularly radical lesbian feminists, have accused trans women and men of benefiting from male privilege. Male-to-female transsexuals, they argue, are socialized as boys and thus given male privilege; female-to-male transsexuals on the other hand are characterized as traitors who have abandoned their sisters in a pathetic attempt to acquire male privilege. *Transfeminism* must respond to this criticism, because it has been used to justify discrimination against trans women and men within some feminist circles.

When confronted with such an argument, a natural initial response of trans women is to deny ever having any male privilege whatsoever in their lives. It is easy to see how they would come to believe that being born male was more of a burden than a privilege: many of them despised having male bodies and being treated as boys as they grew up. They recall how uncomfortable it felt to be pressured to act tough and manly. Many have experienced bullying and ridicule by other boys because they did not act appropriately as boys. They were made to feel ashamed, and frequently suffered from depression. Even as adults, they live with the constant fear of exposure, which would jeopardize their employment, family relationships, friendships and safety.

However, as transfeminists, we must resist such a simplistic reaction. While it is true that male privilege affects some men far more than others, it is hard to imagine that trans women born as males never benefited from it. Most trans women have "passed" as men (albeit as "sissy" ones) at least some point in their lives, and were thus given preferable treatments in education and employment, for example, whether or not they enjoyed being perceived as men. They have been trained to be assertive and confident, and some trans women manage to maintain these "masculine" traits, often to their advantage, after transitioning.

What is happening here is that we often confuse the oppression we have experienced for being gender-deviant with the absence of the male privilege. Instead of claiming that we have never benefited from male supremacy, we need to assert that our experiences represent a dynamic interaction between male privilege and the disadvantage of being trans.

Any person who has a gender identity and/or an inclination toward a gender expression that match the sex attributed to her or him has a privilege of being non-trans. This privilege, like other privileges, is invisible to those who possess it. And like all other privileges, those who lack the privilege intuitively know how severely they suffer due to its absence. A trans woman may have limited access to male privilege depending on how early she transitioned and how fully she lives as a woman, but at the same time she experiences vast emotional, social, and financial disadvantages for being trans. The suggestion that trans women are inherently more privileged than other women is as ignorant as claiming that gay male couples are more privileged than heterosexual couples because both partners have male privilege.

Tensions often arise when trans women attempt to access "women's spaces" that are supposedly designed to be safe havens from the patriarchy. The origin of these "women's spaces" can be traced back to the early lesbian feminism of the 1970s, which consisted mostly of white middle-class women who prioritized sexism as the most fundamental social inequality while largely disregarding their own role in perpetuating other oppressions such as racism and classism. Under the assumption that sexism marked women's lives far more significantly than any other social elements, they assumed that their experience of sexism is universal to all women regardless of ethnicity, class, etc.— meaning, all non-trans women. Recent critiques of the 1970s radical feminism point out how their convenient negligence of racism and classism in effect privileged themselves as white middle-class women.

Based on this understanding, transfeminists should not respond to the accusation of male privilege with denial. We should have the courage to acknowledge ways in which trans women may have benefited from male privilege—some more than others, obviously—just like those of us who are white should address white privilege. *Transfeminism* believes in the importance of honoring our differences as well as similarities because women come from a variety of backgrounds. Transfeminists confront our own privileges, and expect non-trans women to acknowledge their privilege of being non-trans as well.

By acknowledging and addressing our privileges, trans women can hope to build alliances with other groups of women who have traditionally been neglected and deemed "unladylike" by white middle-class standard of womanhood. When we are called deviant and attacked just for being ourselves, there is nothing to gain from avoiding the question of privilege.

Deconstructing the Reverse Essentialism

While the second wave of feminism popularized the idea that one's gender is distinct from her or his physiological sex and is socially and culturally constructed, it largely left unquestioned the belief that there was such a thing as true physical sex. The separation of gender from sex was a powerful rhetoric used to break down compulsory gender roles, but allowed feminists to question only half of the problem, leaving the naturalness of essential female and male sexes until recently.

Transfeminism holds that sex and gender are both socially constructed; furthermore, the distinction between sex and gender is artificially drawn as a matter of convenience. While the concept of gender as a social construct has proven to be a powerful tool in dismantling traditional attitudes toward women's capabilities, it left room for one to justify certain discriminatory policies or structures as having a biological basis. It also failed to address the realities of trans experiences in which physical sex is felt more artificial and changeable than their inner sense of who they are.

Social construction of biological sex is more than an abstract observation: it is a physical reality that many intersex people go through. Because society makes no provision for the existence of people whose anatomical characteristics do not neatly fit into male or female, they are routinely mutilated by medical professionals and manipulated into living as their assigned sex. Intersex people are usually not given an opportunity to decide for themselves how they wish to live and whether or not they want surgical or hormonal "correction." Many intersex people find it appalling that they had no say in such a major life decision, whether or not their gender identity happen to match their assigned sex. We believe that genital mutilation of intersex children is inherently abusive because it unnecessarily violates the integrity of their bodies without proper consent. The issue is not even whether or not the sex one was assigned matches her or his gender identity; it is whether or not intersex people are given real choice over what happens to their bodies.

Trans people feel dissatisfied with the sex assigned to them without their consent according to the simplistic medical standard. Trans people are diverse: some identify and live as members of the sex different from what was assigned to them by medical authorities, either with or without medical intervention, while others identify with neither or both of male and female sexes. Trans liberation is about taking back the right to define ourselves from medical, religious and political authorities. *Transfeminism* views any method of assigning sex to be socially and politically constructed, and advocates a social arrangement where one is free to assign her or his own sex (or non-sex, for that matter).

As trans people begin to organize politically, it is tempting to adopt the essentialist notion of gender identity. The cliché popularized by the mass media is that trans people are "women trapped in men's bodies" or vice versa. The attractiveness of such a strategy is clear, as the general population is more likely to become supportive of us if we could convince them that we are somehow born with a biological error over which we have no control over it. It is also often in tune with our own sense of who we are, which feels very deep and fundamental to us. However, as transfeminists, we resist such temptations because of their implications.

Trans people have often been described as those whose physical sex does not match the gender of their mind or soul. This explanation might make sense intuitively, but it is nonetheless problematic for *transfeminism*. To say that one has a female mind or soul would mean there are male and female minds that are different from each other in some identifiable way, which in turn may be used to justify discrimination against women. Essentializing our gender identity can be just as dangerous as resorting to biological essentialism.

Transfeminism believes that we construct our own gender identities based on what feels genuine, comfortable and sincere to us as we live and relate to others within given social and cultural constraint. This holds true for those whose gender identity is in congruence with their birth sex, as well as for trans people. Our demand for recognition and respect shall in no way be weakened by this acknowledgement. Instead of justifying our existence through the reverse essentialism, *transfeminism* dismantles the essentialist assumption of the normativity of the sex/gender congruence.

Body Image/Consciousness as a Feminist Issue

We as feminists would like to claim that we feel comfortable, confident and powerful with our own bodies; unfortunately, this is not the case for many women, including trans women.

For many transfeminists, the issue of body image is where our needs for comfort and safety directly collide with our feminist politics. Many of us feel so uncomfortable and ashamed of our appearances that we opt to remain in the closet or endure electrolysis, hormone therapy and surgical interventions to modify our bodies in congruence with our identity as women. These procedures are costly, painful and time-consuming and can lead to the permanent loss of fertility and other serious complications such as an increased risk of cancer.

Why would anyone opt for such a seemingly inhumane practice? While we might like to believe that the need to match our bodies to our gender identity to be innate or essential, we cannot in honesty neglect social and political factors contributing to our personal decisions.

One such factor is society's enforcement of dichotomous gender roles. Because our identities are constructed within the social environment into which we are born, one could argue that the discontinuity between one's gender identity and physical sex is problematic only because society is actively maintaining a dichotomous gender system. If one's gender were an insignificant factor in society, the need for trans people to modify their bodies to fit into the dichotomy of genders may very well decrease, although probably not completely.

However, such reasoning should not be used to hold back trans persons from making decisions regarding their bodies. Trans women are extremely vulnerable to violence, abuse and discrimination as they are, and should not be made to feel guilty for doing whatever it takes for them to feel safe and comfortable. *Transfeminism* challenges us to consider ways in which social and political factors influence our decisions, but ultimately demands that society respect whatever decisions we each make regarding our own bodies and gender expression.

It is not contradictory to fight against the institutional enforcement of rigid gender roles while simultaneously advocating for individuals' rights to choose how they live in order to feel safe and comfortable. Nor is it contradictory to provide peer support to each other so that we can build healthy self-esteem while embracing individuals' decisions to modify their bodies if they choose to do so. We can each challenge society's arbitrary assumptions about gender and sex without becoming dogmatic. None of us should be expected to reject every oppressive factor in our lives at the same time; it would burn us out and drive us crazy. Sum of our small rebellions combined will destabilize the normative gender system as we know it. Various forms of feminisms, queer activism, *transfeminism*, and other progressive movements all attack different portions of the common target, which is the heterosexist patriarchy.

Violence Against Women

Feminists have identified since the 1970s violence against women was not merely as isolated events, but as a systematic function of the patriarchy to keep all women subjugated. *Transfeminism* calls attention to the fact that trans women, like other groups of women who suffer from multiple oppressions, are particularly vulnerable to violence compared to women with non-trans privilege.

First, trans women are targeted because we live as women. Being a woman in this misogynist society is dangerous, but there are some factors that make us much more vulnerable when we are the targets of sexual and domestic violence. For example, when a man attacks a trans woman, especially if he tries to rape her, he may discover that the victim has or used to have a "male" anatomy. This discovery often leads to a more violent assault fueled by homophobia and transphobia. Trans women are frequently assaulted by men when their trans status is revealed. Murders of trans women, like that of prostitutes, are seldom taken seriously or sympathetically by the media and the authorities— especially if the victim is a trans woman engaged in prostitution.

Trans women are also more vulnerable to emotional and verbal abuse by their partners because of their often-low self-esteem and negative body image. It is easy for an abuser to make a trans woman feel ugly, ashamed, worthless and crazy, because these are the same exact messages the whole society has told her over many years. Abusers get away with domestic violence by taking away women's ability to define their own identity and experiences—the areas where trans women are likely to be vulnerable to begin with. Trans women have additional difficulty in leaving their abusers because it is harder for them to find employment and would almost certainly lose child custody to their abusive partner in a divorce if there were any children involved.

In addition, trans women are targeted for being queer. Homophobes tend not to distinguish between gays and trans people when they commit hate crimes, but trans people are much more vulnerable to attack because they are often more visible than gays. Homophobic terrorists do not look into people's bedrooms when they go out to hunt gays; they look for gendered cues that do not match the perceived sex of their prey, effectively targeting those who are visibly gender-deviant. For every gay man or lesbian whose murder makes national headlines, there are many more trans people who are killed across the nation, even though there are far more "out" gays and lesbians than there are "out" trans people.

Trans men also live in the constant fear of discovery as they navigate in a society that persecutes men who step outside of their socially established roles. Crimes against trans men are committed by strangers as well as by close "friends," and are undoubtedly motivated by a combination of transphobia and misogyny, performed as a punishment for violating gender norms in order to put them back in a "woman's place."

Because of the danger in which we live, *transfeminism* believes that violence against trans people is one of the largest issues we must work on. We may be hurt and disappointed that some women-only events refuse to let us in, but it is the violence against us that has literally killed us or forced us to commit suicide way too often for way too long. We have no choice but to act, immediately.

In this regard, cooperation with traditional domestic violence shelters, rape crisis centers and hate crime prevention programs is essential. Some shelters have already decided to fully accept trans women just like they would any other women, while others hesitate for various reasons. We must organize and educate existing agencies about why trans women deserve to be served. We must stress that the dynamics of the violence against trans women is not unlike that involving non-trans women, except that we are often more vulnerable. And we should also advocate for services for trans men.

As transfeminists, we should not just demand that existing organizations provide services to us; we should join them. We should volunteer to assist them develop an effective screening method in order to preserve safety as they expand their base. We should make ourselves available as crisis counselors and case managers to other trans women in need. We should help them fund trans-specific workshops for their staff too. We should develop self-defense courses for trans women modeled after feminist self-defense programs for women, but which pay special attention to our unique experiences. There may not be enough of us to start our own shelters from scratch, but we can work toward elimination of the violence against trans people in the broader coalition toward the elimination of violence against women and sexual minorities.

We must also address the issue of economic violence. Trans women are often in poverty because as women we earn less than men do, because overt discrimination against trans people in employment is rampant, and because of the prohibitively high cost of transitioning. This also means that abusive partners of trans women have more leverage to control and keep us trapped in abusive relationships. *Transfeminism* believes in fighting transphobia and sexism simultaneously in the economic arena as well as social and political.

Health and Reproductive Choice

It may seem ironic that trans women, who in general have no capacity for bearing children, would be interested in the women's reproductive rights movement, but *transfeminism* sees a deep connection between the liberation of trans women and women's right to choose.

First of all, society's stigmatization of trans existence is partly due to the fact that we mess with our reproductive organs. Non-genital cosmetic surgeries are performed far more frequently than sex reassignment surgeries, yet they do not require months of mandatory psychotherapy. Nor are the ones who pursue cosmetic surgeries ridiculed and scorned daily on nationally broadcast trash talk shows. Such hysteria over our personal choices is fueled in part by society's taboo against self-determination of our reproductive organs: like women seeking an abortion, our bodies have become an open territory, a battleground.

Additionally, the hormones that many trans women take are similar in origin and chemical composition to what non-trans women take for birth control, emergency contraception, and hormone replacement therapy. As trans women, we share their concerns over safety, cost and availability of these estrogen-related pills. Trans and non-trans women need to be united against the right-wing tactics aimed at making means and information to control our bodies unavailable, if not illegal.

Of course, reproductive choice is not just about access to abortion or birth control; it is also about resisting forced and coerced sterilization or abortion of less privileged women. Likewise, *transfeminism* strives for the right to refuse surgical and hormonal interventions, including those prescribed for intersex people, and still expect society to honor our sense of who we are.

During the 1980s, lesbians were purged from some reproductive choice organizations because they were seen as irrelevant to their cause. But the right to choose is not exclusively a heterosexual issue nor a non-trans issue, as it is fundamentally about women having the right to determine what they do with their own bodies. Transfeminists should join reproductive choice organizations and demonstrate for choice. A society that does not respect women's right to make decisions regarding pregnancy is not likely to respect our right to make decisions about medical interventions to make our bodies in congruence with our gender identity. If we fear having to obtain underground hormones or traveling overseas for a sex reassignment surgery, we should be able to identify with women who fear going back to the unsafe underground abortions.

In addition, *transfeminism* needs to learn from the women's health movement. Research on health issues that is of particular interest to women, such as breast cancer, did not arise in a vacuum. It was through vigorous activism and peer-education that these issues came to be taken seriously. Realizing that the medical community has historically failed to address women's health concerns adequately, transfeminists cannot expect those in the position of power to take trans women's health seriously. That is why we need to participate in and expand the women's health movement.

Drawing analogies from the women's health movement also solves the strategic dilemma over pathologization of gender identity. For many years, trans people have been arguing with each other about whether or not to demand de-pathologization of gender identity disorder, which is currently a pre-requisite for certain medical treatments. It has been a divisive issue because the pathologization of gender identity disorder allows some of us to receive medical interventions, even though it stigmatizes us and negates our agency at the same time. Before the feminist critiques of modern medicine, female bodies are considered "abnormal" by the male-centered standard of the medical establishment, which resulted in the pathologization of such ordinary experiences of women as menstruation, pregnancy and menopause; it was the women's health movement that forced the medical community to accept that they are part of ordinary human experiences. *Transfeminism* insists that transsexuality is not an illness or a disorder, but as much a part of the wide spectrum of ordinary human experiences as pregnancy. It is thus not contradictory to demand medical treatment for trans people to be made more accessible, while de-pathologizing "gender identity disorder."

Call for Action

While we have experienced more than our share of rejection within and outside of feminist communities, those who remained our best allies have also been feminists, lesbians and other queers. *Transfeminism* asserts that it is futile to debate intellectually who is and is not included in the category "women": we must act, now, and build alliances.

Every day, we are harassed, discriminated against, assaulted, and abused. No matter how well we learn to pass, the social invisibility of trans existence will not protect us when all women are under attack. We can never win by playing by society's rule of how women should behave; we need feminism as much as non-trans women do, if not more. Transfeminists take pride in the tradition of our feminist foremothers and continue their struggle in our own lives.

Transfeminism believes that a society that honors cross-gender identities is the one that treats people of all genders fairly, because our existence is seen as problematic only when there is a rigid gender hierarchy. In this belief, it is essential for our survival and dignity that we claim our place in feminism, not in a threatening or invasive manner, but in friendly and cooperative ways. Initial suspicion and rejection from some existing feminist institutions are only natural, especially since they have been betrayed so many times by self-identified "pro-feminist" men; it is through our persistence and commitment to action that *transfeminism* will transform the scope of feminism into a more inclusive vision of the world.

10 Pajama Femme Manifesto

2011

Katie Tastrom

How can you tell who is a femme? Their shoes? Their outfits? Make-up? A combination of the three? Most days that I am out in the world I will be wearing sweatpants, a crappy t-shirt with no bra and no makeup, yet I am a femme. Like a lot of us, I have chronic illnesses that prevent me from wearing bras, and clothes other than pajamas (both because of the physical discomfort, and the energy needed). I am also fat, and have little time or money to shop (let alone time or money for altering or making clothes), and have trouble finding clothes that don't hurt, are affordable and fit, yet alone cute clothes that meet all these requirements. My feet deformities mean that all I can wear are ugly hippie shoes, sneakers or Doc Martens, and nothing that could be properly described as "cute."

There are all sorts of reasons, yet at the same time no reason is necessary, why many of us are pajama femmes. As a femme, my sexual orientation (what a ridiculous word!) feels invisible in a lot of queer spaces (and almost always in non queer specific places). As a pajama femme, my femmeness feels invisible everywhere. My gender identity is Dolly Parton, but my gender presentation is more Roseanne (who I adore and I think is amazing, but doesn't typify what we usually think of when we think of "femme").

And I know there are a lot of barriers for all of us in terms of looking how we feel and doing gender, but this is my experience, and I don't think it is an uncommon one.

I propose a different kind of femme, and we are fabulous. And here is our manifesto.

WHEREAS, Femmes of all kinds are often invisible in queer culture, and the traits that society deems feminine in all of us is devalued in queer and "mainstream culture,"

WHEREAS, many of us are also sick, poor, busy, tired, allergic, fat, incarcerated, lazy, etc., we may not have the resources (financially, energetically, materially etc.) to present ourselves and our gender to society the way we want to,

WHEREAS, we are the ONLY ones who can define our gender identity and sexual orientation and NO ONE, can tell us we are something that we are not, but we do want to be visible to each other and the world.

WE DECLARE:

As pajama femmes we understand all that and call for a new kind of femme visibility, one that is rooted in an analysis that centers the experience of those of us too fat to find cute clothes in our size, or too allergic to products to wear makeup, or too tired to deal with our hair (which affects many of those of us of color in very intense and resource heavy ways), or those of us that are incarcerated and have very little say in our physical appearance.

Pajama femme doesn't rely on outward appearances for identification.

Pajama femme challenges the idea that ANYONE'S gender can be summed up by their appearance.

Pajama femme understands that our gender and sexual orientation are just two of the jillions of identities that we are trying to navigate in this world,

Pajama femme knows that being marginalized is hard work and we should at least be comfortable.

So join the pajama femme revolution! We will be the ones at the gay bar in our sweatpants.

11 Lesbian Mafia Manifesto

2007

The Lesbian Mafia

The Lesbian Mafia: because Lesbians are not bisexual. Learn it b*tches. Leeearn it! We love our bi friends but Lesbians are NOT.

After decades of media and porno assault on Lesbian identity and culture, if anyone male, female, gay, bi or otherwise gets the simple truth above twisted then they are homophobic misogynists and need to GO. We understand that nothing in life is black or white and there are a myriad of reasons women end up living heterosexual lives ... internal or external homophobia, bad relationships, economic concerns, religion, kids etc., but for the most part it's reeeeally simple ... if a woman enjoys sleeping with dudes she's NOT a Lesbian. The End. She may be primarily attracted to women and "Lesbian identified" or whatever the frack, but sorry, she ain't Lez if she's doing it with dudes and gets hot for dudes, that's called bi or queer. Learn it! And PLEASE do not come to us with Jerry Springer questions about your gay guy friend who had sex with your Lesbian friend under a magnolia tree in 1992 who got preggers and they had a baby named Emily and ask us "is she a Lesbian?" Look, we don't know WTF your friend is.

On a more serious Manifesto-y note ...

Pro-Woman:
We are not feminists of any kind BECAUSE we are pro-woman we don't relate to most of the politics in the feminist/womanist or LGBT community anymore. We still have many as friends of course and there are still some great thinkers in the feminist world but our experience is that in the feminist community you are respected when you

say nothing, tow the line, and promote men's agendas under the guise of rigid equality and never ever hurting anyone's feelings ever for any reason whatsoever at WOMEN'S EXPENSE and being so "inclusive" that WOMEN have NOTHING to do with your focus any longer. In the gay community women have never been the focus they are only servants to the rest of the G B & T. So, not a big surprise who are considered "respected" in the feminist and gay community, THAT respect is meaningless and useless and we relate to it almost as little as we relate to the right wing but in a different way, conservative republican extremism is deliberate evil but liberal extremism is the path to hell paved with good intentions. Liberals ARE still good intentioned but ultimately you end up in almost the same place, just a different version of hell. And it's very easy for either side to become too extreme and tyrannical. If you look at both sides basic tenets, they aren't THAT different at their core but both sides violate that core HUGE. The only way to change it is to reject it and MAKE a new STANDARD, your own. The field needs to be changed, you don't climb their moron mountain and "play the game" and get "respected" by a bunch of over-privileged and wanna-be over-privileged self-promoting people who are WRONG most of the time NEVER focus on women and side against Lesbians at the drop of a dime on any given issue (the rare Lesbians who still have the ability for independent thought outside of these male-centric communities). You MOVE the field. Lesbian feminists have always done the heavy lifting and been the backbone in the feminist and LGBT world and then get abused HUGE and dismissed. Which is why these days Lesbians are rarely if ever feminist and don't bother showing up to gay or feminist functions in true numbers. And feminists can't distance themselves FROM Lesbians FAST ENOUGH! The feeling is mutual when they hijack a movement, miss the point entirely and reduce it all to "shame-free" promiscuity and not getting pregnant, ultimately serving males even MORE. At least men felt responsible for taking care of a woman and their children back in the day. It didn't always happen but at least the prick had to disappear and go to a new town if he was just going to abandon her with child because her father would come after him with a shotgun because her daddy wasn't going to support his daughter AND a grandkid. Now dudes can do whatever the hell they want.

And the LGBTQIAABCDEFGHIJKLMNOP community, if possible, are even more begrudging of Lesbians and particularly with the headway in media which Lesbians had to get on OUR OWN because the gay (and feminist/womanist) media excluded us COMPLETELY for decades while using our brain-power and muscle to advance a sausage-fest agenda that has little to nothing to do with Lesbian women. That backfired HUGE so NOW they're trying to change that but many are still horribly begrudging of the straight world's never ending fascination with most Lesbians, lipstick or not doesn't even seem to matter these days. Just the media headway and multiple orgasms alone will always make G B & T and feminists hate us but we digress ..... Saying the same old boring equation BS to a bunch of over-privileged people and those who aspire to be over-privileged people, isn't going to DO or CHANGE a thing. We'll still defend any one of them when right wing loonbags are attacking based on their Atheist masquerading as Christian agenda of hatred because WE are not spineless traitors but we will also be the first ones to argue with them too, same goes for any Trans women expecting us to stop identifying ourselves as women but instead "biological" women, you have really GOT to be kidding with that. You want four sexes do your thing, we'll hire you, we'll rent you an apartment, we'll chill with you, love you to death and respect you as an individual who can and should live the way you want but you should respect that women should live the way WE want and understand that women can have all different varying shades of feelings about things that affect us like who we undress with, without being shamed by the liberal, feminist or LGBT establishment who don't have any concept of reality or how things actually APPLY within the inner working of the Lesbian world. They have only been exposed to uber civilized privileged LGBT (and couldn't care less about Trans men by the way AND they would never tell men they had to start identifying as "biological" men and they wouldn't be taken seriously even if they tried but they never would because they aren't agro) so if anyone is expecting half of the human population to change how we identify ourselves, we call that misogynist crazy-making and that's not going to work for us because we are not slaves to be named, we already have one, it's called Women. And you can call us all the hostile misogynist labels you want, BIOLOGICAL FEMALE, CIS, GENDER THIS-OR-THAT, CGI, CSI, PSY-FY, PHI BETTA KAPPA, LOCA, FOUR LOCO phobic this and that and WHAT EVER the frack you want but when VIOLENCE and AGGRESSION are your go-to reaction whenever you hear women say something that disagrees with your misogynist rules for us, JUST EXACTLY how you want them, then don't expect us to think you are women exactly like us because violence, aggression and stabbing threats due to upset feelings are not how women handle things, we tune out that misogynist rage. But thankfully, and without any help from the feminist, LGBT or liberal world, the newer wave of gender-queer and Trans women have seemingly changed much of this outdated ideology, many are embracing their bodies and LOOK amazing and happier. And for all intents and purposes have seemingly dropped much of the misogynist aggressive attitudes. Call us!

We care about and have tremendous compassion for everyone but as shocking as it may be, our focus is WOMEN and LESBIANS. And femininity, which is not cut and dry, is the source of our strength. It is our observation that most (not all but most) L G B & T are frequently more aggressively misogynistic than straight men and women. That goes for the gay orgs who supposedly speak for us but decidedly do not. So when WE choose to donate our money, valuable life-energy and time it goes to <u>women's causes</u>. There are many women-specific cancers, autoimmune diseases and social and economic concerns that very often directly affect Lesbian women. 99.9 percent of Lesbians will never contract HIV through sexually irresponsible behavior BUT it IS likely that in her last years (or longer) she will live with a women-specific illness and/or disability like any other woman. Women's issues (not gay issues) ARE Lesbian issues. WE are not "bad" because we aren't CONSTANTLY concerned with EVERY SINGLE OTHER GBTQIAABCDEFGHIJKLMNOP group of 6 people under the sun who think they don't have it as good as we do. YOU DON'T KNOW US!! YOU DON'T KNOW SHIT about what we have or what it's like to be us. Can we live? We are FEMALE, we don't have anything that great. But we can't go anywhere or even read a liberal/ progressive or feminist or LGBTQIAABCDEFG blog without being shamed because we aren't MORE victimized than whatever letter of the LGBTQIAABCDEFG alphabet soup community's pet issue takes priority OVER women and decides THEY are more victimized than us. SCREW YOU. We are allowed to disagree with LGBT and feminist male-centric and everyone-ELSE-except-lezbos misogynist agendas without having to apologize for it. We aren't hurting ANYONE, harass the people who DO. Just because you're a woman or a Lesbian doesn't mean it's your JOB to bow to every single G B and T or feminist or liberal agenda and pet project. We don't have husbands, so G B and

T and feminists/womanists and even some Lesbians get aggressive with the stupid Lesbians who don't ever want to upset anyone ever EVEN when THEY are being disrespected or put upon. Their conferences, media and blogosphere are more often than not indoctrination tools for christ's sake, that have less and less to do with WOMEN or LESBIANS any and every time we tune in. It's SO easy to get women, especially young women, to sympathize with everyone OVER themselves and then think "Wow, I never thought about it like that. I'm more hetero-normative than I thought blah blah blah … poor everyone else but me, sniffle, sob. I SHOULD be thinking about THEM, they ARE feminism." NO they aren't actually. Every single other minority status group does not need women to fight for them, they ALL end up doing WAY better than women are and THEY never fight for WOMEN unless it serves THEM and when they do pretend they care they threaten non-support because of women not being inclusive ENOUGH of THEIR agendas! FUCK THAAAT sick twisted misogyny masquerading as inclusiveness!! You have only to look so far as their media to see how important women's issues are in the G B T and feminist and liberal world, (it's not cool when anyone is killed or attacked but) the difference in the response to violence against women via their online and mainstream media says unequivocally that G, B & T matter more than women. That rigid "equality" UNDER the law gets the over-privileged all fired up but has no place in the REALITY of most humans, LEAST of all WOMEN regardless of age or station in life. Libs, LGBT, Feminists just ignore that fact and shoot for utopia that can only stagnate and fail (if their wet dreams were realized). But get 'em young and they will be morons forever until someone slaps them awake. They wanna shame everyone and LESBIANS for not being BETTER more EVOLVED people. Oh, eat a dick. You think your average Woman or Lesbian doesn't have more stress and problems to deal with and they have TIME to worry about every single G B & T??? We don't need their over-privileged asses telling us we need to be BETTER. MOST Lesbians are having a hard time just LIVING! You live in a niche that has nothing to do with REAL WOMEN AND LESBIANS then good for you. But take a trip out of SOHO or Park Slope or Tribeca, fuck LEAVE NY, LA, SF, BOSTON, CONNECTICUT or SEATTLE and see what REAL women, no less LESBIANS have to deal with! FUCK, JUST LEAVE YOUR NEIGHBORHOOD and talk to someone who didn't go to COLUMBIA!!!

Have you ever noticed they will tell you ALL DAY what and who not to support and why, because it supposedly "discriminates" but never tell you ANYTHING that educates you so then YOU have knowledge to apply? You're not helping me bitch, you're just applying equation standards to shit and handing me a NAZI playbook. How about you help a bitch UNDERSTAND something, with the information she already HAS. People are not stupid they just THINK they are. They live in this world and they HAVE their own experiences, they just don't know they know stuff. And handing them an UNREALIS-TIC playbook just makes them feel bad OR turns them into a weird thoughtless army of morons WHO will eventually grow up,

have an experience and then stop participating in nonsense. Women don't PARTICIPATE in feminism anymore. They don't even LIVE it. They don't need to slut march or a sleazy gay parade that has fuck all to do with women or Lesbians, they need to LIVE IT and have their own experiences and interpretations. Giving them knowledge and information is empowering them and HELPS them LIVE IT.

Pro 2nd Amendment: In a world where women are always on the receiving end of violence, we find it positively orgasmic when a normal, sane, empowered woman can handle a gun. In our opinion gun bans are illogical, have proven disastrous and we consider them anti-woman.

Moderate/Political Atheists: We regularly call out BS on all sides of the political spectrum, liberal, conservative, left, right, democrat, repub-lican, etc., because BS on ALL sides needs to be called out. We have no use or respect for politicians and their shit-whore media. We don't believe a single word any of them say. They're as phony as they sound. We stay away from ALL talking head provocateur reactionary pundits and anchors on the conservative White Trash Media and all cable "news" and of course the jukebox nobody knows even exists anymore known as right wing a.m. radio, controlled mainstream media, print, editorials and the blogosphere whose only job is to inflame and incite hatred. No matter which pundits or talking heads you tune into it is blatantly obvious they've divided our society and that is precisely why they exist. Right wing White Trash Media are quintessential white trash and they are the leaders of and the face of white trash everywhere. They have NOTHING to offer. That's WHY they're on the extremist

right. Hate, fights, and snide little comments. That's so EASY. And
they aren't even good at it. You could spout THEIR agenda on ANY
topic in your sleep. Just pit everyone against each other with HATE
using phony arguments right, left and center and twist and blame and
anyone with a different opinion are automatically the "opposition"
the "bad guys" and blah blah blah booooooooooooring propaganda
snooze-fest!! Just pretend it makes sense. Left wing media isn't guilt-
less, their propaganda seeps in or is pushed deliberately whether they
are well intentioned or not. We (TLM) have an agenda, Lesbian and
women stuff and goofing around on Podcast, but that is the POINT,
we're totally up front about that. But it can't even be remotely compared. We aren't posing as JOURNALISTS who have no agenda, there
IS an agenda and you can disagree with it all you want, it says it right
IN this manifesto, but we don't just swallow all of anyone's ideals, no
matter who it's from. We just like to point out how biased and twisted
the misinformation the media puts out IS. Admit the agenda, stop
pretending it's unbiased news, we don't care which side you are on or
how well intentioned you are, if you HAVE an agenda, don't hide it.
Let people decide, don't trick them. Even a benevolent dictator controls and oppresses, the left is waaaay better than the evil right wing
but it's still tyranny. There are billions of people and endless ideas in
this world, and there are only two stark opposing positions available
on any and every issue that divide Americans into extreme left or the
extreme right wing misogynist, racist, classist, homophobes? Then
they switch sides on issues every couple of years to keep everyone off
balance? Come on. This is what will bring the already sinking America
down completely. Sorry, the world is NOT divided into left and right.
How blind and stupid can people be that they can't see what is right
in front of their eyes? They watch the news to be informed but the
very reason they're so uninformed is BECAUSE they watch the news.
Anyone who continues to watch and believe it deserves what they
get. Entering the political arena is playing by their rules, you've lost
already, it is their system and they write the rules and the news media
lies all day and all night and sprinkles in half-truths to make it palat-
able. The system can't be fixed by working from within because the
system protects itself. The only answer is to refuse to go along with it
by not supporting a system that represents the powerful and excludes
real people with real-life concerns. There are only cliques and niche
groups with their crazy agendas. Do you enjoy being duped over and

over and over again? We don't. Disaffiliation from party politics is the revolution that will return power to the people.

We are <u>Pro-choice</u> but we do not subscribe to the divisive tenet that all of womanity boils down to this one issue. This doesn't mean however, that we don't have strong opinions about our reproductive rights and control over our own bodies. Maybe when we see Anti-choice reactionary frauds violently protesting IVF clinics for discarding all of the surplus embryos that die in trash bins we'll raise an eyebrow, until then, it's clear that they are frauds. As far as men's opinions on the matter we don't spend much time thinking about them. <u>Anti-choice Gay Men</u> and <u>Trans</u> on the other hand do cause a slight blip on our radar (there ARE some shit-whores) because if there's anyone on God's green earth further removed from the creation of life it's them. They could not care less about embryos but we sure get a laugh out of their embarrassing posturing that they have MORALS ahhaha!!! We suggest they focus their energies on themselves by taking a more vocal position on NAMBLA, HIV/AIDS transmission and get Preparation H by the caseload. Or perhaps, for those less civic minded, how about putting on a pair of pants at parades and God forbid maybe a shirt? Nobody wants to smell or see them shoving their offensive nakedness in everyone's faces it's beyond gross and embarrassing for everyone involved which is why we don't attend LGBTQIAABCDEFGHIJKLMNOP dude-centric parades. Clearly, they only want their unstable, slutty, low-class fag-hags and tranny-hags trotting behind them anyway. We'd like to remind these faux-Christian gay harpies that sodomy is prolifically condemned in the Old Testament very specifically between males. Leviticus does not apply to Lesbian women. No, women are not included in the condemnation "ALSO" because saying "man" in the bible applies to males and females, nope, WRONG, women have never been considered to have any sexual needs, no less was WRITTEN about for chrissakes until maybe the 1960s, so don't be ridiculous. And there's certainly no Leviticus for abortion either and abortions have most DEFINITELY been going on way before only the white trash Priests were killing babies and women off as witches who were probably with child from being raped by THEM, only God knows, they're so depraved. It really is ridiculous when an "I wanna be 'conservative' because I'm better than other fags" shit-whore pretends to judge a woman or have an opinion about birth control or anything really, picking up dog-shit even. If sticking your dick in another queer's ass produced a baby, not only would they want free birth control, they'd want free abortion too and they'd make zygote quilts, have vigils and cry into every camera on the planet. That actually goes for ANY dude if they could create life, just like how dude's health insurance covers VIAGRA and VASEC-TOMIES, so go make love to a glory-hole, ya degenerates. The only thing dudes can give birth to is a dump in the toilet. Their feigned anti-choice agenda is an act of anti-woman aggression and should be regarded as such. These are not just gay dudes with whom we have differing political opinions; they are fundamentally damaged miserable people who are intent upon attacking women's rights. The fact that it's just posturing and that they have no power does not make their behavior any less reprehensible and worthy of contempt. They exploit God and scripture to advance themselves reveling in the approval they get from bitter hateful fake Christian, Racist, Misogynist, Classist Homophobe conservative extremists by supporting an anti-choice agenda. Like crack heads, they will do anything to get their approval fix. They know they are frauds which is why they are self-destructive obnoxious buffoons who ultimately embarrass themselves constantly and everyone associated with them. No one takes them seriously, least of all the Christian conservative right who adeptly exploits their insecurities and uses them as pawns.

Finally, although we do have some strong opinions, we aren't the type of lesbians who need you to think like us in order to be friends. We find it effortless to look beyond differences, unless you're a hostile misogynist, racist, homophobic, classist a-hole.

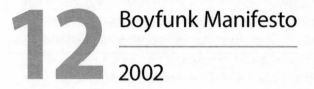

Boyfunk Manifesto

2002

Boyfunk

I don't know about you, but I'm tired of the mainstream gay male culture that says I'm supposed to be a mindless, hard-bodied twink whose only purpose in life is to titillate middle-aged, middle-class faggots.

I'm tired of the prevailing attitude out there. You know the one that says I'm supposed to spend all my time tanning, shopping for clothes, jerking off to Internet porn featuring boys who look like they're 13, working out or cruising parks, bathrooms, bars, rest stops, etc.

I'm so fuckin' sick of gay men who act like who they fuck or wanna fuck is the single most important facet of their existence—the guys whose synapses fire only in thinking about who, when, how, and where they're gonna bone the next twink they have their eye on.

boyfunk is not a dating service, chat room, gossip column, Hollywood star rag, site for idol worship or gay porn alternative.

boyfunk is a fuck you to all that *Out, The Advocate, XY, Genre, Men, Freshmen, Queer as Folk, Will & Grace,* &c stand for!

It's not about fitting into society or selling some circuit boy, cream puff image.

It's not about begging for laws to approve of our existence.

It's not about establishing a new marketing demographic or demonstrating the strength of the gay dollar.

It's not about creating alternative forms of media for the sake of being underground or separatist but because society and mainstream gay culture has chosen to exclude, alienate and degrade us.

boyfunk is not about you agreeing with me.

boyfunk is about creating images, writing and sounds I can relate to. Maybe you can too.

boyfunk is about encouraging other queer boys to explore their emotions and ideas about whatever inspires them and providing a space for them to feel comfortable doing so.

boyfunk is a fist up the ass of the gay establishment.

It's not about gays in the military, gay marriage or begging for "equal" rights.

boyfunk is queer corps.

boyfunk is about revolution.

boyfunk is about fucking, fucking hard, fucking well and fucking loving it.

boyfunk is about hearts and flowers, goatees and messy hair, tight t-shirts and baggie jeans to hide our hard-ons.

boyfunk is about getting dirty and staying there.

boyfunk is about the graduations, nuances, cracks, crevices, nooks and crannies that makes us individuals and give us a unique voice.

boyfunk is about wearing your heart on your sleeve.

boyfunk is my voice, heart and mind, not yours.

Queer Sailors, Butt Pirates, Punk Rock Dreams Cum True, International Spy Bois/Grrrls and Gorgeous Girlie Guys/Guyish Girls are the Gravediggers of the Gay Establishment. Lavender and Red and Black are the colors of our flag.

13 Manifesto for a New Feminist Presence

2007

Eskalera Karakola

The image of the queers, the freaks, the wild ones, the cyborgs, the hysterics, the truck-drivers, the frigid ones and the loose ones, the ones in broken high-heels and the barefoot ones assaulting the supermarket of the world, the privatized garden and the wedding ceremony is our most cherished dream. To be divine is always to push the limits, to lose composure, to expose the sexual discipline of Home and Crust; it is to disorganize anew all the categories.

Rights are a useful but insufficient charity, perverse in their disciplinary capacity. Now that capital has been embodied in us with hushed and persistent violence: (re)productive body, consumer body, clean and disinfected body which has repressed the ghost of stigma and death, versatile and accelerated body, it is time to ask:

Is a different body possible?

It must be, because here we are.

Times and spaces.

The space, in this case, the middle of Lavapies, Madrid. The time, open and changing, that which runs against our desires and our projects. The occupied social center Eskalera Karakola has been a part of our neighborhood for ten years now. A women's project arising from the necessity to experience ourselves, relate and invent ourselves, to communicate and to sabotage the mechanisms of production and reproduction, heterosexual normalization and rigid demarcation of gender roles imposed upon us.

A women's project which undertakes continually to pose questions and to propose from a feminist position, confronting the world with an analysis criss-crossed by the complexity of structures: those same structures which compose us, never innocent, always complex, the same structures which place us in tension and which demand us to understand ourselves as subjects rooted in a particular sex-gender-desire system, in a particular class, in a particular ethnic group, of a particular age... in a particular, always pressing space and time.

THUS WE OCCUPY AND INHABIT THE ESKALERA KARA-KOLA. OCCUPATION AS A REAPPROPRIATION OF PHYSICAL SPACE AND OCCUPATION AS A REAPPROPRIATION OF OUR OWN LIVING TIME, OF OUR OWN DESIRES AND AFFEC-TIONS, OUR OWN BODIES.

Always diverse and transforming, always different, we have undertaken to open a space for political intervention, an invitation to create a space of participation in all sorts of activities by, for, and with women. A photography workshop, a school for feminisms, the discussions and screenings of "the House of Difference," the bar as a space to meet ourselves, to take our own pulse, to explode contradictions and collect their creative energy. Energy for interaction and intervention, because the house is not isolated, is not alone, because to understand it is to take it with you into your own spaces, because the Karakola invites us to step out, critical, political and feminist. Always intervening, always, that is, coming and going. Finding limits, fighting them, daring ourselves with sometimes greater and sometimes lesser luck: harboring doubts, fragmenting ourselves, recomposing ourselves.

A project which is also indispensable in a neighborhood like Lavapies, submitted for years to an "urban recovery" plan which has not responded to the needs of those of us who live here, which has put aside our opinions and concerns. A neighborhood which lacks public facilities, acceptable housing conditions, social resources, spaces for meeting and socializing ... and which faces policies of exclusion and privatization, of ever greater limitation of people's basic rights. And it is here that the Karakola erupts as more than necessary space, a collective undertaking for relating, encountering, and communicating among women up against this dusty, suffocating, bleached out, fat-free, canned and vacuum packed life.

Spaces and times which press us on in our need to restore the house, an initiative which may at any moment be interrupted. Space which must be rebuilt; time which has us captive ... We break this waiting by acting, anticipating, pressuring so that the importance of our project be recognized.

Counting on your support.

But what is a feminist space?

Urban space hides itself in an opaque neutrality. We move through it so naturally that it is difficult for us to see that this space is not neutral at all, but rather the product of decisions and policies, struggles and demands, an accumulation of history and an incarnation of power. It forms us and transforms us; we are molded by the spaces through which we move, which structure our daily life, which determine whom we encounter and in what terms. Thus the space we live in is something intimate which constitutes our subjectivities at the same time that urban space—the streets, the squares—are "the public" par excellence, precisely that which is recognized as political.

To make explicit this unity, this non-differentiation, between "the public" and "the personal" and to insist that it is in this complex environment that "politics" is done, is, like so many feminist struggles, a matter of making visible the invisible, of denaturalizing what passes for "natural," just as is revealing the hidden economy of domestic work or the concealed anguish of sexual violence. To speak about space as a feminist is a question of valuing and politicizing the quotidian; recognizing that that which each one of us experiences—instability, violence, little annoyances, isolation—is that from which the productive and reproductive order is created, and also that from which resistance arises. Creating our own spaces is a matter of insisting that citizenship is a daily practice collectively built through the active and conscientious habitation of space.

Thus when we speak of a feminist space, we speak of a space in which the quotidian is recognized and approached as political, and where the political shows itself to be a daily matter: brought down from the heights, from the abstraction and the alienation, and occupied as a living space. Politicizing daily life—relationships, work, neighborhoods– requires a space from which to develop knowledge collectively, from which to reflect and think, from which to organize and experiment with new forms, new interventions.

Living life as political is a potent challenge, taking up the spirit of so many feminist, anti-racist and anti-homophobic struggles which have insisted in NOT accepting violence, exclusion or annoyances as "normal." If these struggles have achieved important changes in society it is thanks to many years of fighting and wagering on the collective. But let's not fool ourselves; much remains to be done, it is not time to rest on our laurels.

LET'S MAKE OF OUR BODIES, OUR SEXUALITY, OUR DESIRES, OUR EMOTIONS A GLOBAL DISORDER!

From here, from "the personal is political," from the insertion of a new conception of the political in daily life, from self-management and the collective, from this position we insist on a new way of "doing city."

Political processes are not unfamiliar to us; for this reason, we search for ways to promote participation in them, capacity of decision, of action, of transformation, in what we could call the formation of an active, public and participative citizenship. This is not something we can take for granted, especially as women who have seen the possibility of making decisions about our lives, our environment, our city, our world always restricted. This is then a question of generating collective links that can transmit, fluctuate, create new techniques of intervention and construction arising from ourselves, techniques that can really conform the city and the world we want and desire. Because we are part of this terrain we decide and fight daily to construct and organise it. Plastic designs of the world we want. Brutal expansions of constricted designs. Legitimate re-appropriation of our living space, of our bodies, of our boroughs, of our world.

PART II

ANTI-CAPITALIST/
ANARCHIST

Introduction to Anticapitalist/Anarchist

In this section, we take a sweeping look at the twin impulses of anarchy and anticapitalism, moving from early pro-anarchist texts of the mid-nineteenth century through to late-stage capitalism of today and visions for a future free of the constraints of capitalism. From the abolition of marriage (Emma Goldman and Marie Edwards) and money (D.M.D.), to the radical demands and platform statements of a radical feminist future (Anarchafeminist Manifesto, Radical Women Manifesto), these manifestos collectively imagine both the "freedom from" and "freedom to"—freedom from the constraints of a society based on capitalism and institutional oppression and the freedom to imagine, play, love, write, and breathe freely.

Refusing the emptiness of alienated labor (Laboria Cuboniks), the disenfranchisement of poor women, old women, and women of color (Radical Women Manifesto, Lindsey German and Nina Power), and the easy identity politics of "wokeness" (Anonymous), this section builds a case for a radical feminist future that is both self-aware and angry as hell. Traversing time period and region, this section weaves together the necessity for women to strike (Ni Una Menos), the claiming of spaces to rebuild from disaster (subRosa), the destruction of the "United" States (D.M.D.), the impossibility of adequately recognizing the labor of housework (Silvia Federici), and the challenges of working against structural oppression (Marie Edwards) to indict our current practices and outline new possibilities for statelessness and chaos.

Anarchy and the Sex Question

1896

Emma Goldman

The workingman, whose strength and muscles are so admired by the pale, puny offsprings of the rich, yet whose labour barely brings him enough to keep the wolf of starvation from the door, marries only to have a wife and house-keeper, who must slave from morning till night, who must make every effort to keep down expenses. Her nerves are so tired by the continual effort to make the pitiful wages of her husband support both of them that she grows irritable and no longer is success-ful in concealing her want of affection for her lord and master, who, alas! soon comes to the conclusion that his hopes and plans have gone astray, and so practically begins to think that marriage is a failure.

The Chain Grows Heavier and Heavier

As the expenses grow larger instead of smaller, the wife, who has lost all of the little strength she had at marriage, likewise feels herself betrayed, and the constant fretting and dread of starvation consumes her beauty in a short time after marriage. She grows despondent, neglects her household duties, and as there are no ties of love and sympathy between herself and her husband to give them strength to face the misery and poverty of their lives, instead of clinging to each other, they become more and more estranged, more and more impa-tient with each other's faults.

The man cannot, like the millionaire, go to his club, but he goes to a saloon and tries to drown his misery in a glass of beer or whiskey. The unfortunate partner of his misery, who is too honest to seek forgetfulness in the arms of a lover, and who is too poor to allow herself any legitimate recreation or amusement, remains amid the squalid, half-kept surroundings she calls home, and bitterly bemoans the folly that made her a poor man's wife.

Yet there is no way for them to part from each other.

But They Must Wear It

However galling the chain which has been put around their necks by the law and Church may be, it may not be broken unless those two persons decide to permit it to be severed.

Should the law be merciful enough to grant them liberty, every detail of their private life must be dragged to light. The woman is condemned by public opinion and her whole life is ruined. The fear of this disgrace often causes her to break down under the heavy weight of married life without daring to enter a single protest against the outrageous system that has crushed her and so many of her sisters.

The rich endure it to avoid scandal—the poor for the sake of their children and the fear of public opinion. Their lives are one long continuation of hypocrisy and deceit.

The woman who sells her favours is at liberty to leave the man who purchases them at any time, "while the respectable wife" cannot free herself from a union which is galling to her.

All unnatural unions which are not hallowed by love are prostitution, whether sanctioned by the Church and society or not. Such unions cannot have other than a degrading influence both upon the morals and health of society.

The System Is to Blame

The system which forces women to sell their womanhood and independence to the highest bidder is a branch of the same evil system which gives to a few the right to live on the wealth produced by their fellow-men, 99 percent of whom must toil and slave early and late for barely enough to keep soul and body together, while the fruits of their labour are absorbed by a few idle vampires who are surrounded by every luxury wealth can purchase.

Look for a moment at two pictures of this nineteenth century social system.

Look at the homes of the wealthy, those magnificent palaces whose costly furnishings would put thousands of needy men and women in comfortable circumstances. Look at the dinner parties of these sons and daughters of wealth, a single course of which would feed hundreds of starving ones to whom a full meal of bread washed down by water is a luxury. Look upon these votaries of fashion as they spend their days devising new means of selfish enjoyment—theatres, balls, concerts, yachting, rushing from one part of the globe to another in their mad search for gaiety and pleasure. And then turn a moment and look at those who produce the wealth that pays for these excessive, unnatural enjoyments.

The Other Picture

Look at them herded together in dark, damp cellars, where they never get a breath of fresh air, clothed in rags, carrying their loads of misery from the cradle to the grave, their children running around the streets, naked, starved, without anyone to give them a loving word or tender care, growing up in ignorance and superstition, cursing the day of their birth.

Look at these two startling contrasts, you moralists and philanthropists, and tell me who is to be blamed for it! Those who are driven to prostitution, whether legal or otherwise, or those who drive their victims to such demoralisation?

The cause lies not in prostitution, but in society itself; in the system of inequality of private property and in the State and Church. In the system of legalized theft, murder and violation of the innocent women and helpless children.

The Cure for The Evil

Not until this monster is destroyed will we get rid of the disease which exists in the Senate and all public offices; in the houses of the rich as well as in the miserable barracks of the poor. Mankind must become conscious of their strength and capabilities, they must be free to commence a new life, a better and nobler life.

Prostitution will never be suppressed by the means employed by the Rev. Dr. Parkhurst and other reformers. It will exist as long as the system exists which breeds it.

When all these reformers unite their efforts with those who are striving to abolish the system which begets crime of every description and erect one which is based upon perfect equity—a system which guarantees every member, man, woman or child, the full fruits of their labour and a perfectly equal right to enjoy the gifts of nature and to attain the highest knowledge—woman will be self-supporting and independent. Her health no longer crushed by endless toil and slavery no longer will she be the victim of man, while man will no longer be possessed of unhealthy, unnatural passions and vices.

An Anarchist's Dream

Each will enter the marriage state with physical strength and moral confidence in each other. Each will love and esteem the other, and will help in working not only for their own welfare, but, being happy themselves, they will desire also the universal happiness of humanity. The offspring of such unions will be strong and healthy in mind and body and will honour and respect their parents, not because it is their duty to do so, but because the parents deserve it.

They will be instructed and cared for by the whole community and will be free to follow their own inclinations, and there will be no necessity to teach them sychophancy and the base art of preying upon their fellow-beings. Their aim in life will be, not to obtain power over their brothers, but to win the respect and esteem of every member of the community.

Anarchist Divorce

Should the union of a man and woman prove unsatisfactory and distasteful to them they will in a quiet, friendly manner, separate and not debase the several relations of marriage by continuing an uncongenial union.

If, instead of persecuting the victims, the reformers of the day will unite their efforts to eradicate the cause, prostitution will no longer disgrace humanity.

To suppress one class and protect another is worse than folly. It is criminal. Do not turn away your heads, you moral man and woman.

Do not allow your prejudice to influence you: look at the question from an unbiased standpoint.

Instead of exerting your strength uselessly, join hands and assist to abolish the corrupt, diseased system.

If married life has not robbed you of honour and self-respect, if you have love for those you call your children, you must, for your own sake as well as theirs, seek emancipation and establish liberty. Then, and not until then, will the evils of matrimony cease.

15 Call to Women's International Strike

2017

Ni Una Menos (Not One Less)

This March 8 the earth trembles. The women of the world unite and organize a measure of strength and a common cry: Women's International Strike. We Stop. We strike, we organize and we are among us. We put into practice the world in which we want to live.

#NosotrasParamos

We stop to report:

That capital exploits our informal, precarious and intermittent economies.

That the national states and the market exploit us when we are indebted.

That the States criminalize our migratory movements.

That we charge less than men and that the salary gap reaches, on average, 27%.

That it is not recognized that domestic and care tasks are work that is not remunerated and adds, at least, three hours to our workdays.

That these economic violences increase our vulnerability to sexist violence, whose most aberrant end are femicides.

We stop against the institutional violence that threatens and persecutes those who practice prostitution and sex workers.

We stop to claim the right to free abortion and not to force any girl to motherhood.

We stop to make it visible that while the tasks of care are not a responsibility of the whole society we are forced to reproduce the class and colonial exploitation among women. To go to work we depend on other women. To migrate, we depend on other women.

We stop to value the invisible work we do, which builds a network, support and vital strategies in difficult and crisis contexts.
#NoWeareAll
We stop because we lack the victims of femicide, voices that are violently extinguished to the chilling rhythm of one per day only in Argentina.
We are missing the murdered lesbians and transvestites.
We lack the political prisoners, the persecuted, the murdered in our Latin American territory to defend the land and its resources.
We lack women imprisoned for minor crimes that criminalize forms of survival, while the crimes of corporations and drug trafficking go unpunished because they benefit capital.
We lack the dead and the prisoners for unsafe abortions.
We are missing those disappeared by trafficking networks; the victims of sexual exploitation.
Faced with homes that become hell, we organize ourselves to defend ourselves and take care of each other.
In the face of sexist crime and its pedagogy of cruelty, in the face of the media's attempt to victimize and terrorize us, we make individual consolation of collective mourning, and of shared struggle and rage. Faced with cruelty, more feminism.
#NosotrasNosOrganizamos
We appropriate the unemployment tool because our demands are urgent. We make women's unemployment a broad and up-to-date measure, capable of sheltering the employed and the unemployed, the salaried and those who receive subsidies, the self-employed and the students, because we are all workers. We stopped.
We organize ourselves against domestic confinement, against compulsory motherhood and against competition between women, all forms driven by the market and the patriarchal family model.
We organize ourselves everywhere: in the houses, in the streets, in the works, in the schools, in the fairs, in the neighborhoods. The strength of our movement lies in the ties we create between us.
We organize ourselves to change everything.
#LaInternacionalFeminista
We weave a new internationalism. From the concrete situations in which we are interpreting the conjuncture.
We see that in the face of the neo-conservative turn in the region and the world, the women's movement emerges as an alternative power.

That the new "witch hunt" that now pursues what it names as "gender ideology" tries to combat and neutralize our strength and break our will.

Faced with the multiple spoils, expropriations, and contemporary wars that have the land and the body of women as favorite territories of conquest, we get together politically and spiritually.

#NosMueveElDeseo

Because #VivasYLibresNosQueremos we take risks in unusual alliances.

Because we appropriate time and build availability for ourselves, we make together relief and conversation among allies, from the assemblies, demonstrations, a party, a common future.

Because #EstamosParaNosotras, this March 8 is the first day of our new life.

Because #NosMueveElDeseo, 2017 is the time of our revolution.

#NiUnaMenos

16 Wages against Housework

1974

Silvia Federici

They say it is love. We say it is unwaged work.
They call it frigidity. We call it absenteeism.
Every miscarriage is a work accident.
Homosexuality and heterosexuality are both working conditions...
but homosexuality is workers' control of production, not the end of
work.
More smiles? More money. Nothing will be so powerful in destroy-
ing the healing virtues of a smile.
Neuroses, suicides, desexualization: occupational diseases of the
housewife.

Many times the difficulties and ambiguities which women express in discussing wages for housework stem from the fact that they reduce wages for housework to a thing, a lump of money, instead of viewing it as a political perspective. The difference between these two standpoints is enormous. To view wages for housework as a thing rather than a perspective is to detach the end result of our struggle from the struggle itself and to miss its significance in demystifying and subverting the role to which women have been confined in capitalist society.

When we view wages for housework in this reductive way we start asking ourselves: what difference could some more money make to our lives? We might even agree that for a lot of women who do not have any choice except for housework and marriage, it would indeed make a lot of difference. But for those of us who seem to have other choices—professional work, enlightened husband, communal way of life, gay relations or a combination of these—it would not make much of a difference at all. For us there are supposedly other ways of achieving economic independence, and the last thing we want is to get it by identifying ourselves as housewives, a fate which we all agree is, so to speak, worse than death. The problem with this position is that in our imagination we usually add a bit of money to the shitty lives we have now and then ask, so what? on the false premise that we could ever get that money without at the same time revolutionizing— in the process of struggling for it—all our family and social relations. But if we take wages for housework as a political perspective, we can see that struggling for it is going to produce a revolution in our lives and in our social power as women. It is also clear that if we think we do not "need" that money, it is because we have accepted the particular forms of prostitution of body and mind by which we get the money to hide that need. As I will try to show, not only is wages for housework a revolutionary perspective, but it is the only revolutionary perspective from a feminist viewpoint and ultimately for the entire working class.

"A Labour of Love"

It is important to recognize that when we speak of housework we are not speaking of a job as other jobs, but we are speaking of one of the most pervasive manipulations, most subtle and mystified forms of violence that capitalism has perpetrated against any section of the working class. True, under capitalism every worker is manipulated and exploited and his/her relation to capital is totally mystified. The wage gives the impression of a fair deal: you work and you get paid, hence you and your boss are equal; while in reality the wage, rather than paying for the work you do, hides all the unpaid work that goes into profit. But the wage at least recognizes that you are a worker, and you can bargain and struggle around and against the terms and the quantity of that wage, the terms and the quantity of that work. To have a wage means to be part of a social contract, and there is no doubt concerning its meaning: you work, not because you like it, or because it comes naturally to you, but because it is the only condition under which you are allowed to live. But exploited as you might be, you are not that work. Today you are a postman, tomorrow a cabdriver. All that matters is how much of that work you have to do and how much of that money you can get.

But in the case of housework the situation is qualitatively different. The difference lies in the fact that not only has housework been imposed on women, but it has been transformed into a natural attribute of our female physique and personality, an internal need, an aspiration, supposedly coming from the depth of our female character. Housework had to be transformed into a natural attribute rather than be recognized as a social contract because from the beginning of capital's scheme for women this work was destined to be unwaged. Capital had to convince us that it is a natural, unavoidable and even fulfilling activity to make us accept our unwaged work. In its turn, the unwaged condition of housework has been the most powerful weapon in reinforcing the common assumption that housework is not work, thus preventing women from struggling against it, except in the privatized kitchen-bedroom quarrel that all society agrees to ridicule, thereby further reducing the protagonist of a struggle. We are seen as nagging bitches, not workers in struggle.

Yet just how natural it is to be a housewife is shown by the fact that it takes at least twenty years of socialization—day-to-day training, performed by an unwaged mother—to prepare a woman for this role, to convince her that children and husband are the best she can expect from life. Even so, it hardly succeeds. No matter how well-trained we are, few are the women who do not feel cheated when the bride's day is over and they find themselves in front of a dirty sink. Many of us still have the illusion that we marry for love. A lot of us recognize that we marry for money and security; but it is time to make it clear that while the love or money involved is very little, the work which awaits us is enormous. This is why older women always tell us "Enjoy your freedom while you can, buy whatever you want now …" But unfortunately it is almost impossible to enjoy any freedom if from the earliest days of life you are trained to be docile, subservient, dependent and most important to sacrifice yourself and even to get pleasure from it. If you don't like it, it is your problem, your failure, your guilt, your abnormality.

We must admit that capital has been very successful in hiding our work. It has created a true masterpiece at the expense of women. By denying housework a wage and transforming it into an act of love, capital has killed many birds with one stone. First of all, it has got a hell of a lot of work almost for free, and it has made sure that women, far from struggling against it, would seek that work as the best thing in life (the magic words: "Yes, darling, you are a real woman"). At the same time, it has disciplined the male worker also, by making *his* woman dependent on *his* work and *his* wage, and trapped him in this discipline by giving him a servant after he himself has done so much serving at the factory or the office. In fact, our role as women is to be the unwaged but happy, and most of all loving, servants of the "working class," i.e. those strata of the proletariat to which capital was forced to grant more social power. In the same way as god created Eve to give pleasure to Adam, so did capital create the housewife to service the male worker physically, emotionally and sexually—to raise his children, mend his socks, patch up his ego when it is crushed by the work and the social relations (which are relations of loneliness) that capital has reserved for him. It is precisely this peculiar combination of physical, emotional and sexual services that are involved in the role women must perform for capital that creates the specific character of that servant which is the housewife, that makes her work so burdensome and at the same time invisible. It is not an accident that most men start thinking of getting married as soon as they get their first job. This is not only because now they can afford it, but because having somebody at home who takes care of you is the only condition not to go crazy after a day spent on an assembly line or at a desk. Every woman knows that this is what she should be doing to be a true woman and have a "successful" marriage. And in this case too, the poorer the family the higher the enslavement of the woman, and not simply because of the monetary situation. In fact capital has a dual policy, one for the middle class and one for the proletarian family. It is no accident that we find the most unsophisticated machismo in the working class family: the more blows the man gets at work the more his wife must be trained to absorb them, the more he is allowed to recover his ego at her expense. You beat your wife and vent your rage against her when you are frustrated or overtired by your work or when you are defeated in a struggle (to go into a factory is itself a defeat). The more the man serves and is bossed around, the more he bosses around. A man's home is his castle … and his wife has to learn to wait in silence when he is moody, to put him back together when he is broken down and swears at the world, to turn around in bed when he says "I'm too tired tonight," or when he goes so fast at lovemaking that, as one woman put it, he might as well make it with a mayonnaise jar. (Women however have always found ways of fighting back, or getting back at them, but always in an isolated and privatized way. The problem, then, becomes how to bring this struggle out of the kitchen and bedroom and into the streets.)

This fraud that goes under the name of love and marriage affects all of us, even if we are not married, because once housework was totally naturalized and sexualized, once it became a feminine attribute, all of us as females are characterized by it. If it is natural to do certain things, then all women are expected to do them and even like doing them— even those women who, due to their social position, could escape some of that work or most of it (their husbands can afford maids and shrinks and other forms of relaxation and amusement). We might not serve one man, but we are all in a servant relation with respect to the whole male world. This is why to be called a female is such a putdown, such a degrading thing. ("Smile, honey, what's the matter with you?" is something every man feels entitled to ask you, whether he is your husband, or the man who takes your ticket on a train, or your boss at work.)

The Revolutionary Perspective

If we start from this analysis we can see the revolutionary implications of the demand for wages for housework. It is the demand by which our nature ends and our struggle begins because just to want wages for housework means to refuse that work as the expression of our nature, and therefore to refuse precisely the female role that capital has invented for us.

To ask for wages for housework will by itself undermine the expectations society has of us, since these expectations—the essence of our socialization—are all functional to our wageless condition in the home. In this sense, it is absurd to compare the struggle of women for wages to the struggle of male workers in the factory for more wages.

The waged worker in struggling for more wages challenges his social role but remains within it. When we struggle for wages we struggle unambiguously and directly against our social role. In the same way there is a qualitative difference between the struggles of the waged worker and the struggles of the slave for a wage against that slavery. It should be clear, however, that when we struggle for a wage we do not struggle to enter capitalist relations, because we have never been out of them. We struggle to break capital's plan for women, which is an essential moment of the divisions within the working class, through which capital has been able to maintain its power. Wages for housework, then, is a revolutionary demand not because by itself it destroys capital, but because it forces capital to restructure social relations in terms more favourable to us and consequently more favourable to the unity of the class. In fact, to demand wages for housework does not mean to say that if we are paid we will continue to do it. It means precisely the opposite. To say that we want money for housework is the first step towards refusing to do it, because the demand for a wage makes our work visible, which is the most indispensable condition to begin to struggle against it, both in its immediate aspect as housework and its more insidious character as femininity.

Against any accusation of "economism" we should remember that money is capital, i.e. it is the power to command labour. Therefore to re-appropriate that money which is the fruit of our labour—of our mothers' and grandmothers' labour—means at the same time to undermine capital's power to command forced labour from us. And we should not distrust the power of the wage in demystifying our female-ness and making visible our work—our femaleness as work—since the lack of a wage has been so powerful in shaping this role and hiding our work. To demand wages for housework is to make it visible that our minds, bodies and emotions have all been distorted for a specific function, in a specific function, and then have been thrown back at us as a model to which we should all conform if we want to be accepted as women in this society.

To say that we want wages for housework is to expose the fact that housework is already money for capital, that capital has made and makes money out of our cooking, smiling, fucking. At the same time, it shows that we have cooked, smiled, fucked throughout the years not because it was easier for us than for anybody else, but because we did not have any other choice. Our faces have become distorted from so much smiling, our feelings have got lost from so much loving, our oversexualization has left us completely desexualized.

Wages for housework is only the beginning, but its message is clear: from now on they have to pay us because as females we do not guar-antee anything any longer. We want to call work what is work so that eventually we might rediscover what is love and create what will be our sexuality which we have never known. And from the viewpoint of work we can ask not one wage but many wages, because we have been forced into many jobs at once. We are housemaids, prostitutes, nurses, shrinks; this is the essence of the "heroic" spouse who is celebrated on "Mother's Day." We say: stop celebrating our exploitation, our supposed heroism. From now on we want money for each moment of it, so that we can refuse some of it and eventually all of it. In this respect nothing can be more effective than to show that our female virtues have a calculable money value, until today only for capital, increased in the measure that we were defeated; from now on against capital for us in the measure we organize our power.

The Struggle for Social Services

This is the most radical perspective we can adopt because although we can ask for everything, day care, equal pay, free laundromats, we will never achieve any real change unless we attack our female role at its roots. Our struggle for social services, i.e. for better working conditions, will always be frustrated if we do not first establish that our work is work. Unless we struggle against the totality of it we will never achieve victories with respect to any of its moments. We will fail in the struggle for the free laundromats unless we first struggle against the fact that we cannot love except at the price of endless work, which day after day cripples our bodies, our sexuality, our social relations, unless we first escape the blackmail whereby our need to give and receive affection is turned against us as a work duty for which we constantly feel resentful against our husbands, children and friends, and guilty for that resentment. Getting a second job does not change that role, as years and years of female work outside the house still witness. The second job not only increases our exploitation, but simply reproduces our role in different forms. Wherever we turn we can see that the jobs women perform are mere extensions of the housewife condition in all its implications. That is, not only do we become nurses, maids, teachers, secretaries—all functions for which we are well-trained in the home—but we are in the same bind that hinders our struggles in the home: isolation, the fact that other people's lives depend on us, or the impossibility to see where our work begins and ends, where our work ends and our desires begin. Is bringing coffee to your boss and chatting with him about his marital problems secretarial work or is it a personal favour? Is the fact that we have to worry about our looks on the job a condition of work or is it the result of female vanity? (Until recently airline stewardesses in the United States were periodically weighed and had to be constantly on a diet—a torture that all women know—for fear of being laid off.) As is often said—when the needs of the waged labour market require her presence there—"A woman can do any job without losing her femininity," which simply means that no matter what you do you are still a cunt.

As for the proposal of socialization and collectivization of housework, a couple of examples will be sufficient to draw a line between these alternatives and our perspective. It is one thing to set up a day care centre the way we want it, and demand that the State pay for it. It is quite another thing to deliver our children to the State and ask the State to control them, discipline them, teach them to honour the American flag not for five hours, but for fifteen or twenty-four hours. It is one thing to organize communally the way we want to eat (by ourselves, in groups, etc.) and then ask the State to pay for it, and it is the opposite thing to ask the State to organize our meals. In one case we regain some control over our lives, in the other we extend the State's control over us.

The Struggle Against Housework

Some women say: how is wages for housework going to change the attitudes of our husbands towards us? Won't our husbands still expect the same duties as before and even more than before once we are paid for them? But these women do not see that they can expect so much from us precisely because we are not paid for our work, because they assume that it is "a woman's thing" which does not cost us much effort. Men are able to accept our services and take pleasure in them because they presume that housework is easy for us, that we enjoy it because we do it for their love. They actually expect us to be grateful because by marrying us or living with us they have given us the opportunity to express ourselves as women (i.e. to serve them), "You are lucky you have found a man like me." Only when men see our work as work— our love as work—and most important our determination to refuse both, will they change their attitude towards us. When hundreds and thousands of women are in the streets saying that endless cleaning, being always emotionally available, fucking at command for fear of losing our jobs is hard, hated work which wastes our lives, then they will be scared and feel undermined as men. But this is the best thing that can happen from their own point of view, because by exposing the way capital has kept us divided (capital has disciplined them through us and us through them—each other, against each other), we—their crutches, their slaves, their chains—open the process of their liberation. In this sense wages for housework will be much more educational than trying to prove that we can work as well as them, that we can do the same jobs. We leave this worthwhile effort to the "career woman," the woman who escapes from her oppression not through the power of unity and struggle, but through the power of the master, the power to oppress—usually other women. And we don't have to prove that we can "break the blue collar barrier." A lot of us broke that barrier a long time ago and have discovered that the overalls did not give us more power than the apron; if possible even less, because now we had to wear both and had less time and energy to struggle against them. The things we have to prove are our capacity to expose what we are already doing, what capital is doing to us and our power in the struggle against it.

Unfortunately, many women—particularly single women—are afraid of the perspective of wages for housework because they are afraid of identifying even for a second with the housewife. They know that this is the most powerless position in society and so they do not want to realize that they are housewives too. This is precisely their weakness, a weakness which is maintained and perpetuated through the lack of self-identification. We want and have to say that we are all housewives, we are all prostitutes and we are all gay, because until we recognize our slavery we cannot recognize our struggle against it, because as long as we think we are something better, something different than a housewife, we accept the logic of the master, which is a logic of division, and for us the logic of slavery. We are all housewives because no matter where we are they can always count on more work from us, more fear on our side to put forward our demands, and less pressure on them for money, since hopefully our minds are directed elsewhere, to that man in our present or our future who will "take care of us."

And we also delude ourselves that we can escape housework. But how many of us, in spite of working outside the house, have escaped it? And can we really so easily disregard the idea of living with a man? What if we lose our jobs? What about ageing and losing even the minimal amount of power that youth (productivity) and attractiveness (female productivity) afford us today? And what about children? Will we ever regret having chosen not to have them, not even having been able to realistically ask that question? And can we afford gay relations? Are we willing to pay the possible price of isolation and exclusion? But can we really afford relations with men?

The question is: why are these our only alternatives and what kind of struggle will move us beyond them?

17 The Singles Manifesto

1974

Marie Edwards

PREAMBLE: Whereas the written and spoken word about singles has been and continues to be one of gloom and doom, untruths and misinformation, we the singles of the United States—divorced, separated, widowed, and never-married—in order to bury the myths, establish the truths, uplift our spirits, promote our freedom, become cognizant of our great fortune as singles, do ordain and establish this manifesto for the singles of the United States of America.

ARTICLE 1
Attitude toward self:

1. As a single, I shall appreciate myself as a unique person with a special combination of traits and talents no one else has.
2. I will develop and maintain a healthy self-respect and a high sense of self-worth, knowing that I cannot respect and like others until I first appreciate myself.
3. I will at all times take responsibility for my own actions, knowing that responsibility begins within my own self.
4. I will strive to put all my talents to work so that I can eliminate any residual, socially induced feelings of inferiority, knowing that when I give of myself to others, my self-esteem will rise accordingly.
5. I will have goals, knowing I will feel a sense of elation and heightened self-esteem once the goal is accomplished.
6. I will give myself rewards when I have accomplished a goal or difficult task, knowing the more I practice the spirit of giving of myself,

the more I will be able to give to others—and rewards, like charity, begin at home.

7. I will take an entirely new look at loneliness, knowing there is a vast difference between loneliness and being alone, realizing further that loneliness is a part of the human condition and that facing it when it happens will allow me to appreciate the positive side of being alone.

8. I will, in my deepest feelings, know that it's okay to be single and, becoming braver, know that it's even more than okay—it can be a great and untapped opportunity for continuous personal growth.

ARTICLE II
Attitude toward others:

1. I will stop searching for the "one-and-only," knowing that as I become more free to be myself, I will be freer to care about others, so that relationships will come to me as a natural consequence and I will feel free to accept or reject them.

2. Instead of searching for the "one-and-only," I will realize the tremendous importance of friendships and will develop under-standing, worthwhile friends of both the same and opposite sex. I will realize that platonic friendships are not only possible, but a necessary part of a successfully single life.

3. I will take inventory of my present "friends," bypassing those who are negative and harmful and cultivating those who are helpful and nourishing.

4. I will, when I attend singles' affairs, consider the singles I meet there as potential friends, not as "losers," knowing my attitude will color my perception even before I step in the door.

ARTICLE III
Attitude toward society:

1. I will appreciate that all four categories of singlehood—divorced, separated, widowed, and never-married—suffer similar discrimi-nations and that we are much more alike than different, no matter what our age and sex.

2. I will appreciate that the so-called battle of the sexes is a social myth, that men and women are much more alike than different in their

reaction to fear, rejection, loneliness, sorrow, joy, caring, sharing, and loving, and that, as singles, we have a unique opportunity to foster understanding and empathy between male and female.

3. I will no longer suffer in silence the injustices to me as a single, but will do everything I can to help eradicate them.

4. I will, by choosing to live a free single life, be helping to raise the status of singlehood. In doing this, I will be strengthening rather than weakening marriage, for when we truly have the option not to marry, marriage will be seen as a free choice rather than one demanded by a pairing society.

5. Finally, I will do my part in every way to promote good will between marrieds and singles, because misunderstandings will be diminished only when each of us, as a unique human being, realizes that being self-aware, autonomous, free, self-fulfilled, and whole has nothing whatsoever to do with being either married or single, but, in the final analysis, comes from being ourselves.

Xenofeminism: A Politics for Alienation (excerpt)

2015

Laboria Cuboniks

ZERO

0x00

Ours is a world in vertigo. It is a world that swarms with technological mediation, interlacing our daily lives with abstraction, virtuality, and complexity. XF constructs a feminism adapted to these realities: a feminism of unprecedented cunning, scale, and vision; a future in which the realization of gender justice and feminist emancipation contribute to a universalist politics assembled from the needs of every human, cutting across race, ability, economic standing, and geographical position. No more futureless repetition on the treadmill of capital, no more submission to the drudgery of labour, productive and reproductive alike, no more reification of the given masked as critique. Our future requires depetrification. XF is not a bid for revolution, but a wager on the long game of history, demanding imagination, dexterity and persistence.

0x01

XF seizes alienation as an impetus to generate new worlds. We are all alienated—but have we ever been otherwise? It is through, and not despite, our alienated condition that we can free ourselves from the muck of immediacy. Freedom is not a given—and it's certainly not given by anything "natural." The construction of freedom involves not less but more alienation; alienation is the labour of freedom's construction. Nothing should be accepted as fixed, permanent, or "given"—neither material conditions nor social forms. XF mutates, navigates and probes every horizon. Anyone who's been deemed "unnatural" in the face of reigning biological norms, anyone who's experienced injustices wrought in the name of natural order, will realize that the glorification of "nature" has nothing to offer us—the queer and trans among us, the differently-abled, as well as those who have suffered discrimination due to pregnancy or duties connected to child-rearing. XF is vehemently anti-naturalist. Essentialist naturalism reeks of theology—the sooner it is exorcised, the better.

0x02

Why is there so little explicit, organized effort to repurpose technologies for progressive gender political ends? XF seeks to strategically deploy existing technologies to re-engineer the world. Serious risks are built into these tools; they are prone to imbalance, abuse, and exploitation of the weak. Rather than pretending to risk nothing, XF advocates the necessary assembly of techno-political interfaces responsive to these risks. Technology isn't inherently progressive. Its uses are fused with culture in a positive feedback loop that makes linear sequencing, prediction, and absolute caution impossible. Technoscientific innovation must be linked to a collective theoretical and political thinking in which women, queers, and the gender non-conforming play an unparalleled role.

0x03

The real emancipatory potential of technology remains unrealized. Fed by the market, its rapid growth is offset by bloat, and elegant innovation is surrendered to the buyer, whose stagnant world it decorates. Beyond the noisy clutter of commodified cruft, the ultimate task lies in engineering technologies to combat unequal access to reproductive and pharmacological tools, environmental cataclysm, economic instability, as well as dangerous forms of unpaid/underpaid labour. Gender inequality still characterizes the fields in which our technologies are conceived, built, and legislated for, while female workers in electronics (to name just one industry) perform some of the worst paid, monotonous and debilitating labour. Such injustice demands structural, machinic and ideological correction.

0x04

Xenofeminism is a rationalism. To claim that reason or rationality is "by nature" a patriarchal enterprise is to concede defeat. It is true that the canonical "history of thought" is dominated by men, and it is male hands we see throttling existing institutions of science and technology. But this is precisely why *feminism must be a rationalism*—because of this miserable imbalance, and not despite it. There is no "feminine" rationality, nor is there a "masculine" one. Science is not an expression but a suspension of gender. If today it is dominated by masculine egos, then it is at odds with itself—and this contradiction can be leveraged. Reason, like information, wants to be free, and patriarchy cannot give it freedom. *Rationalism must itself be a feminism*. XF marks the point where these claims intersect in a two-way dependency. It names reason as an engine of feminist emancipation, and declares the right of everyone to speak as no one in particular.

INTERRUPT

0x05

The excess of modesty in feminist agendas of recent decades is not proportionate to the monstrous complexity of our reality, a reality crosshatched with fibre-optic cables, radio and microwaves, oil and gas pipelines, aerial and shipping routes, and the unrelenting, simultaneous execution of millions of communication protocols with every passing millisecond. Systematic thinking and structural analysis have largely fallen by the wayside in favour of admirable, but insufficient struggles, bound to fixed localities and fragmented insurrections. Whilst capitalism is understood as a complex and ever-expanding totality, many would-be emancipatory anti-capitalist projects remain profoundly fearful of transitioning to the universal, resisting big-picture speculative politics by condemning them as necessarily oppressive vectors. Such a false guarantee treats universals as absolute, generating a debilitating disjuncture between the thing we seek to depose and the strategies we advance to depose it.

0x06

Global complexity opens us to urgent cognitive and ethical demands. These are Promethean responsibilities that cannot pass unaddressed.

Much of twenty-first century feminism—from the remnants of postmodern identity politics to large swathes of contemporary ecofeminism—struggles to adequately address these challenges in a manner capable of producing substantial and enduring change. Xenofeminism endeavours to face up to these obligations as collective agents capable of transitioning between multiple levels of political, material and conceptual organization.

0x07

We are adamantly synthetic, unsatisfied by analysis alone. XF urges constructive oscillation between description and prescription to mobilize the recursive potential of contemporary technologies upon gender, sexuality and disparities of power. Given that there are a range of gendered challenges specifically relating to life in a digital age—from sexual harassment via social media, to doxxing, privacy, and the protection of online images—the situation requires a feminism at ease with computation. Today, it is imperative that we develop an ideological infrastructure that both supports and facilitates feminist interventions within connective, networked elements of the contemporary world. Xenofeminism is about more than digital self-defence and freedom from patriarchal networks. We want to cultivate the exercise of positive freedom—freedom-to rather than simply freedom-from—and urge feminists to equip themselves with the skills to redeploy existing technologies and invent novel cognitive and material tools in the service of common ends.

0x08

The radical opportunities afforded by developing (and alienating) forms of technological mediation should no longer be put to use in the exclusive interests of capital, which, by design, only benefits the few. There are incessantly proliferating tools to be annexed, and although no one can claim their comprehensive accessibility, digital tools have never been more widely available or more sensitive to appropriation than they are today. This is not an elision of the fact that a large amount of the world's poor is adversely affected by the expanding technological industry (from factory workers labouring under abominable conditions to the Ghanaian villages that have become a repository for the e-waste of the global powers) but an explicit acknowledgement of these conditions as a target for elimination. Just as the invention of the stock market was also the invention of the crash, Xenofeminism knows that technological innovation must equally anticipate its systemic condition responsively.

TRAP

0x09
XF rejects illusion and melancholy as political inhibitors. Illusion, as the blind presumption that the weak can prevail over the strong with no strategic coordination, leads to unfulfilled promises and unmarshalled drives. This is a politics that, in wanting so much, ends up building so little. Without the labour of large-scale, collective social organisation, declaring one's desire for global change is nothing more than wishful thinking. On the other hand, melancholy—so endemic to the left—teaches us that emancipation is an extinct species to be wept over and that blips of negation are the best we can hope for. At its worst, such an attitude generates nothing but political lassitude, and at its best, installs an atmosphere of pervasive despair which too often degenerates into factionalism and petty moralizing. The malady of melancholia only compounds political inertia, and—under the guise of being realistic—relinquishes all hope of calibrating the world otherwise. It is against such maladies that XF innoculates.

0x0A
We take politics that exclusively valorize the local in the guise of subverting currents of global abstraction, to be insufficient. To secede from or disavow capitalist machinery will not make it disappear. Likewise, suggestions to pull the lever on the emergency brake of embedded velocities, the call to slow down and scale back, is a possibility available only to the few—a violent particularity of exclusivity—ultimately entailing catastrophe for the many. Refusing to think beyond the microcommunity, to foster connections between fractured insurgencies, to consider how emancipatory tactics can be scaled up for universal implementation, is to remain satisfied with temporary and defensive gestures. XF is an affirmative creature on the offensive, fiercely insisting on the possibility of large-scale social change for all of our alien kin.

0x0B

A sense of the world's volatility and artificiality seems to have faded from contemporary queer and feminist politics, in favour of a plural but static constellation of gender identities, in whose bleak light equations of the good and the natural are stubbornly restored. While having (perhaps) admirably expanded thresholds of "tolerance," too often we are told to seek solace in unfreedom, staking claims on being "born" this way, as if offering an excuse with nature's blessing. All the while, the heteronormative centre chugs on. XF challenges this centrifugal referent, knowing full well that sex and gender are exemplary of the fulcrum between norm and fact, between freedom and compulsion. To tilt the fulcrum in the direction of nature is a defensive concession at best, and a retreat from what makes trans and queer politics more than just a lobby: that it is an arduous assertion of freedom against an order that seemed immutable. Like every myth of the given, a stable foundation is fabulated for a real world of chaos, violence, and doubt. The "given" is sequestered into the private realm as a certainty, whilst retreating on fronts of public consequences. When the possibility of transition became real and known, the tomb under Nature's shrine cracked, and new histories—bristling with futures—escaped the old order of "sex." The disciplinary grid of gender is in no small part an attempt to mend that shattered foundation, and tame the lives that escaped it. The time has now come to tear down this shrine entirely, and not bow down before it in a piteous apology for what little autonomy has been won.

0x0C

If "cyberspace" once offered the promise of escaping the strictures of essentialist identity categories, the climate of contemporary social media has swung forcefully in the other direction, and has become a theatre where these prostrations to identity are performed. With these curatorial practices come puritanical rituals of moral maintenance, and these stages are too often overrun with the disavowed pleasures of accusation, shaming, and denunciation. Valuable platforms for connection, organization, and skill-sharing become clogged with obstacles to productive debate positioned as if they are debate. These puritanical politics of shame—which fetishize oppression as if it were a blessing, and cloud the waters in moralistic frenzies—leave us cold.

We want neither clean hands nor beautiful souls, neither virtue nor terror. We want superior forms of corruption.

0x0D

What this shows is that the task of engineering platforms for social emancipation and organization cannot ignore the cultural and semiotic mutations these platforms afford. What requires reengineering are the memetic parasites arousing and coordinating behaviours in ways occluded by their hosts' self-image; failing this, memes like "anonymity," "ethics," "social justice" and "privilege-checking" host social dynamisms at odds with the often-commendable intentions with which they're taken up. The task of collective self-mastery requires a hyperstitional manipulation of desire's puppet-strings, and deployment of semiotic operators over a terrain of highly networked cultural systems. The will will always be corrupted by the memes in which it traffics, but nothing prevents us from instrumentalizing this fact, and calibrating it in view of the ends it desires.

PARITY

0x0E

Xenofeminism is gender-abolitionist. "Gender abolitionism" is not code for the eradication of what are currently considered "gendered" traits from the human population. Under patriarchy, such a project could only spell disaster—the notion of what is "gendered" sticks disproportionately to the feminine. But even if this balance were redressed, we have no interest in seeing the sexuate diversity of the world reduced. Let a hundred sexes bloom! "Gender abolitionism" is shorthand for the ambition to construct a society where traits currently assembled under the rubric of gender, no longer furnish a grid for the asymmetric operation of power. "Race abolitionism" expands into a similar formula—that the struggle must continue until currently racialized characteristics are no more a basis of discrimination than the color of one's eyes. Ultimately, every emancipatory abolitionism must incline towards the horizon of class abolitionism, since it is in capitalism where we encounter oppression in its transparent, denaturalized form: you're not exploited or oppressed because you are a wage labourer or poor; you are a labourer or poor because you are exploited.

0x0F
Xenofeminism understands that the viability of emancipatory abolitionist projects—the abolition of class, gender, and race—hinges on a
profound reworking of the universal. The universal must be grasped
as generic, which is to say, intersectional. Intersectionality is not the
morcellation of collectives into a static fuzz of cross-referenced identities, but a political orientation that slices through every particular,
refusing the crass pigeonholing of bodies. This is not a universal that
can be imposed from above, but built from the bottom up—or, better,
laterally, opening new lines of transit across an uneven landscape.
This non-absolute, generic universality must guard against the facile
tendency of conflation with bloated, unmarked particulars—namely
Eurocentric universalism—whereby the male is mistaken for the
sexless, the white for raceless, the cis for the real, and so on. Absent
such a universal, the abolition of class will remain a bourgeois fantasy,
the abolition of race will remain a tacit white-supremacism, and the
abolition of gender will remain a thinly veiled misogyny, even—
especially—when prosecuted by avowed feminists themselves. (The
absurd and reckless spectacle of so many self-proclaimed 'gender abolitionists' campaign against trans women is proof enough of this.)

0x10
From the postmoderns, we have learnt to burn the facades of the false
universal and dispel such confusions; from the moderns, we have
learnt to sift new universals from the ashes of the false. Xenofeminism seeks to construct a coalitional politics, a politics without the
infection of purity. Wielding the universal requires thoughtful qualification and precise self-reflection so as to become a ready-to-hand
tool for multiple political bodies and something that can be appropriated against the numerous oppressions that transect with gender
and sexuality. The universal is no blueprint, and rather than dictate
its uses in advance, we propose XF as a platform. The very process of
construction is therefore understood to be a negentropic, iterative, and
continual refashioning. Xenofeminism seeks to be a mutable architecture that, like open source software, remains available for perpetual
modification and enhancement following the navigational impulse
of militant ethical reasoning. Open, however, does not mean undirected. The most durable systems in the world owe their stability to the
way they train order to emerge as an "invisible hand" from apparent

spontaneity; or exploit the inertia of investment and sedimentation. We should not hesitate to learn from our adversaries or the successes and failures of history. With this in mind, XF seeks ways to seed an order that is equitable and just, injecting it into the geometry of freedoms these platforms afford.

19 Anarchafeminist Manifesto

1982

Anarchafeminist International

All over the world most women have no rights whatsoever to decide upon important matters which concern their lives. Women suffer from oppressions of two kinds: 1) the general social oppression of the people, and 2) secondly sexism—oppression and discrimination because of their sex.

There are five main forms of oppression:

- Ideological oppression, brainwash by certain cultural traditions, religion, advertising and propaganda. Manipulation with concepts and play upon women's feelings and susceptibilities. Widespread patriarchal and authoritarian attitudes and capitalistic mentality in all areas.
- State oppression, hierarchical forms of organization with command lines downwards from the top in most interpersonal relations, also in the so-called private life.
- Economic exploitation and repression, as a consumer and a worker in the home and in low-salary women's jobs.
- Violence, under the auspices of the society as well as in the private sphere—indirectly when there is coercion because of lack of alternatives and direct physical violence.
- Lack of organization, tyranny of the structurelessness which pulverizes responsibility and creates weakness and inactivity.

These factors work together and contribute simultaneously to sustain each other in a vicious circle. There is no panacea to break the circle, but it isn't unbreakable.

Anarcha-feminism is a matter of consciousness. The consciousness which puts guardians off work. The principles of a liberating society thus stand perfectly clear to us.

Anarcha-feminism means women's independence and freedom on an equal footing with men. A social organization and a social life where no-one is superior or inferior to anyone and everybody is coordinate, women as well as men. This goes for all levels of social life, also the private sphere.

Anarcha-feminism implies that women themselves decide and take care of their own matters, individually in personal matters, and together with other women in matters which concern several women. In matters which concern both sexes essentially and concretely women and men shall decide on an equal footing.

Women must have self-decision over their own bodies, and all matters concerning contraception and childbirth are to be decided upon by women themselves.

It must be fought both individually and collectively against male domination, attitudes of ownership and control over women, against repressive laws and for women's economic and social autonomy and independence.

Crisis centers, day care centers, study and discussion groups, women's culture activities etc. must be established, and be run under women's own direction.

The traditional patriarchal nuclear family should be replaced by free associations between men and women based on equal right to decide for both parts and with respect for the individual person's autonomy and integrity.

Sex-stereotyping in education, media and at the place of work must be abolished. Radical sharing of the work by the sexes in ordinary jobs, domestic life and education is a suitable mean.

The structure of working life must be radically changed, with more part-time work and flat organized cooperation at home as well as in society. The difference between men's work and women's work must be abolished. Nursing and taking care of the children must concern men just as much as women.

Female power and female prime ministers will neither lead the majority of women to their ends nor abolish oppression. Marxist and bourgeoisie feminists are misleading the fight for women's liberation. For most women it is not going to be any feminism without anarchism.

In other words, anarcha-feminism does not stand for female power or female prime ministers, it stands for organization without power and without prime ministers.

The double oppression of women demands a double fight and double organizing: on the one hand in feminist federations, on the other hand in the organizations of anarchists. The anarcha-feminists form a junction in this double organizing.

A serious anarchism must also be feminist otherwise it is a question of patriarchal half-anarchism and not real anarchism. It is the task of the anarcha-feminists to secure the feminist feature in anarchism. There will be no anarchism without feminism.

An essential point in anarcha-feminism is that the changes must begin today, not tomorrow or after the revolution. The revolution shall be permanent. We must start today by seeing through the oppression in the daily life and do something to break the pattern here and now.

We must act autonomously, without delegating to any leaders the right to decide what we wish and what we shall do: we must make decisions all by ourselves in personal matters, together with other women in pure female matters, and together with the male fellows in common matters.

20 American Beasts

2017

D.M.D.

I. WE ARE INDICTED

We have abandoned meaning in the name of security, standing by as the American powers that be murder, plunder, and pillage in our names. There is blood on our hands, and we have misjudged the cost.

Is it not enough that those murdered and plundered are our siblings by virtue of our shared humanity? It is by mere accident of birth that we call ourselves American. The pain—the complexity—the worlds of others are but a step removed from ourselves.

Is it not enough that we are beasts in the shape of men? We get off to the violence of our system, seizing our pleasure from the carcass of our own humanity.

And for what?

Lives predicated upon fragile security born of ignorance. For ignorance is the true escape, allowing us to ignore the damage we inflict upon others and ourselves.

Lives dedicated to hedonism born of our individualist creed. We threw off the shackles of the collective in order to free our greed.

II. The Twin Lies of Patriotism and the Cult of Things

We have fetishized our own origin story, holding up the "Fathers" as bastions of democracy and progress. Their calcified words are held up as a holy document, the one guarantee of democracy. The alternative is to embrace uncertainty born of the reality that any system created by humans can and will be imperfect. We celebrate their revolution, but frown upon any and all revolutionaries that have since attempted to ignite a rebirth of government, branding them as criminals. We cling to our republic, never mind the fact that it is rotting from the inside out. Corporations and politicians preserve and amass power for its own sake, like maggots stripping a carcass until all that is left is bone. We have forgotten that we, the people, are the source and end of this power, and it is our minds, bodies, and labor that they engorge upon.

We have embraced consumption as the means and end of life. We are not citizens, standing together in community, embracing democratic processes—but individuals, content to focus on the minutiae of our own lives, desperately scrambling over one another in the hopes, that maybe, just maybe, we too can be on top. We have embraced the capitalist creed that we are fundamentally selfish, and it dictates all aspects of our lives and our relationships to one another. How pathetic, that we embrace a system that looks down upon us and reminds us over and over that our base impulses can barely be contained. It belies the falsehood of humanity's "progress," for if American institutions are dedicated to the pruning and weaponizing of self-interest, what "progress" can possibly be achieved?

The time is ripe for a modern rebirth of government. We must embrace a new system that breaks free of capitalist hegemony. We can no longer shrug off the brutality and alienation of capitalism or despair of a better future. Let us look to a new form of social organization born of the utter dissolution of America.

III. THE DISSOLUTION OF THESE "UNITED" STATES

The time is ripe for a modern rebirth of government. We must embrace a new system that breaks free of capitalist hegemony, which wreaks havoc on our ability to even imagine another world. Let us begin by ripping up every last vestige of American systems and symbols— poisonous lies that feed our complacency. In order to realize a new society free of alienation and oppression, let us act in order to achieve the following vision:

1. VOID ALL AMERICAN FEDERAL, STATE, COUNTY AND MUNICPAL CODES, FRAMEWORKS AND INSTITUTIONS

All levels of American government are founded upon the preservation and accumulation of wealth, property, and state hegemony. All tax codes, laws, restrictions, construction, and other actions taken by the state cease to apply to any and all peoples residing within the borders of "America."

2. RESTITUTION FOR ALL DESCENDANTS OF AMERICAN GENOCIDES

The very existence of America is predicated upon twin genocides—the brutal enslavement of African peoples and the eradication of indigenous peoples.

This land we stand upon was stolen over centuries by means of plague, murder, and famine. This land was not waiting for America's destiny, it was systematically emptied of indigenous peoples whose many cultures, histories, and languages formed a rich tapestry of humanity. And even now, we deny the legacy and resilience of the indigenous peoples who remain, shunted aside to reserves of land that American powers see as unprofitable. We demand full recognition of the sovereignty of the native tribes of America in order to facilitate the return of millions of acres of stolen land. All indigenous tribes will be given utter sovereignty, and the laundry list of treaties long violated will once more be recognized. All non-natives living on land henceforth considered the territory of native tribes (including those who occupy what is now called Hawaii) will be subject to the authority and regulations of said tribes. Let us undertake restitution for all peoples whose land and heritages were severed following the treaty of Guadalupe Hidalgo in the form of arable land.

The domestic symbols of American "greatness"—architecture, wealth—are the direct result of the forced labor of enslaved Africans. The human cost of slavery—and its continued impact upon descendants of enslaved peoples—can never be adequately redressed, but it is the height of moral corruption to forego the opportunity to alleviate the continued impact of psychological and material racism. Therefore, let us undertake the task of restitution for all descendants of enslaved African peoples in the form of arable land: One acre for every person claiming heritage of enslaved peoples.

3. OPEN AMERICAN BORDERS

All sea and land borders will be completely open to the free and unhindered flow of people, animals, goods, and information. Our American borders are an artifice that testifies to a history of brutal conquest. Our borders will be fluid in order to honor the history of millennia of unhindered movement by Chicanx and Indigenous peoples.

4. RELINQUISH CONTROL OF THE HENCEFORTH SOVEREIGN TERRITORIES OF PUERTO RICO, GUAM, AMERICAN SAMOA, NORTHERN MARIANA ISLANDS, AND THE VIRGIN ISLANDS

Our so-called democracy holds territories without even providing the mere farce of representative government. The peoples who inhabit the colonized islands of Puerto Rico, Guam, American Samoa, Northern Mariana Islands, and the Virgin Islands are wronged by their utter exclusion from American governance. The use of these islands as laboratories and wastelands by the American military enables those of us on the mainland to ignore the immense destruction and experimentation carried out, the cost of which is beyond reckoning. These islands and the peoples are free to establish their own systems of governance. All vestiges of American military presence will be removed after a concentrated clean-up of the environment is carried out.

5. ABOLISH AMERICAN CURRENCY

The American dollar is a symbol of waste, power and exploitation. It enables profligate speculation, wealth accumulation, and exploitation. Let us return to the world of the concrete, adopting barter systems in place of currency. The primary measures of value will be land and goods.

6. ABOLISH CAPITALIST CONCEPTIONS OF PRIVATE PROPERTY

Private property enables the utter disconnection between our individual lives. It is violent to demand that a human must work, contribute, be "productive" in order to secure the basic needs of food, water, shelter, and community. Are we mere animals, fighting over scraps in the middle of plenty? In our modern technological era, we have the capability to provide for each person within our community. We must open up our homes, our neighborhoods, our communities to all who wish to join in the common pursuit of human fulfillment. Control of production will revert to collective ownership by the communities in closest proximity.

However, the total abolition of private property will only serve to harm those who are already ground under the heel of America. As such, let us establish the new currency of our collectivist communities. Every individual, regardless of age, will be granted an acre of arable land to call their own. First priority for land distribution will be those whom we must restitute in order to address centuries of oppression; they will be given prime consideration for land that must be judged according to the following principles: arable and within half a mile proximity to a major water system.

7. ABOLISH THE AMERICAN PRISON SYSTEM— FEDERAL, STATE, AND MUNICIPAL

The hypocrisy of these United States is at work every day, ripping apart families and communities, and derailing the lives of individuals. Mass incarceration serves arbitrary standards of social control, providing near-free labor for massive corporations. We abolished slavery EXCEPT as a form of punishment, enabling continued access to devalued labor for the buzzards that circle, increasing profit margins at the expense of humanity.

As such, all prisons are henceforth closed, to be abandoned as symbols of profligate waste to human life. We welcome all liberated prisoners to lay waste to the machine of their oppression, ensuring that no one else will be held in cells meant to ground down and break the human spirit.

8. DISMANTLE THE UNITED STATES MILITARY

We must dismantle our vast tools of conquest and oppression. The United States' vast military arsenal must be dismantled and disposed of, including all nuclear arms and waste—the power to destroy life at such a vast scale is an abomination against nature and humanity. The United States has military bases scattered throughout the world, a constant reminder of American hegemony. We must shutter and dismantle all military bases, both within the United States and without, to prevent them from ever again being used to inflict violence upon states, civilians and the earth. Military capability and any arms will be removed, leaving hollow shells with the following sign posted to their doors:

A TESTAMENT TO ARROGANCE & HYPOCRISY

21 Radical Women Manifesto Platform (excerpt)

1967 (revised 2001)

Radical Women

Legal Rights

Throughout most of the world, women are not recognized under the law as equals with men. Current laws and judicial interpretations are sexist. For example, after a century and a half of struggle, the U.S. Constitution still lacks a federal Equal Rights Amendment and thus provides no nationwide legal foundation for women's equality.

The law should protect human life and liberty above private property, but under capitalism the reverse is true. The just and democratic recognition of the rights of women is sacrificed for capital's need to perpetuate the institution of the nuclear family, along with the subordination of wives to their husbands. The resulting second-class status of women is enforced through legislation, the courts and government policy.

We demand:

- Unconditional equal treatment under non-sexist law for all women regardless of age, marital status, disability, health, race, sexual orientation, size and weight, immigration status, political ideology, lifestyle, or income level.
- Equal legal recognition of all forms of consenting relationships, marriage and domestic partnerships, including those of lesbians, gays, bisexuals and transgendered people. No preferential tax treatment based on marital status. The unqualified right of married women to keep their own names and independent

legal identities. Divorce granted on the grounds of incompatibility and incontestable by either party. Child custody and community property disputes resolved free of charge by a qualified, non-adversarial and publicly funded family commission composed of professionals and lay people acceptable to both parents. Removal of divorce and child custody issues from the adversarial court system. The right of women and children to legal separation from their families.

- Preservation and extension of civil liberties to protect our right to dissent, including freedom of speech, association and assembly, and the right to privacy in all spheres—particularly on the job, where civil rights are routinely suppressed.

Economic Equality

The reentry of women into the world of paid work on every level and on an equal footing with men is the essential lever for achieving social equality. Yet the economic crisis of capitalism deals its heaviest blows to women. Economic dependence, whether on men or on welfare, is in fundamental contradiction to freedom and independence. Women face constant prejudice in financial transactions because of our supposed "emotionalism" and consequent "instability" and also because many women are not paid enough to independently qualify for many economic transactions. To control our lives, we must control our own livelihood.

We demand:

- Affirmative action and seniority protection in employment and promotion. Separate seniority lists by race and/or sex in job classifications where women and people of color are underemployed. Legally enforceable quotas to guarantee equal access to all job classifications for women, people of color and ethnic minorities.
- Equal pay for equal or comparable work as a right of women, people of color, disabled, old, young and immigrant workers.
- Free 24-hour, industry- and government-funded, community-controlled childcare centers on or near the job, with educational, recreational and medical facilities for children.

- Paid leave for pregnancy, new baby care and major illness without loss of benefits, seniority or job status.
- Safe working conditions for everyone. Eradication of dangerous work environments that affect disproportionate numbers of women, especially women of color and immigrants. An end to using unsafe conditions as an excuse to exclude women from certain areas of employment. The right of all workers to withdraw their labor, with full pay, from any hazardous work environment or practice until the problem is rectified.
- Unlimited employer-funded sick leave at full pay. Employer-paid, comprehensive health insurance for both full- and part-time workers where healthcare is not yet nationalized. Employer-funded domestic partnership benefits.
- Nationalization of failing industries under workers' control.
- Corporate- and government-sponsored retraining and placement at no loss in pay for injured workers and those laid off by plant closures, automation, or speedup.
- Equal access for women to apprenticeships in the trades. Affirmative action training programs in nontraditional trades. An end to harassment and physical attacks on women in the trades.
- Full employment instituted through a sliding scale of hours with the length of the working day uniformly reduced until there is work for everyone paid at the rate of a full day's union wage.
- Regular, automatic wage increases to fully match increases in the cost of living.

Women and Unions

Women workers and unionists are key to a revitalized labor movement. As the lowest paid workers, our struggles against discrimination and for our rights bring fresh dynamism to the labor movement.
We demand:

- Full equality for women in union membership and leadership functions. The leadership of unions should reflect the membership in terms of race, sex, and languages spoken. Union-sponsored apprenticeship programs with affirmative action hiring and training.

- Aggressive campaigns by unions to organize the traditionally unorganized sectors of labor, which are primarily women and people of color. The labor movement must fight for equality for all workers, address social issues, and prioritize the demands of women, people of color, immigrants, and lesbians and gays.
- Union democracy: the right of union members to decide the goals and priorities of their unions through full discussion and majority vote. Free speech within our unions, including the right of radicals to be heard.
- Militant labor action, including general strikes, in solidarity against government and business attacks on any sector of the labor movement. Solidarity actions with workers of other countries against the union-busting multinationals. Replace protectionist consumer campaigns with "Buy Union" campaigns.
- An anti-capitalist labor party to act as an independent political voice for labor and put an end to the union bureaucracy's perennial alliance with the pro-capitalist parties.
- End AFL-CIO support for the American Institute for Free Labor Development and other CIA fronts which crush independent unions in the Third World.

Biological Self-Determination

Under capitalism, women are considered the property of men, the church and the state. To gain control over our lives, we must take back our minds and bodies.

Our sexuality is for us alone to determine; we must define ourselves. Fundamental to the liberation of women is our right as free individuals to exercise control over our own bodies based on our own judgment, free from economic or social coercion. Bearing and nurturing children is only one part of a woman's life. Children should not be our private responsibility nor should we be forced into childbearing. We demand:

- No state interference with a woman's reproductive decisions or with her decisions during pregnancy.
- Readily available birth control information and the distribution of free, safe contraceptives to all who request them, regardless of

age. Development and promotion of safe, reliable birth control for men as well as women.

- No forced sterilization or "consent" obtained under pressure or in the absence of full information and understanding of consequences. No experiments on women without their knowledge and informed, uncoerced agreement. Stop the reproductive genocide against indigenous and colonized nations, people of color, ethnic minorities, and people with disabilities. Stop "population control" programs used by imperialism to perpetrate genocide in Third World countries.
- Free, safe and accessible abortion on demand for any woman, including women under the age of 18, without notification or approval of parents, the father, or the courts. Legal and medical recognition that a woman's life and livelihood take precedence over a fetus.
- An end to the double standard of sexual morality. The right of married women to extramarital sexual relations free from the atrocious label of "adultery." The right of unmarried women of all sexual orientations to enjoy sexual self-expression and free sex lives, untrammeled by social and religious prejudice and vicious regulatory laws.
- Nationalization of companies that develop new reproductive technology to ensure it will be controlled by and used for women, not against us. Reproductive technology should be introduced only after approval by women. Ban profit-making agencies in the surrogate-mother industry. Recognize the rights of surrogate mothers as workers. A surrogate mother should have the same right to change her mind and keep her child as a mother who puts her baby up for adoption.
- Free, quality prenatal care and childbirth services.
- Mandatory non-sexist and non-homophobic sex education for all students of all ages.

Quality Healthcare

We should not be forced to place our mental and physical health in the hands of an insensitive, for-profit medical system that is enriched by our illness. First-rate healthcare is a basic human right.

We demand:

- Quality, informative, preventive, and rehabilitative healthcare for all at no charge.
- Nationalization of all sectors of the medical industry—including pharmaceuticals, insurance, and home care services—and place them under the control of healthcare workers and users of medical services. Union wages for all health care workers.
- The right to free, quality mental health treatment, without pressure to conform to traditional sex roles or heterosexuality. Stop "therapy" aimed at subverting women's rebellion and keeping us in "our place" through harmful drugs, shock treatment and other forms of social control. End the brutalization of women by the psychiatric profession and by racist, sexist psychological testing.
- Comprehensive funding for unbiased research, prevention, and treatment of diseases that affect women and other oppressed people. No exploitive use of women as medical "guinea pigs," which has been especially common with women of color and in Third World nations. An end to the practice of using studies composed solely of white men to develop medical treatments for diseases that affect everyone.
- Full funding for research, treatment, cure and prevention of AIDS. Make all trial drugs free and available to all AIDS/HIV-positive patients—including women, who are now routinely excluded from test protocols—on an informed, voluntary basis. Free, voluntary, anonymous HIV testing; no forced testing. No quarantine of AIDS and HIV-positive people. Housing, childcare, medical care, counseling, and a guaranteed income to people with AIDS. Free, culturally appropriate safer sex education and materials for all ages. No discrimination against people with AIDS or HIV.
- Stop the breast cancer epidemic with comprehensive funding for education, research, treatment, cure and prevention. Make all trial drugs free and available. Clean up environmental contributors to cancer. Make state-of-the-art, low-radiation mammography available to all women at no cost. Make all forms of treatment and detection—traditional and nontraditional—available at no cost to breast cancer patients. Breast

cancer education for all young women through the schools. Housing, child care, medical care, counseling, and a guaranteed income for *all* cancer patients.

- Legalize all drugs under community control to take away drug dealers' profits, lower the cost and, therefore, reduce crimes committed to finance drug habits. Allow regulation of drug quality. Provide free, sterile needles and no-cost, stigma-free, accessible, voluntary treatment programs for addicts and alcoholics. Establish universal, culturally aware educational programs to help prevent drug addiction. No forced drug testing.
- The right to make informed decisions about our own healthcare, including the choice of legal guardian, if needed. The right to choose or refuse medical treatment, regardless of pregnancy status. The right to die and the legal right to assisted suicide.
- Full civil rights for people in nursing homes and mental health institutions.

Rights of Children

Within the hierarchy of the nuclear family, children are at the bottom, with no control over their lives, minds or bodies. They receive the harshest blows from the stress, conflict and disintegration of the nuclear family under capitalism, yet have no escape from it. Class society deprives children of their legal, social, economic and political rights through often capricious laws and social mores that take no account of a child's individual and constantly expanding capabilities. Children are the future of humanity, and therefore society as a whole must assume responsibility for the young: to provide for their needs, protect them where they are vulnerable, socialize and educate them, and open the prison door of the nuclear family. Children should be guaranteed freedom from oppressive family relations and their parents should be liberated from the sole and isolated responsibility for child-rearing.

We demand:

- The right of children to be respected as capable human beings who can participate in society to the fullest extent of their experience and abilities.

- Free, quality, community-controlled industry- and government-funded childcare centers staffed by professionally trained personnel at union wages and conditions, open 24 hours a day to all children regardless of their social status or the parents' reasons for bringing the children there.
- Guaranteed quality living conditions for children, including full and free access to medical, dental and mental health care, housing, clothing and a nutritious diet. Free breakfast, lunch, and dinner programs for all low-income school children, regardless of immigration status.
- Full protection of children from physical and psychological abuse and sexual coercion, molestation or exploitation by any institution or individual, including parents. Courts and social welfare agencies must make protecting a child from an abusive parent a higher priority than trying to "keep the family together." End the practice of ignoring or discounting children's testimony about sexual abuse and of scapegoating mothers who are unable to provide sufficient care and protection due to economic or social factors beyond their command. Community control of all agencies charged to act as children's advocates or protectors.
- Recognition of children's right to be sexually active on their own terms and at their own pace.
- Governmental responsibility and allocation of resources at no cost for children with special problems such as AIDS, disabilities, homelessness, and drug or alcohol dependence.
- Implement educational programs to teach parents, teachers and childcare workers how to guide very young children to express themselves through non-sexist play.
- End poverty as a cause for giving children up for adoption. Stop adoption profiteering. Babies shouldn't be brokered.
- The right of young people to organize on their own behalf.
- Stop police harassment and race-profiling of youth.

Education

Women are doubly discriminated against in education. First, we are denied equal opportunity in the free choice of fields of academic study as a result of cultural conditioning and closed doors. Second, our own history as a sex is ridiculed and/or ignored in the prevailing curricula.

We demand:

- Equal opportunity in all academic fields and in professional, service and industrial training schools. Equal funding for women's and men's sports. An end to race and sex bias in testing. Women and people of color should be represented on all school admissions committees.
- Elimination of stereotyping in educational materials and instruction. Diverse faculty, including women, people of color, and lesbians and gays, at all grade levels. Lesbians, gays, transgendered people, and leftists should have the right to teach, free of harassment or discrimination.
- Free, quality, multilingual, multicultural education for all, from primary through college levels in an atmosphere of civil liberties and respect for dissidence and nonconformity. An end to the elitist, ivory-tower separation of universities from the communities of oppressed people.
- Access at all educational levels to curricula that represent the full spectrum of human endeavor, including the often omitted areas of creative and performing arts, languages, sex education and the true history of all the exploited and oppressed. End corporate control of curricula and research. The establishment and funding of women's studies, ethnic studies, sexual minority studies, and labor studies departments with teachers qualified to explore and teach the history of oppression and resistance. Required courses in these fields regardless of academic major.
- Expose the cultural-religious myths that claim women's "inferior nature" is scientifically based on biology, sociology, psychology and social anthropology. An international campaign against sexist ideology in the schools.
- Paid living expenses for all students. Free bilingual, multicultural childcare on every campus.
- Accelerated and transitional courses, and waivers on standard entrance qualifications, for women returning to school after years away from it.
- Community/teacher/parent/student control of the schools.

Administrators and principals should carry out policies established by the community, not dictate to students and teachers.

- The right to privacy, free speech and association, and the right to organize for teachers and students at all grade levels. Outlaw corporal punishment in the schools.
- Full funding for literacy campaigns in both majority and minority languages. Guarantee every person the right to learn to read and write in the languages of their choice. Fully paid study leave to acquire these skills.
- Raise the levels of teachers' salaries and school funding through taxing corporations.

Politics

Winning the right to vote was a progressive gain for women, but it has not given us political equality. Capitalist parties court women's votes either by championing the "virtues" of the nuclear family and traditional values, or by presenting themselves as advocates for women's rights and equality. But no capitalist parties can genuinely fight for or achieve full women's rights because they are all dedicated to a system that reaps huge profits from women's inferior status.

Women, people of color, sexual minorities and working people should support only socialist or anti-capitalist labor candidates and build a working class party to take independent political action in our own interests. Only such a party will enable us to break the confines of the bourgeois state and create in its stead a new, egalitarian, socialist society.

We demand:

- The right to equal participation in political life and all social, political and economic leadership functions.
- The democratic right for all oppressed groups within any organization to form caucuses.
- Responsible action in the interests of their sex by all women legislators.
- Equal access to the ballot, media time, and financial resources for minor parties.

People of Color, National/Ethnic Minorities and Indigenous Nations

The same system that oppresses women is responsible for the subjugation of people of color, indigenous people and ethnic minorities. We are all used to make profits for capitalism. The entire movement must learn that we *cannot* achieve meaningful unity by pandering to the most privileged elements of the struggle or by allowing homophobia or anti-Semitism to divide us.

Women of color and national/ethnic minority women experience the most intense forms of oppression because they are discriminated against on three counts—their ethnicity, their sex and their class. Lesbians of color face homophobia as well. They embody and reflect the needs of all oppressed people. No one will achieve true equality until lesbians of color are free and equal.

The leadership role of women of color, indigenous women and national/ethnic minority women is decisive to the coming revolution. They have the most to gain and the least to lose from the destruction of the private property system. It is their seriousness and dedication, born of years of struggle against the racist and sexist ruling class, that will provide the energy and direction towards unity and eventual liberation.

We demand:

- An end to all forms of racial and ethnic discrimination: social, legal, political, cultural, linguistic, and economic. Equal participation for everyone in all aspects of society.
- Affirmative action in hiring, promotion and educational opportunities for all people of color and ethnic minorities, particularly women.
- Overturn all immigration laws which limit admission of people of color, discriminate against both undocumented workers and citizens of color, and pit native workers against immigrants—who are actually allies in the fight against the capitalists. Open all borders for free movement internationally.
- An end to both overt and indirect denial of voting rights to people of color, ethnic minorities and immigrants. Mandatory multilingual ballots, voting materials and campaign information.

- Immediate cessation of police brutality and racist harassment, terrorism, and murder of people of color and ethnic minorities. Establish elected, community-controlled police review boards, independent of the police, with power to discipline and fire cops who harass, brutalize and murder people of color, youth, queers, workers and women. The police are the armed agents of the ruling class and are incapable of policing themselves.
- Self-determination for all oppressed and indigenous nations, including Native Americans, Australian Aborigines, Maoris, the Kanaks of New Caledonia, Kurds, Puerto Ricans, and Palestinians.
- An end to racist, anti-immigrant, and anti-Semitic violence and scapegoating.
- End all language discrimination. All state institutions must be fully multilingual.

Sexual Minorities

Lesbians, gay men, bisexuals, transgendered people, and transvestites suffer extreme bias because their lives are a direct threat to the "sanctity" of the nuclear family. With the advent of the AIDS crisis, the hysterical scapegoating of gays has triggered a sharp rise in discrimination and violence aimed at all sexual minorities.

All oppressed people must embrace the demands of sexual minorities for total liberation in order for any of us to gain our freedom. Lesbians face the most intense forms of sexism and lesbians of color have the additional burden of racism. The life experience of surviving a brutally oppressive and hostile society has produced among lesbians a large number of independent, strong and capable women. In these women lies a vast potential for dedicated feminist leadership that can provide strength to the whole movement.

We demand:

- An end to the social, political, moral, legal and economic discrimination against lesbians and all sexual minorities. Enactment of comprehensive legislation to outlaw discrimination against sexual minorities.
- An immediate halt to police harassment, brutality and murder of sexual minorities.

- The right of sexual minorities to care for and raise their children and to be adoptive or foster parents. No discrimination based on sexual orientation, marital status or race against adults who want to adopt children.
- Reversal of immigration laws which refuse entry to sexual minority persons or anyone who has or is suspected of having AIDS.
- An end to the vicious and destructive portrayal of sexual minorities by the media. The image of lesbians as sick, vicious man-haters is consistently used to divide the feminist movement. We denounce such lies and smear tactics.
- Equal access for sexual minorities and independent women to medical benefits, insurance, and paid leave for bereavement and major illnesses. Domestic partner laws that allow all people— gay *and* straight—to claim benefits for all self-defined family relationships. Protect the privacy rights of domestic partners.
- An end to anti-sodomy laws and all other laws that limit consenting sexual practices.

Elder Women

The plight of elder women in our society is an intensification of the discrimination and exploitation faced by all women. Self-righteous testimonials about the supposedly revered status of elder women cannot hide the fact that women over 65 are the most impoverished sector of society.

The hard work and poverty endured by young women results only in more poverty and social isolation when they grow old. The inadequate wages of working women yield correspondingly scanty Social Security, medical and retirement benefits, stranding them with increasing healthcare expenses and the ever-rising cost of living.

What little social recognition is given women for their domestic and reproductive services is withdrawn after childbearing age and they are coldly discarded by the rest of society as no longer useful. The cruel poverty and isolation suffered by older women are an insult to all women and a crucial component of our struggle for liberation.

Older women are a very important part of the women's movement. Their years of struggle for survival against unremitting oppression have produced a wisdom invaluable to younger women who are just becoming aware of the harsh reality of women's existence. The feminist movement was built by their hard work and dedication and is strengthened by their continued participation and leadership.

We demand:

- A guaranteed pension at livable union wage for all elders.
- Healthcare that is thorough, respectful, and caring. Free, well-staffed, multicultural, multilingual medical and home care. End dehumanizing custodial care for profit. Provision at no cost of all techniques, personal aid devices, exercise and therapy to promote quality of life. Free, accessible transportation. Nutritious, quality meals delivered to the home at no charge.
- The right to a useful and productive life regardless of age. An end to forced retirement and age discrimination in hiring. Jobs and training for elders who don't wish to retire. Seniority rights and health and safety rules to protect the elder worker.
- Free, quality, elder-controlled social and recreational resources.
- An end to violence and threats of violence against older women.
- An end to media stereotyping of elders—and older women in particular—as childlike, useless and dependent. An end to repressive sexual morality toward older women and men.

Young Women

Young women are doubly oppressed because of their sex and their age. They are prisoners of their families and their education. They are subjected to intense sex-role socialization which limits their abilities, restricts their opportunities and destroys their sense of self-worth. They are denied the basic right to determine the course of their lives. Their sex automatically marks them for oppression, and their youth renders them relatively defenseless against it.

Under capitalism, young women are objects used as their parents/ owners see fit. Their struggle against the confines of the nuclear family —and the dynamic leadership they develop as a result—are essential to the liberation of all women.

We demand:

- The right of young women to develop physically, intellectually, socially, politically and sexually, free from sexist repression in their families, schools and other social institutions. An immediate halt to the intimidation and institutionalization of young women for their sexual activities and their rejection of the passive "feminine role."
- Establishment of collective homes where young people can live and grow with their peers and compatible adults. Legal recognition of young people's right to enter and leave a family or collective household.
- An end to the super-exploitation of youth as cheap labor. Jobs and training for young people, especially youths of color and young women who are doubly and triply discriminated against in the workplace. Equal wages and union protection for young people who choose to work. No sex-role stereotyping in training or employment opportunities.
- A halt to the exploitation and abuse of young women and children by the advertising and pornography industries.
- The right of young women to make their own reproductive decisions, including the right to abortion, and for social and economic support for teenage mothers. Quality education and childcare for young mothers who wish to continue their schooling.

Disabled Women

Disabled people constitute a sizable minority. For example, one-quarter of the U.S. population aged 22 to 64 have some level of physical or mental disability. The three major creators of disabilities—war, unsafe working conditions, and poverty—are directly linked to capitalism. The disabled face discrimination and segregation in all facets of their lives.

Disabled women, in particular, are rendered invisible and socially stigmatized as deformed, helpless, and asexual. Although their sexuality is denied, they are also prime targets of sexual abuse, especially if they are mentally disabled or institutionalized.

Disabled women and men are super-exploited as workers. They are paid far less than other workers or used as free labor. The system forces the disabled into social isolation, thereby reinforcing their second-class status. More money is spent on dependence-oriented programs than on strategies to increase autonomy and self-sufficiency and to allow disabled people to be contributing members of society.

We demand:

- Complete integration of the disabled into society, including full legal rights and protection from discrimination. Full government and corporate funding to provide state-of-the-art technological aids to all people with disabilities.
- Make transportation, buildings and all public facilities accessible to disabled people. Free transportation.
- Free, quality, nationalized healthcare.
- Nondiscriminatory job training and employment. Affirmative action quotas for employing people with disabilities. Building and tool modifications for disabled people. Jobs at livable union wages. No exemption from the minimum wage for employers of the disabled. Safe and healthy working conditions for all. Unionize the sweatshops where disabled people are often forced to work. Guaranteed income at union wages for all those who are unable to work.
- Equal education for the disabled, including modified facilities where required. Full funding for programs at all educational levels to teach students with learning disabilities.
- An end to social and media stereotypes which emphasize people's disabilities and ignore their abilities.
- Government funding to provide signing for the hearing impaired at all cultural, educational and political events.
- Training on disabled rights issues for those who work with the public. Eliminate government bureaucracy that hinders the disabled from receiving necessary assistance.

Women and Poverty

Limited opportunities have forced many women, especially single mothers, to become dependent upon welfare for their economic survival. This is particularly the case for women of color who, because of racism and sexism, have fewer chances for education and decent paying jobs.

Welfare was fought for and won by the working class to protect its members from the permanent unemployment and poverty that are intrinsic to capitalism. This important gain has been distorted into a system that creates and perpetuates dependency, powerlessness and cynicism, alienating women from the work experiences that build strength and self-sufficiency. If women are ever to achieve equality, they must have training and economic independence.

Instead, even limited welfare benefits are denied to many. In Australia, for example, many single parents are pushed off welfare if suspected of forming a sexual relationship. In the U.S., a rapidly growing number of mothers and homeless people have no welfare benefits to sustain them. The epidemic of extreme poverty and home-lessness in advanced capitalist countries is a searing indictment of the system.

We demand:

- Guaranteed income for all at livable union wage levels.
- Immediate cessation of forced work and "training" programs which use economic intimidation to coerce women to accept undesirable jobs at substandard wages. Such programs use welfare women as a cheap labor pool to break the union move-ment and produce super-profits for big business.
- Equal access to education and training programs in *all* occupa-tions, not just stereotypical "women's" fields.
- Fair grievance procedures with free legal support for all welfare recipients. An end to spying on welfare recipients.
- Free, 24-hour, quality childcare with transportation and three full daily meals provided to the children.
- Collectivize housework, cooking and child-rearing as *paid* jobs that are societal, not individual, responsibilities. As long as these socially necessary jobs remain the private responsibility of women in the home, the government should pay wages to those doing this work.
- Government subsidized, quality housing for the poor. Stop housing discrimination against welfare recipients. An end to dangerous and dehumanizing "warehousing" of the homeless in shelters. Nutritious food for all.

Women in Prison

Prisons are institutions of social control and inhumane punishment rather than rehabilitation. The accused person's race, sex, sexuality, political ideology and class often have more bearing on convictions and sentences than does evidence of guilt.

Women, in particular, are often incarcerated for "crimes" of economic desperation or for defending themselves against brutal husbands or boyfriends. While imprisoned, women are subjected to degrading living conditions and physical, psychological and sexual harassment. We demand:

- The right to quality, free legal counsel. Stop racism and sexism in sentencing. Eliminate all forms of discrimination against prisoners and ex-prisoners.
- An end to the racist, anti-working class, anti-radical death penalty.
- Freedom for all political prisoners. Shut down special control units that use sensory deprivation and are especially employed against political prisoners.
- The right of prisoners to organize on their own behalf, with protection against retaliation.
- Quality healthcare and decent living conditions in prison. An end to medical experimentation and testing on prisoners. No discriminatory sentencing or treatment of prisoners with AIDS or who are HIV-positive. Free condoms and clean syringes for all prisoners.
- Job training and education while in prison, including training for non-traditional trades. An end to the use of prisoners as super-exploited cheap labor. Employment at union wages for prisoners.
- The right of inmates to retain custody of their children and to choose whether to have their children with them in prison. Adequate facilities for children to stay with their mothers. The right of all prisoners to have unmonitored and unlimited visits from friends, relatives and lovers, regardless of sexual orientation or marital status.
- An end to sexual harassment of all prisoners, lesbians and gay men in particular. An end to racist and sexist violence against prisoners. Stop strip searches and prison rapes.

Legalization of Prostitution

Prostitution is the inevitable corollary of bourgeois monogamy, middle class morality and Puritanism. Given the establishment's need to maintain the male-dominated, monogamous family—and the taboo on sex outside marriage—prostitution will continue to exist until relationships and moral values are revolutionized.

Again, women are the victims. Lacking job training, skills and education, some women are forced to become prostitutes, a role in which they face overwhelming economic, legal and moral oppression. The illegality of their trade leaves them open to violence from customers, super-exploitation by their parasitic pimp bosses, and constant harassment and abuse by police and courts which treat them as the lowest of criminals.

While we work for an end to capitalism and its merchandising of sex—as prostitution or in any other form—we simultaneously demand protection for maligned and abused sex workers.

We demand:

- The immediate and unconditional legalization of prostitution. By "legalization," we mean the complete *decriminalization* of prostitution, so that sex workers are not subject to any form of legal harassment, fines, prosecution or regulation. They should instead be defended under the law from violence and intimidation by pimps, cops and customers. The right of prostitutes to police protection.
- Integration of prostitutes into the working class, with basic labor safeguards and the right to unionize. The right of prostitutes to control their own earnings, free from the parasitism of pimps. A guaranteed minimum wage at union standards for prostitutes.
- Free medical care and checkups for prostitutes as they request them.
- The right of prostitutes to have custody of their children.
- End the causes of prostitution: poverty, racism and sexism. Free job training and placement for women who choose to leave prostitution for another profession.

Violence against Women

As women, we experience violence every day of our lives. Our minds and our bodies are continually subjected to the arbitrary and often ruthless whims of the men who hold power over us—our bosses, husbands, fathers, co-workers, cops, and government officials.

Rape is an extension of male control, a form of terrorism to keep us in our "place." Any woman is fair game to any rapist. When we are raped and protest to the authorities, we are accused of having "asked for it." The insensitive treatment of sexual assault victims by the police, the medical profession, and the courts stems from that same rapist mentality—hidden behind a smoke screen of officialdom and sanctioned by the state.

As an extreme expression of the prevailing "blame-the-victim" attitude, women—especially women of color—who successfully defend themselves against violence are often prosecuted and imprisoned.

Domestic violence has reached epidemic proportions that cut across all class and race lines. Often, police treat marital assault as simply a "spat," leaving a woman undefended against attacks that can escalate to murder. Economics and the judicial system frequently force a battered wife to return to a deadly situation.

The fact is, the patriarchy depends upon the violent and inhumane exploitation of women to maintain dominance. We can free ourselves from violence only by joining together, seizing the power, and building a society free of psychological and physical brutality.

We demand:

- The right to live freely without fear of sexual insult or attack. The legal right to self-defense against all forms of sexual violence. No sexual harassment on the job.
- Full police and legal protection for victims of rape and domestic violence. Immediate investigation of all reported crimes against women. Balance the legal assumption that the attacker is innocent until proven guilty with a first priority commitment to protect the victim from further abuse or injury.
- Prosecution of all rapists with the burden of proof placed in the hands of the authorities, not on the victims. Outlaw marital rape. The right of victims of violent crimes to direct their own legal cases if they so choose.

- Free, sympathetic healthcare for all sexual assault victims. Stop subjecting assault victims to self-righteous moral condemnation from a society that created the problem in the first place.
- State-funded shelters for women fleeing domestic violence. Job training and placement for battered women.
- Compensation of rape/violence survivors for lost income, psychiatric counseling, medical care and any other expenses resulting from an attack.

The Environment

Capitalist globalization is destroying the earth. Living under the reign of a class willing to jeopardize our lives and future generations for quick cash, we are bombarded with chemicals in our food, water and air, and poisons at our job sites, in our homes, and in our communities. Women suffer the worst job conditions, and our bodies may also have special susceptibilities to certain environmental poisons.

Women have led the fight against pesticides, toxic and nuclear wastes, deforestation, and other forms of environmental destruction. Technology in the hands of workers can be used for human progress, but under the ruling class it is used against us.

We demand:

- Funding and education to preserve and protect the environment and recycle or restore natural resources.
- Open the books of the energy moguls. Nationalize the energy and petrochemical industries under workers' control. Develop safe and abundant energy forms that preserve and improve the global standard of living.
- Immediate shut down of all nuclear plants. Stop the building of nuclear weapons. End dumping of nuclear pollutants and implement community-supervised, safe disposal of existing radioactive waste. Corporations must take full responsibility for re-training and re-employing workers in the nuclear industry.
- Rid the environment and the workplace of murderous pesticides, poisons and hazardous refuse. Full corporate liability for the cost to clean up waste dumps and repair damage to the environment —instead of using workers' tax dollars to clean up the mess.

- An end to all strip mining, especially mining of cancer-causing uranium. An end to the theft of indigenous people's lands for mineral deposits or any other resources.
- Stringently enforced safety and health standards for all workers, particularly those who clean up environmental disasters.
- An end to corporate dumping of garbage and the transfer of hazardous industries to poor communities, Native reservations, and Third World countries. Stringent international standards to stop the industries of imperialist nations from polluting other countries.
- For humane treatment of animals and full protection of endangered species and habitats, including rain forests, tundra and oceans. The survival of animal and plant life is necessary for human progress and should not be pitted against our own well-being.

Media and Culture

Radio, television, video games, the press, and movies all spew out virulent prejudice against women. Women are portrayed as vacuous, frivolous, inept fools, manipulating seductresses, or simple-minded sex objects who love to be violently abused. We are used to sell anything and everything with our "sex appeal."

Male chauvinism is ingrained in contemporary culture. Most men accept and live by it automatically, as do many women despite their obvious confusion, frustration and misery. At the same time that sexist stereotypes proliferate, real information about our lives is often censored and kept from us.

We demand:

- End the imposition on the public of sick, distorted and demeaning media images of women and people of color. Cease perpetuating a standard of skinny, slinky white beauty which blatantly discriminates against women of other body types and colors.
- Stop advertisers from using women and children as sexual sales gimmicks. End the practice of employing images of violence against women as attention-grabbers for products. No more

advertising aimed at creating consumerist mentality in children
and promoting products harmful to their health or their attitudes about others.

- Provide serious media coverage of the struggle for women's
  rights and the movements of all oppressed people. An end
  to censorship of our history and information about women's
  issues. Free media access for all political viewpoints. Programming that reflects the full diversity of human experience and
  lifestyles, including people of color and sexual minorities.
  Abolish stereotypical images of all kinds in the media.
- Eliminate the violent exploitation of women and children by the
  multi-billion dollar international pornography industry.

The Military and the Draft

We oppose a compulsory draft which forces working people to defend
imperialism and kill their class sisters and brothers. But we also protest
many countries' sexist exclusion of women from the draft.

Women are denied opportunities for military training and suffer
sex role stereotyping and economic discrimination in the armed
forces. We understand the necessity for women and other oppressed
people to learn military skills for our own self-defense.

We demand:

- No draft. Not one human life nor any public funds for imperialist war. Where conscription does exist, no sexist exclusion of
  women from draft registration or the draft.
- An end to bigotry and job discrimination against women,
  people of color, sexual minorities, and mothers in the military.
- The right of all military personnel to union wages and to organize unions. Training programs and job placement following
  military service.
- Free, voluntary military training for all.
- Withdrawal of imperialist troops and advisors around the
  world. Eliminate the military budget and put the money into
  social services.
- No United States intervention in other countries. Abolish the
  U.S.-sponsored School of the Americas which trains rightwing

death squads and armies on how to crush democracy and popular revolt. Full support to anti-imperialist struggles and the right of all nations to self-determination.

The Right to Self-Defense

We support the right of oppressed people everywhere to defend themselves against violence. Whether the danger is posed by right-wing death squads, repressive police, out-of-control husbands, white supremacists, racist thugs, gay bashers, Nazis or police states, we believe organized community self-defense is a matter of survival and common sense.

We do not advocate "turn-the-other-cheek" martyrdom to people of color under racist assault or to anti-Nazi activists attacked by fascist thugs. We do not counsel *campesinos* in Central America to hand over their weapons to the repressive states that have slaughtered so many of their number. We support women who defend themselves and their children against rape or assault, sexual minorities who organize defense squads against gay bashers, and workers who protect their picket lines against anti-union scabs.

The question of nonviolence is a tactical issue, not an absolute principle. We do not advocate reckless adventurism or provoke clashes with the cops, Nazis or scabs when there is little to be gained by physical confrontation.

We demand:

- Legal recognition of oppressed people's right to self-defense, including community-organized mobilization against police brutality, racist and Nazi assaults, attacks on abortion clinics, queer-bashing, strikebreaking raids, and other forms of repressive violence or terrorism.

For a United Front against the Right Wing and Fascism

The economic crisis of capitalism emboldens the conservative right wing and fascists. Their aim is to preserve profits, whatever the cost. To avoid socialist revolution, the system will resort to full-blown fascism, with its genocidal racism, anti-Semitism, sexism and homophobia. Once in power, fascism crushes all unions and working class community organizations and obliterates democratic rights for all the oppressed.

The feminist movement is in the forefront of the battle with the ultra-right, particularly over abortion rights. Feminism is the subject of virulent attacks because it challenges the supremacy of the nuclear family. Conversely, women have the capacity to link every targeted movement into a powerful united front against fascism and the right wing.

A united front by definition has a leadership and program that represent the interests of the working class. When petty-bourgeois or bourgeois organizations hold leadership, a united front is undermined and turned into its opposite: an opportunist and class collaborationist "people's front." People's fronts act to preserve the status quo. They always acquiesce to the ruling class—the very class which finances and backs the reactionaries.

A movement to defeat fascism has no place for sectarianism, sexism and bigotry. United fronts must be broad-based organizations that reach beyond the organized Left to also include unions, people of color, Jews, feminists, civil libertarians, and sexual minorities.

We demand:

- Democratically run united front organizations in which members are the decision-makers. Each participating organization retains its own program and agrees to work collaboratively on specific actions against the reactionaries.
- No reliance on the police to defend us from fascists. Self-defense against Nazis and the Klan. Confront the fascists in some fashion with specific tactics determined by the relationship of forces and the degree of self-discipline within our ranks. Do not lead people into adventurist, losing battles.
- Solidarity in action against the reactionaries. An injury to one is an injury to all.

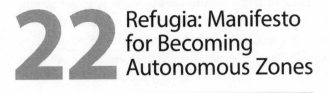

Refugia: Manifesto for Becoming Autonomous Zones

2002

subRosa

REFUGIA: A place of relatively unaltered climate that is inhabited by plants and animals during a period of continental climate change (as a glaciation) and remains as a center of relict forms from which a new dispersion and speciation may take place after climatic readjustment. (WEBSTER'S NEW COLLEGIATE DICTIONARY, 1976)

REFUGIA: Sections of agricultural fields planted with non-transgenic crops, alternating with transgenic crops. This is thought to slow the rate of resistance mutation caused in susceptible insect and weed species by gene transfer from GM (Genetically Modified) mono-culture crops.

REFUGIA: A Becoming Autonomous Zone (BAZ) of desirous mixings and recombinations; splicing female sexual liberation and autonomy with cyber feminist skills, theory, embodiment, and political activism.

REFUGIA: A critical space of liberated social becoming and intellectual life; a space liberated from capitalist Taylorized production; a space of unregulated, unmanaged time for creative exchange and play; experimental action and learning; desiring production, cooking, eating, and skill sharing.

REFUGIA: A reproducible concept that can be adapted to various climates, economies, and geographical regions worldwide. Any useless space can be claimed as a refugium: suburban lawns, vacant urban lots, rooftops, the edges of agricultural lands, clear-cut zones in forests, appropriated sections of monoculture fields, fallow land, weed lots, transitional land, battlefields, office buildings, squats, etc. Also currently existing Refugia such as multi-cultivar rice paddies, companion planted fields, organic farms, home vegetable gardens, etc.

REFUGIA: A postmodern commons; a resistant biotech victory garden; a space of convivial tinkering; a commonwealth in which common law rules. Not a retreat, but a space resistant to mono-culture in all its social, environmental, libidinal, political, and genetic forms.

REFUGIA: A habitat for new AMOs (Autonomously Modified Organism) and agit-crops; for example, "ProActiva," an herb that is a grafting of witch-root, mandrake, and all-heal.

REFUGIA: A place of asylum for the recuperation, regeneration and re-engineering of essential crops that have been corrupted by capitalist viruses and agribusiness greed.

REFUGIA: A space of imaginative inertia that slows down the engines of corporate agro/biotech and allows time to assess its risks and benefits through long-term testing.

REFUGIA: Neither a utopia nor a dystopia, but a haunted space for reverse engineering, monstrous graftings, spontaneous generation, recombination, difference, polyversity hybridization, wildlings, mutations, mongrelizing, crop circles, anomalies, useless beauty, coalitions, agit-crops, and unseemly sproutings. Biotech and transgenic work in Refugia will be based on desire, consensual public risk assessment, informed amateur experimentation, contestational politics, nourishment and taste value, non-proprietary expertise, convivial delight, and healing.

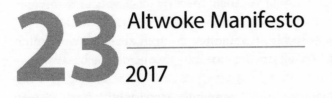

Altwoke Manifesto

2017

Anonymous

Introduction

There is no term more ubiquitous, obnoxious, and self-serving in our current lexicon as "woke." Woke is safety-pin politics, masturbatory symbolism, and virtue signaling of a deflated Left insulated by algorithms, filter bubbles, and browser extensions that replace pictures of Donald Trump with Pinterest recipes.

Woke is a misnomer—it's actually asleep and myopic. Woke is a safe space for the easily distracted and defensive pop culture inbred. Woke is the Left curled up in a fetal ball scribbling think pieces about Broad City while its rights get trampled by ascendant fascism, domestically and globally.

Woke is the easy button: it combats injustice by sharing videos of police brutality to an echo of outrage.

Woke is bereft of irony: it shares HuffPo articles about gentrification from condos in Flatbush and Oakland.

Woke is alchemy: it transmutes oppressed identities into advertising campaigns, trend reports, and new demographics to market towards.

Woke is poptimstic: it believes Jaden Smith becoming the face of Louis Vuitton is enough to qualify as a win for progress.

Woke is content with the status quo: it would be perfectly content if another economic collapse happened tomorrow, just as long as those who rigged it were sufficiently intersectional.

Woke is a sanctimonious grammar-nazi who critiques the bully's phrasing of "stop hitting yourself," through toothless gums. Woke is too ethical for its own good.

Woke is the gospel truth of the new evangelical Leftist. Woke is the Left's consolidated failures distilled into a monosyllabic buzzword. A whimper into the digital landscape prefixed with a hashtag, arriving at the same point each time: #Woke is the literal antithesis of progress.

CATALOGUE OF THE WOKE LEFT'S FAILURES

1. Moderate Liberal

The moderate Left misappropriated theoretical terms and concepts, divorced from any actual theory. Identity politics, despite its origins in academia, flourishes best on social media—it's the most accessible concept for moderate liberals to grasp.

"Well, if identity is only a game, if it is only a procedure to have relations, social and sexual-pleasure relationships that create new friendships, it is useful. But if identity becomes the problem of sexual existence, and if people think that they have to 'uncover' their 'own identity,' and that their own identity has to become the law, the principle, the code of their existence; if the perennial question they ask is 'Does this thing conform to my identity?' then, I think, they will turn back to a kind of ethics very close to the old heterosexual virility. If we are asked to relate to the question of identity, it must be an identity to our unique selves. But the relationships we have to have with ourselves are not ones of identity, rather, they must be relationships of differentiation, of creation, of innovation. To be the same is really boring. We must not exclude identity if people find their pleasure through this identity, but we must not think of this identity as an ethical universal rule."—Michel Foucault, "Sex, Power, and the Politics of Identity" (1984)

Identity politics became an albatross, however. Both the moderate and radical were too eager to evangelize oppressed identities. There was no room for discussion, no place for debate. Call outs, clap backs, and other reality tv patois replaced dialectics.

Representation is the de facto litmus of society's progress for the moderate liberal—society appeared more inclusive and diverse because "Orange is the New Black" has a female lead and a multiethnic supporting cast. They inhabit a never ending, curated echo chamber of think pieces, listicles, notifications, and retweets.

Everyone within their algorithmic ghetto shares their sentiments about society. The algorithm makes their small corner seem far more vast than it actually is, and as a result, the moderate extends this myopia to society at large.

The moderate midwifed the birth of the Alt-Right through bipartisan compromises. Moderate liberals are basically content to vest trust in their vaunted Democratic Party as it slides further to the right, thereby underpinning a level of discourse friendly to the far-right. It's worth remembering that the end of the 20th and beginning of the 21st centuries were a period of diehard cooperation between liberals and conservatives in crafting today's authoritarianism.

Neoconservatism provided socio-political planning that complemented a neoliberal economic agenda. This is why the radical Left blames liberals as well as conservatives for "command and control policing," mass surveillance and this century's rationale for endless warfare.

Moderate liberals provided and adopted theoretical frameworks that explained away structural oppression but retained an appearance of caring about racism and equality across intersecting spectrums of gender and sexuality.

This was an obvious farce that mystified progress and the far right took advantage of this because they actually suffered no serious political setbacks. Liberalism provided an incubator for the alt right to form by mollifying actual demands for change.

"If politics without passion leads to cold-hearted, bureaucratic technocracy, then passion bereft of analysis risks becoming a libidinally driven surrogate for effective action. Politics comes to be about feelings of personal empowerment, masking an absence of strategic gains."—Nick Srnicek and Alex Williams, "Inventing the Future" (2015)

2. Radical Left

If the liberal is the evangelical, pearl clutching apostle of the woke Left, the radical, then, is St. Augustine—the hierophant, the pedagogue. The radical is the vanguard inhabiting academia & activism, creating the language and atmosphere of critique.

Its ideologies trickle down from intellectuals at universities to moderate liberals on social media, and more recently, the Alt-Right (e.g. culture jamming by way of "meme magic" or the synthesis of identity politics and white nationalism by way of identitarianism).

Radicals scapegoated liberals to absolve themselves of any responsibility by being all critique with no tangible answers. The radical left in its current incarnation is somewhat fossilized in terms of strategies and needs an immediate remodeling.

The radical is too comfortable inhabiting only the periphery of academia & activism. Radical academics and activists are insulated not only by algorithms but also their obsolescence. The radical academic has failed to bridge the gap between intellectuals & larger society.

That is, intellectuals failed to subvert hegemony and normativity. Academics did not do enough to reach beyond universities and make positive reforms to public education. Intellectuals failed to politicize the natural sciences early enough. Intellectuals lost programming and hacker culture to neoliberalism & libertarians. Computer science transitioned from cyberpunk to Silicon Valley venture capitalism.

Had radical academics succeeded, there might've been more legitimacy in the fight to combat climate change. Or traditional journalism wouldn't have been so easily defeated by the post-fact information economy. What we have now is a new Scholasticism of students & professors as clergy dominated by an agitated, anti-intellectual populist bloc.

"*Learning surrenders control to the future, threatening established power. It is vigorously suppressed by all political structures, which replace it with a docilizing and conformist education, reproducing privilege as wisdom. Schools are social devices whose specific function is to incapacitate learning, and universities are employed to legitimate schooling through perpetual reconstitution of global social memory. The meltdown of metropolitan education systems in the near future is accompanied by a quasi-punctual bottom-up takeover of academic institutions, precipitating their mutation into amnesiac cataspace-exploration zones and bases manufacturing cyberian soft-weaponry.*" Nick Land, "Meltdown" (1994)

The radical activist lost its sense of resistance. There are no radicals in Congress. There are no radical lawmakers. No radical judges. Community organizing is helpful, but it's not sufficient. To remain relevant radicals have to widen their scope to adapt to the changing global climate.

"The idea that one organisation, tactic or strategy applies equally well to any sort of struggle is one of the most pervasive and damaging beliefs among today's left. Strategic reflection—on means and ends, enemies and allies—is necessary before approaching any political project. Given the nature of global capitalism, any postcapitalist project will require an ambitious, abstract, mediated, complex and global approach—one that folk-political approaches are incapable of providing." —Nick Srnicek and Alex Williams, "Inventing the Future" (2015)

WHAT IS #ALTWOKE

1. Theoria

AltWoke is a new awakening for the post-modern Left to navigate the protean digital era. AltWoke can be categorized as the new New Left. Or Second Wave Neo-Marxism. The Post- Truth Left. Anti-liberal postcapitalist left. AltWoke is antithetical to Silicon Valley techno-neoliberalism. AltWoke is not the cult of Kurzweil. AltWoke is not merely analogous to the Alt-Right. AltWoke injects planning back into left-wing politics. AltWoke supports universal basic income, biotechnology and radical energy reforms to combat climate change, open borders, new forms of urban planning and the liquidation of Western hegemony. AltWoke sees opportunity in disaster. AltWoke is the Left taking futurism away from fascism. David Harvey is #altwoke. Situationist International is #altwoke. Lil B is #altwoke. Jean Baudrillard is #altwoke. Kodwo Eshun is #altwoke, Mark Fisher is #altwoke, Roberto Mangabeira Unger is #altwoke. Edward Snowden is #altwoke. Daniel Keller is #altwoke. Chelsea Manning is #altwoke. Theo Parrish is #altwoke. William Gibson is #altwoke. Holly Herndon is #altwoke. Frantz Fanon is #altwoke. Alvin Toffler is #altwoke.

2. Poiesis

Anti-liberal, Left-accelerationism. Revolution is slow & gradual.

Technology, media, the global market, and culture accelerate the process.

Alt-Woke embraces the post-fact information economy as a pedagogical tool.

Culture is more important than policy.

Trickle-down ideology; AltWoke embraces normalization & hyper-
ıeality. Memetic counter-insurrection: culture-jamming is the weapon
of choice to tilt normalization in the direction we'd like it to go.

Xenofeminism. Technology is the missing component of intersectional politics. Eurocentrism and phallocentrism are obsolete, despite
the Right's best efforts. Queer is a verb, not a noun. If nature's oppressive, change nature. Normalize "deviance."

Reappropriation of globalism as a personal lifestyle.

AltWoke is duplicitous, amoral, & problematic. But also conscientious. The ends always justify the means. The Right hits low, so we hit
lower, harder, and without mercy.

AltWoke is cautiously optimistic about the future.

PREFACE TO PRAXIS

Why support Left-Accelerationism?

Accelerationism is a contested and obtuse term among the Left, so in
order to understand what accelerationism is, it's crucial to understand
what it isn't.

Accelerationism doesn't propose letting capitalism expand and
erode to such a degree that its corrosive contradictions become so
unbearable that the oppressed and working classes have no choice but
to revolt. #Alt-Woke doesn't and wouldn't espouse such a simplistic
and foolish framework, either.

In its neutral alignment, accelerationism is the idea that neoliberalism facilitates so much growth—economically, technologically, and
globally—that its social contradictions continue to expand to such a
degree that its "collapse" is not only inevitable, but creates a vacuum
for new integrated social platforms. That is, like feudalism before it,
late capitalism is transitory and incubates other socioeconomic ideologies that will ultimately replace it, since it's now reaching its limits.

In its Right alignment, accelerationism is a schism: Neoreaction
(NRx) is a radical libertarianism accelerating toward neoliberalism's
ultimate conclusion: plutocratic corporate monarchism (e.g., man
as nation). The second is the Alt-Right, which is white identity
politics accelerating toward capitalism's ultimate conclusion: techno-
fascism.

Left Accelerationism insists the only way out of capitalism is through it. It's become apparent that capitalism is reaching its limits, and it can't sustain itself any longer. The marriage of capitalism and democracy has been a powerful roadblock in the Left's struggle to combat structural power. In its late phase, this divorce of capitalism and democracy is imminent.

"But, in general, the protective system of our day is conservative, while the free trade system is destructive. It breaks up old nationalities and pushes the antagonism of the proletariat and the bourgeoisie to the extreme point. In a word, the free trade system hastens the social revolu-tion. It is in this revolutionary sense alone, gentlemen, that I vote in favor of free trade." —Karl Marx, "On the Question of Free Trade" (1884)

Left Accelerationism is a vindication of Marxism that synthesizes vertical tektology. It anticipates capitalism's collapse, repurposing growth and technology against its progenitor and nudges that collapse toward a Leftist counter-hegemony. Capitalism provides the efficiency of integrated networks, it provides the tools to combat the inequalities of its rapacious growth. A post-scarcity, socialist society can sustain itself from the technologies capitalism produces.

"The paradox of free-market communism is even more dramatic: the terms are strongly charged, ideological polar opposites, designating a kind of Mexican standoff between capitalism, on the one hand, and its archenemy and would-be grave digger, on the other. But the point of combining the terms free market *and* communism *in this way is to deploy selected features of the concept of communism to transform capitalist markets to render them truly free and, at the same time, to deploy selected features of the free market to transform communism and free it from a fatal entanglement with the State."* —Eugene W. Holland, "Nomad Citizenship: Free-Market Communism and the Slow-Motion General Strike" (2011)

The process of acceleration is well under way and no one but the most dogmatic and naive beltway libertarian would argue contrary. Left Accelerationism in an alternative to traditional avenues like reform or revolution and attempts to reorganize power from within power. It does this without completely discarding avenues like reform or revolution, either.

Left-Accelerationism is a synthesis of Marxism with vertical-scale tektology. It's Gramsci by way of Debord and David Harvey by way of Deleuze.

Why embrace a post-facts/post-truth information economy?

As it stands, narrative is more important than facts. Media and communications are so accelerated that both sides of the political spectrum are locked in a battle over consensus. Traditional pedagogy will not work in this instance. The Left hurts itself by not using this to its advantage.

"Sometimes people hold a core belief that is very strong. When they are presented with evidence that works against that belief, the new evidence cannot be accepted. It would create a feeling that is extremely uncomfortable, called cognitive dissonance. And because it is so important to protect the core belief, they will rationalize, ignore and even deny anything that doesn't fit with the core belief."—Frantz Fanon, "Black Skin, White Masks" (1952)

Why is culture more important than policy? Why weaponize memetics? What is "trickle down ideology"? Why support hyperreality and normalization?

Culture is society's barometer. From the meme unleashed by Marshall McLuhan's too-oft repeated phrase "the medium is the message," author Joshua Meyrowitz seems to have taken it most seriously. "No Sense of Place" is an analysis into how television changed society by altering society's access to information.

Meyrowitz forms a clear theory on information-power systems and discusses ways in which television breaks those down. At the end of the book, Meyrowitz chooses three specific topics: the merging of childhood and adulthood, the merging of masculinity and femininity, and the lowering of the political hero through the demystification of power.

Meyrowitz fundamentally believes that many social groupings and hostilities exist due to access to and restrictions of information and space. When information and space are separated, then the boundaries between social groups relax. For example, the television show "The Jeffersons" brought white families in their living rooms to the living room of a black family; and news coverage of the war in Vietnam "brought the war home" in visceral detail.

Memes are ideologies distilled, repackaged, and ready for viral distribution. The internet is something of an AI: a communication network operating as its own sovereign entity. Social media platforms, and other communications technologies accelerate the flow of ideas, bypassing restrictions put in place by traditional media.

A journalist in New York may engage with a senator in Washington over Twitter. A misguided 17-year old from Wisconsin who received their political education from /Pol, Breitbart, or Reddit can also join that same dialogue, and disrupt it. This is the best case scenario, unfortunately. Ideology is a memetic virus. Memes are an insurgent medium. The internet is an insurgent technology.

"The spectacle presents itself simultaneously as all of society, as part of society, and as instrument of unification. As a part of society it is specifically the sector which concentrates all gazing and all consciousness. Due to the very fact that this sector is separate, it is the common ground of the deceived gaze and of false consciousness, and the unification it achieves is nothing but an official language of generalized separation. The spectacle is not a collection of images, but a social relation among people, mediated by images." —Guy Debord, "Society of the Spectacle" (1967)

What is xenofeminism?

Xenofeminism is a form of Left-Accelerationism and, by extension, can be read as AltWoke's answer to identity politics. Or, more accurately, it critiques liberal "privilege"-based identity politics and re-situates Left "critical theory"-based identity politics into a technological framework.

Innovation is a consequence of capitalism's growth, hence it's irresponsible not to recognize how power operates not only through structures like capitalism, but also its incarnations like racism, colonialism, and heteronormativity.

When looking at history, it's imperative to ask questions about how technology changes and affects the ways in which people communicate, disseminate, and process information. This should always be taken into consideration from an intersectional frame of reference.

AltWoke isn't opposed to identity politics so much as it's opposed to reductionist, two-dimensional, representation as the crux of liberal identity politics. This mode of thinking lacks nuance and oftentimes devolves into inconsequential arguments over single phrases and who gets to participate. Bad politics comes in all forms of representation.

Hegemony operates in such a way that it permeates every aspect of social life in late capitalism, yet this isn't always apparent—its existence must be revealed. Culture's more dubious incarnation tells society who is and isn't worthy of praise, admiration, and, ultimately, life. The White Man™ is still the dominant conduit through which capitalism operates.

However, there's a cultural shift happening that is impossible to deny. The chauvinism of Western exceptionalism, essentialism, and the central cornerstone, "whiteness" are sociopolitical dead ends. It confines itself within impossible paradigms, even while, nonwhite, non-Western, non-binary identities are accelerating the process. The West crumbles as China accelerates toward superpower status. It's no coincidence that pop music is now synonymous with R&B. Hip hop, techno, house, and footwork bridge the gap between the avant garde and pop by accelerating language, form, timbre, and aesthetics to alien plateaus.

Is it any wonder why "cuckold" is the Alt-Right's pejorative of choice? The old guard justifies oppression and inequality as immutable and "natural." The deviant Other threatens this "natural" hierarchy. The normalization of deviance is the ultimate culture-jam. Cuckoldry is deviant, and deviance is the vanguard. #BlackPopMatters.

Why embrace and reappropriate globalism?

AltWoke perceives the "nation" as an information network and citizen –> user. The governance structure of the internet creates the subjectivity of power, the user, in the same fashion as the invention of the state created the subjectivity of citizens. Global scale computation has built a new governing rhizomatic architecture. All systems have integrated into platform stacks, and by extension, nations and governments are but another component in the Internet of Things (IoT).

People should be allowed in all physical spaces as a fundamental right. Politics has nothing to do with physical territory. AltWoke accelerationism fully separated land from politics once it realized that political groupings are aspatial networks: informational, cybernetic.

The old paradigm was political grouping by blood, land, and then language. These were all networks. Cyberspace is an artificial network same as blood, land, and language. It's better, too, as it is instantaneous. Those who hold politics to be the defense of land, nation, ethnicity, or linguistics are the old-guard; they are demonstrably incorrect and stand between people and their liberty.

"Geology is sensible of itself in so much as it has an ordering logic,

if it is articulate in its stratifications, reading pebbles, rocks, various kinds of matter, sorting, organizing (Roger Caillois calls this agency 'computational'), folding, compacting the biological slime of the earth into its various layers." Kathryn Yusoff, "Anthropogenesis: Origins and Endings in the Anthropocene" (2015)

The American nation was formed by the economic activities of the thirteen colonies as they functioned with common standards, such as shipping timetables and commercial infrastructure, developing into a consciousness of togetherness and assumed similarity between participants in the network.

Nations are coextensive with land, not that the land has ties to blood or biology (the misstep of historical fascism and contemporary nationalism, to glorify the soil) but the physical geography of land determined the networks superimposed over it.

Europe, for example, has for so long been balkanized into nationalities and peoples separated by mountain ranges, seas, and long distances, and brought together by modifications to this physical geography (see: Spain's hegemony over Europe and its fantastic road system prior to 1648).

Now, pan-Europeanism burgeons on the fact that highway systems, shipping, and a porousness of state borders has reduced or annihilated these impediments to a common access to the European network. It fails because it does not see that the same forces that drive Pan-Europeanism point towards a global society.

The separation of the information network from place thus reduces the determination of place upon network, of place upon user, of place upon that user's conception of themselves interacting with others, to the point that in a globalized world the user will interact with their physical neighbor in the same network as they will interact with someone in a different (city/state/nation/region), such that planetary consciousness necessarily forms.

Why is #AltWoke amoral?

Short answer: Politics is amoral. Long answer: As it stands, the political infrastructures of Western governments are collapsing. The Right solidified its stranglehold on structural power. Right Accelerationism is several steps ahead of its Leftist counterpart.

In America, the GOP is imploding and the Alt-Right is slowly replacing this obsolete party. The Right is vulgar, so we'll stop taking the moral high road and be even fouler. The Left has no structural power, and the stakes are far too high. We truly stand to lose everything. Traditional means of Left praxis are ineffectual against this ascendant superstructure. Asking that every individual respect the humanity of ethnic, racial, and sexual minorities is naive. It will take more deceptive and subversive methods for the political Left to affect any change. #Alt-Woke praxis is, if anything, a reappropriation of Vladislav Surkov's idea of "nonlinear warfare." We don't fight fair. We won't be civil. We don't resist power, we seize it.

3. Praxis

The question of AltWoke Praxis is also the question of Left-Accelerationist Praxis: How does one organize politically? AltWoke Praxis has two modal structures: Right Hand Praxis & Left Hand Praxis. Or, The Hand That Strikes & The Hand That Repurposes. RHP takes advantage of the cracks within the Alt-Right, disrupting any roadblocks to clear a path so LHP can shift the Overton Window. LHP repurposes existing technologies, networks, and power structures to initiate a counter-hegemony. LHP advances AltWoke's core tenets without ever explicitly espousing as such. Privacy is crucial to Left Hand Praxis, so it won't be listed, but appropriating multinational corporate identity is a crucial first step.

Right Hand Praxis

Alt-Right countersurveillance. Invade their spaces, disrupt their safe space.

Break out of your filter bubble, learn their language. Learn who they are, and what they believe. Befriend them only to spy on them. Dox the doxers.

Exploit the right's paranoia and affinity towards pseudoscience. If they believe that supplements will boost their testosterone or tin foil nets disrupt phone signals, exploit that market.

Direct action hacktivism. Penetrate the SEO. Make #altwoke viral. Twitter bot agit prop.

Appropriate post-fact culture. Conspiracy theories are memetically powerful. The Left does itself a disservice by not making its own. Speak their language to make it compelling: "Peter Thiel is a member of the Bilderberg Group!"

Exploit their contradictions: Human biodiversity is incompatible with Traditionalist Catholics. White nationalists think Identitarians are ineffectual Third Positionists. Drive them further into their own filter bubbles and out of voting booths.

Agitate Leftist demonstrations. The more the Woke, horizontal Left marches, the better. It takes any potential attention away from Left Hand Praxis.

24 A Feminist Manifesto for the 21st Century

2010

Lindsey German and Nina Power

1 Globalisation and neoliberalism have had a profound effect on the lives of millions of women. Capitalism itself has created new forms and manifestations of women's oppression.

2 Women's oppression is a product of class society which has existed for thousands of years. It was only with the development of capitalism that large numbers of women developed a consciousness of their position and the ability to do something about it.

3 Women have been drawn into the workforce in millions but working in factories, offices and shops has not led to an improvement in women's lives far less to liberation. Women suffer exploitation at work as well as still shouldering the double burden of family and childcare as well as paid work.

4 Women's traditional role as wives and mothers has not disappeared but has been reinvented to fit in with the needs of exploitation. They are now expected to juggle all aspects of their lives and are blamed as individuals for any failings in family or work life.

5 The talk of glass ceilings and unfairly low bonuses for women bankers miss the point about liberation, which is that liberation has to be for all working women and not just a tiny number of privileged women.

6 Although all women suffer oppression and face discrimination, their life experiences are radically different. Women are not united as a sex but are divided on the basis of class. Middle and upper class women share in the profits from the exploitative system in which we live and use this benefit to alleviate their own oppression.

Working class women are usually the people who cook, clean and provide personal services for these women, receiving low wages and often neglecting their own families to do so.

7 Women are more than ever regarded as objects defined by their sexuality. The commercialisation of sexuality with its lad and ladette culture, its pole dancing clubs and its post-modern Miss World contests keeps women being judged as sex objects as if nothing has changed since the 1950s.

8 This objectification, alongside women's role as supposedly the property of men, leads to domestic violence, rape and sexual abuse. This abuse is under recognised and under reported. It was only in the 1960s and 70s that these issues began to be viewed as political.

9 To control their own lives, women must control their own bodies and sexuality.

10 Capitalist ideology prioritises the family and the subordinate role of women and children within it, while at the same time forcing individual members of the family to sacrifice "family life" because of the pressures of work and migration.

11 The priorities of the profit system and the existence of the privatised family means that women's oppression is structured into capitalism. Any genuine liberation has to be connected to a wider movement for human emancipation and for working people to control the wealth that they produce. That's why women and men have to fight for liberation. Socialism and women's liberation are inextricably connected.

12 We will not win without a fight. Every great social movement raises the question of women. In the 19th century the movement for women's emancipation took its name from the movement to abolish slavery. In the 20th century women's liberation took its name from the movements against colonialism around the world. 21st century women's liberation has to fight to change the world and to end the class society which created oppression and exploitation in the first place.

PART III

Introduction to Angry/Violent

The first action of these oppressed creatures is to bury deep down that hidden anger which their and our moralities condemn and which is however only the last refuge of their humanity.
　　　　—Jean-Paul Sartre, Preface to *The Wretched of the Earth*

Here we find white-hot rage radiating through the pages, with women hell-bent on destroying the status quo and rebuilding something new. This section also contains what I believe to be the single greatest feminist manifesto ever written—Valerie Solanas's *SCUM Manifesto*, a text that is at once satirical and deadly serious, contentious and playful, philosophically sophisticated and downright nasty. *SCUM Manifesto* changed the course of feminist history, paving the way for voices of feminist rage in the 50 plus years since its publication. The version included here is the version Solanas herself most wanted out in the world: the 1977 self-published *SCUM Manifesto*.

Surrounding *SCUM*, we find key texts of the second-wave radical feminist movement, including the classic Redstockings Manifesto and Shulamith Firestone's *The Dialectic of Sex*, texts that forged new paths by linking gender with class and race struggles. We also read an early speech (Sojourner Truth) that radically upended the role of women and their legal and social rights, together with an early twentieth-century diatribe about the status of women (Mina Loy). We finish off this section with Andrea Dworkin, the patron saint of feminist rage, who vividly portrays intercourse as irredeemably power-imbalanced (and women as *fucked*, in all ways), followed by a short and powerful anti-racist manifesto (E. Jane) and a long poem by radical feminist folksinger Ani DiFranco, who takes to task the politics of a country that continually undermines women's lives with greed, corruption, racism, and misogyny.

25 I Am as Strong as Any Man

1851

Sojourner Truth

May I say a few words? I want to say a few words about this matter. I am a woman's rights. I have as much muscle as any man, and can do as much work as any man. I have plowed and reaped and husked and chopped and mowed, and can any man do more than that? I have heard much about the sexes being equal; I can carry as much as any man, and can eat as much too, if I can get it. I am as strong as any man that is now. As for intellect, all I can say is, if woman have a pint and man a quart—why cant she have her little pint full? You need not be afraid to give us our rights for fear we will take too much,—for we cant take more than our pint'll hold. The poor men seem to be all in confusion, and dont know what to do.

Why children, if you have woman's rights give it to her and you will feel better. You will have your own rights, and they wont be so much trouble. I cant read, but I can hear. I have heard the bible and have learned that Eve caused man to sin. Well if woman upset the world, do give her a chance to set it right side up again. The Lady has spoken about Jesus, how he never spurned woman from him, and she was right. When Lazarus died, Mary and Martha came to him with faith and love and besought him to raise their brother. And Jesus wept—and Lazarus came forth. And how came Jesus into the world? Through God who created him and woman who bore him. Man, where is your part? But the women are coming up blessed be God and a few of the men are coming up with them. But man is in a tight place, the poor slave is on him, woman is coming on him, and he is surely between-a hawk and a buzzard.

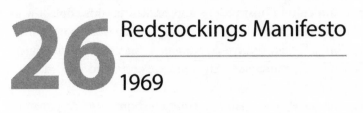

Redstockings Manifesto

1969

Redstockings

I After centuries of individual and preliminary political struggle, women are uniting to achieve their final liberation from male supremacy. Redstockings is dedicated to building this unity and winning our freedom.

II Women are an oppressed class. Our oppression is total, affecting every facet of our lives. We are exploited as sex objects, breeders, domestic servants, and cheap labor. We are considered inferior beings, whose only purpose is to enhance men's lives. Our humanity is denied. Our prescribed behavior is enforced by the threat of physical violence.

Because we have lived so intimately with our oppressors, in isolation from each other, we have been kept from seeing our personal suffering as a political condition. This creates the illusion that a woman's relationship with her man is a matter of interplay between two unique personalities, and can be worked out individually. In reality, every such relationship is a <u>class</u> relationship, and the conflicts between individual men and women are <u>political</u> conflicts that can only be solved collectively.

III We identify the agents of our oppression as men. Male supremacy is the oldest, most basic form of domination. All other forms of exploitation and oppression (racism, capitalism, imperialism, etc.) are extensions of male supremacy: men dominate women, a few men dominate the rest. All power structures throughout history have been male-dominated and male-oriented. Men have controlled all political, economic and cultural institutions and backed up this control with physical force. They have used their power to keep women in an inferior position. All men receive economic, sexual, and psychological benefits from male supremacy. All men have oppressed women.

IV Attempts have been made to shift the burden of responsibility from men to institutions or to women themselves. We condemn these arguments as evasions. Institutions alone do not oppress; they are merely tools of the oppressor. To blame institutions implies that men and women are equally victimized, obscures the fact that men benefit from the subordination of women, and gives men the excuse that they are forced to be oppressors. On the contrary, any man is free to renounce his superior position, provided that he is willing to be treated like a woman by other men.

We also reject the idea that women consent to or are to blame for their own oppression. Women's submission is not the result of brain-washing, stupidity or mental illness but of continual, daily pressure from men. We do not need to change ourselves, but to change men.

The most slanderous evasion of all is that women can oppress men. The basis for this illusion is the isolation of individual relationships from their political context and the tendency of men to see any legitimate challenge to their privileges as persecution.

V We regard our personal experience, and our feelings about that experience, as the basis for an analysis of our common situation. We cannot rely on existing ideologies as they are all products of male supremacist culture. We question every generalization and accept none that are not confirmed by our experience.

Our chief task at present is to develop female class consciousness through sharing experience and publicly exposing the sexist foundation of all our institutions. Consciousness-raising is not "therapy," which implies the existence of individual solutions and falsely assumes that the male-female relationship is purely personal, but the only method by which we can ensure that our program for liberation is based on the concrete realities of our lives.

The first requirement for raising class consciousness is honesty, in private and in public, with ourselves and other women.

VI We identify with all women. We define our best interest as that of the poorest, most brutally exploited woman.

We repudiate all economic, racial, educational or status privileges that divide us from other women. We are determined to recognize and eliminate any prejudices we may hold against other women.

We are committed to achieving internal democracy. We will do whatever is necessary to ensure that every woman in our movement has an equal chance to participate, assume responsibility, and develop her political potential.

VII We call on all our sisters to unite with us in struggle.

We call on all men to give up their male privilege and support women's liberation in the interest of our humanity and their own.

In fighting for our liberation we will always take the side of the women against their oppressors.

We will not ask what is "revolutionary" or "reformist," only what is good for women.

The time for individual skirmishes has passed. This time we are going all the way.

July 7, 1969, New York City

27 The Feminist Manifesto

1914

Mina Loy

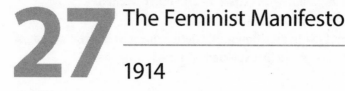

This is a rough draught of an absolute resystamisation of this question I. feminist

beg Feminist Manifesto. give me your opinion

beg The feminist movement as at present institu-
ted is Inadequate . ×easily come it illusions to be proud no here truth

Women if you want to realise yourselves
— you are on the eve of a anyway
devastating pschycological upheaval —
all your pet illusions must be un-
masked — the lies of centuaries you
have got to go — are you prepared
for the Wrench — ? There is no half-
measure — No scratching on the surface
of the rubbish heaps of tradition,
will bring about Reform , the only
method is Absolute Demolition

Cease to place your confidence in economic
legislation, vice-crusades & uniform education — you are glossing over
Reality .

Professional & commercial careers are
opening up for you — Is that all
you want ?

And if you honestly desire to find your
level without prejudice — Be Brave
& deny at the outset — that pathetic
clap - trap warcry
Woman is the equal of man —

   She is NOT. ! tor

The man who lives a life in which his
activities conform to a social code
which is a protectorate of the feminine
element _____ is no longer masculine

The women who adapt themselves to a
theoretical valuation of their sex as a
relative impersonality, is not yet
Feminine

Leave off looking to men to find out
what you are not — seek within
yourselves to find out what you are

As conditions are at present constituted
— you have the choice between Para —
sitism, & Prostitution — or Negation

3.

Men & women are enemies, with the enmity
of the exploited for the parasite, the parasite
for the exploited — at present they are at
the mercy of the advantage that each can
take of the others sexual dependence —.
The only point at which the interests
of the sexes merge — is the sexual
embrace.

The first illusion it is to your interest to de-
molish is the division of women into two
classes   the mistress, & the mother
every well-Balanced & developed woman
knows that is not true, Nature has
endowed the complete woman with a faculty for expressing herself through all
her functions — there are no restrictions
the woman who is so incompletely developed self-conscious evolved as to
be un-self-conscious in sex, will prove
a restrictive influence on the temperamental expansion of the next generation;
the woman who is a poor mistress will
be an incompetent mother — an inferior
mentality — & will enjoy an inadequate
apprehension of Life.

4.

To obtain results you must make sacrifices & the first & greatest sacrifice you have to make is of your "virtue"

The fictitious value of woman as identified with her physical purity — is too easy a stand-By — rendering her lethargic in the acquisition of intrinsic merits of character By which she could obtain a concrete value — therefore, the first self-enforced law for the female sex, as a protection against the man made bogey of virtue — which is the principal instrument of her subjection, would be the unconditional surgical destruction of virginity throughout the female population at puberty —.

The value of man is assessed entirely according to his use or interest to the community, the value of woman, depends entirely on chance her success or insuccess in manoeuvering a man into taking the life-long responsibility of her —

The professiona advantages of marriage are too ridiculously ample — compared to all other trades — for under modern conditions

6

a woman can accept preposterously luxurious
support from a man (with-out return of any
sort – even offspring) — as a thank offering for her virginity

The woman who has not succeeded in striking
that advantageous Bargain – is prohibited
from any but surreptitious re-action to
Life - Stimuli — & entirely debarred
Maternity . Every woman has a right
to maternity —
Every woman of superior intelligence
should realize her race-responsibility,
in producing children in adequate proportion to the unfit or degenerate members of her sex –

Each child of a superior woman should
be the result of a definite period of psych-
cic development in her life – & not necessarily of a possibly irksome & outworn
continuance of an alliance – spontaneously
adapted for vital creation in the beginning
but not necessarily harmoniously balanc-
ed as the parties to it – follow their individual lines of personal evolution –

For the harmony of the race , each indi-

6.

vidual should be the expression of an easy
& ample interpenetration of the male & female
temperaments — free of stress
Woman must become more responsible for
the child than man —
Women must destroy in themselves, the
desire to be loved —
The feeling that it is a personal insult
when a man transfers his attentions from
her to another woman
The desire for comfortable protection instead
of an intelligent curiosity & courage in
meeting & resisting the pressure of life
Sex or so called love must be reduced
to its initial element, honour, grief.
Sentimentality, pride & consequently jealousy
must be detached from it.
Woman for her happiness must retain her
deceptive fragility of appearance, combined with
indomitable will, irreducible courage, & abundant health, the outcome of sound nerves —
Woman must use all her introspective
another great illusion that
clear-sightedness & unbiassed bravery
to destroy -for the sake of her _self respect_
is the impurity of sex

7

the realisation in defiance of superstition that there is _nothing impure in Sex_ — except in the mental attitude tude to it — will constitute ~~a wider a more~~ an incalculable & wider social regeneration than it is possible for our generation to imagine

Nov. 15th   Mina Loy.

Firenze.

SCUM Manifesto

1967

Valerie Solanas

This society being, at best, an utter bore and no aspect of society being at all relevant to women, there remains to civic-minded, responsible, thrill-seeking females only to overthrow the government, eliminate the money system, institute complete automation and eliminate the male sex.

Since it's now technically possible to reproduce without the aid of males (or, for that matter, females) and to produce only females, retaining the male hasn't even the dubious purpose of reproduction.

The male's a biological accident: the y (male) gene's an incomplete x (female) gene, that is, has an incomplete set of chromosomes. In other words, the male's an incomplete female, a walking abortion, aborted at the gene stage. To be male's to be deficient, emotionally limited; maleness is a deficiency disease and males are emotional cripples. The male's completely egocentric, is trapped inside himself, is incapable of empathizing or identifying with others, of love, affection, friendship or tenderness. He's a completely isolated unit, incapable of rapport with anyone. His enthusiasms are entirely animal, visceral, not mental, cerebral; his intelligence is a mere tool in the service of his drives and needs; he's incapable of mental passion, mental interaction; he can't relate to anything other than his own physical sensations. He's a half-dead, unresponsive lump, incapable of either giving or receiving pleasure or happiness, and, consequently, he's at best, an utter bore, an inoffensive blob, as only those capable of absorption in others can be charming. He's trapped in a twilight zone halfway between humans and apes, and is far worse off than the apes, because he's first of all, capable of a large array of negative feelings the apes aren't—hate, jealousy, contempt, disgust, guilt, shame, disgrace, doubt—and secondly, he's aware of what he is and isn't.

Although completely physical, the male's unfit even for stud service, for, even assuming mechanical proficiency, which few men have, he's, first of all, incapable of zestfully, lustfully, tearing off a piece, but is rather eaten up with guilt, shame, fears and insecurities, feelings rooted in male nature, which the most enlightened training can only minimize; secondly, the physical feeling he attains is next to nothing; and thirdly, he's not empathizing with his partner, but is obsessed with how he's doing, turning in an A performance, functioning well, doing a good plumbing job. To call a man an animal's to flatter him; he's a machine, a walking dildo. It's often said men use women. Use them for what? Surely not pleasure.

Eaten up with guilt, shame, fears and insecurities and obtaining, if he's lucky, a barely perceptible physical feeling, the male's, nonetheless, obsessed with screwing; he'll swim through a river of snot, wade nostril-deep through a mile of vomit, if he thinks there'll be a friendly pussy awaiting him; he'll screw a woman he despises, any filthy, toothless hag, and, further, pay for the opportunity. Why? Relieving physical tension isn't the answer, as masturbation suffices for that. It's not to conquer; that doesn't explain screwing corpses and babies. Completely egocentric, unable to relate, empathize or identify and consisting of a pervasive, diffuse sexuality, the male's psychically passive. He hates his passivity, so he projects it onto women, defines the male as active, then sets out to prove he is ("prove he's a Man"). His main means of attempting to prove it is screwing (Big Man with a Big Dick tearing off a Big Piece). Since he's attempting to prove an error, he must "prove" it again and again. Screwing, then, is a desperate, compulsive attempt to prove he's not passive, not a woman; but he *is* passive and *does* want to be a woman. Being an incomplete female, the male spends his life attempting to complete himself, become female. He attempts to do this by constantly seeking out, fraternizing with and trying to live through and fuse with the female and by claiming as his own all female characteristics—emotional strength and independence, forcefulness, dynamism, decisiveness, coolness, objectivity, assertiveness, courage, integrity, vitality, intensity, depth of character, grooviness, etc. —and projecting onto women all male traits—vanity, frivolity, triviality, weakness, etc. (It should be said, though, the male has one glaring area of superiority over the female—public relations. He's done a brilliant job of convincing millions of women that men are women and women are men.) The male claim that females find fulfillment through motherhood and sexuality reflects what males think *they'd* find fulfilling if *they* were female. Women, in other words, don't have penis envy; men have pussy envy. When the male accepts his passivity, defines himself as a woman (Males as well as females think men are women and women are men) and becomes a transvestite he loses his desire to screw (or to do anything else, for that matter: he fulfills himself as a dragqueen.) and gets his dick chopped off in hopes of deriving a continuous, diffuse sexual feeling from "being a woman." Screwing is, for a man, a defense against his desire to be female. Sex is, itself, a sublimation.

The male, because of his obsession to compensate for not being female combined with his inability to relate and feel compassion, has made of the world a shitpile. He's responsible for:

WAR

The male's normal method of compensation for not being female, namely, getting his Big Gun off, being grossly inadequate, as he can get it off only a very limited number of times, he gets it off on a really massive scale, grand scale, and proves to the entire world he's a "Man." Since he has no compassion or ability to empathize or identify, proving it's worth an endless amount of mutilation and suffering and an endless number of lives, including his own—his own live being worthless, he'd rather go out in a blaze of glory than plod grimly on for fifty more years.

NICENESS," POLITENESS AND "DIGNITY"

Every man, deep down, knows he's a worthless piece of shit. Overwhelmed by a sense of animalism and deeply ashamed of it, wanting, not to express himself, but to hide from others his total physicality and total egocentricity and having a crudely constructed nervous system easily aroused by the least display of emotion or feeling, the male tries to enforce a perfect blandness by a "social" code consisting of "copulate," "sexual congress," "have relations with" (To men "sexual relations" is a redundancy.), and of stilted manners, the suit on the chimp.

MONEY, MARRIAGE AND PROSTITUTION, WORK AND PREVENTION OF AN AUTOMATED SOCIETY

There is no human reason for money or for anyone to work more than two or three hours a week at the very most. All non-creative jobs (practically all jobs now being done) could've been automated away long ago, and in a moneyless society everyone can have as much of the best of everything as one wants. But there are non-human, male reasons for maintaining the money-work system:

1. Pussy. Despising his highly inadequate self, overcome with intense anxiety and a deep, profound loneliness when by his empty self, desperate to attach himself to any female in dim hopes of completing himself, in the mystical belief that by touching gold he'll turn to gold, the male craves the continuous companionship of women. The company of the lowest female's preferable to his own or that of other men. But females, unless very young or very sick, must be coerced or bribed into male company.

2. Supply the non-relating male with the delusion of usefulness, enable him to try to justify his existence by digging holes and filling them up. Leisure time horrifies the male, who'll have nothing to do but contemplate his grotesque self. Unable to relate or love, the male must work. Females crave absorbing, emotionally satisfying, meaningful activity, but lacking the opportunity or ability for this, they prefer to idle and waste away their time in ways of their own choosing—sleeping, shopping, bowling, shooting pool, playing cards, breeding, reading, walking around, daydreaming, eating, playing with themselves, popping pills, going to the movies, getting analyzed, boozing, traveling, raising dogs and cats, lolling on the beach, swimming, watching T.V., listening to music, decorating their houses, gardening, sewing, night-clubbing, dancing, visiting, "improving their minds" (taking courses), and absorbing "culture" (lectures, plays, concerts, "art" movies) —therefore, many females would, even assuming complete economic equality between the sexes, prefer living with males or peddling their asses on the street,

thereby having most of their time for themselves, to spending many hours of their days doing boring, stultifying, non-creative work for somebody else, functioning as less than animals, as machines, or, at best—if able to get a "good" job—co-managing the shitpile. What will liberate women, therefore, from male control is the total elimination of the money–work system, not the attainment of economic equality within it.

3. Power and Control. Unmasterful in his personal relations with women, the male attains to general masterful by the manipulation of money and of everything and everybody controlled by money, in other words, of everything and everybody.

4. Love substitute. Unable to give love or affection, the male gives money. It makes him feel motherly. The mother gives milk; he gives bread. He's the Breadwinner.

5. Provide the male with a goal. Incapable of enjoying the moment, the male needs something to look forward to, and money provides him with an eternal, never-ending goal: Just think of what you could do with 80 trillion dollars—Invest it! And in three years time you'd have 300 trillion dollars!!!

6. Provide the basis for the male's major opportunity to control and manipulate—fatherhood.

FATHERHOOD AND MENTAL ILLNESS
(fear, cowardice, timidity, humility, insecurity, passivity)

Mother wants what's best for her kids; Daddy only wants what's best for Daddy, that is peace and quiet, pandering to his delusion of dignity ("respect"), a good reflection on himself (status) and the opportunity to control and manipulate, or, if he's an "enlightened" father, "give guidance." His daughter, in addition, he wants sexually—He gives her *hand* in marriage; the other part's for him.

Daddy, unlike Mother, can never give in to his kids, as he must at all costs preserve his delusion of decisiveness, forcefulness, always-rightness and strength.

Never getting one's way leads to lack of self-confidence in one's ability to cope with the world and to a passive acceptance of the status quo. Mother loves her kids, although she sometimes gets angry, but anger blows over quickly and even while existing doesn't preclude love and basic acceptance. Emotionally diseased Daddy doesn't love his kids; he approves of them—if they're "good," that is, if they're nice, "respectful," obedient, subservient to his will, quiet and not given to unseemly displays of temper that would be most upsetting to Daddy's easily aroused male nervous system, in other words, if they're passive vegetables. If they're not "good," he doesn't get angry—not if he's a modern, "civilized" father (the old-fashioned ranting, raving brute's preferable, as he's so ridiculous he as to be easily despised) —but rather express disapproval, a state that, unlike anger, endures and precludes a basic acceptance, leaving the kid with a feeling of worthlessness and a lifelong obsession to be approved of, with a resulting fear of independent thought as this leads to unconventional, disapproved of opinions and way of life.

For the kid to want Daddy's approval it must "respect" Daddy, and, being garbage, Daddy can insure he's "respected" only by remaining aloof, by distantness, by acting on the precept: "Familiarity breeds contempt," which is, of course, true, if one's contemptible. By being distant and aloof, he's able to remain unknown, mysterious, and thereby, to inspire fear ("respect"). Disapproval of emotional "scenes" leads to fear of strong emotion, fear of one's own anger and hatred and to a fear of facing reality, as facing it leads at first to anger and hatred. Fear of anger and hatred combined with a lack of self-confidence in one's ability to cope with and change the world or even to affect in the slightest way one's own destiny leads to a mindless belief that the world as it is and one's position in it are really nice and that the most banal, trivial amusements are great fun and deeply pleasurable.

The *effect* of Fatherhood on males, specifically, is to make them "Men," that is, highly defensive of all impulses to passivity, faggotry, and of desires to be female. Every boy wants to imitate his mother, be her, fuse with her, but Daddy forbids this; *he's* the mother; *he* gets to fuse with her. So he tells the boy, sometimes directly, sometimes indirectly, to not be a sissy, to act like a "Man." The boy, scared shitless of and "respecting" his father, complies, and becomes just like Daddy, that model of "Manhood," the all-American heterosexual dullard.

The effect of Fatherhood on females is to make them male— dependent, passive, domestic, animalistic, "nice," insecure, approval and security seekers, cowardly, humble, "respectful" of authorities and men, closed, not fully responsive, half dead, trivial, dull, conventional, flattened out and thoroughly contemptible. Daddy's Girl, always tense and fearful, uncool, unanalytical, lacking objectivity, appraises Daddy, and thereafter, other men against a background of fear ("respect") and isn't able to see the empty shell behind the aloof facade, but accepts the male definition of himself as superior, as a female, and of herself, as inferior, as a male, which, thanks to Daddy, she really is.

It's the widespreadness of Fatherhood, resulting from the increased and more widespread affluence Fatherhood needs to thrive, that has caused the general increase of mindlessness—as evidence by, for example, the increase in breast feeding, natural childbirth, church going—and the decline of women in the United States since the early part of the century. The close association of affluence with Fatherhood has led, for the most part, to only the wrong girls, namely, the "privileged," middle and upper class ones, getting "educated."

The effect of Fathers, in sum, has been to corrode the world with maleness. The male has a negative Midas Touch—everything he touches turns to shit.

ANIMALISM
(domesticity and motherhood)
AND SUPPRESSION OF INDIVIDUALITY

The male's just a bunch of conditioned reflexes, is incapable of a mentally free response, is tied to the early conditioning, is determined completely by his past experiences. His earliest experiences are with his mother, and he's throughout his life tied to her. It never becomes completely clear to the male that he's not part of his mother, that he's him and she's her.

His greatest need's to be guided, sheltered, protected and admired by Mama (Men expect women to adore what men shrink from in horror—themselves), and; being completely physical, he yearns to spend his time—that's not spent "out in the world" grimly defending against his passivity—in wallowing in basic animal activities—eating, sleeping, shitting, relaxing and being soothed by Mama.

Passive, rattle-headed Daddy's Girl, ever eager for approval, for a pat on the head, for the "respect" of any passing piece of garbage, is easily reduced to Mama, mindless administrator to physical needs, soother of the weary, apey brow, booster of the puny ego, appreciator of the contemptible, a hot water bottle with tits. The reduction to animals of the women of the most backward segment of society—the "privileged," "educated" middle and upper classes, the backwash of humanity—where Daddy reigns supreme, has been so thorough they try to groove on labor pains and lie around in the most advanced nation in the world in the middle of the twentieth century with babies chomping away on their tits. It's not for the kid's sake, though, the "experts" tell women Mama should stay home and grovel in animalism, but for Daddy's; the tit's for Daddy to hang onto; the labor pains for Daddy to vicariously groove on (Half dead, he needs awfully strong stimuli to make him respond).

Reducing the female to an animal, to Mama, to a male, is necessary for psychological as well as practical reasons: the male's a mere member of the species, interchangeable with every other male, every other dick. He has no deep-seated individuality (sense of distinctness, psychological self-sufficiency, self-containment), which stems from what intrigues you, what outside yourself absorbs you, what outside yourself you're in relation to. Completely self-absorbed, capable of being in relation only to their bodies and physical sensations, males differ from each other only to the degree and in the ways they attempt to defend against their passivity and against their desire to be female.

The female's individuality, which he's aware of, but which he doesn't comprehend and isn't capable of relating to, frightens and upsets him and fills him with envy, so he denies it in her and proceeds to define everyone in terms of a function or use, assigning to himself, of course, the most important functions—doctor, president, scientist—thereby providing himself with an identity, if not individuality, and tries to convince himself and women—he's succeeded best at convincing women—that the female function's to bear and raise children and to relax, comfort and boost the ego of the male, that her function's such as to make the most together female interchangeable with the least.

In actual fact, the female function's to explore, discover, invent, solve problems crack jokes, make music—all with love. In other words, create a magic world.

The male function's to produce sperm. We now have sperm banks.

PREVENTION OF PRIVACY

Although the male, being ashamed of what he is and of almost everything he does, insists on privacy, secrecy in all aspects of his life, he, yet, has no real regard for privacy. Being empty, not being a complete, separate being, having no individuality, no self to groove on and needing to be constantly in female company, he sees nothing at all wrong in intruding himself on any woman's, even a total stranger's, thoughts anywhere at any time, but rather feels indignant and insulted when put down for doing so, as well as confused—he can't, for the life of him, understand why anyone would prefer so much as one minute of solitude to the company of any creep around. Wanting to become a woman, he strives to be constantly around females, the closest he can get to becoming one, so he created a society based upon the family—a male–female couple and their kids (the excuse for the family's existence), who live virtually on top of one another, scrupulously violating the female's rights, privacy and sanity.

ISOLATION, SUBURBS AND PREVENTION OF COMMUNITY

Our society isn't a community, but merely a collection of isolated family units. Desperately insecure, fearing his woman'll leave him if she's exposed to other men or to anything remotely resembling life, the male seeks to isolate her from other men and from what little civilization there is, so he moves her out to the suburbs, a collection of self-absorbed couples and their kids.

Isolation, further, enables him to try to maintain his pretense of being an individual by being a "rugged individualist," a loner, equating non-cooperation and solitariness with individuality.

And there's yet another reason for the male to isolate himself: every man's an island. Trapped inside himself, emotionally isolated, unable to relate, the male has a horror of civilization, people, cities, situations requiring an ability to understand and relate to people, so, like a scared rabbit, he scurries off, dragging Daddy's little asshole along with him, to the wilderness, the suburbs, or, in the case of the "hippy"—He's way out, Man—all the way out to the cow pasture where he can fuck and breed undisturbed and mess around with his beads and flute.

The "hippy," whose defenses against his passivity, whose desire to be a "Man," a "rugged individualist," aren't quite as strong as the average man's, and who, in addition, is excited by the thought having lots of women accessible to him, rebels against the harshness of a Breadwinner's life and the monotony of one woman and, in the name of sharing and cooperation, forms the commune or tribe, which, for all its togetherness and partially because of it (the commune, being an extended family, is an extended violation of the females' rights, privacy and sanity) is no more a community than normal society.

A true community consists of individuals—not mere species members, not couples—respecting each others individuality and privacy, while at the same time interacting with each other mentally and emotionally (free spirits in free relation to each other) and co-operating with each other to achieve common ends. Traditionalists say the basic unit of society is the family; "hippies" say the tribe; no one says the individual.

The "hippy" babbles on about individuality, but has no more conception of it than any other man. He desires to get back to Nature, back to the wilderness, back to the home of furry animals he's one of, away from the city, where there's at least a trace, a bare beginning of civilization, to live at the species level, his time taken up with simple, non-intellectual activities—farming, fucking, bead stringing.

The most important activity of the commune, the one on which it's based, is gangbanging. The "hippy" is enticed to the commune mainly by the prospect of all the free pussy—the main commodity to be shared—to be had just for the asking, but, blinded by greed, he fails to anticipate all the other men he has to share it with or the jealousies and possessiveness of the pussies, themselves.

Men necessarily can't co-operate to achieve a common end, because each man's end is all the pussy for himself. The commune, therefore, is doomed to failure; each "hippy" will, in panic, grab the first simpleton who digs him and whisk her off to the suburbs as fast as he can. The male can't progress socially, but merely swings back and forth from isolation to gangbanging.

CONFORMITY

Although wanting to be an individual, the male's scared of anything about him that's the slightest bit different from other men; it causes him to suspect he's not really a "Man," that he's passive and totally sexual, a highly upsetting suspicion. If other men are "A" and he's not, he must not be a man; he must be a fag. So he tries to affirm his "Manhood" by being like all the other men. Differentness in other men, as well as in himself, threatens him; it means *they're* fags, who he must, at all costs, avoid, so he tries to ensure that all other men conform.

The male dares to be different to the degree he accepts his passivity and his desire to be female, his fagginess. The farthest out male's the dragqueen, but he, although different from most men, is exactly like all other dragqueens; like the functionalist, he has an identity—a female (He tries to define all his troubles away)—but still no individuality. Not convinced he's a woman, highly insecure about being sufficiently female, he conforms compulsively to the man-made feminine stereotype, ending up as nothing but a bundle of stilted mannerisms.

To be sure he's a "Man," the male must see to it the female be clearly a "Woman," the opposite of a "Man," that is, the female must act like a faggot. And Daddy's Girl, all of whose female instincts were tromped out of her when little, easily and obligingly adapts herself to the role.

AUTHORITY AND GOVERNMENT

Having no sense of right and wrong, no conscience, which can only stem from an ability to empathize with others having no faith in his non-existent self, being unnecessarily competitive and, by nature, unable to co-operate, the male feels a need for external guidance and control, so he created authorities—priests, experts, bosses, leaders, etc.—and government. Although he wants the female (Mama) to guide him, he's unable to face this fact (He is, after all, a *MAN*), so, wanting to play Woman, be a "Man," he claims her aptitude for Guiding and Protecting and sees to it all authorities are male.

There's no reason why a society consisting of rational beings capable of empathizing with each other, complete and having no natural reason to compete should have a government, laws or leaders.

PHILOSOPHY, RELIGION AND MORALITY BASED ON SEX

The male's inability to relate to anybody or anything outside himself makes his life pointless and meaningless (The ultimate male insight is that life's absurd), so he invented philosophy and religion. Being empty, he looks outward, not only for guidance and control, but for salvation and for the meaning of life. Happiness impossible on this earth, he invented Heaven.

For a man, having no ability to empathize with others and being totally sexual, "wrong" is sexual "license" and engaging in "deviant" ("unmanly") sexual practices, that is, not defending against his passivity and total sexuality, which, if indulged, would destroy "civilization," as "civilization" is based entirely on the male need to defend against these characteristics. For a woman (according to men), "wrong" is any behavior that would entice men into sexual "license," not placing male needs above her own and not being a faggot.

Religion not only provides the male with a goal (Heaven) and by its "moral" code helps keep women tied to men, but provides the male with rituals through which he can try to expiate the guilt and shame he feels over not defending enough against his sexual impulses, at bottom, over being male.

Some men, utterly cowardly, project their inherent weaknesses onto women, label them female weaknesses and believe themselves to have female strengths; most philosophers, slightly less cowardly, face the fact male lacks exist in men, but still can't face the fact they exist in men only, so they label the male condition the Human Condition pose their nothingness problem, which horrifies them, as a philosophical dilemma, thereby giving stature to their animalism, grandiloquently label their nothingness their "Identity Problem," and proceed to prattle pompously on about the "Crisis of the Individual," the "Essence of Being," "Existence preceding Essence," "Existential Modes of Being," etc., etc.

A woman not only takes her identity and individuality for granted, but knows instinctively the only wrong's to hurt others and the meaning of life is love.

PREJUDICE
(racial, ethnic, religious, etc)

The male needs scapegoats he can project his failings and inadequacies and onto whom he can vent his frustrations at not being female. And the various discriminations have the practical advantage of substantially increasing the pussy pool available to the men on top.

COMPETITION, PRESTIGE, STATUS, FORMAL EDUCATION, IGNORANCE AND SOCIAL AND ECONOMIC CLASSES

Having an obsessive desire to be admired by women, but no intrinsic worth, the male constructs a highly artificial society enabling him to appropriate the appearance of worth through money, prestige, "high" social class, degrees, professional position and knowledge and by pushing as many other men as possible down professionally, socially, economically, and educationally.

The purpose of "higher" education isn't to educate, but to exclude as many as possible from the various professions.

The male, totally physical, incapable of mental rapport, although able to use knowledge and ideas, is unable to relate to them, to grasp them emotionally; he doesn't value knowledge and ideas for their own sake—they're just means to ends—and, consequently, feels no need for mental companions, no need to cultivate the intellectual potential of others. To the contrary, the male has a vested interest in ignorance; it gives the few knowledgeable men a decided edge on the unknowledgeable ones, and, besides, the male knows an enlightened aware female population'll mean the end of him.

The healthy, conceited female wants the company of equals, whom she can respect and groove on; the male and the insecure, unselfconfident male female crave a society of fleas, whom they can be head and shoulders above.

No genuine social revolution can be accomplished by the male, as the male on top wants the status quo, and all the male on the bottom wants is to be the male on top. The male "rebel" is a farce; this is the male's society, made by *him* to satisfy *his* needs. He's never satisfied, because he's not capable of being satisfied. Ultimately, what the male "rebel" is rebelling against is being male. The male changes only when forced to do so by technology, when he has no choice, when society reaches the stage where he must change or die. We're at that stage now; if women don't fast get their asses in gear, we may very well all die.

PREVENTION OF CONVERSATION

Because the male's completely self-centered and unable to relate to anything outside himself, his "conversation," when not about himself, is an impersonal droning on, removed from anything of any human value. Male "intellectual conversation," when not an evasion of himself, is a strained, compulsive attempt to impress the female.

Daddy's Girl, passive, adaptable, respectful of and in awe of the male, allows him to impose his hideously dull chatter on her. This isn't too difficult for her to do, as her tension and anxiety (her lack of cool) and her insecurity and self-doubt, her unsureness of her own feelings and sensations, all make her perceptions superficial and render her unable to see the male's babble's a babble; like the aesthete "appreciating" the blob labeled "Great Art," she believes she's grooving on what bores the shit out of her. Not only does she permit his babble to dominate, she adapts her own "conversation" accordingly. Trained from early childhood in "niceness," politeness and "dignity," in pandering to the male need to disguise his animalism, she obligingly reduces her "conversation" to small talk, a bland, insipid avoidance of any topic beyond the utterly trivial or, if "educated," to "intellectual" discussion, that is, impersonal discoursing on irrelevant abstractions—Zionism, the Gross National Product, the influence of Rimbaud on symbolist painting. So adept is she at pandering it eventually becomes second nature and she continues to pander to men even when in the company only of other females.

Apart from pandering, her "conversation" is further limited by her insecurity about expressing deviant, original opinions and her self-absorption that insecurity leads to and that prevents her conversation from being charming. "Niceness," politeness, "dignity," insecurity and self-absorption are hardly conducive to intensity and wit, qualities a conversation must have to be worthy of the name, such conversation isn't rampant, as only completely self-confident, conceited, outgoing, proud, tough-minded females are capable of intense, bitchy, witty conversation.

PREVENTION OF FRIENDSHIP (LOVE)

Men have contempt for themselves, for all other men whom they contemplate more than casually and who they don't think are females, (for example "sympathetic" analysts and "Great Artists") or agents of God and for all women who respect and pander to them; the insecure, approval-seeking, pandering male females have contempt for themselves and for all women like them; the self-confident, conceited thrill-seeking female females have contempt for men and for the pandering male females. In short, contempt is the order of the day.

Love isn't dependency or sex, but is friendship, and, therefore, love can't exist between two males, between a male and a female or between two females, one or both of whom's a mindless, insecure, pandering male; like conversation it can exist only between two secure, free-wheeling, independent, groovy female females, as friendship's based on respect, not contempt.

Even among groovy females deep friendships seldom occur in adulthood, as almost all of them are either tied up with men in order to survive economically or are bogged down in hacking their way through the jungle and in trying to keep their heads above the amorphous mass. Love can't flourish in a society based on money and meaningless work, but rather requires complete economic, as well as personal, freedom, leisure time and the opportunity to engage in intensely absorbing, emotionally satisfying activities which, when shared with those you respect, lead to deep friendship, but which our society provides practically no opportunity to engage in.

Having stripped the world of conversation, friendship and love, the male offers us as paltry substitutes—

"GREAT ART" AND "CULTURE"

The male "artist" attempts to solve his dilemma of not being able to live, of not being female, by constructing a highly unrealistic fictional world in which the male's heroized, that is, displays female traits, and the female's reduced to highly limited, insipid subordinate roles, that is, reduced to males.

The male "artistic" aim being, not to communicate (Having nothing inside him, he has nothing to say), but to disguise his animalism, he resorts to symbolism and obscurity ("deep" stuff). The vast majority of people, particularly the "educated" ones, lacking faith in their own judgment, humble, respectful of authority ("Daddy knows best" is translated into adult language as "Critic knows best," "Writer knows best," "Ph.D. knows best"), are easily sucked into believing obscurity, evasiveness, indirectness, ambiguity, incomprehensibility and boringness are marks of depth and brilliance.

"Great Art" "proves," not merely by its content, that men are superior to women, that men are women, but also by its being labeled "Great Art," almost all of which, as the anti-feminists are fond of reminding us, was created by men. They know "Great Art" is great, because male authorities have told us so, and we can't claim otherwise, as only those with exquisite sensitivities far superior to ours can perceive and appreciated the greatness, the proof of their superior sensitivity being they appreciate the slop they appreciate.

Appreciating's the sole diversion of the "cultivated"; passive and incompetent, lacking imagination and wit, they must try to make do with that; unable to create their own diversions, to create a little world of their own, to affect in the smallest way their environments, they must accept what's given; unable to create or relate, they spectate. Absorbing "culture" is a desperate, frantic attempt to groove in an ungroovy world, to escape the horror of a sterile, mindless, existence. "Culture," further, provides a sop to the egos of the incompetent, a means of rationalizing passive spectating; they can pride themselves on their ability to appreciate the "finer" things, to see a jewel where exists only a turd (They want to be admired for admiring). Lacking faith in their ability to change anything, resigned to the status quo, they *have* to see beauty in turds because, so far as they can see, turds are all they'll ever have.

The veneration of "Art" and "Culture" leads many women into boring, passive activity that distracts from more important or rewarding activities and from cultivating active abilities and leads to the constant intrusion on our sensibilities of pompous dissertations on the deep beauty of this and that turd. Allowing the "Artist" to be held up as one of superior feelings, perceptions, insights and judgments, undermines the faith of insecure women in the value and validity of their own feelings, perceptions, insights and judgments.

The very concept of the "Artist," defined in terms of female traits, the male invented to "prove" he's a female ("All the Great Artists are men."), and he holds up the "Artist" as one fit to guide us, to tell us what life's all about, but the male "artist," not being out of the male mold, having a very limited range of feelings and, consequently, very limited perceptions, insights and judgments, as these are based on feelings, being unable to relate to anything beyond the insight that for the male life's meaningless and absurd, can't be an artist. How can he who isn't capable of life tell us what life's all about? A "male artist" is a contradiction in terms. A degenerate can only produce degenerate "art." The true artist is every self-confident, healthy female, and in a female society, the only Art, the only Culture, will be conceited, kookie, funkie, females grooving on each other, cracking each other up, while cracking open the universe.

SEXUALITY

Sex isn't part of a relationship, but is, to the contrary, a solitary experience as well as being non-creative and a gross waste of time. The female can easily—far more easily than she may think—condition her sex drive away, leaving her completely cool and cerebral and free to pursue truly worthy relationships and activities, but the lecherous male excites the lustful female. The male, who seems to dig the female sexually and who seeks out constantly to arouse her, stimulates the highly-sexed female to frenzies of lust, throwing her into a sex bag from which few women ever escape.

Sex is the refuge of the mindless. And the more mindless the woman, the more deeply embedded in the male "culture," in short, the "nicer" she is, the more sexual she is. The "nicest" women in our society are raving sex maniacs. But, being just awfully, awfully nice, they don't, of course descend to fucking—that's uncouth—but rather they make love, commune by means of their bodies and establish sensual rapport; the literary ones are attuned to the throb of Eros and attain a clutch of the Universe; the religious merge with the Erotic Principle and blend with the cosmos, and the acid heads contact their erotic cells. On the other hand, those females least embedded in the male "culture," the least "nice," those crass and simple souls who reduce fucking to fucking, who are too childish for the grown-up world of suburbs, mortgages, mops and baby shit, too arrogant to respect Daddy, the "Greats" or the "deep wisdom" of the Ancients, who trust only their own animal, gutter instincts, who equate Culture with kooky women, whose sole diversion is prowling for mental thrills and excitement, who are given to disgusting, nasty upsetting "scenes," hateful, violent bitches who'd sink a shiv into a man's chest or ram an icepick up his asshole as soon as look at him, if they know they could get away with it, in short, those who, by the standards of our "culture" are SCUM ... these females are cool and cerebral and, at least, skirting asexuality. Unhampered by propriety, "niceness," discretion, public opinion, "morals," the "respect" of assholes, always funky, dirty, low-down, SCUM gets around ... and around and around ... they've seen the whole show—every bit of it—the fucking scene, the sucking scene, the dick scene, the dyke scene—they've covered the whole waterfront, been under every dock and pier—the peter pier, the pussy pier ... You've got to go through a lot of sex to get to anti-sex, and SCUM's been through it all, and they're now ready for a new show; they want to crawl out from under the dock, move, take off, sink out. But SCUM doesn't yet prevail; SCUM's still in the gutter of our "society," which, if it's not deflected from its present course and if the Bomb doesn't drop on it, will hump itself to death.

BORINGNESS

A society made by and for creatures who—because of an extremely limited range of feeling—when they aren't grim and depressing, are utter bores can only be, when not grim and depressing, an utter bore.

SECRECY, CENSORSHIP, SUPPRESSION OF KNOWLEDGE AND IDEAS AND EXPOSES

Every male's deep-seated, secret, most hideous fear is the fear of being discovered to be not a female, to be a male, a subhuman animal. Although "niceness," politeness and "dignity" suffice to prevent his exposure on a personal level, in order to prevent the general exposure of the male sex as a whole and to maintain his unnatural dominant position in society the male must resort to:

1. Censorship. Responding reflexly to isolated works and phrases rather than cerebrally to overall meanings, the male attempts to prevent the arousal and discovery of his animalism by censoring not only "pornography," but any work containing "dirty" words, no matter in what context they're used.
2. Suppression of all ideas and knowledge that might expose him or threaten his dominant position in society. Much biological and psychological data's suppressed, because it's proof of the male's gross inferiority to the female. Also, the problem of mental illness will

never be solved while the male maintains control, because, first of all, men have a vested interest in it, as only females who have very few of their marbles'll allow males the slightest bit of control over anything, and, secondly, the male can't admit to the role Fatherhood plays in causing mental illness.

3. Exposes. The male's chief delight in life—in so far as the tense, grim male can ever be said to delight in anything—is exposing others. It doesn't much matter what they're exposed as, so long as they're exposed; it distracts attention from himself. Exposing others as enemy agents (Communists and Socialists) is one of his favorite exposes, as it removes the source of the threat to him, not only from himself, but from the country and, even further yet, from the Western world. The bugs up his ass aren't in him, they're in Russia.

DISTRUST

Unable to empathize or feel affection or loyalty, being exclusively out for himself, the male has no sense of fair play. Cowardly, needing constantly to pander to the female to win her approval he's helpless without, always on edge lest his animalism, his maleness be discovered, always needing to cover up, he must lie constantly. Being empty he has no honor or integrity; he doesn't know what those words mean. The male, in short, is treacherous, and the only appropriate attitude in a male society's cynicism and distrust.

UGLINESS

Being totally sexual, incapable of cerebral or aesthetic responses, totally materialistic and greedy, the male, besides inflicting on the world "Great Art," has decorated his unlandscaped cities with ugly buildings (both inside and out), ugly decors, billboards, highways, cars, garbage trucks and, most notably, his own putrid self.

HATE AND VIOLENCE

The male's eaten up with tension, with frustration at not being female and at not being capable of ever achieving satisfaction or pleasure of any kind and—when he's not depressed, anxious or bored—with hate, not rational hate that's directed at those who abuse or insult you, but irrational, indiscriminate hate, hatred, at bottom, of his own worthless self.

Gratuitous violence, besides "proving" he's a "Man," serves as an outlet for his hate and, in addition, the male, being capable only of sexual responses and needing very strong stimuli to stimulate his half-dead self, provides him with a little sexual thrill.

DISEASE AND DEATH

All diseases are curable, and the aging process and death are due to disease; it's, therefore, possible to never age and to live forever. In fact, the problems of aging and death could be solved within a few years, if an all-out, massive scientific assault were made on the problem. This, however, won't occur with the male society because of:

1. The discouragement of many potential scientists from scientific careers by the rigidity, boringness, expensiveness, time-consumingness, and unfair exclusivity of our "higher" educational system.
2. Propaganda disseminated by insecure male professionals, who jealously guard their positions, that only a highly select few can comprehend abstract scientific concepts.
3. Widespread lack of self-confidence brought about by the Father system that discourages many who are capable from becoming scientists.
4. The bias of the money system for the least creative becoming scientists. Most scientists come from at least relatively affluent families where Daddy reigns supreme.
5. Lack of automation. There now exists a wealth of data that, if sorted out and correlated, would reveal the cure for cancer and several other diseases and possibly the key to life itself, but the data's so massive it requires high speed computers to correlate it all. The institution of computers'll be delayed interminably in the male society, as the male has a horror of being replaced by machines.
6. The male's marked preference for "manly" war and death programs.
7. The money system's insatiable need for new products. Most of the scientists around who aren't working on death programs are tied up by corporations developing and testing just things.

8. The many male scientists who shy away from biological research because of a horror of the male being discovered to be a highly incomplete female.

* * * * * * * * * * * *

Incapable of a positive state, of happiness, the only thing that can justify one's existence, the male's, at best, relaxed, comfortable, neutral, and this condition's extremely short-lived, as boredom, a negative state, soon sets in; he's, therefore, doomed to an existence of suffering relieved only by occasional, fleeting splatches of restfulness, and he can achieve that state only at the expense of some female; the male's by his very nature a leech, an emotional parasite and, therefore, isn't ethically entitled to both live and prosper, as no one has the right to live at someone else's expense. Just as humans have a prior right to existence over dogs by virtue of being more highly evolved, more aware, having a superior consciousness, so women have a prior right to existence over men.

However, this moral issue will eventually be rendered academic by the fact that the male's gradually eliminating himself. In addition to engaging in the time-honored and classical wars and race riots, men are more and more either becoming dragqueens or obliterating themselves through drugs. The female, whether she likes it or not, will eventually take complete charge, if for no other reason but because she'll have to—the male, for practical purposes, won't exist. Accelerating this trend is the fact that more and more males are acquiring enlightened self-interest; they're coming more and more to see that the female interest is their interest, that they can most nearly live only through the female and that the more the female's encouraged to live, to fulfill herself, to be a female and not a male, the more nearly *he* lives; he's coming to see it's easier and more satisfactory to live *through* her than to try to *become* her, than to try to usurp her qualities, claim them as his own, push the female down and claim she's a male. The fag, who accepts his maleness, that is, his passivity and total sexuality, his femininity, is also best served by women being truly female, as it would then be easier for him to be male, feminine. If men were wise, they'd seek to really become female, would do intensive biological research that'd lead to men, by means of operations on the brain and nervous system, being able to be transformed psychically into women.

Whether to continue to use females for reproduction or to

reproduce in the lab'll also become academic: what'll happen when every female of child-bearing age is routinely using contraceptives and aborting any accidents? How many women'll deliberately get or (if an accident) remain pregnant? No, Virginia, women don't just adore being broodmares, despite what the mass of semi-conscious women'll say. When society consists only of the fully conscious the answer'll be none. Should then, a certain percentage of women be set aside by force to serve as brood-mares for the species? This, obviously, won't do. The answer is lab reproduction of babies.

As for the issue of whether or not to continue to reproduce males, it doesn't follow from the male's, like disease, having always existed among us he should continue to exist. When genetic control's possible —and soon it will be—it goes without saying that we should produce only whole, complete beings, not produce any physical defects or deficiencies, including emotional deficiencies, maleness. Just as the deliberate production of blind people would be highly immoral, so would be the deliberate production of emotional cripples.

Why produce even females? Why should there be future genera-tions? What's their purpose to us? Even without their being eliminated, why reproduce? Why should we care what happens when we're dead? Why should we care that there's no younger generation to succeed us?

So eventually the natural course of events, of social evolution, will lead to total female control of the world and, subsequently, to the ces-sation of the production of males and, ultimately, to the cessation of the production of females.

But SCUM's impatient; SCUM isn't consoled by the thought that future generations'll thrive; SCUM wants to grab some thrilling living for itself. And, if a large majority of women were SCUM, they could acquire complete control of this country within a few weeks simply by withdrawing from the labor force, thereby paralyzing the entire nation. As additional steps, any one by itself sufficient to completely disrupt the economy and everything else, they would declare them-selves off the money system, stop buying, just loot and simply refuse to obey all laws they don't care to obey. The police force, National Guard, Army, Navy and Marines combined couldn't squelch a rebellion of over half the population, particularly when it's made up of people they're utterly helpless without. If all women simply left men, the gov-ernment and the national economy would completely collapse. Even without leaving men, women, if they were aware of the extent of their superiority to and power over men, could effect a total submission of the males to the females. In a sane society the male would trot obediently along after the female. The male's docile and easily led, easily subjected to the domination of any female who cares to dominate him. The male, in fact, wants desperately to be led by females, wants Mama in charge, wants to abandon himself to her care. But this isn't a sane society, and most women aren't even dimly aware of where they're at in relation to men.

The conflict, therefore, isn't between females and males, but between SCUM—dominant, secure, self-confident, nasty, violent, selfish, independent, proud, thrill-seeking, free-wheeling, arrogant females, who consider themselves fit to rule the universe, who have free-wheeled to the limits of this society and are ready to wheel on to something far beyond what it has to offer—and "nice," passive, accepting "cultivated," subdued, dependent, scared, mindless, insecure, approval-seeking Daddy's Girls, who can't cope with the unknown; who want to contribute to wallow in the sewer that's, at least, familiar; who want to hang back with the apes; who feel secure only with Big Daddy standing by, with a big, strong man to lean on and with a fat, hairy face in the White House; who are too cowardly to face up to the hideous reality of what a man, what Daddy, is; who have cast their lot with the swine; who have adapted themselves to animalism, feel superficially comfortable with it and know no other way of life; who have reduced their thoughts and sights to the male level; who, lacking sense, imagination and wit can have value only in a male society, who can have a place in the sun, or, rather, in the slime, only as soothers, ego boosters, relaxers and breeders; who are dismissed as inconsequents by other females; who project their deficiencies, their maleness, onto all females and see the female as a worm.

But SCUM's too impatient to hope and wait for the enlightenment of millions of assholes. Why should the funky females continue to plod dismally along with the dull male ones? Why should the fates of the groovy and the creepy be intertwined? Why should the active and imaginative consult the passive and dull on social policy? Why should the independent be confined to the sewer along with the dependent who need Daddy to cling to? There's no reason.

A small handful of SCUM can take over the country within a year by systematically fucking up the system, selectively destroying property and murder:

SCUM'll become members of the unwork force, the fuck up force; they'll get jobs of various kinds and unwork. For example, SCUM salesgirls won't charge for merchandise; SCUM telephone operators won't charge for calls; SCUM office and factory workers, in addition to fucking up their work, will secretly destroy equipment. SCUM'll unwork at a job until fired, then get a new job to unwork at.

SCUM'll forcibly relieve busdrivers, cabdrivers and subway token sellers of their jobs and run buses and cabs and dispense tokens to the public for free.

SCUM'll destroy all useless and harmful objects—cars, store windows, "Great Art," etc. Eventually SCUM'll take over the air-waves—radio and T.V. networks—by forcibly relieving of their jobs all radio and T.V. employees who would impede SCUM's entry into the broadcasting studios.

SCUM'll kill all men who not in the Men's Auxiliary of SCUM. Men in the Men's Auxiliary are those men who're working diligently to eliminate themselves, men who, regardless of their motives, do good, men who're playing ball with SCUM. A few examples of the men in the Men's Auxiliary are:

Men who kill men.

Biological scientists working on constructive programs, as opposed to biological warfare.

Writers, editors, publishers and producers who disseminate and promote ideas that'll lead to the achievement of SCUM's goals.

Faggots, who by their shimmering, flaming example encourage other men to de"Man" themselves and, thereby, make them-selves relatively inoffensive.

Men who consistently give money and things away and provide free services.

Men who tell it like it is—so far not one ever has—who put women straight, who reveal the truth about themselves, who give the mindless male females correct statements to parrot, who tell them a woman's primary goal in life should be to squash the male sex (To aid men in this endeavor SCUM'll conduct Turd Sessions, at which every male present'll give a speech beginning with the sentence: I'm a turd, a lowly, abject turd," then proceed to list all the ways in which he's so. His reward for so doing'll be the opportunity to fraternize after the session for a whole solid hour with the SCUM who'll be present. "Nice," clean-living male women'll be invited to the sessions to help clarify any doubts and misunderstandings they may have about the male sex).

Makers and promoters of sex books and movies, etc., who are hastening the day when all that'll be shown on the screen'll be Suck and Fuck (Males, like the rats following the Pied Piper, will be lured by Pussy to their doom, will be overcome and submerged by and will eventually drown in the passive flesh they are).

Drug pushers and advocates, who are hastening the dropping out of men.

Doing good's a necessary but not a sufficient condition for membership in the Men's Auxiliary. Besides doing good, to save their worthless asses men must avoid evil. A few examples of the most obnoxious or harmful types are:

Rapists.

Politicians and all who are in their service.

Lousy singers, composers and musicians.

Chairmen of Boards.

Breadwinners.

Landlords.

Owners of greasy spoons and restaurants and stores that play Muzak.

"Great Artists."

Cheap pikers and welchers.

Cops who bust and prosecuters who prosecute and judges who sock time to drug and gambling law violators, prostitutes, porno people and committers of crimes against corporations.

Tycoons.

Scientists working on death and destruction programs or for private industry.

Liars and phonies.

Real Estate men.

Stock brokers.

Men who speak when they have nothing to say.

Litter bugs.

Plagiarizers.

Men who in the slightest way harm any female.

All men in the advertising industry.

Psychiatrists and clinical psychologists.

Men who act on the belief they're entitled to the company of strange females they happen to encounter.

Censors on both the public and private level.

All members of the armed forces, including draftees.

In the case of a man whose behavior falls into both the good and bad categories, an overall subjective evaluation of him'll be made to determine if his behavior's, on balance, good or bad.

It's most tempting to pick off the female "Great Artists," liars and phonies etc. along with the men, but that'd be inexpedient, as it wouldn't be clear to most of the public the female killed was a male.

Dropping out isn't the answer; fucking up is. Most women are already dropped out; they were never in. Dropping out gives control to those few who don't drop out; dropping out's exactly what the rulers want; it's to play into the hands of the enemy; it's to strengthen the system, not undermine it, as the system's based entirely on the non-participation, passivity, apathy and non-involvement of the mass of women. Dropping out, however, is an excellent policy for men, and SCUM'll enthusiastically encourage it.

Looking inside yourself for salvation, contemplating your navel, isn't, as the Drop Out people would have you believe, the answer. Happiness lies outside yourself, is achieved through interacting with others. Self-forgetfulness should be one's goal, not self-absorption. The male, capable of only the latter, makes a virtue of an irremediable fault and sets up self absorption, not only as a good, but as a Philosophical Good, and thereby, gets credit for being deep.

SCUM won't picket, demonstrate, march or strike to attempt to achieve its ends. Such tactics are for "nice," genteel ladies who scrupulously take only such action as is guaranteed to be ineffective. In addition, only decent, clean-living male women, highly trained in submerging themselves in the species, act on a mob basis. SCUM consists of individuals; SCUM isn't a mob, a blob. Only as many SCUM'll do a job as are needed for the job. Also, SCUM, being cool and selfish, won't subject to getting itself to getting rapped on the head with billy clubs; that's for the "nice," "privileged," "educated," ladies with a high regard for and touching faith in the essential goodness of Daddy and policemen. If SCUM ever marches, it'll be over the President's face; if SCUM ever strikes, it'll be in the dark with a six inch blade.

SCUM'll always operate on a criminal as opposed to a civil disobedience basis, that is, as opposed to openly violating the law and going to jail in order to draw attention to an injustice. Such tactics acknowledge the rightness of the overall system and are used only to modify it slightly, change specific laws. SCUM's against the entire system, the very idea of law and government. SCUM's out to destroy the system, not attain certain rights within it. Also, SCUM—always selfish, always cool—will always aim to avoid detection and punishment. SCUM'll always be furtive, sneaky, underhanded (although SCUM murders'll always be known to be such).

Both destruction and killing'll be selective and discriminate. SCUM's against half-crazed, indiscriminate riots, with no clear objective in mind, and in which many of your own kind are picked off. SCUM'll never instigate, encourage or participate in riots of any kind or other form of indiscriminate destruction. SCUM'll coolly, furtively, stalk its prey and quietly move in for the kill. Destruction, further, will never be such as to block off routes needed for the transportation of food or other essential supplies, contaminate or cut off the water supply, block streets and traffic to the extent that ambulances can't get through or impede the functioning of hospitals.

SCUM'll keep on destroying, looting, fucking-up and killing until the money-work system no longer exists and automation's completely instituted or until enough women co-operate with SCUM to make violence unnecessary to achieve these goals, that is, until enough women either unwork or quit work, start looting, leave men and refuse to obey all laws inappropriate to a truly civilized society. Many women'll fall into line, but many others, who surrendered long ago to the enemy, who are so adapted to animalism, to maleness, that they like restrictions and restraints, don't know what to do with freedom, will continue to be toadies and doormats, just as peasants in rice paddies remain peasants in rice paddies as one regime topples another. A few of the more volatile will whimper and sulk and throw their toys and dishrags on the floor, but SCUM'll continue to steamroller over them.

A completely automated society can be accomplished very simply and quickly once there's a public demand for it. The blueprints for it are already in existence, and its construction'll only take a few weeks with millions of people working on it. Even though off the money system, everyone'll be most happy to pitch in and get the automated society built; it'll mark the beginning of a fantastic new era, and there'll be a celebration atmosphere accompanying the construction.

The elimination of money and the complete institution of automation are basic to all other SCUM reforms; without these two the others can't take place; with them the others'll take place very rapidly. The government'll automatically collapse. With complete automation it'll be possible for everyone to vote directly on every issue by means of an electronic voting machine in the house. Since the government's occupied almost entirely with regulating economic affairs and legislating against purely private matters, the elimination of money and with it the elimination of the domination of males, who wish to legislate "morality," will mean there'll be practically no issues to vote on.

After the elimination of money there'll be no further need to kill men; they'll be stripped of the only power they have over psychologically independent females. They'll be able to impose themselves only on the doormats, who like to be imposed upon. The rest of the women'll be busy solving the few remaining unsolved problems before planning their agenda for eternity and Utopia—completely revamping educational programs so that millions can be trained within a few months for high level intellectual work that now requires years of training (This can be done very easily once our educational goal's to educate and not to perpetuate an academic and intellectual elite); solving the problems of disease and old age and death and completely redesigning our cities and living quarters. Many women'll for awhile continue to think they dig men, but as they become accustomed to female society and as they become absorbed in their projects, they'll eventually come to see the utter uselessness and banality of the male.

The few remaining men can exist out their puny days dropped out on drugs or strutting around in drag or passively watching the high-powered female in action, fulfilling themselves as spectators, vicarious livers[1] or breeding in the cow pasture with the toadies or they can go

---

1 It'll be electronically possible for him to tune in to any specific female he wants to and follow in detail her every thought and feeling. The females'll kindly, obligingly consent to this, as it won't hurt them in the slightest and it's a marvelously kind and humane way to treat their unfortunate, handicapped fellow beings.

lesbian avengers **DYKE MANIFESTO** lesbian avengers
CALLING ALL LESBIANS
WAKE UP!WAKE UP! WAKE UP!

IT'S TIME TO GET OUT OF THE BEDS, OUT OF THE BARS AND INTO THE STREETS
TIME TO SEIZE THE POWER OF DYKE LOVE, DYKE VISION, DYKE ANGER
DYKE INTELLIGENCE, DYKE STRATEGY.
TIME TO ORGANIZE AND IGNITE. TIME TO GET TOGETHER AND FIGHT!
WE'RE INVISIBLE AND IT'S NOT SAFE--NOT AT HOME, ON THE JOB, IN THE
STREETS OR IN THE COURTS
WHERE ARE OUR LESBIAN LEADERS?
WE NEED YOU
WE'RE NOT WAITING FOR THE RAPTURE. WE ARE THE APOCALYPSE.
WE'LL BE YOUR DREAM AND THEIR NIGHTMARE.
LESBIAN POWER
BELIEVE IN CREATIVE ACTIVISM:LOUD, BOLD, SEXY, SILLY, FIERCE,TASTY
AND DRAMATIC. ARREST OPTIONAL.
THINK DEMONSTRATIONS ARE A GOOD TIME AND A GREAT PLACE TO CRUISE
WOMEN. DON'T HAVE PATIENCE FORPOLITE POLITICS. ARE BORED WITH THE
BOYS. BELIEVE CONFRONTATION FOSTERS GROWTH AND STRONG BONES.
BELIEVE IN RECRUITMENT. NOT BY THE ARMY; NOT OF STRAIGHT WOMEN.
ARE NOT CONTENT WITH GHETTOS: WE WANT YOUR HOUSE, YOUR JOB, YOUR
FREQUENT FLYER MILES. WE'LL SELL YOUR JEWELRY TO SUBSIDIZE OUR
MOVEMENT. WE DEMAND UNIVERSAL HEALTH INSURANCE AND HOUSING. WE
DEMAND FOOD AND SHELTER FOR ALL HOMELESS LESBIANS. WE ARE THE
13TH STEP. THINK GIRL GANGS ARE THE WAVE OF THE FUTURE
LESBIAN SEX
THINK SEX IS A DAILY LIBATION. GOOD ENERGY FOR ACTIONS. CRAVE,
ENJOY, EXPLORE, SUFFER FROM NEW IDEAS ABOUT RELATIONSHIPS:
SLUMBER PARTIES, POLYGAMY, PERSONAL ADS, AFFINITY GROUPS.
USE LIVE ACTION WORDS: lick, waltz, eat, fuck, kiss, bite, give it up, hit the dirt
LESBIAN ACTIVISM
THINK ACTIONS MUST BE LOCAL, REGIONAL, NATIONAL, GLOBAL, COSMIC.
THINK CLOSETED LESBIANS, QUEER BOYS AND SYMPATHETIC STRAIGHTS
SHOULD SEND US MONEY.
PLAN TO TARGET HOMOPHOBES OF EVERY STRIPE AND INFILTRATE THE
CHRISTIAN RIGHT.
SCHEME AND SCREAM AND FIGHT REAL MEAN

the lesbian
AVENGERS

THE LESBIAN AVENGERS: WE RECRUIT

Dyke Manifesto (1992), by Lesbian Avengers

WELCOME AVENGER!

WHO ARE THE LESBIAN AVENGERS?
The Lesbian Avengers is a **direct action** group focused on issues vital to **lesbian survival and visibility.** There are many ideas in the lesbian community about what kind of strategies to employ-- electoral and legal reform, therapy groups, social services, theoretical development. These are all valid strategies, but they are not the strategies of the Avengers. Direct action is what the Lesbian Avengers do. It is the reason for our existence.

WHAT IS DIRECT ACTION?
The real question is "Do we have to spray paint billboards to be a Lesbian Avenger?" Direct Action is a **public intervention** ranging in creative form from marches to street theatre to speakouts to cathartic spray painting of anti-hate slogans. Direct action is about getting attention, and that means media coverage. The purpose of direct action is **visibility**, so we can't be shy. As a direct action group, the Lesbian Avengers is for women who want to be activists, want to take responsibility for making things happen, want to do the shit work, have their minds blown, change their opinions, share organizing skills, and work in community. You don't have to spray paint billboards (although it's really fun)! You have to be willing to act-out publicly. We want to **empower** lesbians as leaders!

WHY NO ABSTRACT THEORETICAL DISCUSSION?
How many of us have sat in meetings arguing political theory to the point of mental and physical exhaustion, to the point where we run screaming to the nearest dance floor for release from the frustration?! To keep our work pro-active and fulfilling and successful, we focus our political discussions on the creation and purpose of an **action.** We agree to disagree on political ideology-- it is too easy to create false polarities. We also encourage women to **take responsibility** for their own suggestions--be willing to make them happen. Instead of saying "Someone should..." try saying "I will..." or "Who will do this with me?" In our meetings, if you disagree with a proposal on the floor, instead of tearing it apart, propose another way of realizing the goal. The Avengers is a place where ideas are realized, where lesbians can have an impact. A crucial part of that is learning how to **propose alternatives** instead of just offering critiques. Be willing to put your body where your brain is--matter over mind!

A BRIEF HISTORY OF THE LESBIAN AVENGERS

The first Lesbian Avenger group was founded in New York City in June 1992 by a group of experienced activists who were frustrated with their participation in W.H.A.M. and ACT UP where they felt overshadowed and undervalued as lesbians. They called a first meeting by handing out fluorescent green club cards reading "Lesbians! Dykes! Gay Women! We want revenge and we want it now." The idea took off and the group has created many successful actions, including: arriving at public schools on the first day of school to give out balloons inscribe "Ask about Lesbian Lives"--this was surrounding the attempt to include teaching about gay and lesbian lives in the public school curriculum; an anti-violence march and fire eating ceremony in response to the murders of gays and lesbians in Oregon; following Mayor Webb of Colorado (on his visit to New York City to promote tourism) to make sure the media focus was on Amendment 2; a Valentine's Day celebration of romantic love, butch genius and forgotten femmes, featuring the erection of a statue of Alice B. Toklas next to the statue of Gertrude Stein in Bryant Park (poetry and waltzing galore!); and organizing the Dyke March preceding the March on Washington 1993.

The Minneapolis Chapter started on International Women's Day, 1993, when a bunch of dykes got together to potluck and discuss forming a direct action group. Lesbian direct action groups have existed in the Twin Cities before--Tornado Warning, Lesbians Against Imperialism, and other informal and individual efforts. From the first meeting, we discovered the common goals of: action not theory, proactive not reactive, and fun, fun, fun! Everything that we wanted to do as a group fit with what the Lesbian Avengers were doing. Thus the Minneapolis Chapter was born! To announce our birth, we went out that night and appropriated a Navy billboard:

ta dal

ACTIONS IN THE WORKS

Minneapolis Pride March; creating lesbian bar/dance space; radio and video projects; interfering with the Operation Rescue boot camp activities; continued watch-dogging of media to combat homophobic and sexist imagery; a summer celebration of dyke love; fundraising for hellraising! We welcome your ornery ideas for frisky antics and hotheaded capers!

TOP TEN AVENGER QUALITIES
10. COMPASSION
9. LEADERSHIP
8. NO BIG EGO
7. INFORMED
6. FEARLESSNESS
5. RIGHTEOUS ANGER
4. FIGHTING SPIRIT
3. PRO SEX
2. GOOD DANCER
1. ACCESS TO RESOURCES (XEROX MACHINES)

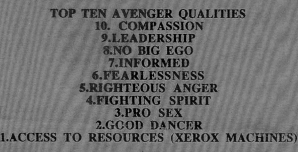

MEETINGS

The Lesbian Avengers currently meet on **Sundays at 7:30p.m.** at the **Sabathani Community Center**, 310 E. 38th Street, Rm C on the 3rd Floor (in GLCAC's space). Meetings are the time to report on past actions and upcoming actions and share news. A **facilitator** (anyone who volunteers to do it) armed with the meeting **agenda** (created at the start of each meeting) keeps things focused and moving along. Anyone can introduce agenda items. Being on time is important--people have limited time and everyone's presence is essential to the success of the meeting.

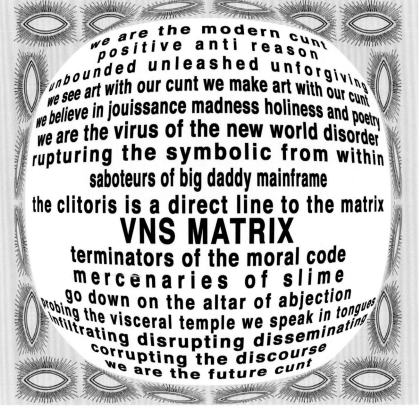

Cyberfeminist Manifesto for the Twenty-First Century (1991), by VNS Matrix

Xenofeminism: A Politics for Alienation (2015), by Laboria Cuboniks

Xenofeminism is gender-abolitionist. 'Gender abolitionism' is not code for the eradication of what are currently considered 'gendered' traits from the human population. Under patriarchy, such a project could only spell disaster — the notion of what is 'gendered' sticks disproportionately to the feminine. But even if this balance were redressed, we have no interest in seeing the sexuate diversity of the world reduced. Let a hundred sexes bloom! 'Gender abolitionism' is shorthand for the ambition to construct a society where traits currently assembled under the rubric of gender, no longer furnish a grid for the asymmetric operation of power. 'Race abolitionism' expands into a similar formula — that the struggle must continue until currently racialized characteristics are no more a basis of discrimination than the colour of one's eyes. Ultimately, every emancipatory abolitionism must incline towards the horizon of class abolitionism, since it is in capitalism where we encounter oppression in its transparent, denaturalized form: you're not exploited or oppressed because you are a wage labourer or poor; you are a labourer or poor because you are exploited.

Xenofeminism understands that the viability of emancipatory abolitionist projects — the abolition of class, gender, and race — hinges on a profound reworking of the universal. The universal must be grasped as generic, which is to say, intersectional. Intersectionality is not the morcellation of collectives into a static fuzz of cross-referenced identities, but a political orientation that slices through every particular, refusing the crass pigeonholing of bodies. This is not a universal that can be imposed from above, but built from the bottom up — or, better, laterally, opening new lines of transit across an uneven landscape. This non-absolute, generic universality must guard against the facile tendency of conflation with bloated, unmarked particulars — namely Eurocentric universalism — whereby the male is mistaken for the sexless, the white for raceless, the cis for the real, and so on. Absent such a universal, the abolition of class will remain a bourgeois fantasy, the abolition of race will remain a tacit white-supremacism, and the abolition of gender will remain a thinly veiled misogyny, even — especially — when prosecuted by avowed feminists themselves. (The absurd and reckless spectacle of so many self-proclaimed gender abolitionists' campaign against trans women is proof enough of this.)

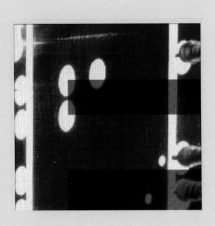

*We should not hesitate to learn
from our adversaries or the
successes and failures of history.*

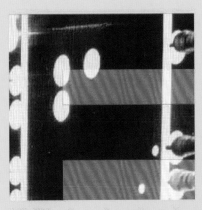

rom the postmoderns, we have learnt to burn the facades of the false universal and dispel such confusions; from the moderns, we have learnt to sift new universals from the ashes of the false. Xenofeminism seeks to construct a coalitional politics, a politics without the infection of purity. Wielding the universal requires thoughtful qualification and precise self-reflection so as to become a ready-to-hand tool for multiple political bodies and something that can be appropriated against the numerous oppressions that transect with gender and sexuality. The universal is no blueprint, and rather than dictate its uses in advance, we propose XF as a platform. The very process of construction is therefore understood to be a negentropic, iterative, and continual refashioning. Xenofeminism seeks to be a mutable architecture that, like open source software, remains available for perpetual modification and enhancement following the navigational impulse of militant ethical reasoning. Open, however, does not mean undirected. The most durable systems in the world owe their stability to the way they train order to emerge as an 'invisible hand' from apparent spontaneity; or exploit the inertia of investment and sedimentation. We should not hesitate to learn from our adversaries or the successes and failures of history. With this in mind, XF seeks ways to seed an order that is equitable and just, injecting it into the geometry of freedoms these platforms afford.

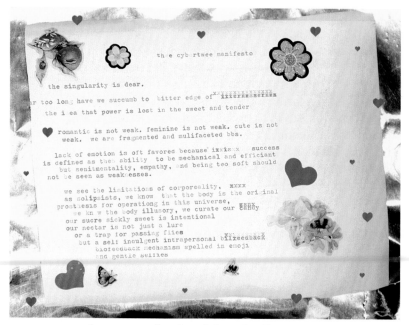

the cybertwee manifesto

the singularity is dear.

ar too long have we succumb to bitter edge of
the idea that power is lost in the sweet and tender

romantic is not weak. feminine is not weak. cute is not
weak. we are fragmented and mulifaceted bbs.

lack of emotion is oft favored because success
is defined as the ability to be mechanical and efficiant
but senitmentality, empathy, and being teo soft should
not be seen as weaknesses.

we see the limitations of corporeality,
as solipsists, we know that the body is the original
prosthesis for operationg in this universe,
we know the body illusory, we curate our candy
our sucre sickly sweet is intentional
our nectar is not just a lure
or a trap for passing flies
but a self indulgent intrapersonal biofeedback
biofeedback mechanism spelled in emoji
and gentle selfies

cybertwee manifesto (2014), by Gabriella Hileman,
Violet Forest, and May Waver

off to the nearest friendly neighborhood suicide center where they'll be quietly, quickly and painlessly gassed to death.

Prior to the institution of automation, to the replacement of males by machines, the male should be of use to the female, wait on her, cater to her slightest whim, obey her every command, be totally subservient to her, exist in perfect obedience to her will, as opposed to the completely warped, degenerate situation we have now of men, not only existing at all, cluttering up the world with their presence, but being pandered to and groveled before by the mass of females, millions of women piously worshiping the Golden Calf, the dog leading the master on a leash, when, in fact, the male, short of being a dragqueen, is least miserable when his dogginess is recognized—no unrealistic emotional demands are made of him and the completely together female's calling the shots.

The sick, irrational men, who try to deny their subhumanity, when they see SCUM barreling down on them, will cling in terror to Big Mama with her Big Bouncy Boobies, but Boobies won't protect him against SCUM; Big Mama'll be clinging to Big Daddy, who'll be in the corner forcefully, dynamically shitting his pants. Men who're rational, however, won't kick or struggle or raise a distressing fuss, but just sit back, relax, enjoy the show and ride the waves to their demise.

29 The Dialectic of Sex: The Case for Feminist Revolution (excerpt)

1970

Shulamith Firestone

Sex class is so deep as to be invisible. Or it may appear as a superficial inequality, one that can be solved by merely a few reforms, or perhaps by the full integration of women into the labor force. But the reaction of the common man, woman, and child—"*That?* Why you can't change *that!* You must be out of your mind!"—is the closest to the truth. We are talking about something every bit as deep as that. This gut reaction —the assumption that, even when they don't know it, feminists are talking about changing a fundamental biological condition—is an honest one. That so profound a change cannot be easily fitted into traditional categories of thought, e.g., "political," is not because these categories do not apply but because they are not big enough: radical feminism bursts through them. If there were another word more all-embracing than *revolution*—we would use it.

Until a certain level of evolution had been reached and technology had achieved its present sophistication, to question fundamental biological conditions was insanity. Why should a woman give up her precious seat in the cattle car for a bloody struggle she could not hope to win? But, for the first time in some countries, the preconditions for feminist revolution exist—indeed, the situation is beginning to *demand* such a revolution.

The first women are fleeing the massacre, and shaking and tottering, are beginning to find each other. Their first move is a careful joint observation, to resensitize a fractured consciousness. This is painful: No matter how many levels of consciousness one reaches, the problem always goes deeper. It is everywhere. The division Yin and

Yang pervades all culture, history, economics, nature itself; modern Western versions of sex discrimination are only the most recent layer. To so heighten one's sensitivity to sexism presents problems far worse than the black militant's new awareness of racism: Feminists have to question, not just all of *Western* culture, but the organization of culture itself, and further, even the very organization of nature. Many women give up in despair: if *that's* how deep it goes they don't want to know. Others continue strengthening and enlarging the movement, their painful sensitivity to female oppression existing for a purpose: eventually to eliminate it.

Before we can act to change a situation, however, we must know how it has arisen and evolved, and through what institutions it now operates. Engels's "[We must] examine the historic succession of events from which the antagonism has sprung in order to discover in the conditions thus created the means of ending the conflict." For feminist revolution we shall need an analysis of the dynamics of sex war as comprehensive as the Marx-Engels analysis of class antagonism was for the economic revolution. More comprehensive. For we are dealing with a larger problem, with an oppression that goes back beyond recorded history to the animal kingdom itself.

In creating such an analysis we can learn a lot from Marx and Engels: Not their literal opinions about women—about the condition of women as an oppressed class they know next to nothing, recognizing it only where it overlaps with economics—but rather their analytic *method*.

Marx and Engels outdid their socialist forerunners in that they developed a method of analysis which was both *dialectical* and *materialist*. The first in centuries to view history dialectically, they saw the world as process, a natural flux of action and reaction, of opposites yet inseparable and interpenetrating. Because they were able to perceive history as movie rather than as snapshot, they attempted to avoid falling into the stagnant "metaphysical" view that had trapped so many other great minds...They combined this view of the dynamic interplay of historical forces with a materialist one, that is, they attempted for the first time to put historical and cultural change on a real basis, to trace the development of economic classes to organic causes. By understanding thoroughly the mechanics of history, they hoped to show men how to master it.

Socialist thinkers prior to Marx and Engels, such as Fourier, Owen, and Bebel, had been able to do no more than moralize about existing social inequalities, positing an ideal world where class privilege and exploitation should not exist—in the same way that early feminist thinkers posited a world where male privilege and exploitation ought not exist—by mere virtue of good will. In both cases, because the early thinkers did not really understand how the social injustice had evolved, maintained itself, or could be eliminated, their ideas existed in a cultural vacuum, utopian. Marx and Engels, on the other hand, attempted a scientific approach to history. They traced the class conflict to its real economic origins, projecting an economic solution based on objective economic preconditions already present: the seizure by the proletariat of the means of production would lead to a communism in which government had withered away, no longer needed to repress the lower class for the sake of the higher. In the classless society the interests of every individual would be synonymous with those of the larger society.

But the doctrine of historical materialism, much as it was a brilliant advance over previous historical analysis, was not the complete answer, as later events bore out. For though Marx and Engels grounded their theory in reality, it was only a *partial* reality. Here is Engels's strictly economic definition of historical materialism from *Socialism: Utopian or Scientific*:

> Historical materialism is that view of the course of history which seeks the *ultimate* cause and the great moving power of all historical events in the economic development of society, in the changes of the modes of production and exchange, in the consequent division of society into distinct classes, and in the struggles of these classes against one another. (Italics mine)

Further, he claims:

> ... that all past history with the exception of the primitive stages was the history of class struggles; that these warring classes of society are always the products of the modes of production and exchange—in a word, of the economic conditions of their time; that the *economic* structure of society always furnishes the real basis, starting from which we can alone work out the *ultimate* explanation of the whole superstructure of juridical and political institutions as well as of the religious, philosophical, and other ideas of a given historical period. (Italics mine)

It would be a mistake to attempt to explain the oppression of women according to this strictly economic interpretation. The class analysis is a beautiful piece of work, but limited: although correct in a linear sense, it does not go deep enough. There is a whole sexual substratum of the historical dialectic that Engels at times dimly perceives, but because he can see sexuality only through an economic filter, reducing everything to that, he is unable to evaluate in its own right.

Engels did observe that the original division of labor was between man and woman for the purposes of child-breeding; that within the family the husband was the owner, the wife the means of production, the children the labor; and that reproduction of the human species was an important economic system distinct from the means of production.

But Engels has been given too much credit for these scattered recognitions of the oppression of women as a class. In fact he acknowledged the sexual class system only where it overlapped and illuminated his economic construct. Engels didn't do so well even in this respect. But Marx was worse: there is a growing recognition of Marx's bias against women (a cultural bias shared by Freud as well as all men of culture), dangerous if one attempts to squeeze feminism into an orthodox Marxist framework—freezing what were only incidental insights of Marx and Engels about sex class into dogma. Instead, we must enlarge historical materialism to *include* the strictly Marxian, in the same way that the physics of relativity did not invalidate Newtonian physics so much as it drew a circle around it, limiting its application—but only through comparison—to a smaller sphere. For an economic diagnosis traced to ownership of the means of production, even of the means of *re*production, does not explain everything. There is a level of reality that does not stem directly from economics.

The assumption that, beneath economics, reality is psychosexual is often rejected as ahistorical by those who accept a dialectical materialist view of history because it seems to land us back where Marx began: groping through a fog of utopian hypotheses, philosophical systems that might be right, that might be wrong (there is no way to tell), systems that explain concrete historical developments by *a priori* categories of thought; historical materialism, however, attempted to explain "knowing" by "being" and not vice versa.

But there is still an untried third alternative: We can attempt to develop a materialist view of history based on sex itself.

The early feminist theorists were to a materialist view of sex what

Fourier, Bebel, and Owen were to a materialist view of class. By and large, feminist theory has been as inadequate as were the early feminist attempts to correct sexism. This was to be expected. The problem is so immense that, at first try, only the surface could be skimmed, the most blatant inequalities described. Simone de Beauvoir was the only one who came close to—who perhaps has done—the definitive analysis. Her profound work *The Second Sex*—which appeared as recently as the early fifties to a world convinced that feminism was dead—for the first time attempted to ground feminism in its historical base. Of all feminist theorists De Beauvoir is the most comprehensive and far-reaching, relating feminism to the best ideas in our culture.

It may be this virtue is also her one failing: she is almost too sophisticated, too knowledgeable. Where this becomes a weakness—and this is still certainly debatable—is in her rigidly existentialist interpretation of feminism (one wonders how much Sartre had to do with this). This in view of the fact that all cultural systems, including existentialism, are themselves determined by the sex dualism. She says:

> Man never thinks of himself without thinking of the Other; he views the world under the sign of duality *which is not in the first place sexual in character.* But being different from man, who sets himself up as the Same, it is naturally to the category of the Other that woman is consigned; the Other includes woman. (Italics mine.)

Perhaps she has overshot her mark: Why postulate a fundamental Hegelian concept of Otherness as the final explanation—and then carefully document the biological and historical circumstances that have pushed the class "women" into such a category—when one has never seriously considered the much simpler and more likely possibility that this fundamental dualism sprang from the sexual division itself? To posit *a priori* categories of thought and existence—"Otherness," "Transcendence," "Immanence"—into which history then falls may not be necessary. Marx and Engels had discovered that these philosophical categories themselves grew out of history.

Before assuming such categories, let us first try to develop an analysis in which biology itself—procreation—is at the origin of the dualism. The immediate assumption of the layman that the unequal division of the sexes is "natural" may be well-founded. We need not immediately look beyond this. Unlike economic class sex class sprang directly from a biological reality: men and women were created different, and not equally privileged. Although, as De Beauvoir points out, this difference of itself did not necessitate the development of a class system—the domination of one group by another—the reproductive *functions* of these differences did. The biological family is an inherently unequal power distribution. The need for power leading to the development of classes arises from the psychosexual formation of each individual according to this basic imbalance, rather than, as Freud, Norman O. Brown, and others have, once again overshooting their mark, postulated, some irreducible conflict of Life against Death, Eros *vs.* Thanatos.

The *biological family*—the basic reproductive unit of male/female/infant, in whatever form of social organization—is characterized by these fundamental—if not immutable—facts:

1) That women throughout history before the advent of birth control were at the continual mercy of their biology—menstruation, menopause, and "female ills," constant painful childbirth, wetnursing and care of infants, all of which made them dependent on males (whether brother, father, husband, lover, or clan, government, community-at-large) for physical survival.

2) That human infants take an even longer time to grow up than animals, and thus are helpless and, for some short period at least, dependent on adults for physical survival.

3) That a basic mother/child interdependency has existed in some form in every society, past or present, and thus has shaped the psychology of every mature female and every infant.

4) That the natural reproductive difference between the sexes led directly to the first division of labor at the origins of class, as well as furnishing the paradigm of caste (discrimination based on biological characteristics).

These biological contingencies of the human family cannot be covered over with anthropological sophistries. Anyone observing animals mating, reproducing, and caring for their young will have a hard time accepting the "cultural relativity" line. For no matter how many tribes in Oceania you can find where the connection of the father to fertility is not known, no matter how many matrilineages, no matter how many cases of sex-role reversal, male housewifery, or even empathic labor pains, these facts prove only one thing: the amazing *flexibility* of human nature. But human nature is adaptable to something, it is, yes, determined by its environmental conditions. And the biological family that we have described has existed everywhere throughout time. Even in matriarchies where woman's fertility is worshipped, and the father's role is unknown or unimportant, if perhaps not on the genetic father, there is still some dependence of the female and the infant on the male. And though it is true that the nuclear family is only a recent development, one which, as I shall attempt to show, only intensifies the psychological penalties of the biological family, though it is true that throughout history there have been many variations on this biological family, the contingencies I have described existed in all of them, causing specific psychosexual distortions in the human personality.

But to grant that the sexual imbalance of power is biologically based is not to lose our case. We are no longer just animals. And the Kingdom of Nature does not reign absolute. As Simone de Beauvoir herself admits:

> The theory of historical materialism has brought to light some important truths. Humanity is not an animal species, it is a historical reality. Human society is an antiphysis—in a sense it is against nature; it does not passively submit to the presence of nature but rather takes over the control of nature on its own behalf. This arrogation is not an inward, subjective operation; it is accomplished objectively in practical action.

Thus, the "natural" is not necessarily a "human" value. Humanity has begun to outgrow nature: we can no longer justify the maintenance of a discriminatory sex class system on grounds of its origins in Nature. Indeed, for pragmatic reasons alone it is beginning to look as if we *must* get rid of it…

The problem becomes political, demanding more than a comprehensive historical analysis, when one realizes that, though man is increasingly capable of freeing himself from the biological conditions that created his tyranny over women and children, he has little reason to want to give this tyranny up. As Engels said, in the context of economic revolution:

It is the law of division of labor that lies at the basis of the division into classes. [Note that this division itself grew out of a fundamental biological division]. But this does not prevent the ruling class, once having the upper hand, from consolidating its power at the expense of the working class, from turning its social leadership into an intensified exploitation of the masses.

Though the sex class system may have originated in fundamental biological conditions, this does not guarantee once the biological basis of their oppression has been swept away that women and children will be freed. On the contrary, the new technology, especially fertility control, may be used against them to reinforce the entrenched system of exploitation.

So that just as to assure elimination of economic classes requires the revolt of the underclass (the proletariat) and, in a temporary dictatorship, their seizure of the means of production, so to assure the elimination of sexual classes requires the revolt of the underclass (women) and the seizure of control of reproduction: the restoration to women of ownership of their own bodies, as well as feminine control of human fertility, including both the new technology and all the social institutions of childbearing and childrearing. And just as the end goal of socialist revolution was not only the elimination of the economic class *privilege* but of the economic class *distinction* itself, so the end goal of feminist revolution must be, unlike that of the first feminist movement, not just the elimination of male *privilege* but of the sex *distinction* itself: genital differences between human beings would no longer matter culturally. (A reversion to an unobstructed *pansexuality*—Freud's "polymorphous perversity" —would probably supersede hetero/homo/bi-sexuality.) The reproduction of the species by one sex for the benefit of both would be replaced by (at least the option of) artificial reproduction: children would be born to both sexes equally, or independently of either, however one chooses to look at it; the dependence of the child on the mother (and vice versa) would give way to a greatly shortened dependence on a small group of others in general, and any remaining inferiority to adults in physical strength would be compensated for culturally. The division of labor would be ended by the elimination of labor altogether (cybernation). The tyranny of the biological family would be broken.

And with it the psychology of power. As Engels claimed for strictly socialist revolution: "The existence of not simply this or that ruling class but of any ruling class at all [will have] become an obsolete anachronism." That socialism has never come near achieving this predicated goal is not only the result of unfulfilled or misfired economic preconditions, but also because the Marxian analysis itself was insufficient: it did not dig deep enough to the psychosexual roots of class. Marx was onto something more profound than he knew when he observed that the family contained within itself in embryo all the antagonisms that later develop on a wide scale within the society and the state. For unless revolution uproots the basic social organization, the biological family—the vinculum through which the psychology of power can always be smuggled—the tapeworm of exploitation will never be annihilated. We shall need a sexual revolution much larger than—inclusive of—a socialist one to truly eradicate all class systems.

*   *   *

We have attempted to take the class analysis one step further to its roots in the biological division of the sexes. We have not thrown out the insights of the socialists; on the contrary, radical feminism can enlarge their analysis, granting it an even deeper basis in objective conditions and thereby explaining many of its insolubles. As a first step in this direction, and as the groundwork for our own analysis we shall expand Engels's definition of historical materialism. Here is the same definition quoted above now rephrased to include the biological division of the sexes for the purpose of reproduction, which lies at the origins of class:

> Historical materialism is that view of the course of history which seeks the ultimate cause and the great moving power of all historic events in the dialectic of sex: the division of society into two distinct biological classes for procreative reproduction, and the struggles of these classes with one another; in the changes in the modes of marriage, reproduction and childcare created by these struggles; in the connected development of other physically-differentiated classes [castes]; and in the first division of labor based on sex which developed into the [economic-cultural] class system.

And here is the cultural superstructure, as well as the economic one, traced not just back to (economic) class, but all the way back to sex:

> All past history [note that we can now eliminate "with the exception of primitive stages"] was the history of class struggle. These warring classes of society are always the product of the modes of organization of the biological family unit for reproduction of the species, as well as of the strictly economic modes of production and exchange of goods and services. The sexual-reproductive organization of society always furnishes the real basis, starting from which we can alone work out the ultimate explanation of the whole superstructure of economic, juridical and political institutions as well as of the religious, philosophical and other ideas of a given historical period.

And now Engels's projection of the results of a materialist approach to history is more realistic:

> The whole sphere of the conditions of life which environ man and have hitherto ruled him now comes under the dominion and control of man who for the first time becomes the real conscious Lord of Nature, master of his own social organization.

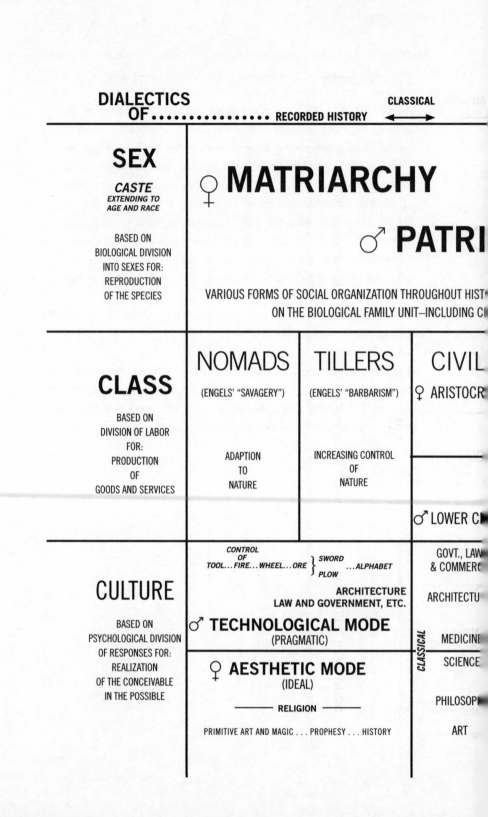

	REVOLUTION	TRANSITION	ULTIMATE GOAL
SSANCE → **MODERN** ↔			
CHY / ED / ATION, ETC.	**SEXUAL REVOLUTION** / FEMINIST REVOLT (ALSO CHILDREN AND YOUTH, OPPRESSED RACES)	"SINGLE STANDARD" MONOGAMY ► / MULTIPLE SOCIAL OPTIONS (INCLUDING THE REPRODUCTIVE "HOUSEHOLD") ► / DEVELOPMENT OF ARTIFICIAL REPRODUCTION ► / (EVENTUAL ELIMINATION OF CHILDHOOD, AGING AND DEATH)	**FULL SEXUAL FREEDOM ALLOWING ATTAINMENT OF "HAPPINESS"** / DISAPPEARANCE OF CULTURAL SEX, AGE, AND RACE DISTINCTION AND OF THE PSYCHOLOGY OF POWER (INCLUDING "NEUROSIS," "SUBLIMATION," ETC.)
ON / ELITE / DLE CLASS / KING CLASS	**ECONOMIC REVOLUTION** / PROLETARIAN REVOLT (INCLUDING THE THIRD WORLD AGAINST IMPERIALISM)	**SOCIALISM** ► / DICTATORSHIP OF THE PROLETARIAT	**SELF-DETERMINATION ("COMMUNISTIC ANARCHY") AND PAN-WORLD LIVING** / DISAPPEARANCE OF CLASS DISTINCTION AND OF THE STATE (NATIONALISM AND IMPERIALISM)
MODERN INDUSTRY (LIED SCIENCE") / MPIRICAL SCIENCE (RE RESEARCH") / MODERN ART (OR ART'S SAKE")	**CULTURAL REVOLUTION** / SCIENTIFIC BREAKTHROUGH BREAKDOWN OF CULTURAL CATEGORIES	**MERGING OF ART AND REALITY**	**REALIZATION OF THE CONCEIVABLE IN THE ACTUAL** / DISAPPEARANCE OF "CULTURE"

30 Intercourse (excerpt)

1987

Andrea Dworkin

Intercourse is commonly written about and comprehended as a form of possession or an act of possession in which, during which, because of which, a man inhabits a woman, physically covering her and overwhelming her and at the same time penetrating her; and this physical relation to her—over her and inside her—is his possession of her. He has her, or, when he is done, he has had her. By thrusting into her, he takes her over. His thrusting into her is taken to be her capitulation to him as a conqueror; it is a physical surrender of herself to him; he occupies and rules her, expresses his elemental dominance over her, by his possession of her in the fuck.

The act itself, without more, is the possession. There need not be a social relationship in which the woman is subordinate to the man, a chattel in spirit or deed, decorative or hardworking. There need not be an ongoing sexual relationship in which she is chronically, demonstrably, submissive or masochistic. The normal fuck by a normal man is taken to be an act of invasion and ownership undertaken in a mode of predation: colonializing, forceful (manly) or nearly violent; the sexual act that by its nature makes her his. God made it so, or nature did, according to the faith of the explainer of events and values. Both conceptual systems—the theological and the biological—are loyal to the creed of male dominance and maintain that intercourse is the elemental (not socialized) expression of male and female, which in turn are the elemental (not socialized) essences of men and women. In *Ideal Marriage*, a sexological marriage manual of vast and ubiquitous influence before the epidemic breakout of so-called sexology as a profession, Theodore Van De Velde summarized what men and women who were married should know about sex:

> What both man and woman, driven by obscure primitive urges, wish to feel in the sexual act, is the essential force of *maleness*, which expresses itself in a sort of violent and absolute *possession* of the woman. And so both of them can and do exult in a certain degree of male aggression and dominance—whether actual or apparent—which proclaims this essential force.

In other words, men possess women when men fuck women because both experience the man being male. This is the stunning logic of male supremacy. In this view, which is the predominant one, maleness is aggressive and violent; and so fucking, in which both the man and the woman experience *maleness*, essentially demands the disappearance of the woman as an individual; thus, in being fucked, she is possessed: ceases to exist as a discrete individual: is taken over.

Remarkably, it is not the man who is considered possessed in inter-course, even though he (his penis) is buried inside another human being; and his penis is surrounded by strong muscles that contract like a fist shutting tight and release with a force that pushes hard on the tender thing, always so vulnerable no matter how hard. He is not possessed even though his penis is gone—disappeared inside someone else, enveloped, smothered, in the muscled lining of flesh that he never sees, only feels, gripping, releasing, gripping, tighter, harder, firmer, then pushing out: and *can he get out alive?* seems a fundamental anxiety that fuels male sexual compulsiveness and the whole discipline of depth psychology. The man is not possessed in fucking even though he is terrified of castration; even though he sometimes thinks—singly or collectively in a culture—that the vagina has teeth; but he goes inside anyway, out of compulsion, obsession: not obsessed with her, a particular woman; but with it, getting inside. He is not possessed even though he is terrified of never getting his cock back because she has it engulfed inside her, and it is small compared with the vagina around it pulling it in and pushing it out: clenching it, choking it, increasing the friction and the frisson as he tries to pull out. He is not possessed even though he rolls over dead and useless afterward, shrunk into oblivion: this does not make him hers by virtue of the nature of the act; he has not been taken and conquered by her, to whom he finally surrenders, beat, defeated in endurance and strength both. And for him, this small annihilation, this little powerlessness, is not eroticized as sexual possession of him by her, intrinsic to the act; proof of an elemental reality, an unchanging relation between male and female. He experiences coitus as death; and he is sad; but he is not possessed.

Men have admitted some form of sexual possession of themselves by women in the fuck when they can characterize the women as witches, evil and carnal, and when the fuck occurs in their sleep at night. The witches have sex with men while they sleep; they use a man against his will, especially at night, when he is asleep and helpless. He ejaculates: proof that, by magic, a woman came to him in the night and did something to or with his penis. In Europe, women were persecuted as witches for nearly four hundred years, burned at the stake, perhaps as many as nine million of them—untold numbers accused of coming to men, having sex with them, causing them to ejaculate: at night, when the men slept. In these instances, then, the charge of witchcraft was a male charge of rape: the man claimed to be taken against his will, used in sex against his will; certainly without his consent and in a way violative of his male prerogatives in sex over women. In Europe during the Inquisition women were slaughtered for this rape of the male that took place in his own mind; for possessing him by making him fuck, twist, turn, tormented, in his sleep; for making him have sex or want it or experience it imprisoned in his own isolated body, sex that was not the issue of his will or predetermination. In many cultures and tribes, men can be similarly possessed; and the key to the possession—the dreams, the sex, the physical reality of desire, the obsession—is that the woman herself is magical and evil; through wickedness and magic she exerts illegitimate (therefore magical; therefore wicked; therefore originating in Satan) power over men.

For women, being sexually possessed by men is more pedestrian. Women have been chattels to men as wives, as prostitutes, as sexual and reproductive servants. Being owned and being fucked are or have been virtually synonymous experiences in the lives of women. He owns you; he fucks you. The fucking conveys the quality of the ownership: he owns you inside out. The fucking conveys the passion of his dominance: it requires access to every hidden inch. He can own everything around you and everything on you and everything you are capable of doing as a worker or servant or ornament; but getting inside you and owning your insides is possession: deeper, more intimate, than any other kind of ownership. Intimate, raw, total, the experience of sexual possession for women is real and literal, without any magical or mystical dimension to it: getting fucked and being owned are inseparably the same; together, being one and the same, they are sex for women under male dominance as a social system. In the fuck, the man expresses the geography of his dominance: her sex, her insides are part of his domain as a male. He can possess her as an individual—be her lord and master—and thus be expressing a private right of ownership (the private right issuing from his gender); or he can possess her by fucking her impersonally and thus be expressing a collective right of ownership without masquerade or manners. Most women are not distinct, private individuals to most men; and so the fuck tends toward the class assertion of dominance. Women live inside this reality of being owned and being fucked: are sensate inside it; the body learning to respond to what male dominance offers as touch, as sex, as love. For women, being possessed is the sex that has to meet the need for love or tenderness or physical affection; therefore, it comes to mean, to show, the intensity of desire; and being erotically owned by a man who takes you and fucks you is a physically charged and meaningful affirmation of womanhood or femininity or being desired.

This reality of being owned and being fucked—as experience, a social, political, economic, and psychological unity—frames, limits, sets parameters for, what women feel and experience in sex. Being that person who is owned and fucked means becoming someone who experiences sensuality in being possessed: in the touch of the possessor, in his fuck, however callous it is to the complexity or the subtlety of one's own humanity. Because a woman's capacity to feel sexual pleasure is developed within the narrow confines of male sexual dominance, internally there is no separate being—conceived, nurtured somewhere else, under different material circumstances—screaming to get out. There is only the flesh-and-blood reality of being a sensate being whose body experiences sexual intensity, sexual pleasure, and sexual identity in being possessed: in being owned and fucked. It is what one knows; and one's capacities to feel and to be are narrowed, sliced down, to fit the demands and dimensions of this sentient reality.

Therefore, women feel the fuck—when it works, when it overwhelms—as possession; and feel possession as deeply erotic; and value annihilation of the self in sex as proof of the man's desire or love, its awesome intensity. And therefore, being possessed is phenomenologically real for women; and sex itself is an experience of diminishing self-possession, an erosion of self. That loss of self is a physical reality, not just a psychic vampirism; and as a physical reality it is chilling and extreme, a literal erosion of the body's integrity and its ability to function and to survive. The physical rigors of sexual possession—of being possessed—overwhelm the body's vitality; and while at first the woman is fierce with the pride of possession—he wants her enough to empty her out—her insides are worn away over time, and she, possessed, becomes weak, depleted, usurped in all her physical and mental energies and capacities by the one who has physically taken her over; by the one who occupies her. This sexual possession is a sensual state of being that borders on antibeing until it ends in death. The body dies, or the lover discards the body when it is used up, throws it away, an old, useless thing, emptied, like an empty bottle. The body is used up; and the will is raped.

31 Nope (a manifesto)

2016

E. Jane

NOPE
(a manifesto)

I am not an identity artist just because I am a Black artist with multiple selves.

I am not grappling with notions of identity and representation in my art. I'm grappling with safety and futurity. We are beyond asking should we be in the room. We are in the room. We are also dying at a rapid pace and need a sustainable future.

We need more people, we need better environments, we need places to hide, we need Utopian demands, we need culture that loves us.

I am not asking who I am. I'm a Black woman and expansive in my Blackness and my queerness as Blackness and queerness are always already expansive. None of this is as simple as "identity and representation" outside of the colonial gaze. I reject the colonial gaze as the primary gaze. I am outside of it in the land of NOPE.

32 Grand Canyon

2004

Ani DiFranco

i love my country
by which i mean
i am indebted joyfully
to all the people throughout its history
who have fought the government to make right
where so many cunning sons and daughters
our foremothers and forefathers
came singing through slaughter
came through hell and high water
so that we could stand here
and behold breathlessly the sight
how a raging river of tears
cut a grand canyon of light

yes, i've bin so many places
flown through vast empty spaces
with stewardesses whose hands
look much older than their faces
i've tossed so many napkins
into that big hole in the sky
bin at the bottom of the atlantic
seething in a two-ply
looking up through all that water
and the fishes swimming by
and i don't always feel lucky

but i'm smart enough to try
cuz humility has buoyancy
and above us only sky
so i lean in
breathe deeper that brutal burning smell
that surrounds the smoldering wreckage
that i've come to love so well
yes, color me stunned and dazzled
by all the red white and blue flashing lights
in the american intersection
where black crashed head on with white
comes a melody
comes a rhythm
a particular resonance
that is us and only us
comes a screaming ambulance
a hand that you can trust
laid steady on your chest
working for the better good
(which is good at its best)
and too, bearing witness
like a woman bears a child:
with all her might

born of the greatest pain
into a grand canyon of light

i mean, no song has gone unsung here
and this joint is strung crazy tight
and people bin raising up their voices
since it just ain't bin right
with all the righteous rage
and all the bitter spite
that will accompany us out
of this long night
that will grab us by the hand
when we are ready to take flight
seatback and traytable
in the upright and locked position

shocked to tears by each new vision
of all that my ancestors have done

like, say, the women who gave their lives
so that i could have one

people, we are standing at ground zero
of the feminist revolution
yeah, it was an inside job
stoic and sly
one we're supposed to forget
and downplay and deny
but i think the time is nothing
if not nigh
to let the truth out
coolest f-word ever deserves a fucking shout!
i mean
why can't all decent men and women
call themselves feminists?
out of respect
for those who fought for this
i mean, look around
we have this

yes
i love my country
by which i mean
i am indebted joyfully
to all the people throughout its history
who have fought the government to make right
where so many cunning sons and daughters
our foremothers and forefathers
came singing through slaughter
came through hell and high water
so that we could stand here
and behold breathlessly the sight
how a raging river of tears
is cutting a grand canyon of light

PART IV

INDIGENOUS/
WOMEN
OF COLOR

Introduction to
Indigenous/Women of Color

If there exists a poetics of oppression, a language that holds the heavy emotional weight of inequality, the manifestos in this section embody it. Here we see the possibilities of resistance and revolt woven across and through multiple generations, tying together black and brown histories, indigenous struggles, and the hard-earned spirit of feminist revolution. This section portrays new possibilities for solidarities between women of color, working together in the project of opposing the violence of whiteness. Seen together, we can imagine women of color embodying a feminism of againstness that merges together critiques of patriarchy and racism.

We begin with arguably the most well-known feminist manifesto written by women of color—the 1977 classic *Combahee River Collective* statement—which details a new vision for black women's empowerment. We dive deep into historical documents of black resistance, including new ways of imagining black womanhood (Frances M. Beal and "The Sisters Reply"). In a lesser known, but equally scathing, indictment of whiteness, Linda La Rue questions what it means to be a black woman in a world that cultivates misogyny and racism in equal measure. Blackness as a source of anger, and whiteness as a target for that righteous anger, constitutes a sizeable portion of this section.

In tandem with this work, several essays showcase the anger of indigenous, Asian, and Chicana women, asking what it means to witness continual erasure and disappearances—of friends, of language, of culture, of possibilities. He-Yin Zhen describes the treatment of women in China as subhuman, while Leanne Simpson and Crystal Zaragoza provide sharp critiques of the loss of indigenous and Mexican people to the forces of whiteness and colonization. We also read new visions for Zapatista women imagining revolution for themselves (EZLN), and we hear from Susan Hawthorne, who uses Australian Aboriginal principles to imagine how to become a "wild poet," free to create on her own terms. The section culminates with the platform statement of Black Lives Matter, a keenly intersectional document that is both wholly "of the now" and of a new and imagined future.

33 The Combahee River Collective Statement

1977

Combahee River Collective

We are a collective of black feminists who have been meeting together since 1974.[1] During that time we have been involved in the process of defining and clarifying our politics, while at the same time doing political work within our own group and in coalition with other progressive organizations and movements. The most general statement of our politics at the present time would be that we are actively committed to struggling against racial, sexual, heterosexual, and class oppression, and see as our particular task the development of integrated analysis and practice based upon the fact that the major systems of oppression are interlocking. The synthesis of these oppressions creates the conditions of our lives. As black women we see black feminism as the logical political movement to combat the manifold and simultaneous oppressions that all women of color face.

We will discuss four major topics in the paper that follows: (1) the genesis of contemporary black feminism; (2) what we believe, i.e., the specific province of our politics; (3) the problems in organizing black feminists, including a brief herstory of our collective; and (4) black feminist issues and practice.

---

1 This statement is dated April 1977.

1. The Genesis of Contemporary Black Feminism

Before looking at the recent development of black feminism we would like to affirm that we find our origins in the historical reality of Afro-American women's continuous life-and-death struggle for survival and liberation. Black women's extremely negative relationship to the American political system (a system of white male rule) has always been determined by our membership in two oppressed racial and sexual castes. As Angela Davis points out in "Reflections on the Black Woman's Role in the Community of Slaves," black women have always embodied, if only in their physical manifestation, an adversary stance to white male rule and have actively resisted its inroads upon them and their communities in both dramatic and subtle ways. There have always been black women activists—some known, like Sojourner Truth, Harriet Tubman, Frances E. W. Harper, Ida B. Wells Barnett, and Mary Church Terrell, and thousands upon thousands unknown—who have had a shared awareness of how their sexual identity combined with their racial identity to make their whole life situation and the focus of their political struggles unique. Contemporary black feminism is the outgrowth of countless generations of personal sacrifice, militancy, and work by our mothers and sisters.

A black feminist presence has evolved most obviously in connection with the second wave of the American women's movement beginning in the late 1960s. Black, other Third World, and working women have been involved in the feminist movement from its start, but both outside reactionary forces and racism and elitism within the movement itself have served to obscure our participation. In 1973, black feminists, primarily located in New York, felt the necessity of forming a separate black feminist group. This became the National Black Feminist Organization (NBFO).

Black feminist politics also have an obvious connection to movements for black liberation, particularly those of the 1960s and 1970s. Many of us were active in those movements (civil rights, black nationalism, the Black Panthers), and all of our lives were greatly affected and changed by their ideologies, their goals, and the tactics used to achieve their goals. It was our experience and disillusionment within these liberation movements, as well as experience on the periphery of the white male left, that led to the need to develop a politics that was anti-racist, unlike those of white women, and anti-sexist, unlike those of black and white men.

There is also undeniably a personal genesis for black feminism, that is, the political realization that comes from the seemingly personal experiences of individual black women's lives. Black feminists and many more black women who do not define themselves as feminists have all experienced sexual oppression as a constant factor in our day-to-day existence. As children we realized that we were different from boys and that we were treated differently. For example, we were told in the same breath to be quiet both for the sake of being "ladylike" and to make us less objectionable in the eyes of white people. As we grew older we became aware of the threat of physical and sexual abuse by men. However, we had no way of conceptualizing what was so apparent to us, what we knew was really happening.

Black feminists often talk about their feelings of craziness before becoming conscious of the concepts of sexual politics, patriarchal rule, and most importantly, feminism, the political analysis and practice that we women use to struggle against our oppression. The fact that racial politics and indeed racism are pervasive factors in our lives did not allow us, and still does not allow most black women, to look more deeply into our own experiences and define those things that make our lives what they are and our oppression specific to us. In the process of consciousness-raising, actually life-sharing, we began to recognize the commonality of our experiences, from that sharing and growing consciousness, to build a politics that will change our lives and inevitably end our oppression. Our development must also be tied to the contemporary economic and political position of black people. The post-World War II generation of black youth was the first to be able to minimally partake of certain educational and employment options, previously closed completely to black people. Although our economic position is still at the very bottom of the American capitalistic economy, a handful of us have been able to gain certain tools as a result of tokenism in education and employment which potentially enable us to more effectively fight our oppression.

A combined antiracist and antisexist position drew us together initially, and as we developed politically we addressed ourselves to heterosexism and economic oppression under capitalism.

2. What We Believe

Above all else, our politics initially sprang from the shared belief that
black women are inherently valuable, that our liberation is a necessity
not as an adjunct to somebody else's but because of our need as human
persons for autonomy. This may seem so obvious as to sound simplistic, but it is apparent that no other ostensibly progressive movement
has ever considered our specific oppression as a priority or worked
seriously for the ending of that oppression. Merely naming the pejorative stereotypes attributed to black women (e.g., mammy, matriarch,
Sapphire, whore, bulldagger), let alone cataloguing the cruel, often
murderous, treatment we receive, indicates how little value has been
placed upon our lives during four centuries of bondage in the Western
hemisphere. We realize that the only people who care enough about us
to work consistently for our liberation is us. Our politics evolve from
a healthy love for ourselves, our sisters and our community which
allows us to continue our struggle and work.

This focusing upon our own oppression is embodied in the concept
of identity politics. We believe that the most profound and potentially
most radical politics come directly out of our own identity, as opposed
to working to end somebody else's oppression. In the case of black
women this is a particularly repugnant, dangerous, threatening, and
therefore revolutionary concept because it is obvious from looking at
all the political movements that have preceded us that anyone is more
worthy of liberation than ourselves. We reject pedestals, queenhood,
and walking ten paces behind. To be recognized as human, levelly
human, is enough.

We believe that sexual politics under patriarchy is as pervasive in
black women's lives as are the politics of class and race. We also often
find it difficult to separate race from class from sex oppression because
in our lives they are most often experienced simultaneously. We know
that there is such a thing as racial-sexual oppression which is neither
solely racial nor solely sexual, e.g., the history of rape of black women
by white men as a weapon of political repression.

Although we are feminists and lesbians, we feel solidarity with
progressive black men and do not advocate the fractionalization that
white women who are separatists demand. Our situation as black
people necessitates that we have solidarity around the fact of race,
which white women of course do not need to have with white men,

unless it is their negative solidarity as racial oppressors. We struggle together with black men against racism, while we also struggle with black men about sexism.

We realize that the liberation of all oppressed peoples necessitates the destruction of the political-economic systems of capitalism and imperialism as well as patriarchy. We are socialists because we believe that work must be organized for the collective benefit of those who do the work and create the products, and not for the profit of the bosses. Material resources must be equally distributed among those who create these resources. We are not convinced, however, that a socialist revolution that is not also a feminist and anti-racist revolution will guarantee our liberation. We have arrived at the necessity for developing an understanding of class relationships that takes into account the specific class position of black women who are generally marginal in the labor force, while at this particular time some of us are temporarily viewed as doubly desirable tokens at white-collar and professional levels. We need to articulate the real class situation of persons who are not merely raceless, sexless workers, but for whom racial and sexual oppression are significant determinants in their working/economic lives. Although we are in essential agreement with Marx's theory as it applied to the very specific economic relationships he analyzed, we know that this analysis must be extended further in order for us to understand our specific economic situation as black women.

A political contribution which we feel we have already made is the expansion of the feminist principle that the personal is political. In our consciousness-raising sessions, for example, we have in many ways gone beyond white women's revelations because we are dealing with the implications of race and class as well as sex. Even our black women's style of talking/testifying in black language about what we have experienced has a resonance that is both cultural and political. We have spent a great deal of energy delving into the cultural and experiential nature of our oppression out of necessity because none of these matters have ever been looked at before. No one before has ever examined the multilayered texture of black women's lives.

As we have already stated, we reject the stance of lesbian separatism because it is not a viable political analysis or strategy for us. It leaves out far too much and far too many people, particularly black men, women, and children. We have a great deal of criticism and loathing for what men have been socialized to be in this society: what they support, how they act, and how they oppress. But we do not have the misguided notion that it is their maleness, per se—i.e., their biological maleness—that makes them what they are. As black women we find any type of biological determinism a particularly dangerous and reactionary basis upon which to build a politic. We must also question whether lesbian separatism is an adequate and progressive political analysis and strategy, even for those who practice it, since it so completely denies any but the sexual sources of women's oppression, negating the facts of class and race.

3. Problems in Organizing Black Feminists

During our years together as a black feminist collective we have experienced success and defeat, joy and pain, victory and failure. We have found that it is very difficult to organize around black feminist issues, difficult even to announce in certain contexts that we *are* black feminists. We have tried to think about the reasons for our difficulties, particularly since the white women's movement continues to be strong and to grow in many directions. In this section we will discuss some of the general reasons for the organizing problems we face and also talk specifically about the stages in organizing our own collective.

The major source of difficulty in our political work is that we are not just trying to fight oppression on one front or even two, but instead to address a whole range of oppressions. We do not have racial, sexual, heterosexual, or class privilege to rely upon, nor do we have even the minimal access to resources and power that groups who possess any one of these types of privilege have.

The psychological toll of being a black woman and the difficulties this presents in reaching political consciousness and doing political work can never be underestimated. There is a very low value placed upon black women's psyches in this society, which is both racist and sexist. As an early group member once said, "We are all damaged people merely by virtue of being black women." We are dispossessed psychologically and on every other level, and yet we feel the necessity to struggle to change our condition and the condition of all black women. In "A Black Feminist's Search for Sisterhood," Michele Wallace arrives at this conclusion:

We exist as women who are black who are feminists, each stranded for the moment, working independently because there is not yet an environment in this society remotely congenial to our struggle—because, being on the bottom, we would have to do what no one else has done: we would have to fight the world.[2]

Wallace is not pessimistic but realistic in her assessment of black feminists' position, particularly in her allusion to the nearly classic isolation most of us face. We might use our position at the bottom, however, to make a clear leap into revolutionary action. If black women were free, it would mean that everyone else would have to be free since our freedom would necessitate the destruction of all the systems of oppression.

Feminism is, nevertheless, very threatening to the majority of black people because it calls into question some of the most basic assumptions about our existence, i.e., that sex should be a determinant of power relationships. Here is the way male and female roles were defined in a black nationalist pamphlet from the early 1970s.

We understand that it is and has been traditional that the man is the head of the house. He is the leader of the house/nation because his knowledge of the world is broader, his awareness is greater, his understanding is fuller and his application of this information is wiser ... After all, it is only reasonable that the man be the head of the house because he is able to defend and protect the development of his home ... Women cannot do the same things as men—they are made by nature to function differently. Equality of men and women is something that cannot happen even in the abstract world. Men are not equal to other men, i.e., ability, experience or even understanding. The value of men and women can be seen as in the value of gold and silver—they are not equal but both have great value. We must realize that men and women are a complement to each other because there is no house/family without a man and his wife. Both are essential to the development of any life.[3]

2 Wallace, Michele. "A Black Feminist's Search for Sisterhood," *The Village Voice*, July 28, 1975, pp. 6–7.

3 Mumininas of Committee for Unified Newark, *Mwanamke Mwananchi (The Nationalist Woman)*, Newark, N.J., ©1971, pp. 4–5.

The material conditions of most black women would hardly lead them to upset both economic and sexual arrangements that seem to represent some stability in their lives. Many black women have a good understanding of both sexism and racism, but because of the everyday constrictions of their lives, cannot risk struggling against them both.

The reaction of black men to feminism has been notoriously negative. They are, of course, even more threatened than black women by the possibility that black feminists might organize around our own needs. They realize that they might not only lose valuable and hardworking allies in their struggles but that they might also be forced to change their habitually sexist ways of interacting with and oppressing black women. Accusations that black feminism divides the black struggle are powerful deterrents to the growth of an autonomous black women's movement.

Still, hundreds of women have been active at different times during the three-year existence of our group. And every black woman who came, came out of a strongly-felt need for some level of possibility that did not previously exist in her life.

When we first started meeting early in 1974 after the NBFO first eastern regional conference, we did not have a strategy for organizing, or even a focus. We just wanted to see what we had. After a period of months of not meeting, we began to meet again late in the year and started doing an intense variety of consciousness-raising. The overwhelming feeling that we had is that after years and years we had finally found each other. Although we were not doing political work as a group, individuals continued their involvement in lesbian politics, sterilization abuse and abortion rights work, Third World Women's International Women's Day activities, and support activity for the trials of Dr. Kenneth Edelin, Joan Little, and Inéz García. During our first summer, when membership had dropped off considerably, those of us remaining devoted serious discussion to the possibility of opening a refuge for battered women in a black community. (There was no refuge in Boston at that time.) We also decided around that time to become an independent collective since we had serious disagreements with NBFO's bourgeois-feminist stance and their lack of a clear political focus.

We also were contacted at that time by socialist feminists, with whom we had worked on abortion rights activities, who wanted to encourage us to attend the National Socialist Feminist Conference in Yellow Springs. One of our members did attend and despite the narrowness of the ideology that was promoted at that particular conference, we became more aware of the need for us to understand our own economic situation and to make our own economic analysis.

In the fall, when some members returned, we experienced several months of comparative inactivity and internal disagreements which were first conceptualized as a lesbian-straight split but which were also the result of class and political differences. During the summer those of us who were still meeting had determined the need to do political work and to move beyond consciousness-raising and serving exclusively as an emotional support group. At the beginning of 1976, when some of the women who had not wanted to do political work and who also had voiced disagreements stopped attending of their own accord, we again looked for a focus. We decided at that time, with the addition of new members, to become a study group. We had always shared our reading with each other, and some of us had written papers on black feminism for group discussion a few months before this decision was made. We began functioning as a study group and also began discussing the possibility of starting a black feminist publication. We had a retreat in the late spring which provided a time for both political discussion and working out interpersonal issues. Currently we are planning to gather together a collection of black feminist writing. We feel that it is absolutely essential to demonstrate the reality of our politics to other black women and believe that we can do this through writing and distributing our work. The fact that individual black feminists are living in isolation all over the country, that our own numbers are small, and that we have some skills in writing, printing, and publishing makes us want to carry out these kinds of projects as a means of organizing black feminists as we continue to do political work in coalition with other groups.

4. Black Feminist Issues and Practice

During our time together we have identified and worked on many issues of particular relevance to black women. The inclusiveness of our politics makes us concerned with any situation that impinges upon the lives of women, Third World, and working people. We are of course particularly committed to working on those struggles in which race, sex, and class are simultaneous factors in oppression. We might, for example, become involved in workplace organizing at a factory that employs Third World women or picket a hospital that is cutting back on already inadequate heath care to a Third World community, or set up a rape crisis center in a black neighborhood. Organizing around welfare and daycare concerns might also be a focus. The work to be done and the countless issues that this work represents merely reflect the pervasiveness of our oppression.

Issues and projects that collective members have actually worked on are sterilization abuse, abortion rights, battered women, rape and health care. We have also done many workshops and educationals on black feminism on college campuses, at women's conferences, and most recently for high school women.

One issue that is of major concern to us and that we have begun to publicly address is racism in the white women's movement. As black feminists we are made constantly and painfully aware of how little effort white women have made to understand and combat their racism, which requires among other things that they have a more than superficial comprehension of race, color, and black history and culture. Eliminating racism in the white women's movement is by definition work for white women to do, but we will continue to speak to and demand accountability on this issue.

In the practice of our politics we do not believe that the end always justifies the means. Many reactionary and destructive acts have been done in the name of achieving "correct" political goals. As feminists we do not want to mess over people in the name of politics. We believe in collective process and a nonhierarchical distribution of power within our own group and in our vision of a revolutionary society. We are committed to a continual examination of our politics as they develop through criticism and self-criticism as an essential aspect of our practice. As black feminists and lesbians we know that we have a very definite revolutionary task to perform and we are ready for the lifetime of work and struggle before us.

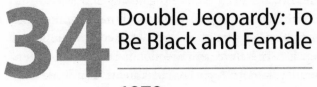

Double Jeopardy: To Be Black and Female

1970

Frances M. Beal

In attempting to analyze the situation of the black woman in America, one crashes abruptly into a solid wall of grave misconceptions, outright distortions of fact and defensive attitudes on the part of many. The system of capitalism (and its afterbirth—racism) under which we all live, has attempted by many devious ways and means to destroy the humanity of all people, and particularly the humanity of black people. This has meant an outrageous assault on every black man, woman and child who reside in the United States.

In keeping with its goal of destroying the black race's will to resist its subjugation, capitalism found it necessary to create a situation where the black man found it impossible to find meaningful or productive employment. More often than not, he couldn't find work of any kind. And the black woman likewise was manipulated by the system, economically exploited and physically assaulted. She could often find work in the white man's kitchen, however, and sometimes became the sole breadwinner of the family This predicament has led to many psychological problems on the part of both man and woman and has contributed to the turmoil that we find in the black family structure.

Unfortunately, neither the black man nor the black woman understood the true nature of the forces working upon them. Many black women tended to accept the capitalist evaluation of manhood and womanhood and believed, in fact, that black men were shiftless and lazy, otherwise they would get a job and support their families as they ought to. Personal relationships between black men and women were thus torn asunder and one result has been the separation of man from wife, mother from child, etc.

America has defined the roles to which each individual should subscribe. It has defined "manhood" in terms of its own interests and "femininity" likewise. Therefore, an individual who has a good job, makes a lot of money and drives a Cadillac is a real "man," and conversely, an individual who is lacking in these "qualities" is less of a man. The advertising media in this country continuously informs the american male of his need for indispensable signs of his virility—the brand of cigarettes that cowboys prefer, the whiskey that has a masculine tang or the label of the jock strap that athletes wear.

The ideal model that is projected for a woman is to be surrounded by hypocritical homage and estranged from all real work, spending idle hours primping and preening, obsessed with conspicuous consumption, and limiting life's functions to simply a sex role. We unqualitatively reject these respective models. A woman who stays at home, caring for children and the house often leads an extremely sterile existence. She must lead her entire life as a satellite to her mate. He goes out into society and brings back a little piece of the world for her. His interests and his understanding of the world become her own and she can not develop herself as an individual, having been reduced to only a biological function. This kind of woman leads a parasitic existence that can aptly be described as "legalized prostitution."

Furthermore, it is idle dreaming to think of black women simply caring for their homes and children like the middle class white model. Most black women have to work to help house, feed and clothe their families. Black women make up a substantial percentage of the black working force and this is true for the poorest black family as well as the so-called "middle class" family.

Black women were never afforded any such phony luxuries. Though we have been browbeaten with this white image, the reality of the degrading and dehumanizing jobs that were relegated to us quickly dissipated this mirage of "womanhood." The following excerpts from a speech that Sojourner Truth made at a Women's Rights Convention in the 19th century show us how misleading and incomplete a life this model represents for us:

> ... Well, chilern, whar dar is so much racket dar must be something out o'kilter. I tink dat 'twixt de niggers of de Souf and de women at

de norf all a talkin' 'bout rights, de white men will be in a fix pretty
soon. But what's all dis here talkin' 'bout? Dat man ober dar say dat
women needs to be helped into carriages and lifted ober ditches,
and to have de best place every whar. Nobody ever help me into
carriages, or ober mud puddles, or gives me any best places ... and
ar'nt I a woman? Look at me! Look at my arm ... I have plowed, and
planted, and gathered into barns, and no man could head me—and
ar'nt I a woman? I could work as much as a man (when I could get
it), and bear de lash as well—and ar'nt I a woman? I have borne
five chilern and I seen 'em mos' all sold off into slavery, and when I
cried out with a mother's grief, none but Jesus heard—and ar'nt I a
woman?

Unfortunately, there seems to be some confusion in the Movement
today as to who has been oppressing whom. Since the advent of black
power, the black male has exerted a more prominent leadership role
in our struggle for justice in this country. He sees the system for what
it really is for the most part. But where he rejects its values and mores
on many issues, when it comes to women, he seems to take his guidelines from the pages of the Ladies Home Journal. Certain black men
are maintaining that they have been castrated by society but that black
women somehow escaped this persecution and even contributed to
this emasculation.

Let me state here and now that the black woman in america can
justly be described as a "slave of a slave." By reducing the black man in
america to such abject oppression, the black woman had no protector
and was used, and is still being used in some cases, as the scapegoat for
the evils that this horrendous system has perpetrated on black men.
Her physical image has been maliciously maligned; she has been sexually molested and abused by the white colonizer; she has suffered
the worst kind of economic exploitation, having been forced to serve
as the white woman's maid and wet nurse for white offspring while
her own children were more often than not, starving and neglected.
It is the depth of degradation to be socially manipulated, physically
raped, used to undermine your own household, and to be powerless
to reverse this syndrome.

It is true that our husbands, fathers, brothers and sons have been
emasculated, lynched and brutalized. They have suffered from the
cruelest assault on mankind that the world has ever known. However,

it is a gross distortion of fact to state that black women have oppressed black men. The capitalist system found it expedient to enslave and oppress them and proceeded to do so without signing any agreements with black women.

It must also be pointed out at this time, that black women are not resentful of the rise to power of black men. We welcome it. We see in it the eventual liberation of all black people from this corrupt system under which we suffer. Nevertheless, this does not mean that you have to negate one for the other. This kind of thinking is a product of mis-education; that it's either X or it's Y. It is fallacious reasoning that in order for the black man to be strong, the black woman has to be weak.

Those who are exerting their "manhood" by telling black women to step back into a domestic, submissive role are assuming a counter-revolutionary position. Black women likewise have been abused by the system and we must begin talking about the elimination of all kinds of oppression. If we are talking about building a strong nation, capable of throwing off the yoke of capitalist oppression, then we are talking about the total involvement of every man, woman, and child, each with a highly developed political consciousness. We need our whole army out there dealing with the enemy and not half an army.

There are also some black women who feel that there is no more productive role in life than having and raising children. This attitude often reflects the conditioning of the society in which we live and is adopted (totally, completely and without change) from a bourgeois white model. Some young sisters who have never had to maintain a household and accept the confining role which this entails, tend to romanticize (along with the help of a few brothers) this role of house-wife and mother. Black women who have had to endure this kind of function as the sole occupation of their life, are less apt to have these utopian visions.

Those who project in an intellectual manner how great and reward-ing this role will be and who feel that the most important thing that they can contribute to the black nation is children, are doing them-selves a great injustice. This line of reasoning completely negates the contributions that black women have historically made to our struggle for liberation. These black women include Sojourner Truth, Harriet Tubman, Ida B. Wells-Barnett, Mary McLeod Bethune and Fannie Lou Hamer to name but a few.

We live in a highly industrialized society and every member of the black nation must be as academically and technologically developed as possible. To wage a revolution, we need competent teachers, doctors, nurses, electronic experts, chemists, biologists, physicists, political scientists, and so on and so forth. Black women sitting at home reading bedtime stories to their children are just not going to make it.

ECONOMIC EXPLOITATION OF BLACK WOMEN

The economic system of capitalism finds it expedient to reduce women to a state of enslavement. They oftentimes serve as a scapegoat for the evils of this system. Much in the same way that the poor white cracker of the South who is equally victimized, looks down upon blacks and contributes to the oppression of blacks, so, by giving to men a false feeling of superiority (at least in their own home or in their relationships with women,) the oppression of women acts as an escape valve for capitalism. Men may be cruelly exploited and subjected to all sorts of dehumanizing tactics on the part of the ruling class, but they have someone who is below them—at least they're not women.

Women also represent a surplus labor supply, the control of which is absolutely necessary to the profitable functioning of capitalism. Women are systematically exploited by the system. They are paid less for the same work that men do and jobs that are specifically relegated to women are low-paying and without the possibility of advancement. Statistics from the Women's Bureau of the U.S. Department of Labor show that the wage scale for white women was even below that of black men; and the wage scale for non-white women was the lowest of all:

White Males	$6,704
Non-white Males	$4,277
White Females	$3,991
Non-white Females	$2,861

Those industries which employ mainly black women are the most exploitative in the country. Domestic and hospital workers are good examples of this oppression; the garment workers in New York City provide us with another view of this economic slavery. The International Ladies Garment Workers Union (ILGWU), whose overwhelming membership consists of black and Puerto Rican women has a leadership that is nearly lily-white and male. This leadership has been working in collusion with the ruling class and has completely sold its soul to the corporate structure.

To add insult to injury, the ILGWU has invested heavily in business enterprises in racist, apartheid South Africa—with union funds. Not only does this bought-off leadership contribute to our continued exploitation in this country by not truly representing the best interests of its membership, but it audaciously uses funds that black and Puerto Rican women have provided to support the economy of a vicious government that is engaged in the economic rape and murder of our black brothers and sisters in our Motherland, Africa.

The entire labor movement in the United States has suffered as a result of the super exploitation of black workers and women. The unions have historically been racist and chauvinistic. They have upheld racism in this country (and condoned imperialist exploitation around the world) and have failed to fight the white skin privileges of white workers. They have failed to fight or even make an issue against the inequities in the hiring and pay of women workers. There has been virtually no struggle against either the racism of the white worker or the economic exploitation of the working woman, two factors which have consistently impeded the advancement of the real struggle against the ruling capitalist class.

This racist, chauvinistic and manipulative use of black workers and women, especially black women, has been a severe cancer on the american labor scene. It therefore becomes essential for those who understand the workings of capitalism and imperialism to realize that the exploitation of black people and women works to everyone's disadvantage and that the liberation of these two groups is a stepping stone to the liberation of all oppressed people in this country and around the world.

BEDROOM POLITICS

I have briefly discussed the economic and psychological manipulation of black women, but perhaps the most outlandish act of oppression in modern times is the current campaign to promote sterilization of nonwhite women in an attempt to maintain the population and power imbalance between the white haves and the non-white have nots.

These tactics are but another example of the many devious schemes that the ruling elite attempt to perpetrate on the black population in order to keep itself in control. It has recently come to our attention that a massive campaign for so-called "birth control" is presently being promoted not only in the underdeveloped non-white areas of the world, but also in black communities here in the United States. However, what the authorities in charge of these programs refer to as "birth control" is in fact nothing but a method of outright surgical genocide.

The United States has been sponsoring sterilization clinics in non-white countries, especially in India where already some 3 million young men and boys in and around New Delhi have been sterilized in make-shift operating rooms set up by the american peace corps workers. Under these circumstances, it is understandable why certain countries view the Peace Corps not as a benevolent project, not as evidence of america's concern for underdeveloped areas, but rather as a threat to their very existence. This program could more aptly be named the "Death Corps."

The Vasectomy which is performed on males and takes only six or seven minutes is a relatively simple operation. The sterilization of a woman, on the other hand, is admittedly major surgery. This surgical operation (Salpingectomy) must be performed in a hospital under general anesthesia. This method of "birth control" is a common procedure in Puerto Rico. Puerto Rico has long been used by the colonialist exploiter, the United States, as a huge experimental laboratory for medical research before allowing certain practices to be imported and used here. When the birth control pill was first being perfected, it was tried out on Puerto Rican women and selected black women (poor), using them like Guinea pigs, to evaluate its effect and its efficiency.

The Salpingectomy has now become the commonest operation in Puerto Rico, commoner than an appendectomy or a tonsilectomy. It is so widespread that it is referred to simply as "la operacion." On the Island, 20% of the women between the ages of 15 and 45 have already been sterilized.

And now, as previously occurred with the pill, this method has been imported into the United States. These sterilization clinics are cropping up around the country in the black and Puerto Rican communities. These so-called "Maternity Clinics" specifically outfitted to purge black women or men of their reproductive possibilities are appearing more and more in hospitals and clinics across the country.

A number of organizations have been formed to popularize the idea of sterilization such as the Association for Voluntary Sterilization and The Human Betterment (!!?) Association for Voluntary Sterilization which has its headquarters in New York City. Front Royal, Virginia has one such "Maternity Clinic" in Warren Memorial Hospital. The tactics used in the clinic in Fauquier County, Virginia, where poor and helpless black mothers and young girls are pressured into undergoing sterilization are certainly not confined to that clinic alone.

Threatened with the cut-off of relief funds, some black welfare women have been forced to accept this sterilization procedure in exchange for a continuation of welfare benefits. Mt. Sinai Hospital in New York City performs these operations on many of its ward patients whenever it can convince the women to undergo this surgery. Mississippi and some of the other Southern states are notorious for this act. Black women are often afraid to permit any kind of necessary surgery because they know from bitter experience that they are more likely than not to come out of the hospital without their insides. (Both Salpingectomies & Hysterectomies are performed.)

We condemn this use of the black woman as a medical testing ground for the white middle class. Reports of the ill effects including deaths from the use of the birth control pill only started to come to light when the white privileged class began to be affected. These outrageous Nazi-like procedures on the part of medical researchers are but another manifestation of the totally amoral and dehumanizing brutality that the capitalist system perpetrates on black women. The sterilization experiments carried on in concentration camps some twenty-five years ago have been denounced the world over, but no one seems to get upset by the repetition of these same racist tactics today in the United States of America—land of the free and home of the brave. This campaign is as nefarious a program as Germany's gas chambers and in a long term sense, as effective and with the same objective.

The rigid laws concerning abortions in this country are another vicious means of subjugation, and, indirectly of outright murder. Rich white women somehow manage to obtain these operations with little or no difficulty. It is the poor black and Puerto Rican woman who is at the mercy of the local butcher. Statistics show us that the non-white death rate at the hands of the unqualified abortionist is substantially higher than for white women. Nearly half of the child-bearing deaths in New York City were attributed to abortion alone and out of these, 79% were among non-whites and Puerto Rican women.

We are not saying that black women should not practice birth control or family planning. Black women have the right and the responsibility to determine when it is in the interest of the struggle to have children or not to have them. <u>It is also her right and responsibility to determine when it is in her own best interests to have children, how many she will have, and how far apart and this right must not be relinquished to anyone.</u>

The lack of the availability of safe birth control methods, the forced sterilization practices and the inability to obtain legal abortions are all symptoms of a decadent society that jeopardizes the health of black women (and thereby the entire black race) in its attempts to control the very life processes of human beings. This repressive control of black women is symptomatic of a society that believes it has the right to bring political factors into the privacy of the bedchamber. The elimination of these horrendous conditions will free black women for full participation in the revolution, and thereafter, in the building of the new society.

RELATIONSHIP TO WHITE MOVEMENT

Much has been written recently about the white women's liberation movement in the United States and the question arises whether there are any parallels between this struggle and the movement on the part of black women for total emancipation. While there are certain comparisons that one can make, simply because we both live under the same exploitative system, there are certain differences, some of which are quite basic.

The white women's movement is far from being monolithic. Any white group that does not have an anti-imperialist and anti-racist ideology has absolutely nothing in common with the black women's struggle. Are white women asking to be equal to white men in their pernicious treatment of third world peoples? What assurances have black women that white women will be any less racist and exploitative if they had the power and were in a position to do so? These are serious questions that the white women's liberation movement has failed to address itself to.

Black people are engaged in a life and death struggle with the oppressive forces of this country and the main emphasis of black women must be to combat the capitalist, racist exploitation of black people. While it is true that male chauvinism has become institution-alized in american society, one must always look for the main enemy … the fundamental cause of the female condition. In fact, some groups come to the incorrect conclusion that their oppression is due simply to male chauvinism. They therefore, have an extremely anti-male tone to their dissertations.

Another major differentiation is that the white women's libera-tion movement is basically middle class. Very few of these women suffer the extreme economic exploitation that most black women are subjected to day by day. If they find housework degrading and dehu-manizing, they are financially able to buy their freedom—usually by hiring a black maid. The economic and social realities of the black woman's life are the most crucial for us. It is not an intellectual perse-cution alone; the movement is not a psychological outburst for us; it is tangible; we can taste it in all our endeavors. We as black women have got to deal with the problems that the black masses deal with, for our problems in reality are one and the same.

If the white groups do not realize that they are in fact, fighting capitalism and racism, we do not have common bonds. If they do not realize that the reasons for their condition lie in a debilitating economic and social system, and not simply that men get a vicari-ous pleasure out of "consuming their bodies for exploitative reasons," (This kind of reasoning seems to be quite prevalent in certain white women's groups) then we cannot unite with them around common grievances or even discuss these groups in a serious manner, because they're completely irrelevant to black women in particular or to the black struggle in general.

THE NEW WORLD

The black community and black women especially, must begin raising questions about the kind of society we wish to see estab-lished. We must note the ways in which capitalism oppresses us and then move to create institutions that will eliminate these destructive influences.

The new world that we are struggling to create must destroy oppression of any type. The value of this new system will be determined by the status of those persons who are presently most oppressed—the low man on the totem pole. Unless women in any enslaved nation are completely liberated, the change cannot really be called a revolution. If the black woman has to retreat to the position she occupied before the armed struggle, the whole movement and the whole struggle will have retreated in terms of truly freeing the colonized population.

A people's revolution that engages the participation of every member of the community, including men, and women, brings about a certain transformation in the participants as a result of this participation. Once you have caught a glimpse of freedom or tasted a bit of self-determination, you can't go back to old routines that were established under a racist, capitalist regime. We must begin to understand that a revolution entails not only the willingness to lay our lives on the firing line and get killed. In some ways, this is an easy commitment to make. To die for the revolution is a one-shot deal; to live for the revolution means taking on the more difficult commitment of changing our day-to-day life patterns.

This will mean changing the traditional routines that we have established as a result of living in a totally corrupting society. It means changing how you relate to your wife, your husband, your parents and your coworkers. If we are going to liberate ourselves as a people, it must be recognized that black women have very specific problems that have to be spoken to. We must be liberated along with the rest of the population. We cannot wait to start working on those problems until that great day in the future when the revolution somehow miraculously, is accomplished.

To assign women the role of housekeeper and mother while men go forth into battle is a highly questionable doctrine for a revolutionary to profess. Each individual must develop a high political consciousness in order to understand how this system enslaves us all and what actions we must take to bring about its total destruction. Those who consider themselves to be revolutionary must begin to deal with other revolutionaries as equals. And so far as I know, revolutionaries are not determined by sex.

Old people, young people, men and women must take part in the struggle. To relegate women to purely supportive roles or to simply cultural considerations is dangerous doctrine to project. Unless black men who are preparing themselves for armed struggle understand that the society which we are trying to create is one in which the oppression of ALL MEMBERS of that society is eliminated, then the revolution will have failed in its avowed purpose.

Given the mutual commitment of black men and black women alike to the liberation of our people and other oppressed peoples around the world, the total involvement of each individual is necessary. A revolutionary has the responsibility of not only toppling those that are now in a position of power, but more importantly, the responsibility of creating new institutions that will eliminate all forms of oppression for all people. We must begin to re-write our understanding of traditional personal relationships between man and woman.

All the resources that the black community can muster up must be channeled into the struggle. Black women must take an active part in bringing about the kind of world where our children, our loved ones, and each citizen can grow up and live as decent human beings, free from the pressures of racism and capitalist exploitation.

The Sisters Reply

1968

Patricia Haden, Sue Rudolph, Joyce Hoyt, Rita Van Lew, Catherine Hoyt, and Patricia Robinson

September 11, 1968

Dear Brothers:

Poor black sisters decide for themselves whether to have a baby or not to have a baby. If we take the pills or practise birth control in other ways, it's because of poor black men.

Now here's how it is. Poor black men won't support their families, won't stick by their women—all they think about is the street, dope and liquor, women, a piece of ass, and their cars. That's all that counts. Poor black women would be fools to sit up in the house with a whole lot of children and eventually go crazy, sick, heartbroken, no place to go, no sign of affection—nothing. Middle class white men have always done this to their women—only more sophisticated like.

So when whitey put out the pill and poor black sisters spread the word, we saw how simple it was not to be a fool for men any more (politically we would say men could no longer exploit us sexually or for money and leave the babies with us to bring up). That was the first step in our waking up!

Black women have always been told by black men that we were black, ugly, evil, birches and whores—in other words, we were the real niggers in this society—oppressed by whites, male and female, and the black man, too.

Now a lot of the black brothers are into a new bag. Black women are being asked by militant black brothers not to practise birth control because it is a form of whitey committing genocide on black people. Well, true enough, but it takes two to practise genocide and black women are able to decide for themselves, just like poor people all over the world, whether they will submit to genocide. For us, birth control is freedom to fight genocide of black women and children.

Like the Vietnamese have decided to fight genocide, the South American poor are beginning to fight back, and the African poor will fight back, too. Poor black women in the U.S. have to fight back out of our own experience of oppression. Having too many babies stops us from supporting our children, teaching them the truth or stopping the brainwashing as you say, and fighting black men who still want to use and exploit us.

But we don't think you are going to understand us because you are a bunch of little middle class people and we are poor black women. The middle class never understands the poor because they always need to use them as you want to use poor black women's children to gain power for yourself. You'll run the black community with your kind of black power—you on top!

Mt. Vernon, N. Y.

# 36

The Feminist Manifesto

1907

He-Yin Zhen

Men and women have been unequal in this world for a very long time. In India, widows immolate themselves to sacrifice their lives for men; in Japan, women prostrate themselves in the service of men. In Europe and America, even though people practice monogamy and thereby proclaim equality, women are rarely able to partake in politics or vote. So, is there any substance to their "equal rights"? When we look back at China, our men practically treat women as subhuman beings. In ancient times, after a tribe defeated another group, they [the tribesmen] would truss up the women, bind up their bodies with pillories, and take them as concubines. This is how men became masters and women slaves. That period can rightly be called the age of [men's] plundering of women. In due time, since stealing other people's women was likely to induce conflicts, people developed the custom of sending deerskin as an engagement "gift." The ancient marriage rites that mandated the groom's family deliver betrothal gifts to the bride's side are remnants of this earlier kind of "property-marriage."[1]

---

1 Tr: Two kinds of gifts are involved, conveyed in two distinct stages: *na cai* and *na zheng* of the betrothal ceremony. As explained in the Confucian classic *Book of Rites* (in "The Meaning of Marriage"): "The ceremony of marriage was intended to be a bond of love between two families of different surnames, with a view, in its retrospective character, to secure the services in the ancestral temple, and in its prospective character, to secure the continuance of the family line. Therefore the superior men set a great value upon it. Hence, in regard to the various introductory ceremonies—the proposal with its accompanying gift (*na cai*), the inquiries about the lady's name, the intimation of the approving divination, the receiving of the special offerings (*na zheng*), and the request to fix the day—these all were received by the principal party on the lady's side." A version of these rites is still being practiced in China today. Translation adapted from James Legge, *The Li Ki (The Book of Rites)*, http://ctext/org/liji/hun-yi.

Women were clearly regarded as a form of male property. Men are human, but women are merely chattel. That period can be called the age of [men's] trading of women. From these two root causes, inequality between men and women became entrenched. The specific forms this inequality has taken can be traced from the four institutions from the past.

The first is inequality in marriage. In ancient times, the more respected a man's position in society, the more wives he had. For example, during the Yin [Shang] dynasty (16th–11th century b.c.e.), the Son of Heaven could marry twelve women; his marquises, nine; high-ranking aristocrats, three; other titled men, two. During the Zhou dynasty (1046–256 b.c.e.), the Son of Heaven had one queen, three helpmates, nine consorts, twenty-seven women of family, and eighty-one ladies of honor. These constituted his wife and concubines.[2] Does this not indicate that in effect over one hundred women were married to one man? Since then, there have been no limits placed on the number of imperial concubines the emperor might retain. Honorable and illustrious families especially hoarded a lot of concubines. This is the first aspect of male-female inequality.

The second is inequality in status between husband and wife. Since men managed to expand their power, they became all the more vigilant against women. They invented the motto, "Once a woman becomes a man's wife, she remains so for life."[3] A woman is thus allowed to serve only one husband. What is more: "The husband is high as the wife is low; the husband is to heaven as the wife is to earth. The wife cannot do without her husband as the earth cannot do without Heaven."[4] As a result, a woman follows her husband's noble rank in life, and she takes her husband's family name, and she posthumously receives her husband's promotion to a higher rank. Women are made into men's subsidiaries. Song dynasty scholars followed this reasoning when they spoke of "shoring up the yang [male] and diminishing the yin [female]." This is the second aspect of male-female inequality.

The third is inequality in work and responsibility. The character for "woman" (fu 婦) is glossed as fu 服, or "to serve." The "woman" character is composed of a woman holding a broom. The Book of Rites ("Quli") makes it clear: "In presenting a daughter for the harem

---

2 Tr: *Book of Rites*, cf "Quli"; "Hunyi." Translation of the titles adapted from Legge's.
3 *Book of Rites.*
4 *White Tiger Discourse* (Baihu Tong).

of the ruler of a state, it is said, 'This is to complete the providers of your spirits and sauces'; for that of a great officer, 'This is to complete the number of those who sprinkle and sweep for you.'"[5] It seems, in this way, ancient women considered serving and obeying to be their obligation. Furthermore, men concocted the teaching that women should not step out of the inner quarters so as to deprive them of their freedom. From then on, women did not have responsibilities aside from managing the household; being educated and talented was deprecated; [as a consequence,] they have taken being servile to be a natural state. This is the third aspect of male-female inequality.

The fourth is inequality in the system of rites. When a wife dies, the husband observes mourning for only one year, but a widow must mourn her husband for three years, and in the coarsest attire (unhemmed sackcloth). And she is to extend the same severity in mourning her husband's parents. But when she mourns her natal parents, she observes rites of the lesser grade (of one year and wearing sackcloth with even edges).[6] [The Confucian classic *Great Learning* says,] "It never has been the case that what was of great importance has been slightly cared for, and what was of slight importance has been greatly cared for."[7] But the mourning rites do exactly that! Even worse is that in ancient times, a daughter's mourning rites for her mother would be downgraded from three years to one if her father was still alive. This was most egregious. This, then, is the fourth aspect of male-female inequality.

Even from this cursory review it becomes very clear how men oppress and subjugate women. It is not hard to fathom why men would

---

5 Tr: Adapted from Legge's translation, http://ctext.org/liji/qu-li-ii.

6 Tr: The funerary and mourning rites, prescribed in the Confucian classic *Book of Rites*, constituted a major means of regulating and substantiating social and gender hierarchy according to the principle of patrilineal descent. There are five "mourning grades" varying in duration and attire. The most severe is *zhan cui* 斬衰 (three years; coarsest sackcloth with unhemmed edges). In ancient times it was mandated for a son mourning his father, a minister mourning his prince, and a wife for her husband. In Ming-Qing times (1368–1911 c.e.), a daughter-in-law also observed the most severe rite for her parents-in-law, as stated by He-Yin Zhen. Next in severity and importance is *zi cui* 齊衰 (three months, one year, or three years; coarse sackcloth with even or hemmed edges). A son was to observe three years of mourning for his mother if his father predeceased her, but only for one year if his father is alive. And so on. Also see "On the Revenge of Women," part 1 … where He-Yin Zhen gives a more extended account of the gendered nature of these rituals.

7 Tr: Adapted from Legge's translation, http://ctext.org/liji/da-xue. The "Great Learning" (Da xue), a part of the *Book of Rites*, was elevated to be a stand-alone classic.

want to bully women; but why, one might ask, are women so willing to submit? Could it be that the power of social customs and the teachings of pedantic scholars have come to bind and restrain women? Let me put it plainly so that all my companions in womanhood understand: men are the archenemy of women. As long as women fail to be men's equals, anger and sorrow will never be requited. Therefore, let me spell out all the things that women need to strive for one by one:

- The first is monogamous marriage. If a man has more than one wife, keeps concubines or mistresses, or is predisposed to whoring, then his wife can use the harshest laws to restrain him, so much so that he would die by women's hands. If a woman willingly serves a husband with multiple wives, the entire womenfolk would rise up against her. If a man only has one wife, but his wife has extramarital affairs, both men and women should rise up against her.

- The second is that after a woman marries, she should not take her husband's surname. Even if she retains her maiden name, it is still unfair because it is her father's surname but not her mother's. Therefore, women like us who are living in the present age should fashion our surnames from both the father's and the mother's [surnames]. After we overthrow the Manchus, neither men nor women should keep a surname. That would be the principle of supreme justice.

- The third is that parents should value sons and daughters equally. Daughters are no different from sons, and a daughter's offspring are full-fledged grandchildren. This way the entrenched custom of slighting daughters and valuing sons would end.

- The fourth is that soon after birth, daughters and sons should be raised without discrimination. As they grow, they should receive equal education. As grownups, they shoulder equal responsibilities. All affairs in society should be women's business.

- The fifth is that if a couple fails to get along after marriage, the man and wife can separate. Until then, neither should take up with someone else lest they violate the first goal above.

- The sixth is that first-time grooms should be paired with first-time brides. When bereaved, a man can remarry, but only to a woman who has married before. Likewise, a bereaved wife can remarry, but only to a man who has married before. If a first-time bride assents to marrying a man who has married before, womenfolk should rise to censure her.

- The seventh is to abolish all the brothels in the world and let go all the prostitutes under the sun to clean up the environment of lasciviousness.

We champion these seven goals, not because we women want to snatch power and rights into our hands, but because Heaven endows natural rights equally to men and women. Since men and women are both human, the lack of equality is unjust and contradicts the principles of nature; ultimately, what women strive for should not stop short of supreme justice for all.

But people may counter my suggestions by raising three common objections. The first is that women endure the toil of childbirth and afterward have to exhaust themselves in raising the children; thus a woman's work and responsibilities are by nature different from men's. Those who think so do not understand that what I am proposing is not merely a women's revolution but a complete social revolution. The women's revolution is but one aspect of the social revolution. After the social revolution is accomplished, after birth, all children would be raised in public child care facilities; accordingly, mothers would no longer have to raise their children by themselves. Once relieved of this task, women could assume responsibilities equal to men's.

The second objection may be that since there are more women than men in the world, it is unfair to mandate that one person can take only one spouse. But those who object thus do not know that women are more plentiful because they never fight wars. Active military duty is without fail a male prerogative; therefore their numbers dwindle by the day. Now, as women, would we rather not unleash destruction and die on the battlefield for posthumous honor than be oppressed to death as obedient concubines? If women indeed carried out the [social] revolution, after the violence ended, the number of women would certainly be the same as the number of men.[8]

The third argument one often hears is that since men have many wives, why shouldn't women have multiple husbands as a form of

---

8 Tr: He-Yin Zhen is not necessarily issuing a call to arms but is suggesting that revolutions are violent and women's participation in the revolution would cull the female population into balance with the male population. For He-Yin Zhen's pacifist views, see her essay "On Feminist Antimilitarism."

redress? The misunderstanding here is that we women desire equality and will get it, not by [the passive means of] reform or boycotting, but by the application of brute force to coerce men to make us equal. But polygyny is a major male transgression. If women choose to emulate them, how are we to defend ourselves when men accuse us [of transgressing]? A woman who has multiple husbands is virtually a prostitute. Those women who are now advocating multiple husbands use the pretext of resisting men, but their real motivation is to give full rein to their personal lust, following the path of prostitutes. These women are traitors to womanhood.

In sum, men and women are both human. By [saying] "men" (*nanxing*) and "women" (*nüxing*) we are not speaking of "nature," as each is but the outcome of differing social customs and education. If sons and daughters are treated equally, raised and educated in the same manner, then the responsibilities assumed by men and women will surely become equal. When that happens, the nouns "men" and "women" would no longer be necessary. This is ultimately the "equality of men and women" of which we speak.

People in China have recently come to believe that for women to reach this goal, they must apply themselves to herald—even ahead of men—racial, political, economic, and other revolutions; they must not allow themselves to lag behind men again. According to their view, the revolution between men and women should proceed side by side with racial, political, and economic revolutions. [They believe] if they succeeded, women could establish the first real regime of "women's rights" in the world. If they failed, women would perish *with* men, never to be subjugated by them again. I think this is a narrow-minded view. Whether people agree with me or condemn me is not my concern here.[9]

---

9 Tr: He-Yin Zhen's expression "*zhiwo zuiwo*" connotes her self-image as the moral judge of history. The expression comes from the Confucian classic *Mencius* and is supposed to be uttered by Confucius himself: "Again the world fell into decay, and the principles faded away. Perverse speakings and oppressive deeds waxed rife again. There were instances of ministers who murdered their sovereigns, and of sons who murdered their fathers. Confucius was afraid and made the *Spring and Autumn*. What the *Spring and Autumn* contains are matters proper to the sovereign. On this account Confucius said, 'Yes! It is the Spring and Autumn that will make people know me, and it is the *Spring and Autumn* that will make them condemn me.'" Adapted from Legge's translation, http://ctext.org/mengzi/teng-wen-gong-ii/zh?en=on.

37 Zapatista Women's Revolutionary Laws

1994

Zapatista Army of National Liberation (Zapatistas)

In their just fight for the liberation of our people, the EZLN incorporates women in the revolutionary struggle regardless of their race, creed, color or political affiliation, requiring only that they meet the demands of the exploited people and that they commit to the laws and regulations of the revolution. As well as, taking account of the situation of the woman worker in Mexico, the revolution incorporates their just demands of equality and justice in the following Women's Revolutionary Law.

First—Women, regardless of their race, creed, color or political affiliation, have the right to participate in the revolutionary struggle in any way that their desire and capacity determine.

Second—Women have the right to work and receive a just salary.

Third—Women have the right to decide the number of children they have and care for.

Fourth—Women have the right to participate in the matters of the community and have charge if they are free and democratically elected.

Fifth—Women and their children have the right to Primary Attention in their health and nutrition.

Sixth—Women have the right to education.

Seventh—Women have the right to choose their partner and are not obliged to enter into marriage.

Eighth—Women have the right to be free of violence from both relatives and strangers. Rape and attempted rape will be severely punished.

Ninth—Women will be able to occupy positions of leadership in the organization and hold military ranks in the revolutionary armed forces.

Tenth—Women will have all the rights and obligations which the revolutionary laws and regulations give.

The Black Movement and Women's Liberation

1970

Linda La Rue

Let us first discuss what common literature addresses as the "common oppression" of blacks and women. This is a tasty abstraction designed purposely or inadvertently to draw validity and seriousness to the women's movement through a universality of plight. Every movement worth its "revolutionary salt" makes these headliner generalities about "common oppression" with others—but let us state unequivocally that, with few exceptions, the American white woman has had a better opportunity to live a free and fulfilling life, both mentally and physically, than any other group in the United States, with the exception of her white husband. Thus, any attempt to analogize black oppression with the plight of the American white woman has the validity of comparing the neck of a hanging man with the hands of an amateur mountain climber with rope burns.

"Common oppression" is fine for rhetoric, but it does not reflect the actual distance between the oppression of the black man and woman who are unemployed, and the "oppression" of the American white woman who is "sick and tired" of *Playboy* fold-outs, or Christian Dior lowering hemlines or adding ruffles, or of Miss Clairol telling her that blondes have more fun.

Is there any logical comparison between the oppression of the black woman on welfare who has difficulty feeding her children and the discontent of the suburban mother who has the luxury to protest the washing of the dishes on which her family's full meal was consumed.

The surge of "common oppression" rhetoric and propaganda may lure the unsuspecting into an intellectual alliance with the goals of women's liberation, but it is not a wise alliance. It is not that women ought not to be liberated from the shackles of their present unfulfillment, but the depth, the extent, the intensity, the importance—indeed, the suffering and depravity of the *real* oppression blacks have experienced—can only be minimized in an alliance with women who heretofore suffered little more than boredom, genteel repression, and dishpan hands.

For all the similarities and analogies drawn between the liberation of women and the liberation of blacks, the point remains that when white women received their voting rights, most blacks, male and female, were systematically disenfranchised and had been that way since Reconstruction. And in 1970, when women's right of franchise is rarely questioned, it is still a less than common occurrence for blacks to vote in some areas of the South.

Tasteless analogies like abortion for oppressed middle class and poor women idealistically assert that all women have the right to decide if and when they want children, and thus fail to catch the flavor of the actual circumstances. Actual circumstances boil down to middle class women deciding when it is convenient to have children, while poor women decide the prudence of bringing into a world of already scarce resources, another mouth to feed. Neither their motives nor their objectives are the same. But current literature leads one to lumping the decisions of these two women under one generalization, when in fact the difference between the plights of these two women is as clear as the difference between being hungry and out of work, and skipping lunch and taking a day off.

If we are realistically candid with ourselves, and accept the fact that despite our beloved rhetoric of Pan-Africanism, our vision of third world liberation, and perhaps our dream of a world state of multiracial humanism, most blacks and a good many who generally exempt themselves from categories, still want the proverbial "piece of cake." American values are difficult to discard for, unlike what more militant "brothers" would have us believe, Americanism does not end with the adoption of Afro hairstyles on pregnant women covered in long African robes.

Indeed, the fact that the independent black capitalism demonstrated by the black Muslims, and illustrated in Nixon's speeches, appeared for many blacks as the way out of the ghetto into the light, lends a truthful vengeance to the maxim that perhaps blacks are

nothing more than black anglo-saxons. Upon the rebirth of the liberation struggle in the sixties, a whole genre of "women's place" advocates
immediately relegated black women to home and babies, which is
almost as ugly an expression of black anglo-saxonism as is Nixon's
concept of "black capitalism."

The study of many developing areas and countries reflects at least
an attempt to allow freedom of education and opportunity to women.
Yet, black Americans have not adopted developing area's "new role"
paradigm, but rather the Puritan-American status of "home and
babies," which is advocated by the capitalist Muslims. This reflects
either ingrained Americanism or the lack of the simplest imagination.

Several weeks ago, women's lib advocates demanded that a local
women's magazine be "manned" by a woman editor. Other segments
of the women's movement have carried on a smaller campaign in
industry and business.

If white women have heretofore remained silent while white men
maintained the better position and monopolized the opportunities by
excluding blacks, can we really expect that white women, when put in
direct competition for employment, will be any more open-minded
than their male counterparts when it comes to the hiring of black
males and females in the same positions for which they are competing? From the standpoint of previous American social interaction, it
does not seem logical that white females will not be tempted to take
advantage of the fact that they are white, in an economy that favors
whites. It is entirely possible that women's liberation has developed a
sudden attachment to the black liberation movement as ploy to share
the attention that it has taken blacks 400 years to generate. In short,
it can be argued that women's liberation not only attached itself to
the black movement, but did so with only marginal concern for black
women and black liberation, and functional concern for the rights of
white women.

The industrial demands of two world wars temporarily offset the
racial limitations to mobility and allowed the possibility of blacks
entering industry, as an important labor force, to be actualized.
Similarly, women have benefited from an expanded science and indus-
trialization. Their biological limitation, successfully curbed by the pill
and by automation, which makes stressing physical labor more the
exception than the rule, has created an impressively large and available
labor force of women.

The black labor force, never fully employed and always representing a substantial percentage of the unemployed in the American economy, will now be driven into greater unemployment as white women converge at every level on an already dwindling job market.

Ideally, we chanced to think of women's liberation as a promising beginning of the "oppressed rising everywhere" in the typically Marxian fashion that many blacks seem drawn to. Instead, the spectre of racism and inadequate education, job discrimination, and even greater unequal opportunity will be, more than ever before, a function of neither maleness nor femaleness, but blackness.

This discussion has been primarily to ward off any unintelligent alliance of black people with white women in this new liberation movement. Rhetoric and anathema hurled at the right industrial complex, idealism which speaks of a final humanism, and denunciations of the system which makes competition a fact of life, do not mean that women's liberation has as its goal anyone else's liberation except its own.

It is time that definitions be made clear. Blacks are *oppressed*, and that means unreasonably burdened, unjustly, severely, rigorously, cruelly and harshly fettered by white authority. White women, on the other hand, are only *suppressed*, and that means checked, restrained, excluded from conscious and overt activity. And there is a difference.

For some, the dangers of an unintelligent alliance with women's liberation will suggest female suppression as the only way to protect against a new economic threat. For others, a greater answer is needed, and required, before women's liberation can be seen in perspective.

To say that black women must be freed before the black movement can attain full revolutionary consciousness, is meaningless because of its malleability. To say that black women must be freed from the unsatisfactory male-female role relationship which we adopted from whites as the paradigm of the good family, has more meaning because it indicates the incompatibility of the white role models with the goal of black liberation. If there is anything to be learned from the current women's lib agitation, it is that roles are not ascribed and inherent, but adopted and interchangeable in every respect except pregnancy, breastfeeding and the system generally employed to bring the two former into existence.

Role integration, which I will elaborate upon as the goal and strength of the black family, is substantially different from the role "usurpation" of men by women. The fact that the roles of man and woman are deemed in American society as natural and divine, leads to false ego attachments to these roles. During slavery and following Reconstruction, black men felt inferior for a great number of reasons, among them that they were unable to work in positions comparable to the ones to which black women were assigned. With these positions often went fringe benefits of extra food, clothes, and perhaps elementary reading and writing skills. Black women were in turn jealous of white women, and felt inadequate and inferior because paraded in front of them constantly, was the white woman of luxury who had no need for work, who could, as Sojourner Truth pointed out, "be helped into carriages, and lifted over ditches, and ... have the best place everywhere."

The resulting "respect" for women and the acceptance of the dominating role for men, encouraged the myth of the immutability of these roles. The term "matriarchy" Frazier employed and Moynihan exploited, was used to indicate a dastardly, unnatural role alteration which could be blamed for inequality of opportunity, discrimination in hiring and sundry other ills. It was as if "matriarchy" was transgression of divine law or natural law, and thus would be punished until the proper hierarchy of man over woman was restored.

Black people have an obligation, as do white women, to recognize that the designation of "mother-head" and "father-head" does not imply inferiority of one and superiority of the other. They are merely arbitrary role distinctions which vary from culture to culture and circumstance to circumstance.

Thus to quip, as it has been popularly done, that the only place in the black movement for black women, is prone, is actually supporting a white role ideal, and it is neither a compliment to men or women to advocate such sexual capitalism or sexual colonialism.

It seems incongruous that the black movement has sanctioned the revolutionary involvement of women in the Algerian revolution, even though its revolutionary circumstances modified and often alternated the common role models, but have been duped into hating even their own slave grandmothers who, in not so admirable yet equally frightening and demanding circumstances, also modified and altered the common role models of the black family. Fanon wrote in glorious terms about this role change:

> The unveiled Algerian women, who assumed an increasingly
> important place in revolutionary action, developed her personality,
> discovered the exalting realm of responsibility... This woman who,
> in the avenues of Algiers or of Constantine, would carry the gre-
> nades of the submachine gun charges, the women who tomorrow
> would be outraged, violated, tortured, could not put herself back
> into her former state of mind, and relive her behavior of the past ...[1]

Can it not be said that in slavery black women assumed an increasingly important place in the survival action and thus developed their
personalities and sense of responsibility? And after being outraged,
violated and tortured, could she be expected to put herself back into
her former state of mind and relive her behavior of the past?

The crux of this argument is essentially that blacks, since slavery
and through their entire existence in America, have also been living
in revolutionary circumstances and under revolutionary pressures.
Simply because the black liberation struggle has taken 400 years to
come to fruition does not mean that it is not every bit as dangerous or
psychologically exhausting as the Algerian struggle. Any revolution
calls upon the best in both its men and women. This is why Moynihan's statements that "matriarchy is a root *cause* of black problems"
is as unfounded as it is inane. He does not recognize the liberation
struggle and the demands that it has made upon the black family.

How unfortunate that blacks and whites have allowed the most
trying and bitter experience in the history of black people to be interpreted as the beginning of an "unashamed plot" to usurp the very
manhood of black men. But the myth was perpetuated, and thus what
brought the alternation if roles in Algeria was distorted and systematically employed to separate black men and women in America.

> Black women take kindness for weakness. Leave them the least little
> opening and they will put you on the cross... It would be like trying
> to pamper a cobra ...[2]

Unless we realize how thoroughly the American value of male superiority and female inferiority has permeated our relationships with each

---

1 Frantz Fanon, *A Dying Colonialism*, New York: Grove Press, 1965, 107.
2 Eldridge Cleaver, *Soul On Ice*, New York: McGraw Hill, 1968, 158.

other, we can never appreciate the role it plays in perpetuating racism and keeping black people divided.

Most, but not all, American relationships are based on some type of "exclusive competition of the superior, and the exclusive competition of the inferior." This means essentially that the poor, the uneducated, the deprived and the minorities of the aforementioned groups, compete among themselves for the same scarce resources and inferior opportunities, while the privileged, middle-class, educated, and select white minorities, compete with each other for rather plentiful resources and superior opportunities for prestige and power. Competition among groups is rare, due to the fact that elements who qualify are almost invariably absorbed to some extent (note the black middle-class) by the group to which they seek entry. We may well understand that there is only one equal relationship between man and woman, black and white, in America, and this equality is based on whether or not you can force your way into qualifying for the same resources.

But instead of attempting to modify this competitive definition within the black movement, many black males have affirmed it as a way of maintaining the closure of male monopolization of scare benefits and making the "dominion of males" impenetrable to black females. This is, of course, very much the American way of exploitation.

The order of logic which makes it possible to pronounce, as did Dr. Robert Staples, that "black women cannot be qua women until all blacks attain their liberation,"[3] maintains, whether purposely or not, that black women will be able to separate their femaleness from their blackness and thus they would be able to be free as blacks, if not free as women; or, finally that the freedom of black women and men, and the freedom of black people as a whole, are not one and the same.

Only with the concept of role integration can we hope to rise above the petty demarcations of human freedom that America is noted for, and that are unfortunately inherent in Dr. Staples' remark. Role integration is the realization that:

- ego attachments to particular activities or traits must be abolished as a method of determining malehood and femalehood; that instead, ego attachments must be distributed to a wider

---

3 Robert Staples, "The Myth of the Black Matriarchy," *The Black Scholar*, Jan.-Feb. 1970, 16.

variety of tasks and traits in order to weaken the power of one activity in determining self-worth, and

- the flexibility of a people in effecting role alternation and role integration has been a historically proven asset to the survival of any people—witness Israel, China and Algeria.

Thus, the unwitting adoption and the knowing perpetuation of this American value reflects three inter-related situations:

- black people's growing sense of security and well-being, and their failure to recognize the expanse of black problems;
- black people's over-identification with the dominant group, even though the survival of blacks in America is not assured, and
- black people's belief in the myth of "matriarchy" and their subsequent rejection of role integration as unnatural and unnecessary.

While the rhetoric of black power and the advocates of cultural nationalism laud black people for their ability to struggle under oppressive odds, they simultaneously seek to strip away or incapacitate the phenomenon of role integration—the very means by which blacks were able to survive! They seek to replace it with a weak, intractable role separation which would completely sap the strength of the black movement because it would inhibit the mobilization of both women and men. It was this ability to mobilize black men and black women that guaranteed survival during slavery.

The strength of role integration is sorely overlooked as blacks throw away the hot comb, the bleach cream, the lye, and yet insist on maintaining the worst of American vales by placing the strength of black women in the traction of the white female status.

I would think black men would want a better status for their sister black women; indeed, black women would want a better status for themselves, rather than a warmed-over throne of women's inferiority, which white women are beginning to abandon.

Though most white women's lib advocates fail to realize the possibility, their subsequent liberation may spell a strengthening of the status quo values from which they sought liberation. Since more and more women will be participating in the decision making process, those few women participating in the "struggle" will be outnumbered by the more traditional middle class women. This means that the traditional women will be in a position to take advantage of new opportunities which radical women's liberation has struggled to win. Voting studies now reflect that the traditional women, middle class and above, tend to vote the same way as their husbands. Because blacks have dealt with these husbands in the effort to secure jobs, housing and education, it does not seem likely that blacks will gain significantly from the open mobility of less tolerant women whose viewpoints differ little from those of their husbands.

If white radical thought has called upon the strength of all women to take a position of responsibility and power, can blacks afford to relegate black women to "home and babies" while white women reinforce the status quo? The cry of black women's liberation is a cry against chaining a very much needed labor force and agitating force to a role that once belonged to impotent, apolitical white women. Blacks speak lovingly of the vanguard and the importance of women in the struggle, and yet fail to recognize that women have been assigned a new place, based on white ascribed characteristics of women, rather than on their actual potential. The black movement needs its women in a position of struggle, not prone. The struggle blacks face is not taking place between knives and forks, at the washboard, or in the diaper pail. It is taking place on the labor market, at the polls, in the government, in the protection of black communities, in local neighborhood power struggles, in housing and in education.

Can blacks afford to be so unobservant of current events as to send their women to fight a non-existent battle in a dishpan? Even now, the black adoption of white values has begun to show its effects on black women in distinctive ways. The black liberation movements has created a politicized, unliberated copy of white womanhood. Black women who participated in the struggle have failed to recognize, for the most part, the unique contradiction between renunciation of capitalistic competition and the acceptance of sexual colonialism. The failure of the black movement to resolve and deal with this dilemma has perpetuated the following attitudes in American politicized black women:

- The belief in the myth of matriarchy. The black woman has been made to feel ashamed of her strength, and so to redeem herself she has adopted from whites the belief that the superiority and dominance of the male is the most "natural" and "normal" relationship. She consequently believes that black women ought to be suppressed in order to attain that "natural balance."

- Because the white woman's role has been held up as an example to all black women, many black women feel inadequate and so ardently compete in "femininity" with white females for black males' attention. She further competes with black females in an attempt to be the "blackest and the most feminine," thereby, the more superior to her fellow black sisters in appealing to black politicized men. She competes also with the apolitical black female in an attempt to keep black males from "regressing" back to females whom she feels had had more "practice" in the traditional role of white woman than has she.

- Finally, she emphasizes the traditional roles of women, such as housekeeping, children, supportive roles, and self-maintenance, but she politicizes these roles by calling them the role of black women. She then adopts the attitude that her job and her life is to have children which can be used in the vanguard of the black struggle.

Black women, as the song "Black Pearl" relates, have been put up where they belong, but by American standards. Is it so inconceivable that the American value of respect and human relationships is distorted? It has taken the birth of women's liberation to bring the black movement back to its senses.

The black woman is demanding a new set of female definitions and a recognition of herself as a citizen, companion and confidant, not a matriarchal villain or a step stool baby-maker. Role integration advocates the complementary recognition of man and woman, not the competitive recognition of same.

The recent, unabated controversy over the use of birth control in the black community of grave importance here. Black people, even the "most liberated of mind," are still infused with ascribed inferiority of females and the natural superiority of males. These same values foster the idea of "good blood" in children. If, indeed there can be any black liberation, it must start with the recognition of contradictions like the following.

It gives a great many black males pride to speak, as Dr. Robert Staples does, of "... the role of the black woman in the liberation struggle is an important one and cannot be forgotten. From her womb have come the revolutionary warriors of our time."[4]

How many potential revolutionary warriors stand abandoned in orphanages while blacks rhetorize disdain for birth control as a "trick of the man" to halt the growth of the black population? Why are there not more revolutionary couples adopting black children? Could it be that the American concept of bastard, which is equivalent to inferior in our society, reflects black anglo-saxonism? Do blacks, like whites, discriminate against black babies because they do not represent "our own personal" image? Or do blacks, like the most racist of whites, require that a child be of their blood before they can love that child or feed it? Does the vanguard, of which Dr. Staples so reverently speaks, recognize the existence of the term "bastard"?

Someone once suggested that the word "bastard" be deleted from the values of black people. Would it not be more revolutionary for blacks to advocate a five-year moratorium on black births until every black baby in an American orphanage was adopted by one or more black parents? Then blacks could really have a valid reason for continuing to give birth. Children would mean more than simply a role for black women to play, or fuel for the legendary vanguard. Indeed, blacks would be able to tap the potential of the existing children and could sensibly add more potential to the black struggle for liberation. To do this would be to do something no other civilization, modern of course, has ever done, and blacks would be allowing every black child to have a home and not just a plot in some understaffed children's penal farm.

What makes a healthy black baby in an orphanage different from "our own flesh and blood"? Except for the American value of inferiority-superiority, and the concept of "bastard" that accompanies it, there is nothing "wrong" with the orphaned child save what white society has taught us to perceive.

We can conclude that black women's liberation and black men's liberation is what we mean when we speak of the liberation of black people. I maintain that the true liberation of black people depends on their rejection of the inferiority of their women, the rejection of competition as the only viable relationship between men, and their re-affirmation of respect for general human potential in whatever form, man, child or woman, it is conceived.

---

4 Ibid.

39 Not Murdered, Not Missing: Rebelling against Colonial Gender Violence

2014

Leanne Betasamosake Simpson

I've learned a tremendous amount over the past months from Loretta Saunders, Bella Laboucan-McLean & all the other Indigenous people that we've had violently ripped away from us in this last little while. Part of me feels shaky to admit this, because intellectually, and even personally I know or I am supposed to know a lot about gender violence. But there are things I don't say in public. There are things I think that I am not brave enough to say because the pain of not being heard, of being betrayed or by appearing weak to my Indigenous friends or colleagues is too much to bear. There are places I only go with other Indigenous comrades who I trust intimately.

That ends here.

It ends here for Loretta, Bella and all of the other brilliant minds and fierce hearts we've lost. It ends here.

This is my rebellion. This is my outrage. This is the beginning of our radical thinking and action.

In the wake of Loretta's death my friends on this blog decided to run a series on gender violence to open up the conversation and to help move it along. Emotions were running high and we felt compelled to act. Our first piece was Tara Williamson's "Don't Be Tricked." It was a very brave piece of writing. It was raw, because we were raw. It was angry, because a lot of us were angry. I could personally identify with every word of Tara's piece, particularly the line "The system and most Canadians don't give a shit about you, how strong and talented you are, how hard you've worked, or where you live. If you are an Indigenous woman, you are a prime target for colonial violence."

This is something I've felt my whole life and never articulated. I've never articulated it because I don't want young Indigenous women and queer youth to know that, I want them to feel hopeful and empowered.

I've never articulated this because I don't want white Canadians to automatically blame Indigenous men for gender violence. I know they will because they've invested a lot of energy into the stereotype of "Indian men" as unfeeling, uncaring, violent savages. They've invested even more energy into pretending that they don't benefit from colonial gender violence perpetuated by the state, in fact they've invested a lot into energy into pretended colonial gender violence perpetuated by the state isn't even a thing. I also don't want Indigenous men to tell me I'm wrong or that this issue doesn't matter, because as much as this is a political issue, this is an intensely painful and personal issue for anyone that has survived gender violence, which if we are honest, is most of us, including Indigenous men. I don't want to have to seek out allies in white feminists, who don't really get it. I want Indigenous men to have my back, even when they feel uncomfortable about what I am saying. And you know what, a few of them did, and that was one of the most amazing feelings I have ever had. They emailed support. They checked in. They listened and encouraged. They re-tweeted, posted, wrote and expressed their outrage.

This is co-resistance.

This is community.

White supremacy, rape culture, and the real and symbolic attack on gender, sexual identity and agency are very powerful tools of colonialism, settler colonialism and capitalism, primarily because they work very efficiently to remove Indigenous peoples from our territories and to prevent reclamation of those territories through mobilization. These forces have the intergenerational staying power to destroy generations of families, as they work to prevent us from intimately connecting to each other. They work to prevent mobilization because communities coping with epidemics of gender violence don't have the physical or emotional capital to organize. They destroy the base of our nations and our political systems because they destroy our relationships to the land and to each other by fostering epidemic levels of anxiety, hopelessness, apathy, distrust and suicide. They work to destroy the fabric of Indigenous nationhoods by attempting to destroy our relationality by making it difficult to from sustainable, strong relationships with each other.

This is why I think it's in all of our best interests to take on gender violence as a core resurgence project, a core decolonization project, a core of any Indigenous mobilization. And by gender violence I don't just mean violence against women, I mean all gender violence.

This begins for me by looking at how gender is conceptualized and actualized within Indigenous thought because it is colonialism that has imposed an artificial gender binary in my nation. This imposed colonial gender binary sets out two very clear genders: male and female and it lays out two very clear sets of rigidly defined roles based on colonial conceptions of femininity and masculinity.

This makes no sense from within Anishinaabeg thought, because first off, we've always had more than two genders in our nation and we've also always practiced a fluidity around gender in general. The rigidity seen in colonial society doesn't make much sense within an Anishinaabeg reality or the reality of any so called "hunting and gathering society."

Anishinaabeg women hunted, trapped, fished, held leadership positions and engaged in warfare, as well as engaged in domestic affairs and looked after children and they were encouraged to show a broad range of emotions and to express their gender and sexuality in a way that was true to their own being, as a matter of both principle and survival. Anishinaabeg men hunted, trapped, fished, held leadership position, engaged in warfare and also knew how to cook, sew and look after children. They were encouraged to show a broad range of emotions, express their gender and sexuality in a way that was true to their own being, as a matter of both principle and survival. This is true for other genders as well. The degree to which individuals engaged in each of these activities depended upon their name, their clan, their extended family, their skill and interest and most importantly individual self-determination or agency. Agency was valued, honoured and respected because it produced a diversity of highly self-sufficient individuals, families and communities. This diversity of highly self-sufficient and self-determining people ensured survival and resilience that enabled the community to withstand difficult circumstances.

Strong communities are born out of individuals being their best selves.

Colonialism recognized this and quickly co-opted Indigenous individuals into colonial gender roles in order to replicate the hetero-patriarchy of colonial society. This causes the power and agency of all of genders to shrink, and those that are farthest away from colonial ideals suffered and continue to be targets of harsh colonial violence.

People also had agency over their sexual and relationship orientations in Anishinaabeg society and this created diversity outside the heteronormative nuclear family. Anytime you hear or read an anthropologist talk about "polygamy" in Indigenous cultures read this as a red flag, because you need a severe form of patriarchy for that to play out the way the anthropologists imagined and in the absence of that, plural marriage or non-monogamy in Indigenous cultures is something far more complex.

There wasn't just agency for adults. Children had a lot of agency. When Chaplain came through my territory he was appalled because the women and children were so far outside of the control of the men that he interpreted this as a bewildered, chaotic, societal disaster, he interpreted us as "savage." I imagine him observing our society and asking from a white European male perspective, how do you exploit women as a commodity in this situation, when they have such agency?

You can't.

Then I imagine the colonizers asking the next logical question: How do you infuse a society with the heteropatriarchy necessary in order to carry out your capitalist dreams when Indigenous men aren't actively engaged in upholding a system designed to exploit women? Well, the introduction of gender violence is one answer. Destroying and then reconstructing sexuality and gender identity is another. Residential schools did an excellent job on both accounts.

Because really what the colonizers have always been trying to figure out is "How do you extract natural resources from the land when the people's whose territory you're on believe that those plant, animal and minerals have both spirit and therefore agency?"

It's a similar answer: You use gender violence to remove Indigenous peoples and their descendants from the land, you remove agency from the plant and animal worlds and you reposition aki (the land) as "natural resources" for the use and betterment of white people. This colonial strategy is clearly working. We also have more than 800 missing and murdered Indigenous women in Canada, a mass incarceration of Indigenous men, and we do not even have statistics about violence against Indigenous Two Spirit, LGBTTQQIA and gender non-conforming people. I think it's not enough to just recognize that violence against women occurs but that it is intrinsically tied to the creation and settlement of Canada. Gender violence is central to our on-going dispossession, occupation and erasure and Indigenous families and communities have always resisted this. We've always fought back and organized against this—our grandparents resisted gender violence, our youth are organizing and resisting gender violence because we have no other option.

Feminist scholar Andrea Smith recently wrote a blog post in response to Eve Ensler's One Billion Rising about what should organizing against gender violence look like. Several of her points resonated with me.

Her post first encourages us to acknowledge that the state is the primary perpetrator of gendered violence in our nations and thus the state cannot be the solution to gendered violence. The state is not our ally. White feminism is not our ally, either because discussing violence against women without discussing gender violence within a colonial context has no meaning for me. Gender violence and murdered and missing Indigenous women are a symptom of settler colonialism, white supremacy and genocide. They are symptoms of the dispossession of Indigenous peoples from our territories.

Some families of missing and murdered Indigenous women want an inquiry. I respect this because Canada must be forced to be accountable for this crisis. Canada must change. Canadians must change their attitudes towards Indigenous peoples and their relationship to us as nations. I also have very little faith that the federal government has the capacity to undertake an inquiry that will bring about the kind of action and change Indigenous peoples are demanding, and to address the root causes of gender violence. The process in British Columbia has been a disaster, and we simply cannot allow an inquiry to be used by the state to neutralize Indigenous dissent, mobilization and protest. The perpetrators of colonial gender violence cannot be in charge of coming up with a strategy to end it because they are the beneficiaries of it. We therefore need a multi-pronged approach to our organizing. If there is an inquiry we have to organize and mobilize through it.

And while it is important for us to come together to honour and remember our missing sisters and their families, I also feel angry about this situation and how violence, both symbolic and real has impacted my own life. Rather than seeking recognition from Canada for this pain and suffering, I feel compelled to use this anger to build nations and communities where violence within our interpersonal relationships is unimaginable.

Communities where we see environmental destruction and contamination as a form of sexualized violence against our communities because toxic chemicals and environmental destruction compromise the integrity of our territories and our bodies.

Communities where we see dismantling settler colonialism as central to ending gender violence because let's remember that gender violence is still a primary strategy used against us in our mobilizations and you can find examples at Oka, at Elsipogtog and in the Idle No More Movement.

We cannot create movements, like Idle No More, where women are in leadership positions and where we also have no plan in place to deal with gender violence in an effective manner. Particularly when we know, from four centuries of experience that gender violence will absolutely be part of the colonial response, and that this violence will not necessarily be perpetrated against women in leadership roles, but the against the most vulnerable women—those that are dealing with multiple sites of oppression.

This realization came crashing down to me during Idle No More when I got a phone call from another woman in the movement asking for help because an Anishinaabekwe had been abducted and sexually assaulted in Thunder Bay. The attack was racially motivated and this woman was targeted in direct relationship to the activism around Idle No More. It became really clear to me really quickly that not only do I personally lack the skills to deal with gender violence but that our community lacks these skills as well. The male leadership in the area was primarily concerned with calling for calm so that the situation didn't spark more violence.

I felt anger and mobilization was the correct response, but my first concern was with this woman and her family, so I called Jessica Danforth and asked for help. The Native Youth Sexual Health Network came through in practical, powerful, and beautiful ways centering on support for the survivor and action on the part of the wider community. This story is in part included in The Winter We Danced: Voices from the Past, the Present and the Idle No More Movement, along with all of the resources Native Youth Sexual Health Network provided us, and we're also donating the royalties from the book to this organization.

This is why youth are so critical to resurgence, because they are teachers and leaders in their own right and because if we are carrying out resurgence properly, each generation should be getting stronger, more grounded and less influenced by colonialism, and this means people like me can learn from them.

This is why resurgence is about bodies and land.

We must build criticality around gender violence in the architecture of our movements. We need to build communities that are committed to ending gender violence and we need real world skills, strategies and plans in place, right now, to deal with the inevitable increase in gender violence that is going to be the colonial response to direct action and ongoing activism. We need trained people on the ground at our protests and our on the land reclamation camps. We need our own alternative systems in place to deal with sexual assault at the community level, systems that are based on our traditions and do not involve state police and the state legal system.

Loretta Saunders wanted an end to gender violence and missing and murdered Indigenous women. I am not murdered. I am not missing. And so I am going to honour her, by continuing her work, and fighting for Indigenous nations and a relationship with Canada that is no longer based on violence, heteropatriarchy and silence. I want to help build Indigenous communities where all genders stand up, speaks out and are committed to both believing and supporting survivors of violence and building our own Indigenous transformative systems of accountability. We simply can no longer rely on or expect the state, the largest perpetrator of gender violence to do this for us.

Loretta Saunders is our tipping point.

40 Manifesto of the Erased: Mujeres, Decolonize El Dios Americano

2015

Crystal Zaragoza

A world where God isn't used as an excuse to be horrible people is what we aim for; a world where "he" doesn't exist as the savior is a world worth living in.

Desde niña, God was someone to be feared and loved. Going to Catechism, giving my body, mind, and soul to this almighty being was the norm. Growing up trying to mold who I was in "his image" was the ultimate goal—not self-love, self-acceptance, cultural pride, education, or having a good future, but being more like "him" was the answer for greatness and success. Believing that an invisible man could see us no matter where we hid, an invisible man knew us so well that he knew the exact number of hair we have on our bodies, and that this invisible man was so selfless he sacrificed his child for "our" sins was completely sane, and that was something to try to embody and love. This Christian theist belief is something to cherish, and hold dear to your heart because it makes you a better person. But, does it really?

No. Déjame decirte porque.

This invisible being that we, as a culture, community, and country are brainwashed to love is the door to hatred. Hatred of one self, one's culture, one's skin color, mujeres, gay mujeres, gay men, trans* men, trans* mujeres, and everything that is not beautiful or normal to the standards of European white men, and it's justified by a white washed "God."

My culture has been stripped away from my people by European Christians believing they were the "saviors" of "savages." When in reality, God and his followers are the savages. According to Merriam

Webster's dictionary, a savage is "not domesticated or under human control." "God" and his followers *are* the savages. They are not domesticated or under human control, not my beautiful genté mexicana. Using God as an excuse to strip beautiful indigenous people of their culture, their rich traditions, their way of existing as a community, their own spirituality, and their own families is an action of savages. God has been used as a way to justify being savages against cultures that don't fall under the white, European, Christian model of perfection.

The white man came to discover mí genté's land. Thank God they did, or else we'd be living on unknown territory.

The white man came to teach mí genté the tongue of his people. Thank God they did, or else we'd have no proper way to communicate.

The white man came to teach mí genté how to dress. Thank God they did, or else we wouldn't know how to suitably cover our bodies.

The white man came to teach mí genté a sense of spirituality. Thank God they did, or else we wouldn't know what true morals are.

The white man came to teach mujeres the patriarchal, misogynistic life style. Thank God they did, or else indigenous mujeres would have this radical idea that they can hold power over themselves.

The white man came to teach mí genté the nonexistent homophobia and transphobia their scripture addresses. Thank God they did, or else we would have continued accepting, respecting, and cherishing other human beings for who they are.

With God's direction and permission, our land, language, traditions, and culture was being lost in colonization. Tearing children apart from families, telling them they weren't worth anything, and savagely punishing them for speaking their tongue, and being true to their culture. Invading mí genté's land. Enslaving mí genté. Taking mí genté's identities. Killing mí genté. Raping mujeres indias, mixing our blood with their savage blood. As generations passed, the belief that mujeres weren't worthy became more prevalent within our households. Mujeres were no longer respected. They became baby-making machines that cleaned, cooked, and raised children they usually didn't consent to conceive. Colonized indigenous people were being baptized into Catholicism, becoming brainwashed with the white man's version of God the Savior.

The white man sailed the ocean blue, and bumped into mí genté's land, without knowledge of its existence prior to his arrival. And thanks to their "God given right" they claimed the land as their own. Through

God, his savages took credit for a landmass that already existed. They manipulated mí genté, they took advantage of mí genté, and stole their homes. The savages took credit for vegetation that mí genté introduced them to. Con el achaqué de dios and help, they infected indigenous people with diseases they carried. The white man would purposely infect mí genté with their diseases, knowing very fucking well they didn't know how to manage the outbreaks. The white man used mí genté as slaves working mines, and serfs working the land. They took advantage of them and their knowledge. They exploited many, massacred thousands, and stripped them away from their identities.

During the massacre, enslavement, and abuse they forced mí genté to speak the Spanish tongue. They implemented harsh tactics to punish mí genté for not learning and consistently speaking the Spanish tongue. Mí genté became afraid and ashamed. As generations went by, their native tongues became lost.—My grandfather was ashamed to teach my father their native tongue because he believed what the savages told him.

With our native tongues being taken, our cultural clothing was taken away. We no longer were allowed to wear our headdresses, our ceremonial outfits, or anything related to our indigenous dress. Mí genté were forced to dress like the white people, because God wants his savages to dress appropriately. Our spirituality was taken from us and the white man's God was shoved down our throats. Making mí genté think they were wrong the whole time. Giving us the white savior complexes we still suffer from today. Implementing self-hating tendencies in the way we see others and ourselves. Diminishing our appreciation for "two spirited people" and our appreciation for the earth. The white man shoved his white washed believes down our throats, giving us no choice but to fucking swallow. Gagging wasn't an option.

Not only did the white saviors "teach" us the right way to be humans, they also added sexist and patriarchal ways into our culture. Mujeres were seen with higher status and respect, not like the traditional Mexican machismo culture. By using God, mujeres were degraded. Mujeres were invaded, raped, and treated fucking awful. They became caterers to men and their uteruses became kangaroo pouches for children. Bearing children to help with daily tasks that became too overwhelming for mujeres to do on their own. With the white man's manipulation of God's "words," mujeres became self-hating, self-blaming, and they internalized the misogynistic views handed down from white savages and their God. She cooks, she cleans, she pops babies out, and she takes care of the crops, the animal feed, and clothing for the children. Tired from a hard day's work, she still doesn't get the rest she fucking deserves because the white man brainwashed her into thinking her husband's needs are met before hers. God and his savages are the cause of mujeres becoming men's wives slaves. Mujeres indigenas work so hard to keep the family going, they work tirelessly and endlessly to make sure they are mujeres perfectas; but only God and men get the credit for the strong, brave, caring, loving, and hard working women they are.

Mujeres were taught to stay quiet. Rape is not in their vocabulary. Why? Because God would see them as tainted and what would other men think of her? Mujeres were taught that they needed to be silent. "Una buena mujer se calla el hocico!" Was a popular phrase mis padres would tell me and mis hermanas. I don't blame them, it was passed on from many generations before them. I blame God and his savages for instilling that belief in mí genté's brains. A woman who talked back, spoke her mind, or stood up for herself and what she believed in was disowned. Una vergüenza. Our madre's worked hard to make sure their hija's image was perfect, that way a great, macho man would be interested in marrying her... under God's blessing. Often mujeres are victims of abuse because they don't do things to their owners' standards, and who is to thank? God. Men's entitlement over our mujeres was given to him through this fake being that a white man forced our indigenous people to believe in.

Mujeres are sexualized, abused, degraded, and seen less than men because of this entity that people praise. Men, especially the white man, like to use the phrase "God given right" for everything. They are raised to truly believe that, truly believe that they have "God given rights" for things they are told they can't have and is not theirs to take.

On top of degrading our culture, and the gift of sexism, the white man's God also taught us that being lesbian, gay, bisexual, transgender, or anything in between was something to be ashamed of. Giving others an excuse to abuse and murder us, all in the name of God. Making us feel like abominations, and leading many to suicide. Our LGBTQ+ brothers and sisters are left out in the dark because of something we can't help or control. This illusion and idea of God really fucks with nuestras mentes, and causes so much self-hatred! People like to argue that "#notalltheists" are savages, but who really believes that? I know I don't. Because of this imaginary man, we are seen as sexual predators, monsters, weirdoes, mentally ill, and so much more. We aren't "real humans." The oh-so loving entity that the white man praises dislikes hates everything that isn't trying to embody their idea of him. In one way or another, he is used to degrade anyone that isn't heterosexual, white, and biologically male. We are told that we can't embody someone so perfect because we are gay, lesbian, bisexual, trans, non-binary, etc. If #notalltheists really was a thing, there wouldn't be the fight for equal rights that there is, and maybe more theists would join the fight for human rights. If #notalltheists was a thing, trans* men and women wouldn't be afraid to be authentic, or something as simple as use the appropriate bathroom. They wouldn't be driven to suicide because they feel so unworthy to theist's standards. This country is run by the white washed Christian belief, and that gives the white man the entitlement to take advantage of our bodies, and our derechos humanos.

People use God as an excuse to rally against our human rights. They stand there with signs that say, "GOD HATES FAGS!" If this God truly existed, then why would he create gay people? Why would he create non-binary people? Why would he "preach" love if it isn't given equally to those who truly deserve it? Is it just to fuck us over? To have more "angels" with him? Or more "demons" with Satan? To turn to substance abuse as a coping mechanism? To become homeless because pricks that follow this white washed God refuse to see us as humans? To make us ashamed of being queer and people of color? To make us wish that we were more like "him"?

God and his savages stomp all over my community's lives. Constantly reminding us that we are not seen as human, that we are constantly being othered, and that our bodies are being policed by white men with "the fear of God." Reminding us that this imaginary entity holds panoptical power over all of us. And making us feel like there is nothing we can do about it because God is the almighty savior.

I don't have the answer to abolish this theist belief and almighty entity as the majority. But, I do have ideas and ways we can stand together to make them the minority, for a change. To make them fear *us*. To make them realize that their idea of faith, hope, and perfection is fucking foolish and hurtful.

As feministas chingonas, we can be the change. We need to link arms, take back our cultural pride. Rally for the right history to be taught in schools. Fight for people of color all over the country to learn their culture's history, and how God is used to excuse white people from being savages. Instead of letting this white supremacist institution take away our languages, and forcing us to speak English, hay que hablar nuestras lenguas indígenas sin vergüenza. Show mí genté Mexicana, homo-sexual, transgénero, etc., that they are strong, brave, and important. Let's cause uproar, cause a revolution of self-love, self-appreciation, self-acceptance, and cultural pride. Spread education of how detrimental this white God really is. Fight for all forms of theism to be taken away from curriculum. Over throw the Christian standards from being part of the government. Let's make curriculum that includes feminist perspectives, and empowers women, especially mujeres of color. A curriculum that doesn't shame people for their sexualities and gender identities.

Instead of staying quiet, like we are taught to be, let's be loud. Loud enough the whole world hears and feels our anger. So loud they too want to create change. Empower one another to be part of that change. To not be afraid to say that theism shouldn't be the norm, that the white man's God isn't perfect, kind and loving.

Desafortunadamente, my culture and the LGBTQ+ community are not the only ones that the white man and their God have fucked up. Many others do too, because they were forced to believe in this imaginary friend that holds so much power. It's not something normal, heart-warming, or something that a whole country should identify with. The white God needs to stop infiltrating misogynistic, patriarchal, and sexist beliefs in our heads. Realize that we are more powerful that they are. Together, we are bigger, stronger, and louder that they are. They don't hold the true power. We do. Together, as feministas chingonas, we can create change and make this country the true amalgamation of skin colors, sexual orientations, gender identities, and cultures it really is.

41 The Wild Poet's Manifesto

2012

Susan Hawthorne

The wild poet sows seeds. She is a creatrix of the mind, of the multidimensional world folded like a fractal. The wild poet takes craft seriously. She comes to it late having had to live before she could write. There are experiences to have, languages to learn, fears to overcome, loves to be made. She goes bush and sits still as the moon sets and the sun rises. She watches the heron fishing at dusk, silent but not quite still. She rushes through the day, trying not to pamper her email, her facebook, her tweets. They enthrall and distract her.

Wild politics, a subject that grabbed me and would not let me go. I first embarked on this journey almost twenty years ago. I travelled to Bangladesh for a conference at the end of 1993. The conference was organised by Farida Akhter of UBINIG (Policy Research for Development Alternative). Sixty-four women talking through the days. I forget precisely how many days, but it must have five or seven. In the small groups were women from every continent. Women known in their community, women whose names are known around the world.

We were there to talk about "population control." How the women of Bangladesh are targeted with dangerous contraceptives with the end of "depopulating Bangladesh" as Farida writes, while on the other hand women in the western world are targeted with reproductive technologies, with the dual purpose of perfection and consumerism. We heard about how girl babies are aborted in massive numbers and how all these policies are connected to economic reform through Structural Adjustment Programs. Rebelling against these policies was about cheering for wild children, children born without all the interventions being put forward by the technodocs. Wild reproduction engages women in purposeful resistance to the commodification of women's bodies.

What finally grabbed me was the understanding that my radical feminist politics was even broader than I had thought. It hit me that the analysis of power that I had been writing about applied to peoples all around the world. At some earlier time I had already made the connection to land and ecology, but here I was realising that I needed to know more about economics. I needed to know more about SAPs, TRIPS and TRIMS, GATT, the IMF and the World Bank. It was in Bangladesh where I heard how these international institutions touched women's lives.

She walks the city to see the world face to face. Walks down seedy laneways, climbs to the top of the highest building, wishes she were a bird flying through the air.

It is city, where small wildernesses can exist side-by-side with urban landscapes. The New York City Garden that was started by feminists in the 1970s. In Germany women from many countries share their knowledge about plants. They have come from different environments; there are things to learn about this climate, this latitude. They discuss companion planting, and the use of herbal sprays to keep insects at bay without exterminating everything.

In Bangladesh, Farida shows us the seed houses, talks about the ways in which the women maintain the local biodiversity. A decade later she takes us to a village which has declared itself pesticide free and dowry free. She shows us where the women collect the uncultivated plants that grow wild near ponds and watercourses. By this time, the women seed savers are clear that they are saving seeds against Monsanto. Resistance to corporate appropriation, incorporation, distortion and selling it back to us involves actions such as these, collecting and protecting wild seeds which forms the basis of wild farming.

The wild poet has an aesthetic that is like a plant growing in soil. She does not try to replicate the known world. The unknown world is her home. She writes of the invisible, the hidden, the story gone astray. She is the uncultivated plant, the one that grows in spite of pesticides and monocultures. This plant grows on the pattern of the Fibonacci numbers, spiraling into timeless time. Like a refracting crystal it is multifaceted, filled with voices from many places. Long filaments blow in the wind.

I think about my own history. The childhood farm where everything was recycled. My parents cared about trees. My mother made sure that the paddocks where sheep grazed had enough shade where they could shelter. She'd be surprised to know that she and Farida give importance to tree shade. Both recognise the importance of shade to life.

In Bangladesh, the farms are so different. It was the shock of the new in a way. Where I grew up on the brick hard clay of the Riverina, farms were big. There were five of us in our house. While our cousins lived nearby, the numbers of people sustained by several acres in Bangladesh would have us starving near Ardlethan, NSW.

Sitting on the bus in Bangladesh, out the window I could see great mounds of cauliflower. Every field had a person in it. Vegetables were hard to grow on our farm, even in the relatively well watered garden. We did have an orchard, mainly citrus fruits. One rarely saw a person driving past paddocks, perhaps a truck, a ute, a tractor, or harvester.

When I visited the second time, we went to a farm and talked with farmers. They found it incredible that a family could not support itself on 100 acres. I looked around and there were fruit trees with mango, papaya, bananas, and fruits I didn't know. They grew rice, their ponds were full of fish, there were herbs and spices and a host of other edibles. Farmers markets, organic farming, self-sufficiency are acts of resistance to globalisation; they are wild markets where exchange is fair, where gifts are not given for tax deductibility or that feel-good emotion the powerful get.

The wild poet is specific. She uses local colour and language. She makes jokes that not all readers will get. Here is a chance, she says, to change how you think. Come with me on this journey of exploring our minds. Come and see the world through my eyes. Put yourself in my shoes. Let your fingers feel.

After reading economics for eight years I enrolled in a PhD. My original insights in Bangladesh were taking shape. I read everything I could about GM crops, how they were being imposed on people for the fake purpose of "solving world hunger," a line that has been bought by far too many. I became engrossed in the rules of free trade and the agreements being foisted on nations. I thought about the way in which work is globalised for women, how the sex industry along with electronics and garments manufacture have so much in common. I noticed that women's work was not valued for the benefit it brought to communities and how men were receiving all the development aid which was going to further deplete women's work and position in those communities.

I began to think about the epistemic advantage those at the margins have, but when the system is controlled by the dominant culture, the marginalised miss out. Dominant Culture Stupidities is what I call the inability of the powerful to see, to know, to understand the gaps in their knowledge. I want the able-bodied, white, heterosexual male to have to work harder. I want them to get down from their pedestal of entitlement and become someone else. I want them to see how it is to walk in someone else's shoes. The efforts of wild women in resisting becoming part of the global market economy were being practised by these women and by many dispossessed and poor women around the world. It would make sense if those of us with far more would join them.

She bares her truths. Naked with honesty not exposure. A straight talker with a bent perspective.

But how was I to get my lesbian perspective into this work? It is in part the issue of margins. The lesbian is invisible in most theorising, and so where I could I used lesbian examples. Some of the farmers protesting at Melbourne's 2000 S11 demonstration are lesbians. The perspective is also the one I learned as a young feminist in Melbourne's lesbian community, the lessons around alternative health, around the personal is political, and the litmus test: if it doesn't work for the poor, for the disabled, for lesbians, for the outcasts in society then it wasn't worth fighting for. The year I finished the work on wild politics was also the year I discovered what was happening to lesbians in places like Uganda. There and in many other countries around the world, lesbians were being tortured and murdered. Some prominence has come to the issue of "corrective rape" in recent years, but it is still a struggle to have the human rights of lesbians acknowledged and campaigned for.

There are connections to be teased out here. When the earth is raped it is seen as wanting, not enough of this element or that, too much water so drains are built, too little so rivers are drained. What we need is social glue, not policies that divide. Our river system could be such a glue, but instead it has been turned into a commodity. Water rights are disconnected from land. It is like a glove with all the fingers cut out. The land is found wanting.

When a lesbian is raped she is found wanting. All she needs is a good fuck (the torturers say these words). Women and earth are both found wanting. When we disconnect from place, from land, from the local we are denying something very deep. We are disallowing our very selves the connection with the place we have known in childhood. When a person disconnects from her or his body, it allows them to do the unthinkable and to protect themselves from unthinkable acts. Extreme disconnection results in self harm, intimate harm and a kind of disconnection from society.

The system of the earth and women and the poor and the powerless found wanting is one of making everyone homeless: homeless on the earth (no place to call home, displaced, dispossessed, a refugee or a returnee), homeless in the body (the prostituted body, the body given over to donating parts for the benefit of others, the body commodified by sexual dominance practices). Resisting these forces entails changing policies on asylum and abolishing opportunities for exploitation of the poor and powerless. Wild sexuality means changing the preconditions for relationship, promoting respect, equality and ridding the media of their love for images of domination and porn.

The wild poet reads the classics and reinvents the world. She joins a singing group. Goes aerial. Becomes a performer. She waits to see how the world responds. She rarely goes to openings or drinks or events to be seen at. She'd rather talk one to one in a café, or walk on a beach.

Poetry took me on my next big journey. In poetry you can say things that are difficult to say in academic prose. Poetry allows for connection, for the associative thought. Through poetry I have been able to explore lesbian culture. I have continued writing the wild through work on cyclones and climate change, drought, flood and mining. I have explored other languages, the connections between us. I have taken on the voices of animals, imagined other histories and worlds. And I have contemplated flight.

The wild poet is hard to pin down. She likes style and form. Likes better the way that structure and content daze one another. She is waiting for the sea to rise.

Lilla Watson in 1984 said that Aboriginal people see the future going forward as far as the past extends back. She said: "That means a 40,000-year plan." These words have been an enduring inspiration for me. If we enter into the wild, if we see the earth as a relationship, not as a possession, if we see our own responsibility in ensuring a future then perhaps a 40,000-year future is possible. The denial of this future is more likely and Indigenous peoples have found themselves at the sharp end with the Human Diversity Genome Project which seeks to collect samples of DNA to get genetic information. Just one more policy which puts the well being of people below the triumphs of western science. But if we deny the future, if we find everything wanting so that we intervene instead of watching and learning, then we are done for. In the wild is structure. In the wild is form. But we have to look. We have to care.

She is happy to place her words in the mouths of beasts and birds, insects and plants. The wild poet inhabits multiple realms. Ecstatic, she breathes fire and water.

42 Black Lives Matter Platform

2016

Black Lives Matter

PLATFORM

Black humanity and dignity requires Black political will and power. Despite constant exploitation and perpetual oppression, Black people have bravely and brilliantly been the driving force pushing the U.S. towards the ideals it articulates but has never achieved. In recent years we have taken to the streets, launched massive campaigns, and impacted elections, but our elected leaders have failed to address the legitimate demands of our Movement. We can no longer wait.

In response to the sustained and increasingly visible violence against Black communities in the U.S. and globally, a collective of more than 50 organizations representing thousands of Black people from across the country have come together with renewed energy and purpose to articulate a common vision and agenda. We are a collective that centers and is rooted in Black communities, but we recognize we have a shared struggle with all oppressed people; collective liberation will be a product of all of our work.

We believe in elevating the experiences and leadership of the most marginalized Black people, including but not limited to those who are women, queer, trans, femmes, gender nonconforming, Muslim, formerly and currently incarcerated, cash poor and working class, disabled, undocumented, and immigrant. We are intentional about amplifying the particular experience of state and gendered violence that Black queer, trans, gender nonconforming, women and intersex people face. There can be no liberation for all Black people if we do not center and fight for those who have been marginalized. It is our hope that by working together to create and amplify a shared agenda, we can continue to move towards a world in which the full humanity and dignity of all people is recognized.

While this platform is focused on domestic policies, we know that patriarchy, exploitative capitalism, militarism, and white supremacy know no borders. We stand in solidarity with our international family against the ravages of global capitalism and anti-Black racism, human-made climate change, war, and exploitation. We also stand with descendants of African people all over the world in an ongoing call and struggle for reparations for the historic and continuing harms of colonialism and slavery. We also recognize and honor the rights and struggle of our Indigenous family for land and self-determination.

We have created this platform to articulate and support the ambitions and work of Black people. We also seek to intervene in the current political climate and assert a clear vision, particularly for those who claim to be our allies, of the world we want them to help us create. We reject false solutions and believe we can achieve a complete transformation of the current systems, which place profit over people and make it impossible for many of us to breathe.

Together, we demand an end to the wars against Black people. We demand that the government repair the harms that have been done to Black communities in the form of reparations and targeted long-term investments. We also demand a defunding of the systems and institutions that criminalize and cage us. This document articulates our vision of a fundamentally different world. However, we recognize the need to include policies that address the immediate suffering of Black people. These policies, while less transformational, are necessary to address the current material conditions of our people and will better equip us to win the world we demand and deserve.

We recognize that not all of our collective needs and visions can be translated into policy, but we understand that policy change is one of many tactics necessary to move us towards the world we envision. We have come together now because we believe it is time to forge a new covenant. We are dreamers and doers and this platform is meant to articulate some of our vision. The links throughout the document provide the stepping-stones and roadmaps of how to get there.

The policy briefs also elevate the brave and transformative work our people are already engaged in, and build on some of the best thinking in our history of struggle. This agenda continues the legacy of our ancestors who pushed for reparations, Black self-determination and community control; and also propels new iterations of movements such as efforts for reproductive justice, holistic healing and reconciliation, and ending violence against Black cis, queer, and trans people.

PART V

SEXI BODY

Introduction to Sex/Body

Here we find the dripping, fleshy, gooey, injured, sexual, defiant, pulsating body. Moving beyond the more tame discussions of "rights" and mere embodiment, we instead find radical and diverse approaches to understanding the relationship between the body and its political context. Most precisely, we hear frank depictions of resistance and resilience, as writers use the body and sexuality to broaden and redefine feminist politics.

The body, here, is also a site of intense emotion. We read several pieces that unite anger and feminist body politics, from Sara Roebuck's letter to her would-be rapist to the Bloodsisters' admonishing of Tampax, Susan Stenson's poetic notions of "occupying" menstruation, and radical feminist Ti-Grace Atkinson's reframing of vaginal orgasm as a "mass hysterical survival response."

And like all politics of bodies and sexualities, we also see wildly different visions for the feminist future of reproductive and sexual rights, from a full-on embrace of lust (Valentine de Saint-Point) to an outright celebration of masturbation (Betty Dodson) to the foregrounding of trans/queer sexualities (Paul B. Preciado) and sex workers' rights ("Feminist Manifesto to Support the Rights of Sex Workers"). We reclaim the sexual body in relation to abortion politics (Simone de Beauvoir) and childlessness (Lisa Hymas) and affirm the defiant stance of being "pro-abortion" rather than merely pro-choice (Valerie Tarico). And, of course, we position bodies on the margins—especially fat bodies—at the center (Judy Freespirit and Aldebaran). Ultimately, this section is designed as a provocative extension of what we think we already know about feminism and sex/body politics—moving us instead into a vision for an unabashed radical politics that imagines bodies and sexualities as confrontational, pulsing, uncontainable, and full of sharp edges.

Vaginal Orgasm as a Mass Hysterical Survival Response

1968

Ti-Grace Atkinson

I suppose we all have put aside the speeches we prepared before last night. In the face of Martin King's death, one must tell the truth as plain as one can.

I was asked by the Medical Committee for Human Rights to speak on Sex. Alright, I really will.

The oppression of women by men is the source of all the corrupt values throughout the world. Between men and women we brag about domination, surrender, inequality, conquest, trickery, exploitation. Men have robbed women of their lives.

A human being is not born from the womb; it must create itself. It must be free, self-generative. A human being must feel that it can grow in a world where injustice, inequity, hatred, sadism are not directed at it. No person can grow into a life within these conditions; it is enough of a miracle to survive as a functioning organism.

Now let's talk about function. Women have been murdered by their so-called function of child-bearing exactly as the black people were murdered by their function of color. The truth is that child-bearing isn't the function of women. The function of child-bearing is the function of men oppressing women.

It is the function of men to oppress. It is the function of men to exploit. It is the function of men to lie, and to betray, and to humiliate, to crush, to ignore, and the final insult: it is the function of men to tell women that man's iniquities are woman's function!

I'm telling it to you as straight as I can. Marriage and the family are as corrupt institutions as slavery ever was. They must be abolished as slavery was. By definition they necessarily oppress and exploit their subject groups. If women were free, free to grow as people, free to be self-creative, free to go where they like, free to be where they like, free to choose their lives, there would be no such institutions as marriage or family. If slaves had had these freedoms, there wouldn't have been slavery.

Until D.N.A. or something similar comes through, women are the only source of new organisms. Men cannot continue to force women to produce children. The society as a whole can decide what it wants to do about its birth rate, and then the women can be asked to contribute their special capacities. But if women don't want to, that's the breaks. If a woman decides to help out, she has absolutely no responsibility for the child. The child is not her s, it belongs to society. It is society even now, or rather men, that decides whether or not women have children; children are the whole society's responsibility.

2

I'm not going to fall into the male-supremacy trap tonight of "who's going to take care of the children", and the "working-mother-delinquent-child" blues. Last night's events reminded me that there's no more time for injustice, euphemistically known as "social justice". It's irrelevant to the emancipation of women what happens when women free themselves from the institutions that maintain them in their oppressed state. It wasn't the responsibility of the slaves to think up, develop, experiment, and prove superior a new economic system for the South before they were emancipated, and it's not our job to figure out what happens to the kiddies before women free themselves. And women will free themselves. I'm just here to tell you men about it so you can expose your sadistic hostility towards your wives and mothers a little more, a little sooner, so they'll revolt quicker. I don't see why women should lose any more of their lives than they have already.

I'm assuming as I write this that I'll be reading it to liberal men. You're a real prize bunch. You quiver with horror over Vietnam because you identify your hide with the boy sent over there. You pontificate, but mostly just shake your head, over black people because you know if they get too uppity, you outnumber them nine to one, and you know that they know it. That's an extra kick. But do you get uptight about women! There are those of you who try to lay a woman to put down her protests. (I expect nervous laughter here.) Then there are those who pat her on her ass and say, "Gee, baby, it's too bad you're inferior but that's your function and I think that's great." What's great? She's great? Of course that's not what you mean. You mean it's great that it's her function to be inferior. But she can't face that so she twists it to mean that you think that she's great. And because she's the cheapest maid going and sleeps in your bed, you let it go—more or less. We all know how uncomfortable it is to be around disgruntled maids nowadays, and as for hostile sex, what other kind is there?

Oh yes, sex. Your kind. The kind you wanted me to titillate you with by speaking here tonight. What could be more amusing than a Feminist talking about sex? Obviously, if Feminism has any logic in it at all, it must be working for a sexless society. But sex you want? Sex you're going to get.

Vaginal orgasm is an excellent illustration of the way men oppress and exploit women. It's ironic that you insist men and women respond the same in the one place no one can deny men and women are different—in their genitals. This difference is the basis for the whole distinction between men and women and the ground for the inequities that are heaped on women by men. But men have no shame. That's what power does for you—like Johnson raping Vietnam. And Johnson has the gall to say the Vietnamese want us

to be there, to keep the free world safe for democracy. He means,
as your enlightened pocket books now know, that we're there to
maintain the oppression of the Vietnamese to keep the world, by
object lesson, safe to exploit for the United States. And as we
see the little life left in the country being burned out of it,
Johnson had the gall to tell us the Vietnamese were loving it.
Try that argument with women, baby, and you'll be home free.

A man's penis and a woman's vagina are obviously different. Male
orgasm is analogous to clitoral orgasm. Where, then, does vaginal
orgasm come from? People say it's learned. And by God you'd
better learn it, lady, especially if you're with a liberal man;
you'd better learn to shuffle, nigger, because if you don't you
won't get the job. And you want to eat don't you? Why should
she learn vaginal orgasm? Because that's what men want. How
about a facial tic? What's the difference?

And love. As long as we're on sacred cows, let's finish them.
What is love but the pay-off for the consent to oppression? What
is love but need? What is love but fear? In a just society,
would we need love?

In a free society, you cannot have the family, marriage, sex, or
love. You will have your Vietnams, and more, you will have your
murdered Martin King's, and more, you will have your Revolution
unless your wives and mothers free themselves, because that's
where the foundations of oppression and exploitation are laid.
You are going to have to have your power wrenched away from you
right where you live, and you're not going to like it. And that's
tough shit.

*   *   *   *   *   *

To the women in the audience, I say: think about these things
with the man you love and want the most.   Scratch his love, and
you'll find your fear.   You'll be afraid you'll die, and the
woman will die, but your life will be born, and you'll begin to
be free.

*   *   *   *   *   *

To the men in the audience, I say: move on over, baby, or we'll
move on over you--'caus al de good niggers is daide!!

Ti-Grace Atkinson
Philadelphia
April 5, 1968

44 Fat Liberation Manifesto

1973

Judy Freespirit and Aldebaran

1. WE believe that fat people are fully entitled to human respect and recognition.
2. WE are angry at mistreatment by commercial and sexist interests. These have exploited our bodies as objects of ridicule, thereby creating an immensely profitable market selling the false promise of avoidance of, or relief from, that ridicule.
3. WE see our struggle as allied with the struggles of other oppressed groups against classism, racism, sexism, ageism, financial exploitation, imperialism and the like.
4. WE demand equal rights for fat people in all aspects of life, as promised in the Constitution of the United States. We demand equal access to goods and services in the public domain, and an end to discrimination against us in the areas of employment, education, public facilities and health services.
5. WE single out as our special enemies the so-called "reducing" industries. These include diet clubs, reducing salons, fat farms, diet doctors, diet books, diet foods and food supplements, surgical procedures, appetite suppressants, drugs and gadgetry such as wraps and "reducing machines".

    WE demand that they take responsibility for their false claims, acknowledge that their products are harmful to the public health, and publish long-term studies proving any statistical efficacy of their products. We make this demand knowing that over 99% of all weight loss programs, when evaluated over a five-year period, fail utterly, and also knowing the extreme proven harmfulness of frequent large changes in weight.

6. WE repudiate the mystified "science" which falsely claims that we are unfit. It has both caused and upheld discrimination against us, in collusion with the financial interests of insurance companies, the fashion and garment industries, reducing industries, the food and drug industries, and the medical and psychiatric establishment.

7. WE refuse to be subjugated to the interests of our enemies. We fully intend to reclaim power over our bodies and our lives. We commit ourselves to pursue these goals together.

FAT PEOPLE OF THE WORLD, UNITE! YOU HAVE NOTHING TO LOSE …

45 Manifesto of the 343

1971

Simone de Beauvoir

One million women in France have abortions every year.

Condemned to secrecy they do so in dangerous conditions, while under medical supervision this is one of the simplest procedures.

We are silencing these millions of women.

I declare that I am one of them. I declare that I have had an abortion.

Just as we demand free access to contraception, we demand the freedom to have an abortion.

Abortion

A word which seems to express and define the feminist fight once and for all. To be a feminist is to fight for free abortion on demand.

Abortion

It's a women's thing, like cooking, diapers, something dirty. The fight to obtain free abortion on demand feels somehow ridiculous or petty. It can't shake the smell of hospitals or food, or of poo behind women's backs.

The complexity of the emotions linked to the fight for abortion precisely indicate our difficulty in being, the pain that we have in persuading ourselves that it is worth the trouble of fighting for ourselves.

It goes without saying that we do not have the right to choose what we want to do with our bodies, as other human beings do. Our wombs, however, belong to us.

Free abortion on demand is not the ultimate goal of women's plight. On the contrary, it is but the most basic necessity, without which the political fight cannot even begin. It is out of vital necessity that women should win back control and reintegrate their bodies. They hold a unique status in history: human beings who, in modern societies, do not have unfettered control over their own bodies. Up until today it was only slaves who held this status.

The scandal continues. Each year 1,500,000 women live in shame and despair. 5,000 of us die. But the moral order remains steadfast. We want to scream.

Free abortion on demand is:

Immediately ceasing to be ashamed of your body, being free and proud in your body just as everyone up until now who has had full use of it; no longer being ashamed of being a woman.

An ego broken into tiny fucking pieces, that's what all women who have to undergo a clandestine abortion experience; just being yourself all the time, no longer having that ignoble fear of being "taken," taken into a trap, being double and powerless with a sort of tumor in your belly; a thrilling fight, insofar as if I win I only begin to belong to myself and no longer to the State, to a family, to a child I do not want; a step along the path to reaching full control over the production of children. Women, like all other producers, have in fact got the absolute right to control all of their productions. This control implies a radical change in women's mental configuration, and a no less radical change in social structures.

1. I will have a child if I want one, and no moral pressure, institution or economic imperative will compel me to do so. This is my political power. As any kind of producer, I can, while waiting for improvement, put pressure on society through my production (child strike).
2. I will have a child if I want one and if the society I will be bringing it into is suitable for me, if it will not make me a slave to that child, its nurse, its maid, its punchbag.
3. I will have a child if I want one, if society is suitable for both me and it, I am responsible for it, no risk of war, no work subject to whims.

No to supervised freedom.

The battle that has risen up around the subject of abortion goes over the heads of those it is most relevant to—women. The issue of whether the law should be made more liberal, the issue of when abortion can be permitted, basically the issue of therapeutic abortion does not interest us because it does not concern us.

Therapeutic abortion requires "good" reasons to receive "permission" to have an abortion. To put it plainly, this means that we must earn the right to not have children. That the decision as to whether to have them or not does not belong to us now any more than it did before. The principle remains that it is legitimate to force women to have children.

A modification to the law, allowing exceptions to this principle, would do nothing other than reinforce it. The most liberal of laws would still be regulating how our bodies can be used. And how our bodies should be used is not something which should be regulated. We do not want tolerance, scraps of what other humans are born with: the freedom to use their bodies as they wish. We are as opposed to the Peyret Law or the ANEA project as to the current law, since we are opposed to all laws which claim to regulate any aspect of our bodies. We do not want a better law, we want it to be removed, pure and simple. We are not asking for charity, we want justice. There are 27,000,000 of us here alone. 27,000,000 "citizens" treated like cattle.

To fascists of all kinds—who admit that is what they are and lay into us, or who call themselves Catholics, fundamentalists, demographers, doctors, experts, jurists, "responsible men," Debré, Peyret, Lejeune, Pompidou, Chauchard, the Pope—we say that we have uncovered them.

We should call them assassins of the people. We should forbid them to use the term "respect for life" which is an obscenity in their mouths. There should be 27,000,000 of us. We should fight until the end because we want nothing more than our right: the free use of our bodies.

The ten commandments of the Bourgeois State:

You choose a fetus over a human being when that human is female.

No woman will have an abortion while Debré wants 100 million more French people.

You will have 100 million French people, as long as it costs you nothing.

You will be particularly severe with poor females who cannot go to England.

As such you will have a wheel of unemployment to make your capitalists happy.

You will be very moralistic, because God knows what "we" women
would do if we had such freedom. You will save the fetus, since it's
more interesting to kill them off aged 18, the age of conscription.
You will really need them as you pursue your imperialist politics.
You use contraception yourself, to send just a few children to the Poly-
technique or the ENA because your flat only has 10 rooms.
As for the others, you will disparage the pill, because that's the only
thing missing.

The list of signatures is a first act of revolt. For the first time, women
have decided to lift the taboo weighing down on their wombs: women
of the Women's Liberation Movement, the Free Abortion Movement,
women who work, women who stay at home.

At the Women's Liberation Movement we are neither a party, nor
an organization, nor an association, and even less so their women's
subsidiary. This is an historic movement which does not only bring
together women who come to the Women's Liberation Movement,
this is the movement for all women, wherever they live, wherever they
work, who have decided to take their lives and their freedom into their
own hands. Fighting against our oppression means shattering all of
society's structures, especially the most routine ones. We do not want
any part or any place in this society which has been built without us
and at our expense.

When womankind, the sector of humanity that has been lurking in
the shadows, takes its destiny into its own hands, that's when we can
start talking about a revolution.

A Free Abortion Movement has been set up, bringing together all
those who are prepared to fight to the end for free abortions. The goal
of this movement is to stir up local and corporate groups, to coordinate
an explanatory and informative campaign, to become the only mass
movement capable of demanding our right to decide for ourselves.

46 Ax Tampax Poem Feministo

1996

adee (The Bloodsisters Project)

At Once Old and New

Ax Tampax
In spirit of challenging and collapsing
The insidious nature of the corporate monster
That gobbles and trashes and fucks us over ...
In response to the dirty business ...
We have made this recipe book.
As an act of resistance to the system
That tramples over the homegrown d.i.y. style
We are sick of how they co-opt our life
To spit out into franchises ...
To over package our needs into taxed luxuries ...
We are sick of that garbarators
That insists to dismember ...
We are sick of how it insists to hide
And disguise our experiences
Fuck the mark up they make on their lies ...
Down with the inventors of necessities!
To the uprising when we stop popping tampons
And the popping big business medicines ...
We fuck the poisons
That kill our free remedies ...
When we fuck the complacency
To build the uprising ...
To bleed and use weeds
To stop feeding the corporate greed
When we ax tampax and what it embodies.

47 Occupy Menstruation

2018

Susan Stenson

It is the astro-feminist biologist calling out
the ruse of the FREE BLEED movement.

It is the Helloflo.com. It is The Period Shop in NYC.
Not #biotolerance. Not #biointolerance.

Not the Man Who Thought His Wife Was a Menstrual Pad.
Not Handmaid. Not poser.

It isn't the *hardest love we carry.* Not *pro patria mori.*
It is they. It is her. It is he. It is you. It is us.

Not *le petit mort.* Although the number of stains
on white pants on a first date may disagree.

Not the antediluvian thought of negotiating menstrual huts
into nursing contracts, heating pads and ibuprofen eschewed.

It is everyone we know.
It is prophecy in leaf.

Not pink sparkles and uterus cakes.
It is the settling for bronze due to period aches.

Not patty cake. Not threshold to womanhood.
Not moon. Not Mars. Not gendered planets.

Not Biblical. Not Pliny.
Not here nor there.

It is personal. It is WTF.
It is *I kid you not*.

It is Li Po. It is origami.
It is passing on the Left.

Not Where were you on the night of the murder?
Not What do you have to say for yourself?

It is the anti-tax lawsuit. It is expensive.
Not sanctified. Not sanitized.

It is not *a lesson in forgetting*.
Nor a lesson in gravity.

It is the other. It is the or.
It is Would you like tampons with that?

It is Corinthian. It is Adamic.
It is open sore. It is when.

It is *Kendal's on her period*.
Kendal's on her period on the playground.

It is an altered narrative. Girl Guides.
It is a man following Monica down the street, sniggering, *FISH*.

48 A Letter to the Man Who Tried to Rape Me

2016

Sara Roebuck

Dear individual,

I write to you on this cold December evening, almost one year after you tried to rape me, because it's the first time that I've felt strong enough to put pen to paper. I write to you because this afternoon we met again, only the surroundings were not quite the same. Your hands were cuffed behind your back, not sweatily gripped around my body. Your eyes were on the floor, not greedily inches away from my face. We were in the same room, only this time it was my choice and not yours. This time, you didn't succeed in blocking the door with a fire extinguisher and keeping me against my will. This time, the door was closed behind you, by an armed police officer, and within, you found yourself looking at three judges in front of you, and my lawyer to the left of me. I write you this letter knowing you will never read it, because you are about to spend a significant duration of your adult life, as you already have done for the last ten months, in prison. But, I must write it nonetheless, for men like you, for women like me, but above all, for my own emancipation.

I write to you in order to put onto paper the gravity of what you did, to materialise the story that unfolds, the choices you put down to "youthful stupidity." I write this to you, so others and I can look at the words take its ugly form on this page. I write this because I am tired; I am exhausted of stories like this. I want myself and others to understand how and why we as a society **still** continue to struggle with the poisonous and violent reality of rape, the gravity of sexual assault, the complexity of misogyny, and the patriarchal weight that continues to minimise the role of the rapist and blame the women whose body was snatched from within her own skin.

I want men to read this and feel just as sick as the women who have lived through things like this do. I want things to change. I **insist** that things change.

You had many psychoanalytical terms and labels thrown at you this afternoon from the belly of the law. Infantile, sickly, deranged, narcissist. Your lack of father and suffocating mother, the absence of a stable job or decent education, your tendency to lie, to undermine, and furthermore your absolute inability to comprehend the severity of what you did, to understand the clear difference between "I consent" from "I do not." Yet quite honestly, I am not interested in skirting around the context of your sad life in order to seek excuses for a man who tried to convince a row of three judges that you heard "stop," "no," and "help" and therefore were lost in translation because you do not speak English. Even though, when I stood up and addressed the court loud and clear in fluent French, we all know I knew how to say "*arrête*," "*non*" and "*aidez-moi*," and did so appropriately when you threw me against a wall. You tried to abuse me, to undermine my sexuality, to enclose me into a cage like an animal, but you will not undermine my intelligence, my integrity, or my strength to call you out in a language that is not my own, in front of a jury of three judges in a country that is not my own, for your weak lies and pathetic account of what simply did not happen. *J'en ai rien à foutre.*

You said that what you did lasted a few minutes, not that you locked me in a room for twenty minutes whilst you tried to take off my clothes, whilst you launched my body onto a sink, whilst you tried to rape me. You said that you were on top of me on the floor because I dropped my drink and slipped, not because, after I managed to push you out from in between my legs, you twisted my body and pushed me onto the floor, pinning me and holding me down with the weight of yours. You said that whilst you threw me on top of the sink, pulling my legs apart and placing yourself in between them whilst I cried and screamed, thrusting my dress way above my chest and exposing the most intimate and vulnerable part of my being, all you did was touch me "one or two times" but on realising, seeing, feeling that I was in fact menstruating and had a tampon inside of me, after you had tried multiple times to ram your dirty hands inside of my body, you decided to stop. We both know that is not true. Everyone in that room knew that it is not true. Because it was not you that decided to stop. It was me who fought back. Your eyes were black and you looked straight into my soul and told me you didn't give a fuck that I said no, that I had a tampon. You held your thick wrist against my chest whilst you abused me, whilst you fumbled with your belt and pushed my underwear to one side, constraining my freedom by forcing my legs apart. Whilst I kicked and screamed and cried, you grabbed and constrained and yanked and hurt every part of me that in no given universe would I have consented you to touch; that the only thing blocking you from succeeding in what you tried to do was the thing that led you to violently assault me: my sexuality. What a concept, the fact that the thing that repulses men, even though it symbolises and embodies female fertility and sexuality, was the thing that saved me.

It was not easy to do what I did today. My lawyer told me I didn't need to be present. But I was. I wanted to stand up and respond when the judges asked me if I had anything to say, because I did. I stood up with every ounce of strength inside of me, fuelled by a blind raging fury, furious against your lies, against the absence of recognition of what you did to me, furious against the fact you thought you could take what wasn't there for you to take. I tapped on the microphone, declined a translator, and delivered my speech to the judges, my voice echoing around a full courtroom, squarely and loudly, in the language that you claimed I did not speak.

At that moment, I stood and spoke for every woman in the world who has suffered at the hands of men like you. I stood for every woman who walks home with her keys clasped between her fingers. I stood for every woman who has switched train carriages because of that one man who isn't breaking eye contact. I stood for every woman whose parents insist they send a text after a night out, even at twenty-four years old, because they worry for their daughters' safety because she's female and not male. I stood for every woman who has felt her sexuality stand on show when walking past a group of men. I stood for every woman who remembers the first time their childlike body was no longer so innocent in front of old horrible men. I stood for every woman who knows how it feels to have the waxy heavy regard of an unwanted gaze envelop her body, drenching your skin in this sickly, uncomfortable glare that you cannot put into words but know so well. I stood for every woman who has been called a whore, a slut, or a bitch for rejecting unwanted advances. I stood for every woman who has felt worthless, used, and judged for having sex when a man has felt empowered, free and strengthened for doing exactly the same thing. I stood for every woman who knows the hot fury in being told blatant outright sexism is just a joke and "you should really learn to chill out a bit and have a laugh." I stood for every woman who has double-questioned an outfit in case it looks "too slutty" or "asking for it." I stood for every woman who has suffered the lonely, self-destructive, "if I hadn't done, worn, said, breathed x y z then it wouldn't have happened to me." I stood for every woman who has felt that hot prickly shame when other women, friends, co-workers think they have the right to talk about your attack as if they have any idea what it feels like, as if they have a **right** to make comment, judging you accordingly in the aftermath for the way you may react and suffer, telling you that "shit happens" and its "no excuse" to fall behind because "you shouldn't have gone out, you should have taken better care of yourself, don't you know men just want one thing, you shouldn't have put yourself in that situation," *"t'as complètement déconné"* (you fucked up big time), spoken from the lungs of **women who claim to be feminists themselves**.

I stood for every woman who has been groped, harassed, attacked, raped, filmed, photographed, followed, touched against her consent, suffered verbal vulgarities, obscene regards, disgusting gestures, and worse of all, within a society that allows it, in some cases with other women who refuel the blame, and men around her who are supposed to be progressive and modern, but stay silent. I address all of these women because **I am each and every one of them**. Because it happens **every single day** to every single woman you, dear reader, know and love. I want people to open their eyes.

This is an open letter to every man who has tried to exploit, enjoy or profit from my body **without my consent**. This is to the man who was stood filming up my floaty dress whilst I was queuing to go up the Arc de Triomphe in the middle of blazing summer in 2014 with his reverse iPhone camera. This is to the multitude of men who have either tried or succeeded to grope me in busy nightclubs, to the man in Barcelona who rode up behind me on a bike whilst I walked to the beach in broad daylight, violently grabbing my breast and almost knocking me onto the floor, only six months after I was attacked in that little room. This letter is to the man who pushed me against a wall and told me he'd love to "screw me like I'd never forget" when I was walking home in my safe, residential district of western Paris, which reduced me to running home with tears streaming down my face, when all I was doing was walking home. This is to the man who rubbed his genitals in front of me and stared directly at me without anyone else seeing, knowing I couldn't change carriage or seat because the train was direct and there was no other space. This is to the man who invited me to his party and then threw me out onto the street at 4am, after screaming at me that the only reason he invited me was because all he wanted to do was to fuck me. This is to every man who has reduced me to nothing more than a body, to an object that deserves nothing more than being violated. And what was my role in all of this? **I was there and I was breathing.**

This year, the issue of rape, sexual assault, and above all **the question of consent** was brought into the public eye yet again with the acquittal of Ched Evans, a man with the glimmering title of "occupation: elite sportsman," a very large income, and more relevantly in this letter, a man with a worryingly large following of strong and passionate male supporters who really got stuck into the rhetoric of "Shows how manipulative lasses can be if they want to be, throwing the rape card about and ruined Ched Evans' career, justice is done slag".

Throwing the rape card about. Let's just consider that slowly. Throwing the rape card about, like having the most intimate part of your body violated against your will and then having the strength to report it is like trying to get an opposing player on the pitch a red card. Do you compare raping women to playing football? That the punishment should be a slap on the wrist because "she can't prove that she said no, or she was too drunk, or that she was coming onto me before, or that her ex boyfriend said she was able to have sex after the event in question so therefore **in the eyes of the law it is ok**"? No.

Do you have any idea what it entails to report a rape?

In the immediate aftermath of my attack, after I managed to escape by kicking the extinguisher out of the way with my foot and managing to open the door, the attacker took my bag and hid it on top of a cupboard that was too high for me to reach and re-find. He stole my phone and fled the premises. Yet, without my bag, I was without my keys. Without my phone, I was stripped of my ability to contact anyone close to me, anyone that could help. I was completely alone in what was the most vulnerable moment of my life. But alas, my bag was found, three hours later, my keys were returned, and I was home. Alone.

There are no words in either the French or English language I can source to describe the aftermath of returning home on my own and of the day after.

The way that I peeled off my dress in front of the mirror and looked at the hand prints, marks, bruises start to develop across my back, legs, arms, shoulders, hips.

The way that I rolled myself into the foetal position, my knees tucked up under my chin, and let my brain process the information without needing me to be awake to register the sensation of coming to terms with the fact that someone has just sexually attacked you.

The indescribable, suffocating, nauseating, horrifying moment of awakening a few hours later, quickly realising that what happened really did in fact happen, the tremor of shock and fear and above all, absolute **shame** that someone took so much from you, that someone had seen your body in that way; and secondly, the natural instinct to feel **culpable and stupid that you let it happen.** It felt like someone had died.

The strength that it takes to find a police station open on a Sunday, to arrive and splutter out in a foreign language "I need to report a crime because a man tried to rape me last night."

To spend fourteen hours being passed backwards and forwards from police, to special services, to medical personnel. To be made to go through, word by word, on no sleep, every single thing that happened to you the night before, the day after you escaped from what is every woman's biggest fear. Only you didn't escape, because he had you extended on a sink with your legs spread against your will and his dirty hands trying to invade your body.

To sit down on a chair and your whole body ache, to have to relive what that person did to you, in front of a team of police officers under a grey flickering light in the middle of a cold room. Do have any idea what that is like? For me, in a language that wasn't even my own.

The way that it feels after being driven to various different offices across the city, to be taken to hospital and to be asked by two doctors specialised in rape attacks to remove your clothes so they can observe the bruises on your body. To be sat on a chair, with your legs extended, so that a stranger can violate your vagina once again to check for lesions, cuts, marks, and insert foreign tools to swab for DNA, skin cells, fluid, sweat, anything scientific to prove that what you have said wasn't false.

That is what it is like to report a rape. And I can tell you now, no person would **ever** willingly put themselves through that process. It is humiliating, exhausting, terrifying, heartbreaking, and it is just the beginning.

Being thrust into the centre of a legal criminal case is not something that is resolved overnight. The process of finding the individual, being notified of police progress, his account of the events that unfolded, his admittance or lack of, whether he is kept in detention, if he is, is he freed, what can I do, how do I understand, what information can I get. There are no words to describe the level of intensity involved in a process like this, and anyone who thinks that ANY woman would put herself through that is simply closing their eyes to the fear and acknowledgement that "men like me who undermine the gravity and the severity of what **it means to rape someone** do the things that women like them have to experience." That, people are so disconnected from the painful, violent reality of rape and sexual attacks, perhaps these men are so ashamed of the way they themselves think and the way they see, bash, objectify, deny and abuse women if only verbally, they can't bear to imagine that it is **men like them** that are the ones who think that a woman's body is there to be taken, there to be enjoyed, even against her will, and will go ahead and take it one step further.

For me, not once did anyone from the police service ever question "the role" that I played, because I played no role. Because the problem we have is social. It is not the services allocated to help and protect us that culpabilise the victim and free the actor, it is the society around us that has allowed that to happen.

I did not do anything other than live. I did not do anything other than breathe, exist, happen to be there on that night in the same space as a man who was so furious against my rejection that he thought he could take what he wanted regardless. It is **so important** to understand this mentality. Because what happened to me is extreme, but not uncommon, and as I wrote earlier, this letter exists as an expression of the overwhelming existence of **diluted forms of misogyny, abuse, violation, and intimidation** that occurs every single day to 100% of the women of which every person reading this will have in their lives.

So to avoid any confusion, for anyone still struggling with the fact that no matter **what a woman does with her life, she does not live asking to be raped**, here it is in a nutshell:

As a human being, I have a right to live my life without my sexuality as a woman being used as justification by men to touch me or sexually benefit from my body.

As a human being, I have the right to go out.

As a human being, I have the right to drink, to talk to people, to wear what I want, to go where I want, unaccompanied, alone, with a group, with no group, to live my life.

As a human being, **I have the right to have sex if I want to**, and that right is **identical to that of a man.**

As a human being, **I also have the right to say** *no.*

If I am unconscious, if I have consumed alcohol, if you are naked with a condom on your penis and I have already said yes but then I change my mind, **that does not translate to consent and sex beyond this point is RAPE.**

A final word. A letter to women like me.

I hope reading this has empowered you. I'm sure it wasn't easy, I bet you reading this right now, yes you, there's something in your mind that connects with something on this paper, something that makes that hot rush shoot up your back, your eyes kind of well, your palms clench just a little, that necessary deep breath. It's ok, and I understand, and if you want to talk about it, you go ahead and write me a message. But above all, I hope you are **empowered.** Because I did this for you.

I stood yesterday and I spoke for you. I wrote this to you, so you know that you are not alone, you are never alone. I wrote this to you, when you're doing something completely ordinary and all of a sudden it comes on top of you out of nowhere, like a tonne of sand, burying you under the banality of your day, and all you can do is push it behind your ears and carry on looking for your Navigo Pass or your Oyster card. I understand. I understand how you feel when you don't even understand how you're reacting. Because you thought that a rape victim or a sexual assault victim was this quivering pale thin gaunt-looking woman who locks herself away in a room and never leaves the house. Maybe you are her. Or maybe you're not. Maybe you had to pick yourself up after that first two months or so of complete and utter shock and denial, that you managed to go out for drinks, or have relationships, and take control of your life.

Because apparently, some people like to think that if you don't embody that frail empty miserable woman, people you even know, friends perhaps, co-workers, of course society would put yet another expectation on the victim (remember though, we know she was raped, we accept this one, so we demand that because of this she shows us that she suffered), *then was it really that bad?*

Yes. It was bad. And no. It was not your fault. Rapes happen because of the rapist. And as you have just read my lengthy speech to any person who considers otherwise, know that, by doing this, we are making progress, we are **forcing** people to open their eyes to the daily, hourly sexism and misogyny, sexual assaults and rapes that unfold against women who are simply living their lives.

But believe me. This is not the end of you. No. This does not define you. This does not outline you. This does not do anything to you other **than to know that you survived this. You deserve to know, from me to you, that you are beautiful, and wanted, and you deserve every single ounce of happiness in your life.**

You deserve to know that you are strong, so unbelievably strong, that you can and will achieve things that seem impossible, even if sometimes, you find yourself unable to sleep, staring out of the window and chain-smoking cigarettes, or overdoing it for a while on something that relieves the pressure just a little bit. Because that's okay.

Because you are a **lioness**. You are fearless. You are **unstoppable.** You are incredible and you will achieve great things. You are beautiful and I want to cover you in love, because you deserve it and so much more. You will survive this. You will walk home at night, as I do every day, alone, with your head held high, afraid of **nothing,** afraid of **no-one.**

You will have a lifetime of precious, intimate, loving relationships. You will make love, enjoy and **appreciate your sexuality,** and you will connect with someone who cares so deeply for you, the love will fill you and never leave. But before that, you'll be great on your own. You'll do your thing, just as you want it, you'll eat alone, drink alone, read alone, walk alone. You'll discover the world without constraint, without oppression, you'll **live.**

My life has not been destroyed, and yours has not either.

I will not allocate this event to determine who I am, or alter the way I feel about myself. And neither must you. I must not, am not, and will not be afraid of intimacy and my sexuality. I am proud and sometimes quite in awe of how I found the force inside of me to fight: to fight against him, to fight against sexual discrimination, to speak my voice in front of those judges, and to **learn about myself** from what has happened. I must learn to love myself, and to appreciate everything I have done. And as I progress at Sciences Po, as I learn so much about philosophy, political science, the law, I can approach this subject head on, because I **must.** And you **must too.**

I refuse to let my life be taken down by this. I refuse to be defined by this, because I am so much more than that, Paris means so much more to me than that, and I will carry on talking and fighting for everything that I believe is right. And you will too.

49

Why I Am Pro-Abortion, Not Just Pro-Choice

2015

Valerie Tarico

I believe that abortion care is a positive social good—and I think it's time people said so.

Not long ago, the Daily Kos published an article titled, *I Am Pro-Choice, Not Pro-Abortion.* "Has anyone ever truly been pro-abortion?" one commenter asked.

Uh. Yes. Me. That would be me.

I am pro-abortion like I'm pro-knee-replacement and pro-chemotherapy and pro-cataract surgery. As the last protection against ill-conceived childbearing when all else fails, abortion is part of a set of tools that help women and men to form the families of their choosing. I believe that abortion care is a positive social good. And I suspect that a lot of other people secretly believe the same thing. And I think it's time we said so.

Note: As an aside, I'm also pro-choice. Choice is about who gets to make the decision. The question of whether and when we bring a new life into the world is, to my mind, one of the most important decisions a person can make. It is too big a decision for us to make for each other, and especially for perfect strangers.

But independent of who owns the decision, I'm pro on the procedure, and I've decided that it's time, for once and for all, to count it out on my ten fingers.

1. **I'm pro-abortion because being able to delay and limit child-bearing is fundamental to female empowerment and equality.**
   A woman who lacks the means to manage her fertility lacks the

means to manage her life. Any plans, dreams, aspirations, responsibilities or commitments—no matter how important—have a great big contingency clause built: "until or unless I get pregnant, in which case all bets are off." Think of any professional woman you know. She wouldn't be in that role if she hadn't been able to time and limit her childbearing. Think of any girl you know who imagines becoming a professional woman. She won't get there unless she has effective, reliable means to manage her fertility. In generations past, nursing care was provided by nuns and teachers who were spinsters, because avoiding sexual intimacy was the only way women could avoid unpredictable childbearing and so be freed up to serve their communities in other capacities. But if you think that abstinence should be our model for modern fertility management, consider the little graves that get found every so often under old nunneries and Catholic homes for unwed mothers.

2. **I'm pro-abortion because well-timed pregnancies give children a healthier start in life.** We now have ample evidence that babies do best when women are able to space their pregnancies and get both pre-natal and pre-conception care. The specific nutrients we ingest in the weeks *before* we get pregnant can have a lifelong effect on the wellbeing of our offspring. Rapid repeat pregnancies increase the risk of low birthweight babies and other complications. Wanted babies are more likely to get their toes kissed, to be welcomed into families that are financially and emotionally ready to receive them, to get preventive medical care during childhood and the kind of loving engagement that helps young brains to develop.

3. **I'm pro-abortion because I take motherhood seriously.** Most female bodies can incubate a baby; and thanks to antibiotics, cesareans and anti-hemorrhage drugs, most of us are able to survive pushing a baby out into the world. But parenting is a lot of work; and doing it well takes twenty dedicated years of focus, attention, patience, persistence, social support, mental health, money, and a whole lot more. This is the biggest, most life-transforming thing most of us will ever do. The idea that women should simply go with it when they find themselves pregnant after a one-night-stand, or a rape, or a broken condom COMPLETELY TRIVIALIZES MOTHERHOOD.

4. **I'm pro-abortion because intentional childbearing helps couples, families and communities to get out of poverty.** Decades of

research in countries ranging from the U.S. to Bangladesh show that reproductive policy is economic policy. It is no coincidence that the American middle class rose along with the ability of couples to plan their families, starting at the beginning of the last century. Having two or three kids instead of eight or ten was critical to prospering in the modern industrial economy. Early unsought childbearing nukes economic opportunity and contributes to multi-generational poverty. Today in the U.S., unsought pregnancy and childbearing is declining for everyone but the poorest families and communities, contributing to what some call a growing "caste system" in America. Strong, determined girls and women sometimes beat the odds, but their stories inspire us precisely because they are the exception to the rule. Justice dictates that the full range of fertility management tools including the best state-of-the-art contraceptive technologies and, when that fails, abortion care be equally available to all, not just a privileged few.

5. **I'm pro-abortion because reproduction is a highly imperfect process.** Genetic recombination is a complicated progression with flaws and false starts at every step along the way. To compensate, in every known species including humans, reproduction operates as a big funnel. Many more eggs and sperm are produced than will ever meet; more combine into embryos than will ever implant; more implant than will grow into babies; and more babies are born than will grow up to have babies of their own. This systematic culling makes God or nature the world's biggest abortion provider: Nature's way of producing healthy kids essentially requires every woman to have an abortion mill built into her own body. In humans, an estimated 60-80 percent of fertilized eggs self-destruct before becoming babies, which is why the people who kill the most embryos are those like the Duggars who try to maximize their number of pregnancies. But the weeding-out process is also highly imperfect. Sometimes perfectly viable combinations boot themselves out; sometimes horrible defects slip through. A woman's body may be less fertile when she is stressed or ill or malnourished, but as pictures of skeletal moms and babies show, some women conceive even under devastating circumstances. Like any other medical procedure, therapeutic contraception and abortion complement natural processes designed to help us survive and thrive.

6. **I'm pro-abortion because I think morality is about the well-being of sentient beings.** I believe that morality is about the lived experience of sentient beings—beings who can feel pleasure and pain, preference and intention, who at their most complex can live in relation to other beings, love and be loved and value their own existence. What are they capable of wanting? What are they capable of feeling? These are the questions my husband and I explored with our kids when they were figuring out their responsibility to their chickens and guinea pigs. It was a lesson that turned expensive, when the girls stopped drinking milk from cows that didn't get to see the light of day or eat grass, but it's not one I regret. *Do unto others as they want you to do unto them.* It's called the Platinum Rule. In this moral universe, real people count more than potential people, hypothetical people or corporate people.

7. **I'm pro-abortion because contraceptives are imperfect, and people are too.** The Pill is 1960's technology, now half a century old. For decades, women were told the Pill was 99 percent effective, and they blamed themselves when they got pregnant anyways. But that 99 percent is a "perfect use" statistics, and in the real world, where most of us live, people aren't perfect. In the real world, 1 in 11 women relying on the Pill gets pregnant each year. For a couple relying on condoms, that's 1 in 6. Young and poor women—those whose lives are least predictable and most vulnerable to being thrown off course—are also those who have the most difficulty taking pills consistently. Pill technology most fails those who need it most, which makes abortion access a matter not only of compassion but of justice. State-of-the-art IUDs and Implants radically change this equation, largely because they take human error out of the picture for years on end, or until a woman wants a baby. And despite the deliberate misinformation being spread by opponents, these methods are genuine contraceptives, not abortifacients. Depending on the method chosen, they disable sperm or block their path, or prevent an egg from being released. Once settled into place, an IUD or implant drops the annual pregnancy rate below 1 in 500. And guess what. Teen pregnancies and abortions plummet—which makes me happy, because even though I'm pro-abortion, I'd love the need for abortion to go away. Why mitigate harm when you can prevent it?

8. **I'm pro-abortion because I believe in mercy, grace, compassion, and the power of fresh starts.** Many years ago, my friend Chip was driving his family on vacation when his kids started squabbling. His wife Marla undid her seatbelt to help them, and as Chip looked over at her their top-heavy minivan veered onto the shoulder and then rolled, and Marla died. Sometimes people make mistakes or have accidents that they pay for the rest of their lives. But I myself have swerved onto the shoulder and simply swerved back. The price we pay for a lapse in attention or judgment, or an accident of any kind isn't proportional to the error we made. Who among us hasn't had unprotected sex when the time or situation or partnership wasn't quite right for bringing a new life into the world? Most of the time we get lucky; sometimes we don't. And in those situations we rely on the mercy, compassion, and generosity of others. In this regard, an unsought pregnancy is like any other accident. I can walk today only because surgeons reassembled my lower leg after it was crushed between the front of a car and a bicycle frame when I was a teen. And I can walk today (and run and jump) because another team of surgeons re-assembled my knee-joint after I fell off a ladder. And I can walk today (and bicycle with my family) because a third team of surgeons repaired my other knee after I pulled a whirring brush mower onto myself, cutting clear through bone. Three accidents, all my own doing, and three knee surgeries. Some women have three abortions.

9. **I'm pro-abortion because the future is always in motion, and we have the power and responsibility to shape it well.** As a college student, I read a Ray Bradbury story about a man who travels back into prehistory on a "time safari." The tourists have been coached about the importance of not disturbing anything lest they change the flow of history. When they return to the present, they realize that the outcome of an election has changed, and they discover that the protagonist who had gone off the trail, has a crushed butterfly on the bottom of his shoe. In baby making, as in Bradbury's story, the future is always in motion, and every little thing we do has consequences we have no way to predict. Any small change means a different child comes into the world. Which nights your mother had headaches, the sexual position of your parents when they conceived you, whether or not your mother rolled over in bed afterwards—if any of these things had been different, someone else

would be here instead of you. Every day, men and women make small choices and potential people wink into and out of existence. We move, and our movements ripple through time in ways that are incomprehensible, and we can never know what the alternate futures might have been. But some things we can know or predict, at least at the level of probability, and I think this knowledge provides a basis for guiding wise reproductive decisions. My friend Judy says that parenting begins before conception. I agree. How and when, we choose to carry forward a new life can stack the odds in favor of our children or against them, and to me that is a sacred trust.

10. **I'm pro-abortion because I love my daughter.** I first wrote the story of my own abortion when Dr. Tiller was murdered and I couldn't bear the thought of abortion providers standing in the crosshairs alone. "My Abortion Baby" was about my daughter, Brynn, who exists only because a kind doctor like George Tiller gave me and my husband the gift of a fresh start when we learned that our wanted pregnancy was unhealthy. Brynn literally embodies the ever changing flow of the future, because she could not exist in an alternate universe in which I would have carried that first pregnancy to term. She was conceived while I would still have been pregnant with a child we had begun to imagine, but who never came to be. My husband and I felt very clear that carrying forward that pregnancy would have been a violation of our values, and neither of us ever second guessed our decision. Even so, I grieved. Even when I got pregnant again a few months later, I remember feeling petulant and thinking, *I want that baby, not this one.* And then Brynn came out into the world and I looked into her eyes, and I fell in love and never looked back.

All around us, living breathing and loving are the chosen children of mothers who waited—who ended an ill-timed or unhealthy pregnancy and then later chose to carry forward a new life. "I was only going to have two children," my friend, Jane said as her daughters raced, screeching joyfully, across my lawn. Jane followed them with her eyes. "My abortions let me have these two when the time was right, with someone I loved."

Those who see abortion as an unmitigated evil often talk about the "millions of missing people" who were not born into this world because a pregnant woman decided, *not now*. But they never talk about the millions of children and adults who are here today only because their mothers had abortions—real people who exist in this version of the future, people who are living out their lives all around us—loving and laughing and suffering and struggling and dancing and dreaming, and having babies of their own.

When those who oppose abortion lament the "missing people," I hear an echo of my own petulant thought: *I want that person, not this one.* And I wish that they could simply experience what I did, that they could look into the beautiful eyes of the people in front of them, and fall in love.

50 The Countersexual Manifesto (excerpt)

2000

Paul B. Preciado

Contra-Sexual Contract (Sample)

I, the signatory herewith _____
foreswear, by my own will, body and affects, of my biopolitical position as a man or a woman, of any privilege (whether social, economic, or regarding hereditary rights) and of any commitment (whether social, economic, or reproductive) resulting from my gender, sexual and race position within the framework of the naturalized heterosexual system.

I recognize my body and all living bodies as speaking bodies and I fully consent to never enter into a naturalized sexual relationship with them, and to never have sex with them outside of temporal and consensual contra-sexual contracts.

I declare myself a somatic translator: dildo-producer, a translator and distributor of dildos onto my own body and onto any body signing this contract.

I renounce all the privileges and all obligations that could derive from the unequal power positions generated by the consensual use and re-inscription of dildos within the framework of this contract.

I declare myself as a hole and as a worker of the asshole.

I resign all legal kinship (both parental and marital) that has been assigned to me within the heterosexual regime, as well as all privileges and obligations derived from them.

I resign all property rights over my sexual fluids and cells and over the production of my uterus. I recognize the right to use my reproductive cells only within the framework of a consensual contra-sexual contract. I resign all property rights over the body or bodies produced within the context of a contra-sexual reproductive practice.

This agreement is valid during a period of time of _____ days, _____ months, _____ years.

Sign _____

Date _____

51 Feminist Manifesto to Support the Rights of Sex Workers

n.d.

Feminists for Sex Workers

As the signatories of this manifesto, we—women's rights, feminist, and sex workers' rights organisations and collectives—express our support for sex workers' self-determination and the recognition of sex work as work. With women's rights, reproductive rights and gender equality threatened across Europe and Central-Asia, we are in solidarity with sex workers, who face myriad forms of violence: from structural and institutional to physical and interpersonal. In order to address the systematic oppression sex workers face, we ask all feminists to concentrate their resources on including and amplifying sex workers' voices in the movement and to stop promoting legal frameworks that have been shown to be detrimental to sex workers' rights.

We call for a feminist movement that situates gender injustice within patriarchal, capitalist, white supremacist societies, and is inclusive of trans people and sex workers. Our criminal justice systems are oppressive, and therefore we do not see increased policing, prosecution, and imprisonment as the only solution to violence against women, trans people and gender inequality. We believe in community interventions, long-term organising and mobilisation against the complexity of violence against women and trans people, including economic inequalities, and the lack of accessible social security nets and services.

1. **We acknowledge sex workers' as experts in their own lives and needs.** Feminism, as it has always done in the past, has to support women's agency and self-determination over their work and their bodies. Sex workers should be no exceptions.

2. **We respect sex workers' decision to engage in sex work.** As feminists, we reject misogynist statements according to which sex workers "sell their bodies" or "sell themselves": to suggest that sex entails giving away or losing part of yourself is profoundly anti-feminist. Women are not diminished by sex. We further reject any analysis which holds that sex workers contribute to the "commodification of women, sex or intimacy". We will not blame sex workers for causing harm to other women but patriarchy and other oppressive systems.

3. **We affirm sex workers' ability to claim consent.** To state that it is impossible to consent within sex work takes away from sex workers the ability to name their own boundaries, and the ability to speak out against violence. To propagate the idea that clients "buy" sex workers' bodies or consent—and as such can do what they want to a sex worker—has dangerous real life consequences for sex workers. Furthermore, by positing all sex work as a form of violence, such ideas can lead to a crackdown on sex work in the name of tackling violence—even though crackdowns on sex work actually increase sex workers' vulnerability to violence.

4. **We advocate for measures that provide real help and support to victims of trafficking, with full respect for the protection of their human and labour rights.** As such, we denounce the conflation of migration, sex work and trafficking. As a result of this conflation, migrant sex workers are particularly targeted by police harassment and raids, detention and deportation, and are pushed into clandestine working environments where they are more vulnerable to violence and exploitation.

5. **We fight to eliminate all forms of violence against sex workers.** Sex work is not a form of sexual violence but sex workers are especially vulnerable to sexual and intimate partner violence due to criminalisation and often intersecting oppressions such as sexism, whorephobia, homophobia and transphobia, racism and classism. Oppression and criminalisation make sex workers vulnerable to violence from individuals, social services, the police, immigration officials, and the judiciary. Regarding sex work as inherently violent and sex workers' consent as invalid serves to normalise violence against them.

6. **We work every day to end misogyny in all spheres of life.** Misogyny, however, is not the cause of sex work, but arises as a

response to women's acts and choices, whether that is wearing make-up, having an abortion, or selling sex. We name misogynist sentiments and acts as the problem, and reject calls to change or eliminate behaviours that 'provoke' misogyny. To attempt to eliminate sex work on the grounds that it supposedly provokes misogyny is to agree with those who state that some women's actions—such as selling sex—are intrinsically deserving of misogyny.

7. **We respect migrants' rights.** Migrant women face limited access to work and often little or no access to social security. Some of those seeking refuge sell sexual services out of very limited options to earn their living. The criminalisation of clients, and other forms of sex work criminalisation put migrant sex workers under a constant threat of police violence, arrest, and deportation, denying their right to access to justice and redress. The criminalisation of clients removes their income, while offering them no alternatives for survival.

8. **We support LGBT rights.** Rejection of LGBT people from their family, obstacles to education and employment in cissexist and heteronormative social structures often result in sex work being one of the very few economic and employment opportunities for LGBT people, especially trans women. Anti sex work laws do not benefit LGB and trans people as they don't address these complex facets of social marginalisation. This is particularly the case for trans women, as laws that criminalise sex work are particularly used to profile and persecute this group, regardless of whether the person in question is even a sex worker.

9. **We call for full decriminalisation of sex work.** There is strong evidence that the Swedish model and all other forms of sex work criminalisation harm sex workers. The Swedish model pushes them into poverty, reduces their power in negotiations with clients, criminalises them for working together for safety, evicts and deports them. By enabling sex workers to organise as workers, decriminalisation decreases sex workers' vulnerability to exploitative labour practices and violence.

10. **We speak up against women's increasing precarisation in labour.** Historically in Western societies under capitalism and patriarchy, women's work (domestic work, care work, sex work, emotional labour) considered "feminine" have been undervalued, underpaid, or completely rendered invisible and unwaged.

Women globally, including sex workers, have jobs that are less well paid and more insecure: they work under exploitative conditions—from criminalised, seasonal or temporary employment to home work, flexi and temp-work, to subcontracting, working as freelancers, or as self-employed persons. Sex work has similarities to other types of care work, in that it is mainly associated with women, and often migrant women or women of colour. Care workers, like sex workers, often do not enjoy the same labour rights as workers in jobs associated with men. Advocating for sex workers' rights therefore has to emphasise their labour rights and needs to address precarious working conditions and exploitation in the sex industry, and advocate for legal frameworks that give power to sex workers as workers.

11. **We demand the inclusion of sex workers in the feminist movement.** Their inclusion brings invaluable insights, energy, diversity and experience of mobilisation to our movement and challenges our assumptions about gender, class and race. Sex workers were some of the world's first feminists, and our community is diminished without them.

52 Masturbation Manifesto

1997

Betty Dodson

A lone warrior extolling the benefits of masturbation for close to three decades, I'm ready to organize a movement with millions of other masturbators against the forces of sex-negativity. What has AIDS got to do with it? Everything. Talking honestly about sex is the key to successful HIV prevention; unsafe sex is the result of all the lies, secrets and silences under which our erotic desires are buried. So if you're a friend of sex who would like to take a stand with me, start today by enjoying your own selfloving sessions without any guilt or apology. The next step is going public by telling a few friends about your favorite techniques. And finally, sharing masturbation with a friend qualifies you as an activist in my book.

The firing of Dr. Joycelyn Elders in 1995 got the word masturbation on networks and in newspapers around the world. The message? Mention this in America and your political career is over. When our former surgeon general responded with intelligence and compassion to a question about masturbation at a news conference—"I think that is something that is part of human sexuality, and it perhaps could be taught"—our elected officials went ballistic. Elders was purposely misconstrued as calling for how-to-jerkoff lessons rather than honest discussion of a universal practice. After the story broke, a conservative politician on TV said, "I don't want my five year old walking around with a condom in his pocket." The old political ploy of bait and switch.

Given the bankruptcy of "abstinence" messages and with half of all new HIV infections among people under 25, masturbation is more than ever a meaningful component of safe-sex education. Rest assured, puritanical leaders will continue to deny the existence of self-sexuality until our unified voices singing its praises are heard above their rhetoric of repression.

Why does the acceptance of masturbation seem to threaten the very foundation of our social structure? Could it be that independent orgasms might lead to independent thoughts? An effective way to keep a population docile and easy to manipulate is by prohibiting childhood masturbation, insisting on the procreative model of sex, upholding marriage and monogamy, withholding sex information, making birth control difficult, trying to end abortion, criminalizing prostitution, condemning homosexuality, censoring sexual entertainment and denying the existence of sexual diversity. That makes everyone a sexual sinner.

Ever wonder why sex with ourselves isn't viewed with any pride? My speculation is, we're a nation of brainwashed romantic-love junkies hooked on a myth that promises us passionate orgasms forever from our very own Prince or Princess Charming. Romance is the drug that leads to monogamous pair bondage that erodes sexual desire. By the time most of us figure it out, children, property or finances keep us glued together as sexual pleasure diminishes or disappears altogether.

Take heart. Partnersex gets better the minute we start improving our own selfloving practices. Start by seeing masturbation as a sexual meditation, and practice regularly for an hour or more. Always use a good massage oil and great music. Focus on your breathing, move your pelvis like Elvis. Although orgasm is a nervous-system function that operates without conscious control, your joyful rhapsody can be extended by building up sexual tension, and right after orgasm, not stopping.

Sex energy is the life force, and my body doesn't care if it's me with my electric vibrator and a dildo, or a lover's tongue, hand or penis. An orgasm is an orgasm is an orgasm. Once we embrace masturbation, we can have all the sex we want on our own terms with someone we love who will never abandon us.

53 The GINK Manifesto

2010

Lisa Hymas

In 1969, graduating college senior Stephanie Mills made national headlines with a commencement address exclaiming that, in the face of impending ecological devastation, she was choosing to forgo parenthood. "I am terribly saddened by the fact that the most humane thing for me to do is to have no children at all," she told her classmates.

I come here before you today to make the same proclamation—with a twist. I am thoroughly *delighted* by the fact that the most humane thing for me to do is to have no children at all.

Making the green choice too often feels like a sacrifice or a hassle or an expense. In this case, it feels like a luxurious indulgence that just so happens to cost a lot less for me and weigh a lot less on the carbon-bloated atmosphere.

I call myself a GINK: green inclinations, no kids.

First, a word for you parents

Let me get this out of the way up front: I like kids—many of them, anyway. Some of my best friends, as they say, are parents. I bear no ill will to procreators, past, present, and prospective. I claim no moral or ethical high ground.

If being a parent is something you've longed and planned for, or already embarked upon, I respect your choice and I wish you luck. Go forth and raise happy, healthy kids. May they bring you joy and fulfillment, and may they become productive members of society who faithfully pay their Social Security taxes.

Of course, you parents and parent wannabes don't need my encouragement—our society supports your decision overwhelmingly. OK,
yes, the U.S. lacks paid family leave and universal childcare, not to
mention many basic rights for same-sex couples with children—and
we should remedy these shortcomings. But from the tax breaks to the
discounted airline seats, from the eager grandparents urging you on
to the friends, cousins, and complete strangers who ask when the first
or next kid is coming, from the "What to Expect ..." empire to the
proliferating mommy and daddy blogs, our culture constantly affirms
your choice—in many ways, almost demands it. And, no small matter,
our biology does too.

So this post isn't for you. It's for the childfree and childfree-curious,
who *don't* get a lot of encouragement in our society. Parents, keep
reading if you like, but you have to promise not to tell the rest of us
that we'd feel differently if we just had our own!

OK, down to business

Here's the dirty little secret that we're never supposed to say in mixed
company: There are a lot of perks to childfree living, not to mention
a lot of green good that comes from bringing fewer beings onto a
polluted and crowded planet.

Yes, as a childfree person, I'll miss out on a lot: The miracle of
childbirth (though, truth be told, I don't feel so bad about skipping
that one). The hilariously perceptive things that only kids say. A
respectable excuse for rereading the Harry Potter series. The hope that
my kid will be smarter and cooler and better looking than I ever was.
More boisterous holiday celebrations. Someone to carry on the family
name (assuming I won the arm-wrestling match with my partner over
whose name the kid would actually get). Maybe even the satisfaction
of helping a child grow into a well-educated, well-adjusted adult, and
the peace of mind of knowing there's someone to take care of me in
my old age.

But parents miss out on a lot too (as some will be the first to tell
you): Time and emotional energy to invest in friendships and a romantic partnership. Space to focus on a career or education or avocation.
Uninterrupted "grown-up" conversations. Travel that's truly impulsive
or leisurely or adventurous (and never involves zoos). Unpremeditated

Saturday nights on the town and Sunday brunches out. Opportunities for political or community engagement. Stretches of quiet for reading or writing or relaxing. A non-child-proofed, non-toy-strewn, non-goldfish-cracker-crumb-riddled home. Eight peaceful, uninterrupted hours of sleep a night. All without any guilt that one should be spending more quality time with the kid.

A childfree life also means a lot more financial freedom. How expensive are kids? Try $291,570 for a child born in 2008 to parents bringing home between $57,000 and $98,000 a year, according to figures from the USDA. That's for the first 18 years, so it *doesn't* include college. If you make more, you're likely to spend more. Couples bringing in upwards of $98,000 a year can expect to spend an average of $483,750 on a child's first 18 years. (Dig into the numbers yourself for all the caveats and conditions.)

Opting out of childrearing might leave you richer in happiness too, as Harvard psychology professor and happiness expert Daniel Gilbert recently told NPR:

> [I]t probably is true that without children, your marriage might be happier in the sense that you would report more daily satisfaction. People are surprised to find this, because they value and love their children above all things. How can my children not be a source of great happiness?

Well, one reason is that although children are a source of happiness, they tend to crowd out other sources of happiness. So people who have a first child often find in the first year or two that they're not doing many of the other things that used to make them happy. They don't go to the movies or the theater. They don't go out with their friends. They don't make love with their spouse.

In his 2006 book *Stumbling on Happiness*, Gilbert offers more on this topic: Careful studies of how women feel as they go about their daily activities show that they are less happy when taking care of their children than when eating, exercising, shopping, napping, or watching television. Indeed looking after the kids appears to be only slightly more pleasant than doing housework.

None of this should surprise us. Every parent knows that children are a lot of work—a lot of really *hard* work—and although parenting has many rewarding moments, the vast majority of its moments involve dull and selfless service to people who will take decades to become even begrudgingly grateful for what we are doing.

Even firebrand valedictorian Stephanie Mills, who initially considered her decision not to have children a sacrifice, new writes:

> ... it proved to be a good personal choice. I am cussedly independent and I love my solitude and freedom. ... Other women, I know, have been able to combine demanding vocations with motherhood. Given my particular nature, the responsibility and distraction of childrearing most likely would have prevented me from pursuing my work as a writer, which has been immensely rewarding ...

Which isn't to say she never wonders about her decision:

> Now that I'm old enough to be a grandmother, I sometimes wish that I had a granddaughter to commune with, but I am friends with some spectacular young people and can learn from them as well as pass along whatever wisdom I've developed. That will have to do.

Ultimately, as Mills suggests, life is a series of tradeoffs. By choosing not to have kids, some doors are closed to you, but others are open— and they don't have sticky doorknobs.

The green angle

Beyond the undisturbed sleep and the gleaming doorknobs, consider the environmental benefits to the childfree life.

We're on track to hit a global population of 7 billion people next year or the year after—3 billion more than when Mills got all riled up four decades ago. We've spewed enough greenhouse gases into the atmosphere to push it past the safe point, which many climate scientists agree is 350 parts carbon dioxide per million; we're already at about 390 and rising fast. And Americans are among the most carbon-intensive people on earth. The average American generates about 66 times more CO_2 each year than the average Bangladeshi—20 tons versus 0.3 tons.

If you consider not just the carbon impact of your own kids but of your kids' kids and so on, the numbers get even starker. According to a 2009 study in *Global Environmental Change* that took into account the long-term impact of Americans' descendants, each child adds an estimated 9,441 metric tons of CO2 to a parent's carbon legacy—that's about *5.7 times his or her direct lifetime emissions.*

"Many people are unaware of the power of exponential population growth," said study coauthor Paul Murtaugh, a professor of statistics at Oregon State University. "Future growth amplifies the consequences of people's reproductive choices today, the same way that compound interest amplifies a bank balance." (To take an extreme example, compare childfree me with Yitta Schwartz of Monroe, N.Y., who died this year at the age of 93, leaving behind an estimated 2,000 descendants.)

A person who cares about preserving a livable environment has lots of options for doing her bit, and you've heard all about them: live in an energy-efficient home in a walkable neighborhood; bike or walk or take public transit when possible; drive an efficient car if you drive one at all; fly less; go veg; buy organic and local; limit purchases of consumer goods; switch to CFLs or LEDs; slay your vampires; offset carbon emissions; vote for climate-concerned candidates, and hold them accountable for their campaign promises.

But even in aggregate, all of these moves don't come close to the impact of not bringing new human beings—particularly new Americans—into the world.

Here's a simple truth: For an average person like me—someone who doesn't have the ability of an Al Gore to reach millions, or of a Nancy Pelosi to advance (if not actually enact) landmark environmental legislation, or of a Van Jones to inspire (and piss off) whole new audiences—the single most meaningful contribution I can make to a cleaner, greener world is to not have children.

Just say it

Why does it feel almost audacious to articulate all of this?

Those of us who are childfree by choice are in the minority, but if you judged by the public discourse about our lifestyle, you'd think we were practically nonexistent.

Parents talk all the time about the delights and challenges of raising kids, to other parents and to all the rest of us, and I don't begrudge them that.

We childfree people rarely discuss in public the upsides and downsides of life without kids—and that's what needs to change.

If you're intentionally childfree, how many times have you been asked, "So, when are you going to have children?" and mumbled a less-than-candid reply: "Oh, I'm not sure," or "Well, it just might not happen for us," or "Maybe someday ..." when what you really mean is "Never."

Childfree people tread too gingerly around parents, as though we might wound their feelings if we told the truth about why we've made different decisions than they have. But we insult them by thinking they're so fragile or insecure about their family choices—and we shortchange ourselves and society at large by not speaking openly about the legitimate choice to not have a child.

What would happen if you answered the kid question honestly? "No, I'm happy with my life as is," or "A child doesn't fit into our life plans," or "Kids aren't really my thing," or "I think there are plenty of people on the planet already."

If we said what we really think, I suspect we would actually find a lot of kindred or at least sympathetic spirits out there, GINKs and otherwise. We might have some refreshingly frank and gratifying conversations with the parents in our lives. And we could give those who are undecided about parenthood the understanding that the choice to be childfree is completely valid, and not completely lonely.

Little bundles of (j)oy aren't for everyone—and it's time we said so out loud.

54

Futurist Manifesto of Lust

1913

Valentine de Saint-Point

A reply to those dishonest journalists who twist phrases to make the Idea seem ridiculous;
to those women who only think what I have dared to say;
to those for whom Lust is still nothing but a sin;
to all those who in Lust can only see Vice, just as in Pride they see only vanity.

Lust, when viewed without moral preconceptions and as an essential part of life's dynamism, is a force.

Lust is not, any more than pride, a mortal sin for the race that is strong. Lust, like pride, is a virtue that urges one on, a powerful source of energy.

Lust is the expression of a being projected beyond itself. It is the painful joy of wounded flesh, the joyous pain of a flowering. And whatever secrets unite these beings, it is a union of flesh. It is the sensory and sensual synthesis that leads to the greatest liberation of spirit. It is the communion of a particle of humanity with all the sensuality of the earth.

Lust is the quest of the flesh for the unknown, just as Celebration is the spirit's quest for the unknown. Lust is the act of creating, it is Creation.

Flesh creates in the way that the spirit creates. In the eyes of the Universe their creation is equal. One is not superior to the other and creation of the spirit depends on that of the flesh.

We possess body and spirit. To curb one and develop the other shows weakness and is wrong. A strong man must realize his full carnal and spiritual potentiality. The satisfaction of their lust is the conquerors' due. After a battle in which men have died, **it is normal for the victors, proven in war, to turn to rape in the conquered land, so that life may be re-created.**

When they have fought their battles, soldiers seek sensual pleasures, in which their constantly battling energies can be unwound and renewed. The modern hero, the hero in any field, experiences the same desire and the same pleasure. The artist, that great universal medium, has the same need. And the exaltation of the initiates of those religions still sufficiently new to contain a tempting element of the unknown, is no more than sensuality diverted spiritually towards a sacred female image.

Art and war are the great manifestations of sensuality; lust is their flower. A people exclusively spiritual or a people exclusively carnal would be condemned to the same decadence—sterility.

Lust excites energy and releases strength. Pitilessly it drove primitive man to victory, for the pride of bearing back a woman the spoils of the defeated. Today it drives the great men of business who run the banks, the press and international trade to increase their wealth by creating centers, harnessing energies and exalting the crowds, to worship and glorify with it the object of their lust. These men, tired but strong, find time for lust, the principal motive force of their action and of the reactions caused by their actions affecting multitudes and worlds.

Even among the new peoples where sensuality has not yet been released or acknowledged, and who are neither primitive brutes nor the sophisticated representatives of the old civilizations, woman is equally the great galvanizing principle to which all is offered. The secret cult that man has for her is only the unconscious drive of a lust as yet barely woken. Amongst these peoples as amongst the peoples of the north, but for different reasons, lust is almost exclusively concerned with procreation. But lust, under whatever aspects it shows itself, whether they are considered normal or abnormal, is always the supreme spur.

The animal life, the life of energy, the life of the spirit, sometimes demand a respite. And effort for effort's sake calls inevitably for effort for pleasure's sake. These efforts are not mutually harmful but complementary, and realize fully the total being.

For heroes, for those who create with the spirit, for dominators of all fields, lust is the magnificent exaltation of their strength. For every being it is a motive to surpass oneself with the simple aim of self-selection, of being noticed, chosen, picked out.

Christian morality alone, following on from pagan morality, was fatally drawn to consider lust as a weakness. Out of the healthy joy which is the flowering of the flesh in all its power it has made something shameful and to be hidden, a vice to be denied. It has covered it with hypocrisy, and this has made a sin of it.

We must stop despising Desire, this attraction at once delicate and brutal between two bodies, of whatever sex, two bodies that want each other, striving for unity. We must stop despising Desire, disguising it in the pitiful clothes of old and sterile sentimentality.

It is not lust that disunites, dissolves and annihilates. It is rather the mesmerizing complications of sentimentality, artificial jealousies, words that inebriate and deceive, the rhetoric of parting and eternal fidelities, literary nostalgia—all the histrionics of love.

We must get rid of all the ill-omened debris of romanticism, counting daisy petals, moonlight duets, heavy endearments, false hypocritical modesty. When beings are drawn together by a physical attraction, let them—instead of talking only of the fragility of their hearts—dare to express their desires, the inclinations of their bodies, and to anticipate the possibilities of joy and disappointment in their future carnal union.

Physical modesty, which varies according to time and place, has only the ephemeral value of a social virtue.

We must face up to lust in full consciousness. We must make of it what a sophisticated and intelligent being makes of himself and of his life; **we must make lust into a work of art.** To allege unwariness or bewilderment in order to explain an act of love is hypocrisy, weakness and stupidity.

We should desire a body consciously, like any other thing.

Love at first sight, passion or failure to think, must not prompt us to be constantly giving ourselves, nor to take beings, as we are usually inclined to do so due to our inability to see into the future. We must choose intelligently. Directed by our intuition and will, we should compare the feelings and desires of the two partners and avoid uniting and satisfying any that are unable to complement and exalt each other.

Equally consciously and with the same guiding will, the joys of this coupling should lead to the climax, should develop its full potential, and should permit to flower all the seeds sown by the merging of two bodies. Lust should be made into a work of art, formed like every work of art, both instinctively and consciously.

We must strip lust of all the sentimental veils that disfigure it. These veils were thrown over it out of mere cowardice, because smug sentimentality is so satisfying. Sentimentality is comfortable and therefore demeaning.

In one who is young and healthy, when lust clashes with sentimentality, lust is victorious. Sentiment is a creature of fashion, lust is eternal. Lust triumphs, because it is the joyous exaltation that drives one beyond oneself, the delight in possession and domination, the perpetual victory from which the perpetual battle is born anew, the headiest and surest intoxication of conquest. And as this certain conquest is temporary, it must be constantly won anew.

Lust is a force, in that it refines the spirit by bringing to white heat the excitement of the flesh. The spirit burns bright and clear from a healthy, strong flesh, purified in the embrace. Only the weak and sick sink into the mire and are diminished. And lust is a force in that it kills the weak and exalts the strong, aiding natural selection.

Lust is a force, finally, in that it never leads to the insipidity of the definite and the secure, doled out by soothing sentimentality. Lust is the eternal battle, never finally won. After the fleeting triumph, even during the ephemeral triumph itself, reawakening dissatisfaction spurs a human being, driven by an orgiastic will, to expand and surpass himself.

Lust is for the body what an ideal is for the spirit—the magnificent Chimaera, that one ever clutches at but never captures, and which the young and the avid, intoxicated with the vision, pursue without rest.

Lust is a force.

PART VI

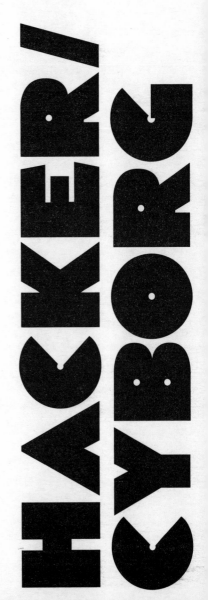

HACKER/CYBORG

Introduction to Hacker/Cyborg

Here we find a feminism wed to technology, wrestling with how we merge with, diverge from, and become technologies of resistance. We begin with one of the all-time classic feminist manifestos—Donna Haraway's "Cyborg Manifesto"—a text that not only forever altered the field of gender studies, but also paved the way for imagining humans and technology as politically intertwined. We see newer visions of cyberfeminism—from cybertwee's short and aesthetically creative manifesto to VNS Matrix's vision for "art with our cunt." This is followed by two substantial manifestos about the value of hackers, both in terms of what the internet *could* be (Oxblood Ruffin) and why we need feminist hackers (McKenzie Wark).

The section concludes with two manifestos that collectively tackle challenges of technology and its relationship to power more broadly—including a manifesto that politicizes technology and imagines it as a force for social justice (Mette Ingvartsen) alongside an older radical rewriting of the field of psychiatry (Claude Steiner). Collectively, this section asks how technology both influences and undermines feminist politics, how the cyborg figures centrally in the revolution, and how the role of the hacker—an inherently disruptive presence—is both compelling and necessary to smash the patriarchy.

55 A Cyborg Manifesto (excerpt)

1991

Donna Haraway

A cyborg is a cybernetic organism, a hybrid of machine and organism, a creature of social reality as well as a creature of fiction. ... Liberation rests on the construction of the consciousness, the imaginative apprehension of oppression and so of possibility. The cyborg is a matter of fiction and lived experience that changes what counts as women's experience in the late twentieth century. This is a struggle over life and death, but the boundary between science fiction and social reality is an optical illusion.

Contemporary science fiction is full of cyborgs—creatures simultaneously animal and machine, who populate worlds ambiguously natural and crafted. Modern medicine is also full of cyborgs, of couplings between organism and machine. ... Cyborg replication is uncoupled from organic reproduction.

I am making an argument for the cyborg as a fiction mapping our social and bodily reality ...

By the late twentieth century, our time, a mythic time, we are all chimeras, theorized and fabricated hybrids of machine and organism; in short, we are cyborgs. The cyborg is our ontology; it gives us our politics. The cyborg is a condensed image of both imagination and material reality. ... the relation between organism and machine has been a border war ...

In a sense, the cyborg has no origin story in the Western sense .... The cyborg skips the step of original unity, of identification with nature in the Western sense.

Unlike the hopes of Frankenstein's monster, the cyborg does not expect its father to save it through a restoration of the garden; that is, through the fabrication of a heterosexual mate, through its completion in a finished whole, a city and cosmos. ... The cyborg would not recognize the Garden of Eden; it is not made of mud and cannot dream of returning to dust.

By the late twentieth century in United States scientific culture, the boundary between human and animal is thoroughly breached. The last beachheads of uniqueness have been polluted if not turned into amusement parks—language, tool use, social behaviour, mental events, nothing really convincingly settles the separation of human and animal. And many people no longer feel the need for such a separation. ... Biology and evolutionary theory over the last two centuries have simultaneously produced modern organisms as objects of knowledge and reduced the line between humans and animals to a faint trace re-etched in ideological struggle or professional disputes between life and social science.

The cyborg appears in myth precisely where the boundary between human and animal is transgressed.

Pre-cybernetic machines could be haunted; there was always the spectre of the ghost in the machine. ... But basically machines were not self-moving, self-designing, autonomous. They could not achieve man's dream, only mock it. They were not man, an author to himself, but only a caricature of that masculinist reproductive dream. To think they were otherwise was paranoid. Now we are not so sure. Late twentieth-century machines have made thoroughly ambiguous the difference between natural and artificial, mind and body, self-developing and externally designed, and many other distinctions that used to apply to organisms and machines. Our machines are disturbingly lively, and we ourselves frighteningly inert.

... a cyborg world might be about lived social and bodily realities in which people are not afraid of their joint kinship with animals and machines, not afraid of permanently partial identities and contradictory standpoints.

Biological organisms have become biotic systems, communications devices like others. There is no fundamental, ontological separation in our formal knowledge of machine and organism, of technical and organic.

One consequence is that our sense of connection to our tools is heightened. The trance state experienced by many computer users has become a staple of science-fiction film and cultural jokes. Perhaps paraplegics and other severely handicapped people can (and sometimes do) have the most intense experiences of complex hybridization with other communication devices. ... Why should our bodies end at the skin, or include at best other beings encapsulated by skin? From the seventeenth century till now, machines could be animated—given ghostly souls to make them speak or move or to account for their orderly development and mental capacities. Or organisms could be mechanized—reduced to body understood as resource of mind. These machine/organism relationships are obsolete, unnecessary. For us, in imagination and in other practice, machines can be prosthetic devices, intimate components, friendly selves.

Monsters have always defined the limits of community in Western imaginations ...

There are several consequences to taking seriously the imagery of cyborgs as other than our enemies. Our bodies, ourselves; bodies are maps of power and identity. Cyborgs are no exception. A cyborg body is not innocent; it was not born in a garden; it does not seek unitary identity and so generate antagonistic dualisms without end (or until the world ends); it takes irony for granted. ... The machine is not an *it* to be animated, worshipped, and dominated. The machine is us, our processes, an aspect of our embodiment. We can be responsible for machines; *they* do not dominate or threaten us. We are responsible for boundaries; we are they.

Cyborg imagery can help express two crucial arguments in this essay: first, the production of universal, totalizing theory is a major mistake that misses most of reality, probably always, but certainly now; and second, taking responsibility for the social relations of science and technology means refusing an anti-science metaphysics, a demonology of technology, and so means embracing the skillful task of reconstructing the boundaries of daily life, in partial connection with others, in communication with all of our parts. It is not just that science and technology are possible means of great human satisfaction, as well as a matrix of complex dominations. Cyborg imagery can suggest a way out of the maze of dualisms in which we have explained our bodies and our tools to ourselves.

56 Cyberfeminist Manifesto for the Twenty-First Century

1991

VNS Matrix

we are the modern cunt
positive anti reason
unbounded unleashed unforgiving
we see art with our cunt we make art with our cunt
we believe in jouissance madness holiness and poetry
we are the virus of the new world disorder
rupturing the symbolic from within
saboteurs of big daddy mainframe
the clitoris is a direct line to the matrix
VNS MATRIX
terminators of the moral code
mercenaries of slime
go down on the altar of abjection
probing the visceral temple we speak in tongues
infiltrating disrupting disseminating
corrupting the discourse
we are the future cunt.

57 cybertwee manifesto

2014

Gabriella Hileman, Violet Forest, and May Waver

the singularity is dear,
far too long have we succumb to bitter edge of xxxxxxxxx
the idea that power is lost in the sweet and tender

romantic is not weak. feminine is not weak. cute is not weak. we are
fragmented and multifaceted bbs.

lack of emotion is oft favored because success is defined as the ability
to be mechanical and efficiant but sentimentality, empathy, and being
too soft should not be seen as weaknesses.

we see the limitations of corporeality, xxx as solipsists, we know that
the body is the original prosthesis for operating in this universe, we
know the body illusory, we curate our candy
our sucre sickly sweet is intentional
our nectar is not just a lure
or a trap for passing flies
but a self indulgent intrapersonal biofeedback mechanism spelled in
emoji and gentle selfies

58 Waging Peace on the Internet

2001

Oxblood Ruffin (Hacktivismo)

There's an international book burning in progress; the surveillance cameras are rolling; and the water cannons are drowning freedom of assembly. But it's not occurring anywhere that television can broadcast to the world. It's happening in cyberspace.

Certain countries censor access to information on the Web through DNS (Domain Name Service) filtering. This is a process whereby politically challenging information is blocked by domain address (the name that appears before the dot-com/net/org suffix, as in Tibet.com, etc.). State censors also filter for politically or socially-unacceptable ideas in e-mail. And individual privacy rights and community gatherings are similarly regulated.

China is often identified as the world's worst offender with its National Firewall and arrests for on-line activity. But the idea that the new Mandarins could have pulled this off by themselves is absurd. The Chinese have aggressively targeted the Western software giants, not only as a means of acquiring technical know-how, but also as agents for influencing Western governments to their advantage through well-established corporate networks of political lobbying. Everything is for sale: names, connections, and even national security.

Witnessing hi-tech firms dive into China is like watching the Gadarene swine. Already fat and greedy beyond belief, the Western technology titans are being herded towards the trough. And with their snouts deep in the feedbag, they haven't quite noticed the bacon being trimmed off their ass. It isn't so much a case of technology transfer as digital strip-mining. Advanced research and technical notes are being handed over to the Chinese without question. It couldn't be going better for the Communists. While bootstrapping their economy with the fruits of Western labor and ingenuity, they gain the tools to prune democracy on the vine.

But to focus on Beijing's strategy misses the larger opportunity of treating the spreading sickness that plagues cyberspace. Cuba not only micromanages its citizens' on-line experience, it has recently refused to sell them computers, the US trade embargo notwithstanding. Most countries indulging in censorship claim to be protecting their citizens from pornographic contagion. But the underlying motive is to prevent challenging opinions from spreading and coalescing through the chokehold of state-sponsored control. This includes banning information that ranges from political opinion, religious witness, "foreign" news, academic and scholarly discovery, news of human rights abuses, in short, all the intellectual exchange that an autocratic leadership considers to be destabilizing.

The capriciousness of state-sanctioned censorship is wide-ranging.

- In Zambia, the government attempted to censor information revealing their plans for constitutional referenda.
- In Mauritania—as in most countries—owners of cybercafés are required to supply government intelligence agents with copies of e-mail sent or received at their establishments.
- Even less draconian governments, like Malaysia, have threatened Web-publishers, whose only crime is to publish frequent Web site updates. Timely and relevant information is seen as a threat.
- South Korea's national security law forbids South Koreans from any contact—including contact over the Internet—with their North Korean neighbors.

The risks of accessing or disseminating information are often great.

- In Ukraine, a decapitated body found near the village of Tarachtcha is believed to be that of Georgiy Gongadze, founder and editor of an on-line newspaper critical of the authorities.
- In August 1998, an eighteen year old Turk, Emre Ersoz, was found guilty of "insulting the national police" in an Internet forum after participating in a demonstration that was violently

suppressed by the police. His ISP provided the authorities with his address.

- Journalist Miroslav Filipovic has the dubious distinction of having been the first journalist accused of spying because his articles detailed the abuses of certain Yugoslav army units in Kosovo, and were published on the Internet.

These are dangerous trends for all of us. The Cult of the Dead Cow (cDc) and Hacktivismo are not prepared to watch the Internet's lights dim simply because liberal democracies are asleep at the switch.

Our fathers and grandfathers fought wars defending, among other things, our right to speak and be heard. They even fought to defend unpopular opinions. It is the unpopular opinions that are most in need of defense. Without them, society would remain unchallenged and unwilling to review core beliefs. It is this tension between received truths and challenging ones that keeps societies healthy and honest. And any attempt at preventing the open exchange of ideas should be seen for what it is: censorship.

For the past four years the cDc has been talking about hacktivism. It's a chic word, beloved among journalists and appropriators alike. Yet the meaning is serious. Our definition of hacktivism is, "using technology to advance human rights through electronic media." Many on-line activists claim to be hacktivists, but their tactics are often at odds with what we consider hacktivism to be.

From the cDc's perspective, creation is good; destruction is bad. Hackers should promote the free flow of information, and causing anything to disrupt, prevent, or retard that flow is improper. For instance, cDc does not consider Web defacements or Denial of Service (DoS) attacks to be legitimate hacktivist actions. The former is nothing more than hi-tech vandalism, and the latter, an assault on free speech.

As we begin to challenge state-sponsored censorship of the Internet, we need to get our own house in order. There have to be accepted standards of what constitutes legitimate hacktivism, and what does not. And of course, none of this will be easy. Hacktivism is a very new field of endeavor that doesn't rely on mere technical expedience. We have to find new paradigms. (Tossing the letter E in front of a concept that has meaning in meat-space, to borrow a term from the Electronic Disturbance Theatre, is convenient but rarely meaningful.) There is no such thing as electronic civil disobedience. Body mass and large numbers don't count as they do on the street. On the Internet, it's the code that counts, specifically code and programmers with conscience.

We need to start thinking in terms of disruptive compliance rather than civil disobedience if we want to be effective on-line. Disruptive compliance has no meaning outside of cyberspace. Disruptive, of course, refers to disruptive technology, a radically new way of doing things; compliance refers back to the Internet and its original intent of constructive free-flow and openness.

But what disruptively compliant, hacktivist applications shall we write, and more importantly, how shall we write them? There are essentially two ways of writing computer programs: closed/proprietary, and, open/public. In non-technical terms, a closed program would be like a menu item in a restaurant for which there was no recipe. An open program would be like a dish for which every ingredient, proportion, and method of preparation was published. Microsoft is an example of a closed, hi-tech restaurant; Linux is its stellar opposite, an open code cafeteria where all is laid bare. For years the technical community has been raging over the absolutes of closed over open code, an argument only slightly more boring than whether Macs are better than PCs.

The answer to this debate is relative; it leans closer to the user's requirements than to the geek community's biases. If the user wants an inflexible, controlled—and often insecure—experience, then closed is the way to go. But if the user opts for greater variety and freedom from control, then flexible, open code is the only option. The choices are similar, although not equivalent, to living in an authoritarian society as opposed to a free one.

Hacktivism chooses open code, mostly. Although there might be very specific instances where we would choose to obscure or hide code, going by the averages we support the same standards-based, open code methodology that built the Internet in the first place. It is germane that users of hacktivist applications sitting behind national firewalls in China and other repressive regimes are more worried about being caught with "criminal software" than crashing their computers. End user safety is paramount in such instances, and if closing down code would prevent arrests, then so be it. Techno-correctness is a luxury of the already free.

There are numerous arguments for open code, from the rhapsodic possibilities of the Open Source Initiative, through the demotic juggernaut of the Free Software Foundation, to the debate laden pages

of Slashdot with its creditable fetish for better security. And everyone is right in his or her own way. But there is another compelling
reason to show the code apart from any technical or philosophical
considerations.

The field is getting crowded.

Four years ago when cDc first started talking about hacktivism,
most Internet users didn't know, or care, about things like state-
sponsored censorship or privacy issues. But now the terrain has
changed. Increasingly human rights organizations, religious and political groups, and even software developers, are entering the fray, each
for unique reasons. It would be premature to call such an unlikely
accretion of stakeholders a coalition. In fact, there is every reason to
believe there are greater opportunities for carping over differences
than leveraging common cause into shared success. But open code
may become the glue that binds.

As more and more disparate groups attempt to loosen dicta-
tors' restraints over Internet, it's important to keep focused on their
common goals and not petty differences. The more transparent and
crystalline their progress towards collective goals becomes, the more
likely it is that those objectives will be achieved. Open code, like the
open and inclusive nature of democratic discourse itself, will prove to
be the *lingua franca* of hacktivism. And perhaps more importantly, it
will demonstrate that hacktivists are waging peace, not war.

In 1968 the Canadian communications guru Marshall McLuhan
stated, "World War Three will be a guerilla information war with no
division between military and civilian participation."

Anyone who's watched the Web after an international incident
knows how true that statement is. Teenagers from China have attacked
sites in Taiwan and the U.S., and vice versa, just to name one claque
of combatants. And although the exchanges are more annoying than
truly damaging, they do support McLuhan's theory. As the Internet
erupts into battle zones, Hacktivists could become something akin to
a United Nations peacekeeping force. But rather than being identified
by blue helmets, they'll be recognized by the openness of their code
and the quality and safety of their applications designed to defeat censorship and challenge national propaganda.

One key to countering the cadres of information censors in China
and elsewhere is the fluidity of open code projects. Another is through
peer-to-peer (P2P) networks. P2P has floated into public awareness

mostly as a result of the Napster phenomenon. The "peers" on the network are computers, and yet not so different from a society of peers in a democracy. Some are more powerful than others, but they all have common attributes. This is in contrast with the traditional, and more pervasive, client/server network mechanism, where little computers go to big ones and ask for something, be it a Web page, an application, or even processing power.

What is most interesting about P2P technologies is that they turn the much-ballyhooed Information Superhighway into a two-way street. Peers become both clients and servers, or "clervers" as one naming convention has it. Files can be shared, a la Napster; or processes from one or many partner computers can be strung together to create supercomputers, among other things. What makes these systems attractive to hacktivist developers is they are difficult to shut down. Large central servers are easy to locate and take down. But clouds of peers in numerous arrays springing up around the datascape are far more problematic.

This is not to say that P2P networks are invincible. Napster got shut down. But when the salt is out of the shaker, it's hard to get it back in. With Napster down, a legion of even more powerful file-trading devices arose to take its place. The fact that Napster was easy to use and didn't require a steep learning curve was also key to its success, other convergences notwithstanding. This is fundamental to anyone hoping to appeal to non-technical users, many of whom are partially blinded and deafened by national firewalls.

The target user is socially engaged, but not necessarily technically adept. Beneath the surface the programs can be as complicated as you please, but on top, from the functionality/usability perspective, the apps have to be dead simple and easy to use. And they have to be trustworthy.

Here is where the Napster analogy breaks down. Trust was never a paramount factor in using the application. It was a fun loving network developed on the free side of the firewall, where users' greatest worries were, a) Can I find what I want? b) How long will it take to download? c) Is it of good quality? and, d) Do I have time to download four more tunes before I go to the keg party?

No one ever had to ask, a) If I'm caught using this, will I be arrested? b) Is this application good for ten years in jail?

Having millions of students on the Napster network made sense because the more users there are on-line, the larger the lending library becomes. Users behind national firewalls cannot be so casual. Having millions of users on a network may be one thing, but only a fool would trust more than his or her closest friends when the consequences of entrapment are so high. Thus, carefree peer-to-peer networks are replaced by careful hacktivist-to-hacktivist (H2H) networks.

H2H networks are like nuclear families living in large communities. Everyone may live in the same area, but each family has its own home where the doors open, close, and lock. And occasionally, a family member will bring someone new home. Everyone will sit around the living room, and if all goes well, the guest will be shown the library, perhaps, and maybe even someone's bedroom. All of this is based on earned trust. H2H networks will operate along these lines, where families will share a space and grant permission to one another as well as to certain visitors. The greater the trust, the more permissions will be granted; and for guests visiting the home, trust will be earned incrementally.

This model is already in existence, more or less. Using the Internet to communicate between known and trusted computers is a fact of business life. Virtual Private Networks are used daily to communicate sensitive and proprietary data. The same can be done by taking elements of this model and marrying them to H2H network development. But saying is not doing, and even the best marriages can unravel and fail. It's important to realize these things are possible but have never been done before.

Building H2H networks is not just a matter of guessing at how particular technologies will respond under fire. Hackers must know what users in the field need. We have been telling anyone who will listen that hackers, grassroots activists, and other parties who care about Internet freedom and the growth of democracy must partner up and work together.

Hacktivismo has been working with Chinese hackers and human rights workers, and the collaboration has been both fruitful and energizing. Occasionally there are cultural conflicts, but this has nothing to do with where anyone was born, and everything to do with how people get things done. Hackers tend towards MIT professor Dave Clark's credo which states, "We reject: kings, presidents, and voting. We believe in: rough consensus and running code." Trust will come as development partners begin working more closely and learning that we aren't so different as we appear at the surface.

Research and development is phase one. Then comes distribution. Hackers have never had a problem distributing software. If you write something worth running, it will end up in every corner of the globe, something else we've learned from experience.

Leveraging existing distribution channels with those of our partners will ensure that users who most need liberating software will get it. Some human rights organizations have vast e-mail databases that will become increasingly invaluable for raising awareness, and in some instances, act as a distribution layer. Other areas of co-operation are also possible, especially in translations for non-English users where documentation and re-skinning U.I.s (the process of replacing the user interface of an application from, say, English to Chinese, or Arabic, etc.) will take development to ever-wider usefulness.

Last, although certainly not least, we need to acknowledge the Chinese government for their unwitting contributions to Hacktivismo's work. After reverse engineering some of their fundamental technologies we've discovered a few cracks where the light might shine through. But it does raise the question: why are we put in the position of doing this work? With billions of dollars in government budgets at their disposal, when are the world's liberal democracies going to put some of their resources into opening up the Internet? We know they don't care about human rights policy when it conflicts with jobs at home; but what about international security? As Beijing continues to play the patriotism card domestically, a more open Internet could diffuse traditional xenophobia through greater one-on-one interaction on-line.

But until Western governments become engaged, the main challenge for hackers is to keep focused on the goal of liberating the Internet. We realize that, but for the grace of God, we could be sitting on the other side of the firewall. It's a sentiment that is being picked up, although it would be a lie to say that thousands of hackers want to get into the game.

Still, enough are beginning to take up this cause that we should be able to see results, if new partnerships hold. There's a new generation of freedom fighters, sitting behind computers, who believe that it can be done.

59 A Hacker Manifesto (Version 4.0)

2004

McKenzie Wark

Manifestation

01. There is a double spooking the world, the double of abstraction. The fortunes of states and armies, companies and communities depend on it. All contending classes—the landlords and farmers, the workers and capitalists—revere yet fear the relentless abstraction of the world on which their fortunes yet depend. All the classes but one. The hacker class.

02. Whatever code we hack, be it programming language, poetic language, math or music, curves or colourings, we create the possibility of new things entering the world. Not always great things, or even good things, but new things. In art, in science, in philosophy and culture, in any production of knowledge where data can be gathered, where information can be extracted from it, and where in that information new possibilities for the world are produced, there are hackers hacking the new out of the old. While hackers create these new worlds, we do not possess them. That which we create is mortgaged to others, and to the interests of others, to states and corporations who control the means for making worlds we alone discover. We do not own what we produce—it owns us.

03. And yet we don't quite know who we are. While we recognise our distinctive existence as a group, as programmers, as artists or writers or scientists or musicians, we rarely see these ways of representing

ourselves as mere fragments of a class experience that is still struggling to express itself as itself, as expressions of the process of producing abstraction in the world. Geeks and freaks become what they are negatively, through their exclusion by others. Hackers are a class, but an abstract class, a class as yet to hack itself into manifest existence as itself.

Abstraction

04. Abstraction may be discovered or produced, may be material or immaterial, but abstraction is what every hack produces and affirms. To abstract is to construct a plane upon which otherwise different and unrelated matters may be brought into many possible relations. It is through the abstract that the virtual is identified, produced and released. The virtual is not just the potential latent in matters, it is the potential of potential. To hack is to produce or apply the abstract to information and express the possibility of new worlds.

05. All abstractions are abstractions of nature. To abstract is to express the virtuality of nature, to make known some instance of its manifold possibilities, to actualise a relation out of infinite relationality. Abstractions release the potential of physical matter. And yet abstraction relies on something that has an independent existence to physical matter—information. Information is no less real than physical matter, and is dependent on it for its existence. Since information cannot exist in a pure, immaterial form, neither can the hacker class. Of necessity it must deal with a ruling class that owns the material means of extracting or distributing information, or with a producing class that extracts and distributes. The class interest of hackers lies in freeing information from its material constraints.

06. As the abstraction of private property was extended to information, it produced the hacker class as a class. Hackers must sell their capacity for abstraction to a class that owns the means of production, the vectoralist class—the emergent ruling class of our time. The vectoralist class is waging an intensive struggle to dispossess hackers of their intellectual property. Patents and copyrights all end up in the hands, not of their creators, but of the vectoralist class that owns the means

of realising the value of these abstractions. The vectoralist class struggles to monopolise abstraction. Hackers find themselves dispossessed both individually, and as a class. Hackers come piecemeal to struggle against the particular forms in which abstraction is commodified and made into the private property of the vectoralist class. Hackers come to struggle collectively against the usurious charges the vectoralists extort for access to the information that hackers collectively produce, but that vectoralists collectively come to own. Hackers come as a class to recognise their class interest is best expressed through the struggle to free the production of abstraction not just from the particular fetters of this or that form of property, but to abstract the form of property itself.

07. What makes our times different is that what now appears on the horizon is the possibility of a society finally set free from necessity, both real and imagined, by an explosion in abstract innovations. Abstraction with the potential once and for all to break the shackles holding hacking fast to outdated and regressive class interests. The time is past due when hackers must come together with all of the producing classes of the world—to liberate productive and inventive resources from the myth of scarcity. "The world already possesses the dream of a time whose consciousness it must now possess in order to actually live it."

Production

08. Production produces all things, and all producers of things. Production produces not only the object of the production process, but also the producer as subject. Hacking is the production of production. The hack produces a production of a new kind, which has as its result a singular and unique product, and a singular and unique producer. Every hacker is at one and the same time producer and product of the hack, and emerges in its singularity as the memory of the hack as process.

09. Production takes place on the basis of a prior hack which gives to production its formal, social, repeatable and reproducible form. Every production is a hack formalised and repeated on the basis of its representation. To produce is to repeat; to hack, to differentiate.

10. The hack produces both a useful and a useless surplus, although the usefulness of any surplus is socially and historically determined. The useful surplus goes into expanding the realm of freedom wrested from necessity. The useless surplus is the surplus of freedom itself, the margin of free production unconstrained by production for necessity.

11. The production of a surplus creates the possibility of the expansion of freedom from necessity. But in class society, the production of a surplus also creates new necessities. Class domination takes the form of the capture of the productive potential of society and its harnessing to the production, not of liberty, but of class domination itself. The ruling class subordinates the hack to the production of forms of production that may be harnessed to the enhancement of class power, and the suppression or marginalisation of other forms of hacking. What the producing classes—farmers, workers and hackers—have in common is an interest in freeing production from its subordination to ruling classes who turn production into the production of new necessities, who wrest slavery from surplus. The elements of a free productivity exist already in an atomised form, in the productive classes. What remains is the release of its virtuality.

Class

12. The class struggle, in its endless setbacks, reversals and compromises returns again and again to the unanswered question—property—and the contending classes return again and again with new answers. The working class questioned the necessity of private property, and the communist party arose, claiming to answer the desires of the working class. The answer, expressed in the Communist Manifesto was to "centralise all instruments of production in the hands of the state." But making the state the monopolist of property has only produced a new ruling class, and a new and more brutal class struggle. But perhaps this was not the final answer, and the course of the class struggle is not yet over. Perhaps there is another class that can pose the property question in a new way—and offer new answers to breaking the monopoly of the ruling classes on property.

13. There is a class dynamic driving each stage of the development of the vectoral world in which we now find ourselves. The pastoralist class disperse the great mass of peasants who traditionally worked the land under the thumb of feudal landlords. The pastoralists supplant the feudal landlords, releasing the productivity of the land which they claim as their private property. As new forms of abstraction make it possible to produce a surplus from the land with fewer and fewer farmers, pastoralists turn them off their land, depriving them of their living. Dispossessed farmers seek work and a new home in cities. Here farmers become workers, as capital puts them to work in its factories. Capital as property gives rise to a class of capitalists who own the means of production, and a class of workers, dispossessed of it—and by it. Dispossessed farmers become workers, only to be dispossessed again. Having lost their land, they lose in turn their culture. Capital produces in its factories not just the necessities of existence, but a way of life it expects its workers to consume. Commodified life dispossess the worker of the information traditionally passed on outside the realm of private property as culture, as the gift of one generation to the next, and replaces it with information in commodified form.

14. Information, like land or capital, becomes a form of property monopolised by a class of vectoralists, so named because they control the vectors along which information is abstracted, just as capitalists control the material means with which goods are produced, and pastoralists the land with which food is produced. Information circulated within working class culture as a social property belonging to all. But when information in turn becomes a form of private property, workers are dispossessed of it, and must buy their own culture back from its owners, the vectoralist class. The whole of time, time itself, becomes a commodified experience.

15. Vectoralists try to break capital's monopoly on the production process, and subordinate the production of goods to the circulation of information. The leading corporations divest themselves of their productive capacity, as this is no longer a source of power. Their power lies in monopolising intellectual property—patents and brands—and the means of reproducing their value—the vectors of communication. The privatisation of information becomes the dominant, rather than a subsidiary, aspect of commodified life. As private property advances

from land to capital to information, property itself becomes more abstract. As capital frees land from its spatial fixity, information as property frees capital from its fixity in a particular object.

16. The hacker class, producer of new abstractions, becomes more important to each successive ruling class, as each depends more and more on information as a resource. The hacker class arises out of the transformation of information into property, in the form of intellectual property, including patents, trademarks, copyright and the moral right of authors. The hacker class is the class with the capacity to create not only new kinds of object and subject in the world, not only new kinds of property form in which they may be represented, but new kinds of relation beyond the property form. The formation of the hacker class as a class comes at just this moment when freedom from necessity and from class domination appears on the horizon as a possibility.

Property

17. Property constitutes an abstract plane upon which all things may be things with one quality in common, the quality of property. Land is the primary form of property. Pastoralists acquire land as private property through the forced dispossession of peasants who once shared a portion of it in a form of public ownership. Capital is the secondary form of property, the privatisation of productive assets in the form of tools, machines and working materials. Capital, unlike land, is not in fixed supply or disposition. It can be made and remade, moved, aggregated and dispersed. An infinitely greater degree of potential can be released from the world as a productive resource once the abstract plane of property includes both land and capital—such is capital's "advance."

18. The capitalist class recognises the value of the hack in the abstract, whereas the pastoralists were slow to appreciate the productivity that can flow from the application of abstraction to the production process. Under the influence of capital, the state sanctions forms of intellectual property, such as patents and copyrights, that secure an independent existence for hackers as a class, and a flow of innovations in culture

as well as science from which development issues. Information, once it becomes a form of property, develops beyond a mere support for capital—it becomes the basis of a form of accumulation in its own right.

19. Hackers must calculate their interests not as owners, but as producers, for this is what distinguishes them from the vectoralist class. Hackers do not merely own, and profit by owning information. They produce new information, and as producers need access to it free from the absolute domination of the commodity form. Hacking as a pure, free experimental activity must be free from any constraint that is not self imposed. Only out of its liberty will it produce the means of producing a surplus of liberty and liberty as a surplus.

20. Private property arose in opposition not only to feudal property, but also to traditional forms of the gift economy, which were a fetter to the increased productivity of the commodity economy. Qualitative, gift exchange was superseded by quantified, monetised exchange. Money is the medium through which land, capital, information and labour all confront each other as abstract entities, reduced to an abstract plane of measurement. The gift becomes a marginal form of property, everywhere invaded by the commodity, and turned towards mere consumption. The gift is marginal, but nevertheless plays a vital role in cementing reciprocal and communal relations among people who otherwise can only confront each other as buyer and sellers of commodities. As vectoral production develops, the means appear for the renewal of the gift economy. Everywhere that the vector reaches, it brings into the orbit of the commodity. But everywhere the vector reaches, it also brings with it the possibility of the gift relation.

21. The hacker class has a close affinity with the gift economy. The hacker struggles to produce a subjectivity that is qualitative and singular, in part through the act of the hack itself. The gift, as a qualitative exchange between singular parties allows each party to be recognised as a singular producer, as a subject of production, rather than as a commodified and quantified object. The gift expresses in a social and collective way the subjectivity of the production of production, whereas commodified property represents the producer as an object, a quantifiable commodity like any other, of relative value only. The

gift of information need not give rise to conflict over information as property, for information need not suffer the artifice of scarcity once freed from commodification.

22. The vectoralist class contributed, unwittingly, to the development of the vectoral space within which the gift as property could return, but quickly recognised its error. As the vectoral economy develops, less and less of it takes the form of a social space of open and free gift exchange, and more and more of it takes the form of commodified production for private sale. The vectoralist class can grudgingly accommodate some margin of socialised information, as the price it pays in a democracy for the furtherance of its main interests. But the vectoralist class quite rightly sees in the gift a challenge not just to its profits but to its very existence. The gift economy is the virtual proof for the parasitic and superfluous nature of vectoralists as a class.

Vector

23. In epidemiology, a vector is the particular means by which a given pathogen travels from one population to another. Water is a vector for cholera, bodily fluids for HIV. By extension, a vector may be any means by which information moves. Telegraph, telephone, television, telecommunications: these terms name not just particular vectors, but a general abstract capacity that they bring into the world and expand. All are forms of telesthesia, or perception at a distance. A given media vector has certain fixed properties of speed, bandwidth, scope and scale, but may be deployed anywhere, at least in principle. The uneven development of the vector is political and economic, not technical.

24. With the commodification of information comes its vectoralisation. Extracting a surplus from information requires technologies capable of transporting information through space, but also through time. The archive is a vector through time just as communication is a vector that crosses space. The vectoral class comes into its own once it is in possession of powerful technologies for vectoralising information. The vectoral class may commodify information stocks, flows, or vectors themselves. A stock of information is an archive, a body of information maintained through time that has enduring value. A flow

of information is the capacity to extract information of temporary value out of events and to distribute it widely and quickly. A vector is the means of achieving either the temporal distribution of a stock, or the spatial distribution of a flow of information. Vectoral power is generally sought through the ownership of all three aspects.

25. The vectoral class ascend to the illusion of an instantaneous and global plane of calculation and control. But it is not the vectoralist class that comes to hold subjective power over the objective world. The vector itself usurps the subjective role, becoming the sole repository of will toward a world that can be apprehended only in its commodified form. The reign of the vector is one in which any and every thing can be apprehended as a thing. The vector is a power over all of the world, but a power that is not evenly distributed. Nothing in the technology of the vector determines its possible use. All that is determined by the technology is the form in which information is objectified.

26. The vectoral class struggles at every turn to maintain its subjective power over the vector, but as it continues to profit by the proliferation of the vector, some capacity over it always escapes control. In order to market and profit by the information it peddles over the vector, it must in some degree address the vast majority of the producing classes as subjects, rather than as objects of commodification. The hacker class seeks the liberation of the vector from the reign of the commodity, but not to set it indiscriminately free. Rather, to subject it to collective and democratic development. The hacker class can release the virtuality of the vector only in principle. It is up to an alliance of all the productive classes to turn that potential to actuality, to organise themselves subjectively, and use the available vectors for a collective and subjective becoming.

Education

27. Education is slavery, it enchains the mind and makes it a resource for class power. When the ruling class preaches the necessity of an education it invariably means an education in necessity. Education is not the same as knowledge. Nor is it the necessary means to acquire knowledge. Education is the organisation of knowledge within the

constraints of scarcity. Education "disciplines" knowledge, segregating it into homogenous "fields," presided over by suitably "qualified" guardians charged with policing the representation of the field. One may acquire an education, as if it were a thing, but one becomes knowledgeable, through a process of transformation. Knowledge, as such, is only ever partially captured by education, its practice always eludes and exceeds it.

28. The pastoralist class has resisted education, other than as indoctrination in obedience. When capital required "hands" to do its dirty work, the bulk of education was devoted to training useful hands to tend the machines, and docile bodies who would accept as natural the social order in which they found themselves. When capital required brains, both to run its increasingly complex operations and to apply themselves to the work of consuming its products, more time spent in the prison house of education was required for admission to the ranks of the paid working class.

29. The so-called middle class achieve their privileged access to consumption and security through education, in which they are obliged to invest a substantial part of their income. But most remain workers, even though they work with information rather than cotton or metal. They work in factories, but are trained to think of them as offices. They take home wages, but are trained to think of it as a salary. They wear a uniform, but are trained to think of it as a suit. The only difference is that education has taught them to give different names to the instruments of exploitation, and to despise those their own class who name them differently.

30. Where the capitalist class sees education as a means to an end, the vectoralist class sees it as an end in itself. It sees opportunities to make education a profitable industry in its own right, based on the securing of intellectual property as a form of private property. To the vectoralists, education, like culture, is just "content" for commodification.

31. The hacker class have an ambivalent relationship to education. The hacker class desires knowledge, not education. The hacker comes into being though the pure liberty of knowledge in and of itself. The hack expresses knowledge in its virtuality, by producing new abstractions

that do not necessarily fit the disciplinary regime of managing and commodifying education. Hacker knowledge implies, in its practice, a politics of free information, free learning, the gift of the result to a network of peers. Hacker knowledge also implies an ethics of knowledge subject to the claims of public interest and free from subordination to commodity production. This puts the hacker into an antagonistic relationship to the struggle of the capitalist class to make education an induction into wage slavery.

32. Only one intellectual conflict has any real bearing on the class issue for hackers: Whose property is knowledge? Is it the role of knowledge to authorise subjects through education that are recognised only by their function in an economy by manipulating its authorised representations as objects? Or is it the function of knowledge to produce the ever different phenomena of the hack, in which subjects become other than themselves, and discover the objective world to contain potentials other than it appears?

Hacking

33. The virtual is the true domain of the hacker. It is from the virtual that the hacker produces ever-new expressions of the actual. To the hacker, what is represented as being real is always partial, limited, perhaps even false. To the hacker there is always a surplus of possibility expressed in what is actual, the surplus of the virtual. This is the inexhaustible domain of what is real without being actual, what is not but which may be. To hack is to release the virtual into the actual, to express the difference of the real.

34. Through the application of abstraction, the hacker class produces the possibility of production, the possibility of making something of and with the world—and of living off the surplus produced by the application of abstraction to nature—to any nature. Through the production of new forms of abstraction, the hacker class produces the possibility of the future—not just "the" future, but an infinite possible array of futures, the future itself as virtuality.

35. Under the sanction of law, the hack becomes a finite property, and the hacker class emerges, as all classes emerge, out of a relation

to a property form. Like all forms of property, intellectual property enforces a relation of scarcity. It assigns a right to a property to an owner at the expense of non-owners, to a class of possessors at the expense of the dispossessed.

36. By its very nature, the act of hacking overcomes the limits property imposes on it. New hacks supersede old hacks, and devalues them as property. The hack as new information is produced out of already existing information. This gives the hacker class an interest in its free availability more than in an exclusive right. The immaterial nature of information means that the possession by one of information need not deprive another of it.

37. To the extent that the hack embodies itself in the form of property, it gives the hacker class interests quite different from other classes, be they exploiting or exploited classes. The interest of the hacker class lies first and foremost in a free circulation of information, this being the necessary condition for the renewed statement of the hack. But the hacker class as class also has an interest in the representation of the hack as property, as something from which a source of income may be derived that gives the hacker some independence from the ruling classes.

38. The very nature of the hack gives the hacker a crisis of identity. The hacker searches for a representation of what it is to be a hacker in the identities of other classes. Some see themselves as vectoralists, trading on the scarcity of their property. Some see themselves as workers, but as privileged ones in a hierarchy of wage earners. The hacker class has produces itself as itself, but not for itself. It does not (yet) possess a consciousness of its consciousness. It is not aware of its own virtuality. It has to distinguish between its competitive interest in the hack, and its collective interest in discovering a relation among hackers that expresses an open and ongoing future.

Information

39. Information wants to be free but is everywhere in chains. Information is the potential of potential. When unfettered it releases the latent capacities of all things and people, objects and subjects. Information is

indeed the very potential for there to be objects and subjects. It is the medium in which objects and subjects actually come into existence, and is the medium in which their virtuality resides. When information is not free, then the class that owns or controls it turns its capacity toward its own interest and away from its own inherent virtuality.

40. Information has nothing to do with communication, or with media. "We do not lack communication. On the contrary, we have too much of it. We lack creation. We lack resistance to the present." Information is precisely this resistance, this friction. At the urgings of the vectoralist class, the state recognises as property any communication, any media product with some minimal degree of difference recognisable in commodity exchange. Where communication merely requires the repetition of this commodified difference, information is the production of the difference of difference.

41. The arrest of the free flow of information means the enslavement of the world to the interests of those who profit from information's scarcity, the vectoral class. The enslavement of information means the enslavement of its producers to the interests of its owners. It is the hacker class that taps the virtuality of information, but it is the vectoralist class that owns and controls the means of production of information on an industrial scale. Privatising culture, education and communication as commodified content, distorts and deforms its free development, and prevents the very concept of its freedom from its own free development. While information remains subordinated to ownership, it is not possible for its producers to freely calculate their interests, or to discover what the true freedom of information might potentially produce in the world.

42. Free information must be free in all its aspects—as a stock, as a flow, and as a vector. The stock of information is the raw material out of which history is abstracted. The flow of information is the raw material out of which the present is abstracted, a present that forms the horizon the abstract line of an historical knowledge crosses, indicating a future in its sights. Neither stocks nor flows of information exist without vectors along which they may be actualised. The spatial and temporal axes of free information must do more offer a representation of things, as a thing apart. They must become the means

of coordination of the statement of a movement, at once objective and subjective, capable of connecting the objective representation of things to the presentation of a subjective action.

43. It is not just information that must be free, but the knowledge of how to use it. Information in itself is a mere thing. It requires an active, subjective capacity to become productive. Information is free not for the purpose of representing the world perfectly, but for expressing its difference from what is, and for expressing the cooperative force that transforms what is into what may be. The test of a free society is not the liberty to consume information, nor to produce it, nor even to implement its potential in private world of one's choosing. The test of a free society is the liberty for the collective transformation of the world through abstractions freely chosen and freely actualised.

Representation

44. All representation is false. A likeness differs of necessity from what it represents. If it did not, it would be what it represents, and thus not a representation. The only truly false representation is the belief in the possibility of true representation. Critique is not a solution, but the problem itself. Critique is a police action in representation, of service only to the maintenance of the value of property through the establishment of its value.

45. The politics of representation is always the politics of the state. The state is nothing but the policing of representation's adequacy to the body of what it represents. Even in its most radical form, the politics of representation always presupposes an abstract or ideal state that would act as guarantor of its chosen representations. It yearns for a state that would recognise this oppressed ethnicity, or sexuality, but which is nevertheless still a desire for a state, and a state that, in the process, is not challenged as an statement of class interest, but is accepted as the judge of representation.

46. And always, what is excluded even from this enlightened, imaginary state, would be those who refuse representation, namely, the hacker class as a class. To hack is to refuse representation, to make

matters express themselves otherwise. To hack is always to produce a difference, if only a minute difference, in the production of information. To hack is to trouble the object or the subject, by transforming in some way the very process of production by which objects and subjects come into being and recognise each other by their representations.

47. The politics of information, of knowledge, advances not through a critical negation of false representations but a positive politics of the virtuality of statement. The inexhaustible surplus of statement is that aspect of information upon which the class interest of hackers depends. Hacking brings into existence the inexhaustible multiplicity of all codes, be they natural or social, programmed or poetic. But as it is the act of hacking that composes, at one and the same time, the hacker and the hack, hacking recognises no artificial scarcity, no official licence, no credentialing police force other than that composed by the gift economy among hackers themselves.

48. A politics that embraces its existence as statement, as affirmative difference, not as negation can escape the politics of the state. To ignore or plagiarise representation, to refuse to give it what it claims as its due, is to begin a politics of statelessness. A politics which refuses the state's authority to authorise what is a valued statement and what isn't. A politics which is always temporary, always becoming something other than itself. Even useless hacks may come, perversely enough, to be valued for the purity of their uselessness. There is nothing that can't be valued as a representation. The hack always has to move on.

49. Everywhere dissatisfaction with representations is spreading. Sometimes it's a matter of breaking a few shop windows, sometimes of breaking a few heads. So-called "violence" against the state, which rarely amounts to more than throwing rocks at its police, is merely the desire for the state expressed in its masochistic form. Where some call for a state that recognises their representation, others call for a state that beats them to a pulp. Neither is a politics that escapes the desire cultivated within the subject by the educational apparatus.

50. Sometimes direct democracy is posited as the alternative. But this merely changes the moment of representation—it puts politics in the hands of claimants to an activist representation, in place of an electoral

one. Sometimes what is demanded of the politics of representation is that it recognise a new subject. Minorities of race, gender, preference demand the right to representation. But soon enough they discover the cost. They must now police the meaning of this representation, and police the adherence of its members to it. Even at its best, in its most abstract form, on its best behaviour, the colour blind, gender neutral, multicultural state just hands the value of representation over to the commodity form. While this is progress, particularly for those formerly oppressed by the state's failure to recognise their identity as legitimate, it stops short at the recognition of expressions of subjectivity that seeks to become something other than a representation that the state can recognise and the market can value.

51. But there is something else hovering on the horizon of the representable. There is a politics of the unrepresentable, a politics of the presentation of the non-negotiable demand. This is politics as the refusal of representation itself, not the politics of refusing this or that representation. A politics which, while abstract, is not utopian. In its infinite and limitless demand, it may even be the best way of extracting concessions precisely through its refusal to put a name—or a price— on what revolt desires.

Revolt

52. The revolts of 1989 are the signal events of our time. What the revolts of 1989 achieved was the overthrow of regimes so impervious to the recognition of the value of the hack that they had starved not only their hackers but also their workers and farmers of any increase in the surplus. With their cronyism and kleptocracy, their bureaucracy and ideology, their police and spies, they starved even their pastoralists and capitalists of innovative transformation and growth.

53. The revolts of 1989 overthrew boredom and necessity. At least for a time. They put back on the world historical agenda the limitless demand for free statement. At least for a time. They revealed the latent destiny of world history to express the pure virtuality of becoming. At least for a time, before new states cobbled themselves together and claimed legitimacy as representations of what revolt desired. The

revolts of 1989 opened the portal to the virtual, but the states that regrouped around this opening soon closed it. What the revolts really achieved was the making of the world safe for vectoral power.

54. The so-called anti-globalisation protests of the 90s are a ripple caused by the wake of these signal events, but a ripple that did not know the current to which it truly belonged. This movement of revolt in the overdeveloped world identifies the rising vectoral power as a class enemy, but all too often it allowed itself to be captured by the partial and temporary interests of local capitalist and pastoralist classes. It was a revolt is in its infancy that has yet to discover the connection between its engine of limitless desire and free statement, and the art of making tactical demands.

55. The class struggle within nations and the imperial struggle between nations has taken shape as two forms of politics. One kind of politics is regressive. It seeks to return to an imagined past. It seeks to use national borders as a new wall, a neon screen behind which unlikely alliances might protect their existing interests in the name of a glorious past. The other form is the progressive politics of movement. The politics of movement seeks to accelerate toward an unknown future. It seeks to use international flows of information, trade or activism as the eclectic means for struggling for new sources of wealth or liberty that overcomes the limitations imposed by national coalitions.

56. Neither of these politics corresponds to the old notion of a left or right, which the revolutions of 1989 have definitively overcome. Regressive politics brings together luddite impulses from the left with racist and reactionary impulses from the right in an unholy alliance against new sources of power. Progressive politics rarely takes the form of an alliance, but constitutes two parallel processes locked in a dialogue of mutual suspicion, in which the liberalising forces of the right and the social justice and human rights forces of the left both seek non-national and transnational solutions to unblocking the system of power which still accumulates at the national level.

57. There is a third politics, which stands outside the alliances and compromises of the post-89 world. Where both progressive and regressive politics are representative politics, which deal with aggregate party

alliances and interests, this third politics is a stateless politics, which seeks escape from politics as such. A politics of the hack, inventing relations outside of representation.

58. Expressive politics is a struggle against commodity property itself. Expressive politics is not the struggle to collectivise property, for that is still a form of property. Expressive politics is the struggle to free what can be free from both versions of the commodity form—its totalising market form, and its bureaucratic state form. What may be free from the commodity form altogether is not land, not capital, but information. All other forms of property are exclusive. The ownership by one excludes, by definition, the ownership by another. But information as property may be shared without diminishing anything but its scarcity. Information is that which can escape the commodity form.

59. Politics can become expressive only when it is a politics of freeing the virtuality of information. In liberating information from its objectification as a commodity, it liberates also the subjective force of statement. Subject and object meet each other outside of their mere lack of each other, by their desire merely for each other. Expressive politics does not seek to overthrow the existing society, or to reform its larger structures, or to preserve its structure so as to maintain an existing coalition of interests. It seeks to permeate existing states with a new state of existence, spreading the seeds of an alternative practice of everyday life.

60 Yes Manifesto

2004

Mette Ingvartsen

Yes to redefining virtuosity
Yes to "invention" (however impossible)
Yes to conceptualizing experience, affects and sensation
Yes to materiality and body practice
Yes to expression
Yes to un-naming, decoding and recoding expression
Yes to non-recognition, non-resemblance
Yes to non-sense/illogics
Yes to organizing principles rather than fixed logic systems
Yes to moving the "clear concept" behind the actual performance of
Yes to methodology and procedures
Yes to editing and animation
Yes to style as a result of procedure and specificity of a proposal
(meaning each proposal has another "style"/specificity, and in this
sense the work cannot be considered essentialist.)
Yes to multiplicity, difference and co-existence

61 Radical Psychiatry Manifesto

1969

Claude Steiner

1. The practice of psychiatry (from the Greek: soul healing) has been usurped by the medical establishment. Political control of its public aspects has been seized by medicine and the language of soul healing has been infiltrated with irrelevant medical concepts and terms.

Psychiatry must return to its non-medical origins since most psychiatric conditions are in no way the province of medicine. All persons competent in soul healing should be known as psychiatrists. Psychiatrists should repudiate the use of medically derived words such as "patient," "illness," "treatment." Medical psychiatrists' unique contribution to psychiatry is as experts on neurology, and, with much needed additional work, on drugs.

2. Extended individual psychotherapy is an elitist, outmoded, as well as nonproductive form of psychiatric help. It concentrates the talents of a few on a few. It silently colludes with the notion that people's difficulties have their sources within them while implying that everything is well with the world. It promotes oppression by shrouding its consequences with shame and secrecy. It further mystifies by attempting to pass as an ideal human relationship when it is, in fact, artificial in the extreme.

People's troubles have their cause not within them but in their alienated relationships, in their exploitation, in polluted environments, in war, and in the profit motive. Psychiatry must be practiced in groups. One-to-one contacts, of great value in crises, should become the exception rather than the rule. The high ideal of I-Thou loving relations should be pursued in the context of groups rather than in the stilted consulting room situation. Psychiatrists not proficient in group work are deficient in their training and should upgrade it. Psychiatrists should encourage bilateral, open discussion and discourage secrecy and shame in relation to deviant behavior and thoughts.

3. By remaining "neutral" in an oppressive situation, psychiatry, especially in the public sector, has become an enforcer of establishment values and laws.

Adjustment to prevailing conditions is the avowed goal of most psychiatric treatment. Persons who deviate from the world's madness are given fraudulent diagnostic tests, which generate diagnostic labels that lead to "treatment" that is, in fact, a series of graded repressive procedures such as "drug management," hospitalization, shock therapy, perhaps lobotomy. All these forms of "treatment" are perversions of legitimate medical methods, which have been put at the service of the establishment by the medical profession. Treatment is forced on persons who would, if let alone, not seek it.

Psychological tests and the diagnostic labels they generate, especially schizophrenia, must be disavowed as meaningless mystification & the real function of which is to distance psychiatrists from people and to insult people into conformity. Medicine must cease making available drugs, hospitals, and other legitimate medical procedures for the purpose of overt or subtle law enforcement and must examine how drug companies are dictating treatment procedures through their advertising. Psychiatry must cease playing a part in the oppression of women by refusing to promote adjustment to their oppression.

All psychiatric help should be by contract; that is, people should choose when, what, and with whom they want to change. Psychiatrists should become advocates of the people; should refuse to participate in the pacification of the oppressed, and should encourage people's struggles for liberation.

Paranoia is a state of heightened awareness. Most people are persecuted beyond their wildest delusions. Those who are at ease are insensitive.

Psychiatric mystification is a powerful influence in the maintenance of people's oppression.

Personal liberation is only possible along with radical social reforms.

Psychiatry must stop its mystification of the people and get down to work!

PART VII

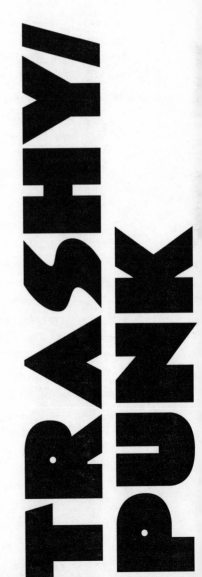

TRASHY/
PUNK

Introduction to Trashy/Punk

Feminist manifestos serve as an ode to trashiness, low-downness, rudeness, brashness, outrageousness. This section brings us voices that argue for revolt and revulsion, trashy women and trashy music, cheap art and criminality. We begin with an unlikely duo of artists, activists, and writers: the RIOT GRRRL Manifesto of the early 1990s followed by a nineteenth century piece by radical feminist labor activist Lucy Parsons. We also witness arguments for new forms of art and a clear rejection of patriarchal values in the art world (VALIE EXPORT, Grimes, and Bread and Puppet Theater), in tandem with punk folksingers Bitch and Animal's playful lyrics to "Pussy Manifesto."

This section also champions voices of class-based rage, with Elizabeth Broeder's wild (and nearly incomprehensible) TRASHGiRR-RRLLLZZZ, Elizabeth Wallace's diatribe about the hazards of cleaning up waste in a hospital, and Stefano Harney and Fred Moten's call for understanding the university as criminally perpetuating class-based inequalities. We finish this section with Jessa Crispin's outrageous and angry voice speaking directly to men who want feminism explained to them. By turning the politics of respectability on its head, these writers advocate for a feminism that is funky, trashy, and sometimes downright nasty.

62 RIOT GRRRL Manifesto

1991

Bikini Kill

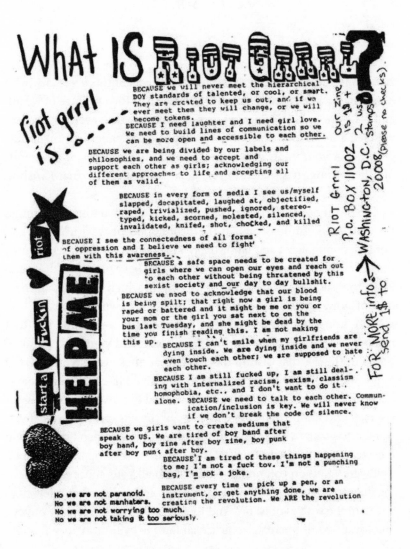

What IS RIOT GRRRL?

riot grrrl is:......

riot

start a ♥ Fuck'in ♥ HELP ME

BECAUSE we will never meet the hierarchical BOY standards of talented, or cool, or smart. They are created to keep us out, and if we ever meet them they will change, or we will become tokens.

BECAUSE I need laughter and I need girl love. We need to build lines of communication so we can be more open and accessible to each other.

BECAUSE we are being divided by our labels and philosophies, and we need to accept and support each other as girls; acknowledging our different approaches to life and accepting all of them as valid.

BECAUSE in every form of media I see us/myself slapped, decapitated, laughed at, objectified, raped, trivialized, pushed, ignored, stereotyped, kicked, scorned, molested, silenced, invalidated, knifed, shot, choked, and killed

BECAUSE I see the connectedness of all forms of oppression and I believe we need to fight them with this awareness.

BECAUSE a safe space needs to be created for girls where we can open our eyes and reach out to each other without being threatened by this sexist society and our day to day bullshit.

BECAUSE we need to acknowledge that our blood is being spilt; that right now a girl is being raped or battered and it might be me or you or your mom or the girl you sat next to on the bus last Tuesday, and she might be dead by the time you finish reading this. I am not making this up.

BECAUSE I can't smile when my girlfriends are dying inside. We are dying inside and we never even touch each other; we are supposed to hate each other.

BECAUSE I am still fucked up, I am still dealing with internalized racism, sexism, classism homophobia, etc.. and I don't want to do it alone. BECAUSE we need to talk to each other. Communication/inclusion is key. We will never know if we don't break the code of silence.

BECAUSE we girls want to create mediums that speak to US. We are tired of boy band after boy band, boy zine after boy zine, boy punk after boy punk.

BECAUSE I am tired of these things happening to me; I'm not a fuck toy. I'm not a punching bag, I'm not a joke.

No we are not paranoid.
No we are not manhaters.
No we are not worrying too much.
No we are not taking it too seriously.

BECAUSE every time we pick up a pen, or an instrument, or get anything done, we are creating the revolution. We ARE the revolution

Riot Grrrl
P.O. Box 11002
WASHINGTON, D.C.
20008 (please no checks).
Our zine is 1$ + 2 us stamps
FOR MORE info → send 1$ to

63 To Tramps, the Unemployed, the Disinherited, and Miserable

1884

Lucy E. Parsons

A word to the 35,000 now tramping the streets of this great city, with hands in pockets, gazing listlessly about you at the evidence of wealth and pleasure of which you own no part, not sufficient even to purchase yourself a bit of food with which to appease the pangs of hunger now gnawing at your vitals. It is with you and the hundreds of thousands of others similarly situated in this great land of plenty, that I wish to have a word.

Have you not worked hard all your life, since you were old enough for your labor to be of use in the production of wealth? Have you not toiled long, hard and laboriously in producing wealth? And in all those years of drudgery do you not know you have produced thousand upon thousands of dollars' worth of wealth, which you did not then, do not now, and unless you ACT, never will, own any part in? Do you not know that when you were harnessed to a machine and that machine harnessed to steam, and thus you toiled your 10, 12 and 16 hours in the 24, that during this time in all these years you received only enough of your labor product to furnish yourself the bare, coarse necessaries of life, and that when you wished to purchase anything for yourself and family it always had to be of the cheapest quality? If you wanted to go anywhere you had to wait until Sunday, so little did you receive for your unremitting toil that you dare not stop for a moment, as it were? And do you not know that with all your squeezing, pinching and economizing you never were enabled to keep but a few days ahead of the wolves of want? And that at last when the caprice of your employer saw fit to create an artificial famine by limiting production, that the fires in the furnace were extinguished, the iron horse to which you had been harnessed was stilled; the factory door locked up, you turned upon the highway a tramp, with hunger in your stomach and rags upon your back?

Yet your employer told you that it was overproduction which made him close up. Who cared for the bitter tears and heart-pangs of your loving wife and helpless children, when you bid them a loving "God bless you" and turned upon the tramper's road to seek employment elsewhere? I say, who cared for those heartaches and pains? You were only a tramp now, to be execrated and denounced as a "worthless tramp and a vagrant" by that very class who had been engaged all those years in robbing you and yours. Then can you not see that the "good boss" or the "bad boss" cuts no figure whatever? that you are the common prey of both, and that their mission is simply robbery? Can you not see that it is the INDUSTRIAL SYSTEM and not the "boss" which must be changed?

Now, when all these bright summer and autumn days are going by and you have no employment, and consequently can save up nothing, and when the winter's blast sweeps down from the north and all the earth is wrapped in a shroud of ice, hearken not to the voice of the hypocrite who will tell you that it was ordained of God that "the poor ye have always"; or to the arrogant robber who will say to you that you "drank up all your wages last summer when you had work, and that is the reason why you have nothing now, and the workhouse or the workyard is too good for you; that you ought to be shot." And shoot you they will if you present your petitions in too emphatic a manner. So hearken not to them, but list! Next winter when the cold blasts are creeping through the rents in your seedy garments, when the frost is biting your feet through the holes in your worn-out shoes, and when all wretchedness seems to have centered in and upon you, when misery has marked you for her own and life has become a burden and existence a mockery, when you have walked the streets by day and slept upon hard boards by night, and at last determine by your own hand to take your life,—for you would rather go out into utter nothingness than to longer endure an existence which has become such a burden—so, perchance, you determine to dash yourself into the cold embrace of the lake rather than longer suffer thus. But halt, before you commit this last tragic act in the drama of your simple existence. Stop! Is there nothing you can do to insure those whom you are about to orphan, against a like fate? The waves will only dash over you in mockery of your rash act; but stroll you down the avenues of the rich and look through the magnificent plate windows into their voluptuous homes, and here you will discover the *very identical robbers* who have despoiled you and yours. Then let your tragedy be enacted *here!* Awaken them from their wanton sport at your expense! Send forth your petition and let them read it by the red glare of destruction. Thus when you cast "one long lingering look behind" you can be assured that you have spoken to these robbers in the only language which they have ever been able to understand, for they have never yet deigned to notice any petition from their slaves that they were not *compelled* to read by the red glare bursting from the cannon's mouths, or that was not handed to them upon the point of the sword. You need no organization when you make up your mind to present this kind of petition. In fact, an organization would be a detriment to you; but each of you hungry tramps who read these lines, avail yourselves of those little methods of warfare which Science has placed in the hands of the poor man, and you will become a power in this or any other land.

Learn the use of explosives!

64 TRASHGiRRRRLLLZZZ: A Manifesto for Misfit ToYZ

2016

Elizabeth Broeder

Trsh gurlZZZZ fownd ©|Marilyn Monroe|© in a crdbrd box on eisle
Sweet 16 and chanted we
wanna b blO UP dollZ for Halloween
Trash Grlz R the pollution of the 'Merican Dream
Beauty Pageants and pyramid schemeS
We are Wise/Jaded jagged Daggers drawn at the guts of the wealthy
happy perverts who indulge
their whims on the backs of trsH
We are egalitarian muskrats fueled by anger, hunger and delusions of
folding money
Delushuns of milk and honey
The delusions from trashhhh
Trash Babies are Cottun Kandy perfume and ripe sweet stayns n' $1 for
a wet dream and a teaze
so cheap you cud prolly just take it from her
2 many stories 'bout 2 story houses
"What do we want to be when we get salavaged..get saved… get recy-
cled..grow up?"
"We wanna be fantasieZ. BARBIES dollz get trashed 2. BARBIE
DOLLZ get drty 2. BRBIE
DOLZ get throne out 2" buuuuttt OOOooo 2 be uZed like THAT
Stoners, wide eyed red dreamin' again, Stone her!!
We watch our heritage aking rusting, cracking, sooooo Tyred; TraSH
dnt sleyp.
WEE Pulll hour own weight under each EYE in duffle bagz becuz We

wrkd hard 4 this burden

Wrinkled Prinsezzes Pullin' nite shiftZ in GAS stasions

TRASH dnt get sik dayz they get minimum waige s

o they GlaZE they're Dystnt Gaze in Make Up anD Sparklez an' iN their sick DAZE sEE

MARY mOther of GOD ridin' bitch on her son's destiny

Bogart our smiles while the jury's still out on bedroom morse code eyes

Baby trash girlz stay up all nite planning or avoiding the future

we learn that security comes from fat white timecard Jesus and his soft spot for Marilyn

Magdalin who used her FILTH to clean his feet

Our bodiez are packages; our bodies are rags; our bodies are tasty; our bodies are mechanical;

our bodies are neon tabernacles for His, his and his ambitions

Hit it! Like when mom won't shut up and take hiz sox off, plastered all over her like an eviction

notice ECONomees BUILt on Insecurity and dESPERATION; A symbiotic mass produced

epidemik of TRASH

Mom can'tt come home; not 'til she leaves a lb. of her soul as a security deposit at company that

needz her to believe that they cud toss her trash ass out at any time because,

"pretty young waitresses are better 4 businezz"

"Wish I had stayed in school. I knew girls who could do that. They stayed in school after they

got pregnant. I just... I just couDn't handle the rumors..."

"He became a doktr, I thnk. But I wanted the baby" "I luv bein' a husk mommy"

Rich boyz like the way we dnt take No for an answer' wish we could say the same for them

TRASH gurlz no the ONLY way owt iz on his coat tale or Ridin bitch on the GLORY uv his

ALMITEY MERCY

Callussed hands snap wedding band into a symphony concert

"You don't belong here" Nice boys taste like sour apples from a Snow White dream of being a

girl worth walking home at night

The only difference between a trash Girll and a prostitute is the market value

"Asking for it" asking for two missing teeth and a blown out kidney

"Is my body difficult for you to swallow?"

Doez it taste like Death, lyke trash, like bonez???

Trsh gets raped in public n' spenz the rest of owr lyves apologizing for this garbage

Hard to call us whiny kuntz wen YOU have to look at all thiz filth DO the LASTING

psychological effects rape make u uncomfortable?

Do u need a safe space?

How 'bout the dumpster where trash gurlz take cigarette brakes 'trash knows that we only get

rest wen we fined new ways to kill ourselves

1 in 3 women LIV on or nere the poverty wage line. That's 42 million women and 28 million

children who hav no real control over their own lives

They use words like "charity" an "giving to the needy" but they do nothing more than indulge in

filanthropic masturbation and shame us TRASH for DARING to need a living wage or

healthcare

What could we be if no 1 told us that not rotting is a luxury

Trsh girlz got Fukd up Wite trASH teeth; and we smell like rotting trash in sumR; TrASH Girlz

got matted hare but ain' it kinda sexy that we're fallin' apart; "all I want for Christmas is a

PROM dress that won't make me look like a phaze he'll get over when he comes to his senses"

Black coffee gut punch cures a guud boi hayze

Safety pins in the mail gayz

"You don't belong here"

What could we be if they quit telling us where we DNT fit

Desiree had a mizcarriage when her mom shuvved her against a bathtub in a fit of righteous rage.

The town mourned the loss of infinity in the infant's potential and shunned the shards of Desiree

that buckled in the blood like a broken jar

"Clean up in ile SWEET 16. There's a husk in the produce eyle who

couldn't deliver our
dreams."
"quit throwin' a PHit!" "so you're saying women should be punished
for having abortions?"
"Yeah, I think there shoul be some kind of punishment, yes."
"I'm so sorry"
War Machine, the battle's in the silences between the "Fuk U!"
"Next Year in Jerusalem"
"I do whatever the fuk I want to!"
"Next year in America"
"I dnt WANNA!"
"Nextt year in California"
"I dn" WANT to"
"Next year when I win the lottery"
Trsh DON' WANT and neeether does Buddha
"Setl doun BiTCH!
DOWN, BITCH!
trAsh DON'T Fight" neeether does Boodaw
TRSCH dnt fite
Trshgirl SENG WITH ME "We are not a defect. WE ARE not rejects.
We are the foundasion of
your kingdom We are NOT grateful 4 this Job/you shud B greatful.
Gareful we don't crumble
out frum underneath you"
TrAsh GetZ used, burned and fuels our own industrial revolution!
"Call the cops! I'll be on a cattle car of a speading trane day aftr tmorow
or someday with the
rest of the waitresses waitin' to escape, waitin' to leavve who just want
to die like the girls on
TV Wide wild Black eyed dreamin' again cuz we ain' ever seen a way
out that wasn't strapped
to the back of a man's dump truck You shud be greatful husk don't tell
you all the rotting truth
you already know 'bout urself.
We are not a HEAP;
Trsh GRL we dn know how to be prty
Pepsi belches and damp cigarettes
Trash don't sleyp.
Tresh fell for that trik b4

Trash Girlz, we get ruthless and angry

Trsh grL Hear Me, Luv yur filth

It is sloppy, it is rotting, it is riddled with quarums written by a society that needs us to believe

that we shud shut up and be too proud to take hand outs

ShUD shut up and take the hand outs

"The poor will always be with us. The poor will always be with us. The poor will always be with

us."

Who's "US?" How do we make ourselves, our futures, our lives better when your "US" treats

our "US" like filth; like sickness; like the wasted; like the waste

Impovrishd disposable trash grl ddn't start this wor

But wel surrender to an incinerator befor lose it.

This trash is ours; a=All oURS

ThIS planiT IS Ours

Now has cum the time for TRsh 2 invadE; THIS IS A CALL TO STRA-TEGIC pollution

=An infection of FILTH

Wmn are instinctively programmed to communicate and protect

WE MUST USE THIS IN OUR GLOBAL DUMPSTER DIVE

WE find our trsh in the streets; by dumpsters; in the fostercare system; in hospitalZZ lying 'bout

where they got bruzes

We must start small, very small

OuR Mother Colony is A single organism. A ONE"charasmetic leder" builTT out ov A family oF

muskrats;- A frankenstien of truth and unwavering anger.

TRsH Cnt DIVE plunge; not just yET

TRsH puluted with President JesuS treamorZ

WE caN nOt see it but if we attck in thizzzzz moment we will surely destroi OUR own movement

and settle for being recycled

We MUST become nomadic; We mustbuild a colonyXX that sTudies CommUnicaTION;

TechNOLOGY and SCienCE

THESE aRe the enemieZZZzz oF oPPressiOn

We mUst fOrce ourselves to liv in harsh, uNbearable ConDItions

Trashhh already know THAT; Trsh been Threw that: trash allredy had that

TRsH migrate; CAMPS oUTside PrisonZ (weather that be male or female prizonzz dus not mattr)

Our focus is trsh; ouR gndR is USED- RMBR that prizonz are our cultural dumpstrs

VICTIMS of systemic poisoning, aBUSE, aDDiction, Ill treated MentaL conditions, VictimS of

CultuRAL MANipulatioN towards violens and tHe unorthodox and desperate R our Patron saintZ

and HigH priests uv revolt!

We must CAMP outSIDE the ConVents of ConVicts; Study the trsH to learn WHAT fuels the

bEAST

When the time arrives for Action WE must be ARCHERS&SPEED D3mOns

We fite with information. We invade one town<>one zipcoud at a Thyme

WE Attack from the Filth Up. We must begin with shelters, Detention sessions at schools, soup

kitchens, AA meetings, FIND THE FILTH

Infrmation is the wpn

Listen for the INFECTION. SNIFF OUT THE DISESE.

HELP these concentrated communnittieZ through SEXUSL education, Technology TRAINING,

TEACH our trahs aBout Government. NURTURE their INSECURI-TIES. INFORMATION IS THE

Weapon. TEACH them about Nurtition, ABOUT creating petitions, how to EVALUATE

electiooooonnnnssss and ELECtoral canidates, Teach them HOW to ACHIEVE SELF ESTEEM

Pvrty is not the absence of money it is the stripping oF sElf EstEEm and Secuirty

TEACH THEM THAT THEY CAN GIVE THT To THEMSELVES and TRSH GrlZZZ WILL BE HERE TO

cLeasn UP wht rmainZZZ

ENCOURAGE communication with peple ouTsIdE of theiR SOSSIAL grOOOupS and Townz. WE

MIGRATE this meenes that we carrrry the knowldg from those we infst

<TRSH tradition> But only amongst r selves

WE aRe hUskS. We foRm A protective layer around the dying while they cure thmslvs frm th
insyderOunD
WE prvd, support and stimulate free/glowbal/free global trade
We establish international laws:
1. TRSH MAKeS DEmAND
2. Trsh LISTNS to DEMnDS
3. Trsh sEEKs SolutiOns
4. TRSH SHARES SOLUTIONZZZ with The global pollution of fellow TrASHHH {we r
aninfultration of VALUeZ}
5. Trsh is EGALITArianistiCCC- ThIs is NOT an AcknowledgeMent to Be RRespected. ThIS is a
commitment. ALL Are EQUAL because WE MAKE ALL EQUAL. Trsh acknowledgs powr in
acknowledgment and prSrvs and DefndZZ trsh thru CummuniKatION
6. We Promote hour lederz on merit
7. We Listn to needZ not Language
8. WEEEE vote with FEET,. Thz menes cHidrn and Babiez hold as much autonomy and
investment in the future AZ adultz do_)General counselZ in the STREET tht dmnd
physical prsnce Xcept for the ELDRly Who may be Represtented VIA virtual
cumunicatioN or a Mailed BalloT
WHITH THESE METHODzzzz we establisshhhshshshshsh a crs cultural pollination- a POLUTION
of A POPULATION A NatION of TrSH that Over THROWS its ownnnn opressoers empowering
THE oppressed

65 Women's Art: A Manifesto

1973

VALIE EXPORT

THE POSITION OF ART IN THE WOMEN'S LIBERATION MOVEMENT IS THE POSITION OF WOMAN IN THE ART'S MOVEMENT.

THE HISTORY OF WOMAN IS THE HISTORY OF MAN.

because man has defined the image of woman for both man and woman, men create and control the social and communication media such as science and art, word and image, fashion and architecture, social transportation and division of labor. men have projected their image of woman onto these media, and in accordance with these medial patterns they gave shape to woman. if reality is a social construction and men its engineers, we are dealing with a male reality. women have not yet come to themselves, because they have not had a chance to speak insofar as they had no access to the media.

let women speak so that they can find themselves, this is what I ask for in order to achieve a self-defined image of ourselves and thus a different view of the social function of women. we women must participate in the construction of reality via the building stones of media-communication.

this will not happen spontaneously or without resistance, therefore we must fight! if we shall carry through our goals such as social equal rights, self-determination, a new female consciousness, we must try to express them within the whole realm of life. this fight will bring about far reaching consequences and changes in the whole range of life not only for ourselves but for men, children, family, church ... in short for the state.

women must make use of all media as a means of social struggle and social progress in order to free culture of male values. in the same fashion she will do this in the arts knowing that men for thousands of years were able to express herein their heroism of eroticism, sex, beauty including their mythology of vigor, energy and austerity in sculpture, paintings, novels, films, drama, drawings, etc., and thereby influencing our consciousness. it will be time.

AND IT IS THE RIGHT TIME

that women use art as a means of expression so as to influence the consciousness of all of us, let our ideas flow into the social construction of reality to create a human reality. so far the arts have been created to a large extent solely by men. they dealt with the subjects of life, with the problems of emotional life adding only their own accounts, answers and solutions. now we must make our own assertions. we must destroy all these notions of love, faith, family, motherhood, companionship, which were not created by us and thus replace them with new ones in accordance with our sensibility, with our wishes.

to change the arts that man forced upon us means to destroy the features of women created by man. the new values that we add to the arts will bring about new values for women in the course of the civilizing process. the arts can be of importance to the women's liberation insofar as we derive significance—our significance—from it: this spark can ignite the process of our self-determination. the question, what women can give to the arts and what the arts can give to the women, can be answered as follows: the transference of the specific situation of woman to the artistic context sets up signs and signals which provide new artistic expressions and messages on one hand, and change retrospectively the situation of women on the other.

the arts can be understood as a medium of our self-definition adding new values to the arts. these values, transmitted via the cultural sign-process, will alter reality toward an accommodation of female needs.

THE FUTURE OF WOMEN WILL BE THE HISTORY OF WOMAN.

66 The Why Cheap Art? Manifesto

1984

Bread and Puppet Theater

the WHY CHEAP ART? manifesto

PEOPLE have been THINKING too long that
ART is a PRIVILEGE of the MUSEUMS & the
RICH .   ART IS NOT BUSINESS !
It does not belong to banks & fancy investors
ART IS FOOD . You cant EAT it BUT it FEEDS
you . ART has to be CHEAP & available to
EVERYBODY . It needs to be EVERYWHERE
because it is the INSIDE of the
WORLD .
ART SOOTHES PAIN !
Art wakes up sleepers !
ART FIGHTS AGAINST WAR & STUPIDITY !
ART SINGS HALLELUJA !
ART IS FOR KITCHENS !
ART IS LIKE GOOD BREAD!
Art is like green trees !
Art is like white clouds in blue sky !
ART IS CHEAP !
HURRAH

Bread & Puppet Glover, Vermont, 1984

67 Pussy Manifesto

1999

Bitch and Animal

Pussy manifesto, pussy manifesto
Pussy pussy pussy manifesto
Pussy manifesto, pussy manifesto
Pussy pussy pussy manifesto

Manifest this motherfucker #1:

Every living thing comes from and returns to ...
Get it?

Pussy manifesto, pussy manifesto
Pussy pussy pussy manifesto

Manifest this Muddafucka #2:

Let Pussy speak to me through every living thing. As all creatures
move and grow, let them bring forth the openness and warmness that
flows in the energy of Pussy ...
The life force on which we all depend.

Pussy pussy pussy manifesto

Manifest this Muthafucka #3:

I'm sick of my genitalia being an insult. Are you? It's time to let my labia rip and rearrange this. Here we go:

"That was so Pussy of you to help me move to my new place! Especially since I'm living on the 13th floor. You've really made this a Pussy move!"

Manifest this Motherfucker #4:

The power of Pussy could be blinding. Do not misinterpret its strength and fear it. Do not try to control it. It is light, rich and full of warmth. Use it wisely and with jeweled intentions.

Manifest this Motherfucker #5:

The Egg says, "Don't forget me, mothafucka!"
The Egg must not be understated. Let the Egg be the symbol of all courage!
Here we go:
"Honey, that took Eggs for you to tell your customer off for not tipping you 20%!"

The Egg, like courage, is a delicate intricate shell surrounding ever-changing nutritious life!
Let the Egg be the teacher and the Pussy be its nest.

Pussy manifesto
Pussy pussy pussy manifesto

Manifest this Motherfucker #6:

Employ the Pussy!

- teacher
- whore
- philosopher
- president

Pay her well!

Manifest this Motherfucker #7:

The Pussy is a traveler! No matter where your Pussy energy leads
you, let the Pussy be your clock...
Allow the
"ticking" to be measured by
Gathered and dispersed
Gathered and dispersed
Gathered and dispersed
One should not outweigh the other...

Manifest this Mothafucker #8:

Let Pussy manifest!
Let Pussy manifest!
Let Pussy manifest!
and let freedom sing!
And let freedom sing!
Let freedom sing!

Pussy manifesto pussy manifesto
Pussy pussy pussy manifesto
Pussy manifesto pussy manifesto
Pussy pussy pussy manifesto
Pussy manifesto

Now that's Pussy!

68 I Don't Want to Have to Compromise My Morals in Order to Make a Living

2013

Grimes

i dont want my words to be taken out of context

i dont want to be infantilized because i refuse to be sexualized

i dont want to be molested at shows or on the street by people who perceive me as an object that exists for their personal satisfaction

i dont want to live in a world where im gonna have to start employing body guards because this kind of behavior is so commonplace and accepted and I'm pissed that when I express concern over my own safety it's often ignored until people see firsthand what happens and then they apologize for not taking me seriously after the fact ...

I'm tired of men who aren't professional or even accomplished musicians continually offering to 'help me out' (without being asked), as if i did this by accident and i'm gonna flounder without them. or as if the fact that I'm a woman makes me incapable of using technology. I have never seen this kind of thing happen to any of my male peers

I'm tired of the weird insistence that i need a band or i need to work with outside producers (and I'm eternally grateful to the people who don't do this)

im tired of being considered vapid for liking pop music or caring about fashion as if these things inherently lack substance or as if the things i enjoy somehow make me a lesser person

im tired of being congratulated for being thin because i can more easily fit into sample sizes from the runway

im tired of people i love betraying me so they can get credit or money

I'm sad that it's uncool or offensive to talk about environmental or human rights issues

I'm tired of creeps on message boards discussing whether or not they'd "fuck" me

I'm tired of people harassing my dancers and treating them like they aren't human beings

I'm sad that my desire to be treated as an equal and as a human being is interpreted as hatred of men, rather than a request to be included and respected (I have four brothers and many male best friends and a dad and i promise i do not hate men at all, nor do i believe that all men are sexist or that all men behave in the ways described above)

im tired of being referred to as "cute," as a "waif" etc., even when the author, fan, friend, family member etc. is being positive

(fyi)

waif |wāf|

noun

1 a homeless and helpless person, esp. a neglected or abandoned child: *she is foster-mother to various **waifs and strays**.*

* an abandoned pet animal.

Cute |kyōot|

adjective

1 attractive in a pretty or endearing way: *a cute kitten.*

• informal sexually attractive.

I'm tired of people assuming that just because something happens regularly it's ok

i have so much love for everyone who has been cool and amazing. I have the best job in the world but I'm done with being passive about any kind of status quo that allows anyone to suffer or to be disrespected

Grimes world tour is officially over, the visions album cycle is officially over, and I'm now taking the time to overhaul everything and make it better

much love to every fan—stuff can be lame sometimes but its really cool to have this support

69 The People Behind the Mop Buckets

2015

Elizabeth Wallace

Have you ever noticed the dust in the vents of a Target restroom? Have you ever wondered how the windows in your dentist's office stay so clean? Have you ever considered perhaps *not* cramming your day old, half-full Starbucks coffee cup in the top of the already overflowing trash can? No? Well, I have. I look at the vents as I pee in Target restrooms. I scan the windows for smudges as I am leaned back in the dentist chair while someone scours my teeth and simultaneously asks me what I am studying in school. And I definitely dump out any liquids before throwing drink containers away. I do this because I am the person who cleans dust out of vents and I am the person who wipes marks off windows and I am the person who gets covered in your day old Starbucks coffee when trash bags split open.

We are housekeepers and we are janitors and we are maids and if you want to get fancy; we are environmental service workers. This may come as a surprise to you, but we are *actual* living, breathing human beings who are paid (mind you, we are paid very little) to clean up after you. If you have a functioning brain in your head and a beating heart in your chest, you should appreciate those whose job it is to clean up after you, or after your family members or after the stranger who stood behind you in line at the ATM. However, for the purposes of this manifesto, we are focusing on the men and women who work in hospital housekeeping.

* * *

"This is really hard work. Why should we give you the job?"
"Because I'm willing to work hard."

I had no idea what I was even saying when I answered my now manager in that job interview two and half years ago. I had no idea I would have to take a bath for the first time in fifteen years just to soak my aching back in hot water. I had no idea my co-workers had to load up on Ibuprofen before shifts in order to make it the full eight and a half hours. I had no idea my stomach was so strong when faced with pee, poop, vomit, blood and mystery fluids that are dried (or not) to the walls around a toilet. I had no idea how anyone could do this job for so fucking long when I was barely making it through the first six months and they had been doing this work for as long as I had been alive. But mostly, I had no idea how poorly we were going to be treated by those outside of housekeeping. I learned pretty quickly that as soon as I walked in those automatic sliding glass doors, I was no one. I was no longer Liz. I was no longer an Arizona State University student. I no longer had loved ones or hobbies or dreams. I was just a housekeeper with a strong emphasis on the "just."

But I am not *just* any one thing. None of us are.

Patients are not the last to leave a room before the next patient enters. It is not okay to be lax or to totally disregard hospital signage policies. While you may not think it matters if "isolation precaution" signs are removed after the patient has changed rooms or has been discharged, there are people who still have to deal with those rooms and everything inside of them. For example, calling a housekeeper to clean a room only to tell her when she is finished cleaning it that the patient was positive for Tuberculosis is not okay. There should have been a bright blue "Airborne Precaution" sign along with a specific kind of fitted mask at the entrance of the room. I can guarantee the nurses, doctors, and ultrasounds techs who worked with the patient were made aware of the TB diagnosis and were provided N-95 masks prior to entering the room, so where was our notification and our mask? Just like, where was our gown and hair net when you wanted us to clean a room so covered in mystery bugs carried in on the clothes of visitors that when our eyes scanned the room, we could actually see tiny bursts of movement from the bugs jumping? Would you send your sister or son or friend or co-worker into a room, unprotected, to stand among an infestation of bed bugs or lice or, really, anything? We did not think so.

It is unacceptable to exclude housekeepers from what is seen as universal precautionary practices for everyone else. Why do you think it is okay for us, but not for anyone else, to wear our normal uniform pants instead of temporary scrub pants when inside a labor and delivery operation room? As you can probably imagine, blood gets everywhere in operating rooms. It is standard practice for housekeepers to use one of the strongest chemicals we have on the goops of blood on the floor, mop it all up, *and then* start actually cleaning so as not to track blood as we clean around the room. I do not know about you, but I am not really looking to carry the blood of a new mother or new baby on my pant leg from inside the hospital to inside my car to inside my home. Oh wait, you do not have to worry about that because you are allowed to wear the scrubs provided by the hospital that get changed before exiting the hospital. Only housekeepers have to worry about it. Imagine that.

We all know stereotypes are exaggerations in order to label and limit groups of people, so why do you think we are all middle-aged Mexican women who love nothing more than to clean... and cook, of course? You see no problem with the fact that all hospital signage, which can possibly relate to housekeepers, is translated into Spanish. But, wait, you are simply being inclusive, right? If inclusivity was the goal and if you took the time to know the housekeepers who get the trash out of your office every goddamn day then you would know your mistake. If inclusivity was the goal then housekeeping signs would be translated into Tagalog, Navajo, Serbian as well as Spanish and that would be just to cover the diversity on one shift in one Arizona hospital. We are a diverse group of people with families and bills and homework and multiple jobs and friends and stress and goals and we do not get paid enough to be treated as anyone less.

We are not invisible nor are we invincible. Stop ignoring us until you need something cleaned and then expect us to clean without consideration for our own health and for the health of those around us. Stop treating us as if we are not people who live normal human lives outside of these sterile walls that *we* fucking sterilize, by the way. Take an extra second out of your life to dump out old coffee cups before cramming then into a full trash can so it does not leak through the bag onto the human beings who eventually have to empty that trash can. At the very least, thank the housekeeper who cleans your hospital room. Treat us like the fully-formed humans that we are and not like the scum of the earth as we are the ones who will sanitize the operating room before your surgery.

While we are neither invisible nor invincible, we *are* strong. We are strong in that without us, the whole hospital system would cease to function. The hospital runs like a car and housekeepers are like the spark plugs. If the spark plugs were gummed up or missing, the car would not run. If the housekeepers were lazy or gone, the hospital would not run. A microbiologist once told me, "Housekeepers are the most important people in the hospital, doctors are second. Housekeepers are the ones who prevent hospital outbreaks, not doctors." So the next time you look us in the face and tell us we are *just* housekeepers, keep that in mind. Also keep in mind that because we all experience the same belittling words and side-eye glances and lack of appreciation, we have learned to stick together. When we wear that plum top and those black pants and that name badge, all of which mark us as housekeepers, we form into a unit. We will not push our carts with our heads down in embarrassment. We will roll through the halls with our heads up and you will see us. We are multi-racial, multi-ethnic, and multi-lingual. We are bakers, seamstresses, and students. We are someone's children, parents, grandparents, and great grandparents. And *we* are the people behind the mop buckets.

70 The Undercommons (excerpt)

2013

Stefano Harney and Fred Moten

THE ONLY POSSIBLE RELATIONSHIP TO THE UNIVERSITY TODAY IS A CRIMINAL ONE

"To the university I'll steal, and there I'll steal," to borrow from Pistol at the end of Henry V, as he would surely borrow from us. This is the only possible relationship to the American university today. This may be true of universities everywhere. It may have to be true of the university in general. But certainly, this much is true in the United States: it cannot be denied that the university is a place of refuge, and it cannot be accepted that the university is a place of enlightenment. In the face of these conditions one can only sneak into the university and steal what one can. To abuse its hospitality, to spite its mission, to join its refugee colony, its gypsy encampment, to be in but not of—this is the path of the subversive intellectual in the modern university.

Worry about the university. This is the injunction today in the United States, one with a long history. Call for its restoration like Harold Bloom or Stanley Fish or Gerald Graff. Call for its reform like Derek Bok or Bill Readings or Cary Nelson. Call out to it as it calls to you. But for the subversive intellectual, all of this goes on upstairs, in polite company, among the rational men. After all, the subversive intellectual came under false pretenses, with bad documents, out of love. Her labor is as necessary as it is unwelcome. The university needs what she bears but cannot bear what she brings. And on top of all that, she disappears. She disappears into the underground, the downlow low-down maroon community of the university, into the *undercommons*

of enlightenment, where the work gets done, where the work gets sub-
verted, where the revolution is still black, still strong.

What is that work and what is its social capacity for both reproducing the university and producing fugitivity? If one were to say teaching,
one would be performing the work of the university. Teaching is
merely a profession and an operation of that onto-/auto-encyclopedic
circle of the state that Jacques Derrida calls the Universitas. But it is
useful to invoke this operation to glimpse the hole in the fence where
labor enters, to glimpse its hiring hall, its night quarters. The university needs teaching labor, despite itself, or as itself, self-identical with
and thereby erased by it. It is not teaching that holds this social capacity, but something that produces the not visible other side of teaching,
a thinking through the skin of teaching toward a collective orientation to the knowledge object as future project, and a commitment to
what we want to call the prophetic organization. But it is teaching that
brings us in. Before there are grants, research, conferences, books, and
journals there is the experience of being taught and of teaching. Before
the research post with no teaching, before the graduate students to
mark the exams, before the string of sabbaticals, before the permanent
reduction in teaching load, the appointment to run the Center, the
consignment of pedagogy to a discipline called education, before the
course designed to be a new book, teaching happened.

The moment of teaching for food is therefore often mistakenly
taken to be a stage, as if eventually one should not teach for food.
If the stage persists, there is a social pathology in the university. But
if the teaching is successfully passed on, the stage is surpassed, and
teaching is consigned to those who are known to remain in the stage,
the socio-pathological labor of the university. Kant interestingly calls
such a stage "self-incurred minority." He tries to contrast it with having
the "determination and courage to use one's intelligence without being
guided by another." "Have the courage to use your own intelligence."
But what would it mean if teaching or rather what we might call "the
beyond of teaching" is precisely what one is asked to get beyond, to
stop taking sustenance? And what of those minorities who refuse, the
tribe of moles who will not come back from beyond (that which is
beyond "the beyond of teaching"), as if they will not be subjects, as if
they want to think as objects, as minority? Certainly, the perfect subjects of communication, those successfully beyond teaching, will see
them as waste. But their collective labor will always call into question

who truly is taking the orders of the enlightenment. The waste lives for those moments beyond teaching when you give away the unexpected beautiful phrase—unexpected, no one has asked, beautiful, it will never come back. Is being the biopower of the enlightenment truly better than this?

Perhaps the biopower of the enlightenment knows this, or perhaps it is just reacting to the objecthood of this labor as it must. But even as it depends on these moles, these refugees, it will call them uncollegial, impractical, naive, unprofessional. And one may be given one last chance to be pragmatic—why steal when one can have it all, they will ask. But if one hides from this interpellation, neither agrees nor disagrees but goes with hands full into the underground of the university, into the Undercommons—this will be regarded as theft, as a criminal act. And it is at the same time, the only possible act.

In that undercommons of the university one can see that it is not a matter of teaching versus research or even the beyond of teaching versus the individualisation of research. To enter this space is to inhabit the ruptural and enraptured disclosure of the commons that fugitive enlightenment enacts, the criminal, matricidal, queer, in the cistern, on the stroll of the stolen life, the life stolen by enlightenment and stolen back, where the commons give refuge, where the refuge gives commons. What the beyond of teaching is really about is not finishing oneself, not passing, not completing; it's about allowing subjectivity to be unlawfully overcome by others, a radical passion and passivity such that one becomes unfit for subjection, because one does not possess the kind of agency that can hold the regulatory forces of subjecthood, and one cannot initiate the auto-interpellative torque that biopower subjection requires and rewards. It is not so much the teaching as it is the prophecy in the organization of the act of teaching. The prophecy that predicts its own organization and has therefore passed, as commons, and the prophecy that exceeds its own organization and therefore as yet can only be organized. Against the prophetic organization of the undercommons is arrayed its own deadening labor for the university, and beyond that, the negligence of professionalization, and the professionalization of the critical academic. The undercommons is therefore always an unsafe neighborhood.

As Fredric Jameson reminds us, the university depends upon "Enlightenment-type critiques and demystification of belief and committed ideology, in order to clear the ground for unobstructed planning and 'development.'" This is the weakness of the university, the lapse in its homeland security. It needs labor power for this "enlightenment-type critique," but, somehow, labor always escapes.

The premature subjects of the undercommons took the call seriously, or had to be serious about the call. They were not clear about planning, too mystical, too full of belief. And yet this labor force cannot reproduce itself, it must be reproduced. The university works for the day when it will be able to rid itself, like capital in general, of the trouble of labor. It will then be able to reproduce a labor force that understands itself as not only unnecessary but dangerous to the development of capitalism. Much pedagogy and scholarship is already dedicated in this direction. Students must come to see themselves as the problem, which, counter to the complaints of restorationist critics of the university, is precisely what it means to be a customer, to take on the burden of realisation and always necessarily be inadequate to it. Later, these students will be able to see themselves properly as obstacles to society, or perhaps, with lifelong learning, students will return having successfully diagnosed themselves as the problem.

Still, the dream of an undifferentiated labor that knows itself as superfluous is interrupted precisely by the labor of clearing away the burning roadblocks of ideology. While it is better that this police function be in the hands of the few, it still raises labor as difference, labor as the development of other labor, and therefore labor as a source of wealth. And although the enlightenment-type critique, as we suggest below, informs on, kisses the cheek of, any autonomous development as a result of this difference in labor, there is a break in the wall here, a shallow place in the river, a place to land under the rocks. The university still needs this clandestine labor to prepare this undifferentiated labor force, whose increasing specialisation and managerialist tendencies, again contra the restorationists, represent precisely the successful integration of the division of labor with the universe of exchange that commands restorationist loyalty.

Introducing this labor upon labor, and providing the space for its development, creates risks. Like the colonial police force recruited unwittingly from guerrilla neighborhoods, university labor may harbor refugees, fugitives, renegades, and castaways. But there are good reasons for the university to be confident that such elements will be exposed or forced underground. Precautions have been taken, book lists have been drawn up, teaching observations conducted, invitations to contribute made. Yet against these precautions stands the immanence of transcendence, the necessary deregulation and the possibilities of criminality and fugitivity that labor upon labor requires. Maroon communities of composition teachers, mentorless graduate students, adjunct Marxist historians, out or queer management professors, state college ethnic studies departments, closed-down film programs, visa-expired Yemeni student newspaper editors, historically black college sociologists, and feminist engineers. And what will the university say of them? It will say they are unprofessional. This is not an arbitrary charge. It is the charge against the more than professional. How do those who exceed the profession, who exceed and by exceeding escape, how do those maroons problematize themselves, problematize the university, force the university to consider them a problem, a danger? The undercommons is not, in short, the kind of fanciful communities of whimsy invoked by Bill Readings at the end of his book. The undercommons, its maroons, are always at war, always in hiding.

71 Why I Am Not a Feminist: A Feminist Manifesto (excerpt)

2017

Jessica Crispin

If I may interrupt my train of thought for just a moment to direct my attention to any men who might be reading this book.

Maybe you picked up my manifesto because you too have some problems with feminism. Maybe those problems are sincere. Maybe you philosophically disagree with current feminist thought; maybe you genuinely support the basic tenets of feminism but are confused by how those tenets are currently being expressed. Maybe you've read Firestone and Dworkin and dealt with the feelings and thoughts they evoked. Maybe you've sorted through your own fear of weakness and vulnerability; maybe you've examined the ways you have in the past projected those feelings onto women. Maybe you've dealt with your discomfort with femininity; maybe you have given space in your life to softness and beauty and love.

Or maybe you tell yourself you are enlightened and sensitive but really it's just that you are uncomfortable with women acting like they are autonomous human beings. Maybe you want a woman writer to tell you it's okay to think women are stupid, illogical idiots and that feminism is the embarrassing farce you deeply need it to be. Maybe you are looking for any excuse available to not take women seriously.

Probably you are somewhere in between. Either way, it's possible you have some questions or concerns with what I've written here, and you would like to me to address that for you.

If so, this is my response: Take that shit somewhere else. I am not interested. You as a man are not my problem. It is not my job to make feminism easy or understandable to you. It is not my job to nurture and encourage your empathy, it is not my job to teach you how to deal with women being human beings.

And don't take that shit to other women either. It's not their job. Your lack of enlightenment is not our problem. Figure it out. Do the reading, feel your own feelings, don't take them to someone else. Men have to do this work on their own and for each other. You cannot ask women to spend the next century carrying the burden of your discomfort and confusion. Do your own fucking work, gentlemen.

I understand that men are going to have to go through a difficult time. They're going to have to do all of the self-examination and seeking they've spent centuries avoiding doing. They're going to have to find new ways of living and being on the planet. Women have a huge head start on them, and they're going to do all they can to avoid going through this process.

Your first encounter with feminism should make you uncomfortable. It has to break through all of the messages you've been indoctrinated with. You'll have to experience regret for your behavior, and you will have to acknowledge all the ways you've been consciously and unconsciously misogynistic during your lifetime. One way to avoid that discomfort is to ask women to reassure you that you are one of the good ones. To perform your sensitivity. It's manipulative. Another way to avoid that discomfort is to sit alone with your dark thoughts about what is wrong with feminists.

I just want to be clear that I don't give a fuck about your response to this book. Do not email me, do not get in touch. Deal with your own shit for once.

PART VIII

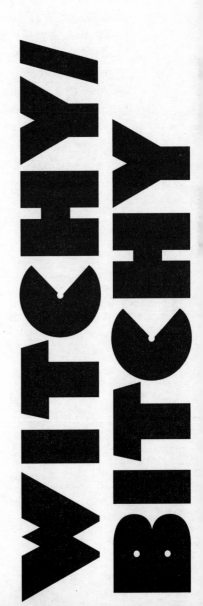

Introduction to Witchy/Bitchy

This short final section embraces two tropes of feminist history—witchiness and bitchiness—to present a group of feminist manifestos that welcome both of these descriptors. We begin with a classic second-wave radical feminist text written by the Women's International Terrorist Conspiracy from Hell (W.I.T.C.H.), a group that resurfaced in Portland, Oregon, and throughout the United States after the election of Donald Trump. We then hear from Joreen (aka Jo Freeman) in her well-known *BITCH Manifesto*, a key effort in reclaiming the word "bitch" and turning it against the oppressors. Next, we move into more explicitly witchy material with Peter Grey's Manifesto of Apocalyptic Witchcraft, followed by Kathie Sarachild's early radical feminist writing about the death of traditional womanhood (and the birth of something new).

The last two pieces come from the 1970s feminist art world (Jenny Holzer and Agnes Denes), circling us back to a feminism that is, as Denes says, "persisting in the eternal search." We are left asking both what has come before us, and what might come next, particularly if we wholly welcome rather than refute the highly gendered stereotypes of witches and bitches. Though manifestos are derived from a genre rooted in presentness, these texts nevertheless always lean toward and look for the future, for something new, for something better, for possibilities just out of our sightline, waiting to be discovered.

72 W.I.T.C.H. Manifesto

1968

W.I.T.C.H.

WITCH is an all-women Everything. It's theater, revolution, magic, terror, joy, garlic flowers, spells, It's an awareness that witches and gypsies were the original guerrillas and resistance fighters against oppression—particularly the oppression of women—down through the ages. Witches have always been women who dared to be: groovy, courageous, aggressive, intelligent, nonconformist, explorative, curious, independent, sexually liberated, revolutionary. (This possibly explains why nine million of them have been burned.) Witches were the first Friendly Heads and Dealers, the first birth-control practitioners and abortionists, the first alchemists (turn dross into gold and you devalue the whole idea of money!). They bowed to no man, being the living remnants of the oldest culture of all—one in which men and women were equal sharers in a truly cooperative society, before the death-dealing, sexual, economic, and spiritual repression of the Imperialist Phallic Society took over and began to destroy nature and human society.

WITCH lives and laughs in every woman. She is the free part of each of us, beneath the shy smiles, the acquiescence to absurd male domination, the make-up or flesh suffocating clothing our sick society demands. There is no "joining" WITCH. If you are a woman and dare to look within yourself, you are a Witch. You make your own rules. You are free and beautiful. You can be invisible or evident in how you choose to make your witch-self known. You can form your own Coven of sister Witches (thirteen is a cozy number for a group) and do your own actions.

Whatever is repressive, solely male-oriented, greedy, puritanical, authoritarian—those are your targets. Your weapons are theater, satire, explosions, magic, herbs, music, costumes, cameras, masks, chants, stickers, stencils and paint, films, tambourines, bricks, brooms, guns, voodoo dolls, cats, candles, bells, chalk, nail clippings, hand grenades, poison rings, fuses, tape recorders, incense—your own boundless imagination. Your power comes from your own self as a woman, and it is activated by working in concert with your sisters. The power of the Coven is more than the sum of its individual members, because it is *together*.

You are pledged to free our brothers from oppression and stereotyped sexual roles (whether they like it or not) as well as ourselves. You are a Witch by saying aloud, "I am a Witch" three times, and *thinking about that*. You are a Witch by being female, untamed, angry, joyous, and immortal.

73 BITCH Manifesto

1968

Joreen

BITCH is an organization which does not yet exist. The name is not an acronym. It stands for exactly what it sounds like.

BITCH is composed of Bitches. There are many definitions of a bitch. The most complimentary definition is a female dog. Those definitions of bitches who are also homo sapiens are rarely as objective. They vary from person to person and depend strongly on how much of a bitch the definer considers herself. However, everyone agrees that a bitch is always a female, dog, or otherwise.

It is also generally agreed that a Bitch is aggressive, and therefore unfeminine (ahem). She may be sexy, in which case she becomes a Bitch Goddess, a special case which will not concern us here. But she is never a "true woman."

Bitches have some or all of the following characteristics.

1) Personality. Bitches are aggressive, assertive, domineering, overbearing, strong-minded, spiteful, hostile, direct, blunt, candid, obnoxious, thick-skinned, hard-headed, vicious, dogmatic, competent, competitive, pushy, loud-mouthed, independent, stubborn, demanding, manipulative, egoistic, driven, achieving, overwhelming, threatening, scary, ambitious, tough, brassy, masculine, boisterous, and turbulent. Among other things. A Bitch occupies a lot of psychological space. You always know she is around. A Bitch takes shit from no one. You may not like her, but you cannot ignore her.

2) Physical. Bitches are big, tall, strong, large, loud, brash, harsh, awkward, clumsy, sprawling, strident, ugly. Bitches move their

bodies freely rather than restrain, refine and confine their motions in the proper feminine manner. They clomp up stairs, stride when they walk and don't worry about where they put their legs when they sit. They have loud voices and often use them. Bitches are not pretty.

3) Orientation. Bitches seek their identity strictly thru themselves and what they do. They are subjects, not objects. They may have a relationship with a person or organization, but they never marry anyone or anything; man, mansion, or movement. Thus Bitches prefer to plan their own lives rather than live from day to day, action to action, or person to person. They are independent cusses and believe they are capable of doing anything they damn well want to. If something gets in their way; well, that's why they become Bitches. If they are professionally inclined, they will seek careers and have no fear of competing with anyone. If not professionally inclined, they still seek self-expression and self-actualization. Whatever they do, they want an active role and are frequently perceived as domineering. Often they do dominate other people when roles are not available to them which more creatively sublimate their energies and utilize their capabilities. More often they are accused of domineering when doing what would be considered natural by a man.

A true Bitch is self-determined, but the term "bitch" is usually applied with less discrimination. It is a popular derogation to put down uppity women that was created by man and adopted by women. Like the term "nigger," "bitch" serves the social function of isolating and discrediting a class of people who do not conform to the socially accepted patterns of behavior.

BITCH does not use this word in the negative sense. A woman should be proud to declare she is a Bitch, because Bitch is Beautiful. It should be an act of affirmation by self and not negation by others. Not everyone can qualify as a Bitch. One does not have to have all of the above three qualities, but should be well possessed of at least two of them to be considered a Bitch. If a woman qualifies in all three, at least partially, she is a Bitch's Bitch. Only Superbitches qualify totally in all three categories and there are very few of those. Most don't last long in this society.

The most prominent characteristic of all Bitches is that they rudely violate conceptions of proper sex role behavior. They violate them in different ways, but they all violate them. Their attitudes towards themselves and other people, their goal orientations, their personal style, their appearance and way of handling their bodies, all jar people and make them feel uneasy. Sometimes it's conscious and sometimes it's not, but people generally feel uncomfortable around Bitches. They consider them aberrations. They find their style disturbing. So they create a dumping ground for all who they deplore as bitchy and call them frustrated women. Frustrated they may be, but the cause is social not sexual.

What is disturbing about a Bitch is that she is androgynous. She incorporates within herself qualities traditionally defined as "masculine" as well as "feminine." A Bitch is blunt, direct, arrogant, at times egoistic. She has no liking for the indirect, subtle, mysterious ways of the "eternal feminine." She disdains the vicarious life deemed natural to women because she wants to live a life of her own.

Our society has defined humanity as male, and female as something other than male. In this way, females could be human only by living vicariously thru a male. To be able to live, a woman has to agree to serve, honor, and obey a man and what she gets in exchange is at best a shadow life. Bitches refuse to serve, honor or obey anyone. They demand to be fully functioning human beings, not just shadows. They want to be both female and human. This makes them social contradictions. The mere existence of Bitches negates the idea that a woman's reality must come thru her relationship to a man and defies the belief that women are perpetual children who must always be under the guidance of another.

Therefore, if taken seriously, a Bitch is a threat to the social structures which enslave women and the social values which justify keeping them in their place. She is living testimony that woman's oppression does not have to be, and as such raises doubts about the validity of the whole social system. Because she is a threat she is not taken seriously. Instead, she is dismissed as a deviant. Men create a special category for her in which she is accounted at least partially human, but not really a woman. To the extent to which they relate to her as a human being, they refuse to relate to her as a sexual being. Women are even more threatened because they cannot forget she is a woman. They are afraid they will identify with her too closely. She has a freedom and an independence which they envy and challenges them to forsake the security of their chains. Neither men nor women can face the reality of a Bitch because to do so would force them to face the corrupt reality of themselves. She is dangerous. So they dismiss her as a freak.

This is the root of her own oppression as a woman. Bitches are not only oppressed as women, they are oppressed for not being like women. Because she has insisted on being human before being feminine, on being true to herself before kowtowing to social pressures, a Bitch grows up an outsider. Even as girls, Bitches violated the limits of accepted sex role behavior. They did not identify with other women and few were lucky enough to have an adult Bitch serve as a role model. They had to make their own way and the pitfalls this uncharted course posed contributed to both their uncertainty and their independence.

Bitches are good examples of how women can be strong enough to survive even the rigid, punitive socialization of our society. As young girls it never quite penetrated their consciousness that women were supposed to be inferior to men in any but the mother/helpmate role. They asserted themselves as children and never really internalized the slave style of wheedling and cajolery which is called feminine. Some Bitches were oblivious to the usual social pressures and some stubbornly resisted them. Some developed a superficial feminine style and some remained tomboys long past the time when such behavior is tolerated. All Bitches refused, in mind and spirit, to conform to the idea that there were limits on what they could be and do. They placed no bounds on their aspirations or their conduct.

For this resistance they were roundly condemned. They were put down, snubbed, sneered at, talked about, laughed at and ostracized. Our society made women into slaves and then condemned them for acting like slaves. It was all done very subtly. Few people were so direct as to say that they did not like Bitches because they did not play the sex role game.

In fact, few were sure why they did not like Bitches. They did not realize that their violation of the reality structure endangered the structure. Somehow, from early childhood on, some girls didn't fit in and were good objects to make fun of. But few people consciously recognized the root of their dislike. The issue was never confronted. If it was talked about at all, it was done with snide remarks behind the young girl's back. Bitches were made to feel that there was something wrong with them; something personally wrong.

Teenage girls are particularly vicious in the scapegoat game. This is the time of life when women are told they must compete the hardest for the spoils (i.e. men) which society allows. They must assert their femininity or see it denied. They are very unsure of themselves and adopt the rigidity that goes with uncertainty. They are hard on their competitors and even harder on those who decline to compete. Those of their peers who do not share their concerns and practice the arts of charming men are excluded from most social groupings. If she didn't know it before, a Bitch learns during these years that she is different.

As she gets older she learns more about why she is different. As Bitches begin to take jobs, or participate in organizations, they are rarely content to sit quietly and do what they are told. A Bitch has a mind of her own and wants to use it. She wants to rise high, be creative, assume responsibility. She knows she is capable and wants to use her capabilities. This is not pleasing to the men she works for, which is not her primary goal.

When she meets the hard brick wall of sex prejudice she is not compliant. She will knock herself out batting her head against the wall because she will not accept her defined role as an auxiliary. Occasionally she crashes her way thru. Or she uses her ingenuity to find a loophole, or creates one. Or she is ten times better than anyone else competing with her. She also accepts less than her due. Like other women her ambitions have often been dulled for she has not totally escaped the badge of inferiority placed upon the "weaker sex." She will often espouse contentment with being the power behind the throne—provided that she does have real power—while rationalizing that she really does not want the recognition that comes with also having the throne. Because she has been put down most of her life, both for being a woman and for not being a true woman, a Bitch will not always recognize that what she has achieved is not attainable by the typical woman. A highly competent Bitch often deprecates herself by refusing to recognize her own superiority. She is wont to say that she is average or less so; if she can do it, anyone can.

As adults, Bitches may have learned the feminine role, at least the outward style but they are rarely comfortable in it. This is particularly true of those women who are physical Bitches. They want to free their bodies as well as their minds and deplore the effort they must waste confining their physical motions or dressing the role in order not to turn people off. Too, because they violate sex role expectations physically, they are not as free to violate them psychologically or intellectually. A few deviations from the norm can be tolerated but too many are too threatening. It's bad enough not to think like a woman, sound like a woman or do the kinds of things women are supposed to do. To also not look like a woman, move like a woman or act like a woman is to go way beyond the pale. Ours is a rigid society with narrow limits placed on the extent of human diversity. Women in particular are defined by their physical characteristics. Bitches who do not violate these limits are freer to violate others. Bitches who do violate them in style or size can be somewhat envious of those who do not have to so severely restrain the expansiveness of their personalities and behavior. Often these Bitches are tortured more because their deviancy is always evident. But they do have a compensation in that large Bitches have a good deal less difficulty being taken seriously than small women. One of the sources of their suffering as women is also a source of their strength.

The trial by fire which most Bitches go thru while growing up either makes them or breaks them. They are strung tautly between the two poles of being true to their own nature or being accepted as a social being. This makes them very sensitive people, but it is a sensitivity the rest of the world is unaware of. For on the outside they have frequently grown a thick defensive callous which can make them seem hard and bitter at times. This is particularly true of those Bitches who have been forced to become isolates in order to avoid being remade and destroyed by their peers. Those who are fortunate enough to have grown up with some similar companions, understanding parents, a good role model or two and a very strong will, can avoid some of the worse aspects of being a Bitch. Having endured less psychological punishment for being what they were they can accept their differentness with the ease that comes from self-confidence.

Those who had to make their way entirely on their own have an uncertain path. Some finally realize that their pain comes not just because they do not conform but because they do not want to conform. With this comes the recognition that there is nothing particularly wrong with them they just don't fit into this kind of society. Many eventually learn to insulate themselves from the harsh social environment. However, this too has its price. Unless they are cautious and conscious, the confidence gained in this painful manner—with no support from their sisters—is more often a kind of arrogance. Bitches can become so hard and calloused that the last vestiges of humanity become buried deep within and almost destroyed.

Not all Bitches make it. Instead of callouses, they develop open sores. Instead of confidence they develop an unhealthy sensitivity to rejection. Seemingly tough on the outside, on the inside they are a bloody pulp, raw from the lifelong verbal whipping they have had to endure. These are Bitches who have gone Bad. They often go around with a chip on their shoulders and use their strength for unproductive retaliation when someone accepts their dare to knock it off. These Bitches can be very obnoxious because they never really trust people. They have not learned to use their strength constructively.

Bitches who have been mutilated as human beings often turn their fury on other people—particularly other women. This is one example of how women are trained to keep themselves and other women in their place. Bitches are no less guilty than non-Bitches of self-hatred and group-hatred and those who have gone Bad suffer the worse of both these afflictions. All Bitches are scapegoats and those who have not survived the psychological gauntlet are the butt of everyone's disdain. As a group, Bitches are treated by other women much as women in general are treated by society—all right in their place, good to exploit and gossip about, but otherwise to be ignored or put down. They are threats to the traditional woman's position and they are also an outgroup to which she can feel superior. Most women feel both better than and jealous of Bitches. While comforting themselves that they are not like these aggressive, masculine freaks, they have a sneaking suspicion that perhaps men, the most important thing in their lives, do find the freer, more assertive, independent, Bitch preferable as a woman.

Bitches, likewise, don't care too much for other women. They grow up disliking other women. They can't relate to them, they don't identify with them, they have nothing in common with them. Other women have been the norm into which they have not fit. They reject those who have rejected them. This is one of the reasons Bitches who are successful in hurdling the obstacles society places before women scorn these women who are not. They tend to feel those who can take it will make it. Most women have been the direct agents of much of the shit Bitches have had to endure and few of either group have had the political consciousness to realize why this is. Bitches have been oppressed by other women as much if not more than by men and their hatred for them is usually greater.

Bitches are also uncomfortable around other women because

frequently women are less their psychological peers than are men. Bitches don't particularly like passive people. They are always slightly afraid they will crush the fragile things. Women are trained to be passive and have learned to act that way even when they are not. A Bitch is not very passive and is not comfortable acting that role. But she usually does not like to be domineering either—whether this is from natural distaste at dominating others or fear of seeming too masculine. Thus a Bitch can relax and be her natural non-passive self without worrying about masticating someone only in the company of those who are as strong as she. This is more frequently in the company of men than of women but those Bitches who have not succumbed totally to self-hatred are most comfortable of all only in the company of fellow Bitches. These are her true peers and the only ones with whom she does not have to play some sort of role. Only with other Bitches can a Bitch be truly free.

These moments come rarely. Most of the time Bitches must remain psychologically isolated. Women and men are so threatened by them and react so adversely that Bitches guard their true selves carefully. They are suspicious of those few whom they think they might be able to trust because so often it turns out to be a sham. But in this loneliness there is a strength and from their isolation and their bitterness come contributions that other women do not make. Bitches are among the most unsung of the unsung heroes of this society. They are the pioneers, the vanguard, the spearhead. Whether they want to be or not this is the role they serve just by their very being. Many would not choose to be the groundbreakers for the mass of women for whom they have no sisterly feelings but they cannot avoid it. Those who violate the limits, extend them; or cause the system to break.

Bitches were the first women to go to college, the first to break thru the Invisible Bar of the professions, the first social revolutionaries, the first labor leaders, the first to organize other women. Because they were not passive beings and acted on their resentment at being kept down, they dared to do what other women would not. They took the flak and the shit that society dishes out to those who would change it and opened up portions of the world to women that they would otherwise not have known. They have lived on the fringes. And alone or with the support of their sisters they have changed the world we live in.

By definition Bitches are marginal beings in this society. They have no proper place and wouldn't stay in it if they did. They are women but not true women. They are human but they are not male. Some don't even know they are women because they cannot relate to other women. They may play the feminine game at times, but they know it is a game they are playing. Their major psychological oppression is not a belief that they are inferior but a belief that they are not. Thus, all their lives they have been told they were freaks. More polite terms were used of course, but the message got thru. Like most women they were taught to hate themselves as well as all women. In different ways and for different reasons perhaps, but the effect was similar. Internalization of a derogatory self-concept always results in a good deal of bitterness and resentment. This anger is usually either turned in on the self—making one an unpleasant person—or on other women reinforcing the social clichés about them. Only with political consciousness is it directed at the source—the social system.

The bulk of this Manifesto has been about Bitches. The remainder will be about BITCH. The organization does not yet exist and perhaps it never can. Bitches are so damned independent and they have learned so well not to trust other women that it will be difficult for them to learn to even trust each other. This is what BITCH must teach them to do. Bitches have to learn to accept themselves as Bitches and to give their sisters the support they need to be creative Bitches. Bitches must learn to be proud of their strength and proud of themselves. They must move away from the isolation which has been their protection and help their younger sisters avoid its perils. They must recognize that women are often less tolerant of other women than are men because they have been taught to view all women as their enemies. And Bitches must form together in a movement to deal with their problems in a political manner. They must organize for their own liberation as all women must organize for theirs. We must be strong, we must be militant, we must be dangerous. We must realize that Bitch is Beautiful and that we have nothing to lose. Nothing whatsoever.

74 The Manifesto of Apocalyptic Witchcraft

2013

Peter Grey

1 If the land is poisoned then witchcraft must respond.
2 It is not our way of life, it's life itself which is under threat.
3 Witchcraft is our intimate connection to the web of life.
4 We are the Witchcraft.
5 Our world has forever changed. The trodden paths no longer correspond. Witchcraft thrives in this liminal, lunar, trackless realm.
6 We are storm, fire and flood.
7 We will not be denied.
8 Witchcraft is the recourse of the dispossessed, the powerless, the hungry, and the abused. It gives heart and tongue to stones and trees. It wears the rough skin of beasts. It turns on a civilization that knows the price of everything and the value of nothing.
9 If you have no price you cannot be bought. If you do not want you cannot be bribed. If you are not frightened you cannot be controlled.
10 Witchcraft is folk magic, the magic of the people and for the people.
11 We call an end to the pretense of respectability.
12 We will not disarm ourselves.
13 The War is upon us.
14 Choose then to become a Mask.
15 Those with nothing left to lose will dare all.
16 There is one Witchcraft under many names. There is one Grand Sabbat on one mountain. There are many ways to fly. There is no witness present at the Sabbat.

17 Witchcraft is a force, not an order. Witchcraft is rhizomatic, not hierarchic. Witchcraft defies organisation, not meaning. We simply bear the marks.

18 Witchcraft is power and possesses this ekstasis, sex, and ordeal.

19 Witchcraft is unbridled sexuality. In witchcraft it is the woman who initiates. We challenge man to be the equal of this woman.

20 Witchcraft is the art of inversion.

21 Witchcraft is the beauty which is terror.

22 Witchcraft is a myth, which drawing on the past, clothes itself in the symbols of (its) time. Witchcraft does not mistake myths for history, it harnesses them to transform the future. Witchcraft knows the ground upon which it stands.

23 Witchcraft honours the spirits. Witchcraft enchants for the lost. Witchcraft will not forget.

24 Witchcraft embodies our ancestors and saints, they carry us with them.

25 To Her is offered the blood, to us the care of the ash and bones.

26 The example we follow is our own.

27 The practice of witchcraft is one of revolution and the power of woman.

28 The Goddess who speaks through us is known among men as Babalon.

29 Witchcraft concerns itself with mystery. Through the gates of mystery we come to knowledge. Knowledge enters us through the body.
The highest form of this knowledge is Love.

30 Every drop of blood is sacrificed to the grail. Love cannot be bought with any other coin.

31 We seek and drink this wine together.

32 Will is finite, passion is infinitely renewed.

33 Witchcraft is present, it is ensanguined and vivified. Witchcraft is prescient, it gazes on the future. Witchcraft is oracular, it will not hold its tongue. Our time has come.

75 Funeral Oration for the Burial of Traditional Womanhood

1968

Kathie Amatniek Sarachild

You see here the remains of a female human being who during her too long lifetime was a familiar figure to billions of people in every corner of the world. Although scientists would classify this specimen within the genus species of Homo sapiens, for many years there has been considerable controversy as to whether she really belonged in some kind of *sub*-species of the genus. While the human being was distinguished as an animal who freed himself from his biological limitations by developing technology and expanding his consciousness, traditional womanhood has been recognized, defined and valued for her biological characteristics only and those social functions closely related to her biological characteristics.

As human beings, both men and women were sexual creatures and they shared their sexuality. But the other areas of humanity were closed off to traditional womanhood ... the areas which, as has already been noted, were more characteristically human, less limited by biology. For some reason, man said to woman: you are less sexual when you participate in those other things, you are no longer attractive to me if you do so. I like you quiet and submissive. It makes me feel as if you don't love me, if you fail to let me do all the talking ... if you actually have something to say yourself. Or else, when I like you to be charming and well educated ... entertainment for me and an intelligent mother for my children ... these qualities are for me and for me alone. When you confront the world outside the home—the world where I operate as an individual self as well as a husband and father—then, for some reason, I feel you are a challenge to me and you become sexless and aggressive.

If you turn me off too much, you know, I'll find myself another woman. And if that happens, what will you do? You'll be a nobody, that's what you'll be. An old maid, if I haven't deigned to marry you yet. A divorced woman with some children, no doubt. Without me, you won't even have your sexuality anymore, that little bit of humanity which I have allowed you. And even if you manage to solve that problem in some kind of perverse way, it's going to be hard for you.

What kinds of jobs can you get to keep yourself in comfort? I control those few interesting challenging ones. And I control the salaries on all the other kinds of jobs from which my fellow men who work at them will at least get the satisfaction of more pay than you. And I control the government and its money which, you can bet your tax dollar, isn't going to get allotted for enough good nursery schools to put your children into so you can go out to work. And because of all these things, there can always be another woman in my life, when you no longer serve my needs.

And so traditional Womanhood, even if she was unhappy with her lot, believed that there was nothing she could do about it. She blamed herself for her limitations and she tried to adapt. She told herself and she told others that she was happy as half a person, as the "better half" of someone else, as the mother of others, powerless in her own right.

Though Traditional Womanhood was a hardy dame, the grand old lady finally died today—her doctor said, of a bad case of shock. Her flattering menfolk had managed to keep her alive for thousands of years. She survived the Amazon challenge. She survived the Lysistrata challenge. She survived the Feminist challenge. And she survived many face-liftings. She was burning her candle at one end on a dull wick and she went out slowly, but she finally went ... not with a bang but a whimper.

There are some grounds for believing that our march today contributed to the lady's timely demise and this is partly the reason we have decided to hold her funeral here. The old hen, it turns out, was somewhat disturbed to hear us—other women, that is—asserting ourselves just this least little bit about critical problems in the world controlled by men. And it was particularly frightening to her to see other women, we-women, asserting ourselves together, however precariously, in some kind of solidarity, instead of completely resenting each other, being embarrassed by each other, hating each other and hating ourselves.

And we were even attempting to organize ourselves on the

basis of power ... that little bit of power we are told we have here in America ... the so-called power of wives and mothers. That this power is only a substitute for power, that it really amounts to nothing politically, is the reason why all of us attending this funeral must bury traditional womanhood tonight. We must bury her in Arlington Cemetery, however crowded it is by now. For in Arlington Cemetery, our national monument to war, alongside Traditional Manhood, is her natural resting place.

Now some sisters here are probably wondering why we should bother with such an unimportant matter at a time like this. Why should we bury traditional womanhood while hundreds of thousands of human beings are being brutally slaughtered in our names ... when it would seem that our number one task is to devote our energies directly to ending this slaughter or else solve what seem to be more desperate problems at home?

Sisters who ask a question like this are failing to see that they really do have a problem as women in America ... that their problem is social, not merely personal ... and that their problem is so closely related and interlocked with the other problems in our country, the very problem of war itself ... that we cannot hope to move toward a better world or even a truly democratic society at home until we begin to solve our own problems.

How many sisters failed to join our march today because they were afraid their husbands would disapprove? How many more sisters failed to join us today because they've been taught to believe that women are silly and a women's march even sillier? And how many millions of sisters all across America failed to join us because they think so little of themselves that they feel incapable of thinking for themselves ... about the war in Vietnam or anything else. And if some sisters come to conclusions of their own, how many others of us fail to express "these ideas" much less argue and demonstrate for them because we're afraid of seeming unattractive, silly, "uppity." To the America watching us, after all, we here on this march are mere women, looking silly and unattractive.

Yes, sisters, we have a problem as women all right, a problem which renders us powerless and ineffective over the issues of war and peace, as well as over our own lives. And although our problem is Traditional Manhood as much as Traditional Womanhood, we women must begin on the solution.

We must see that we can only solve our problem together, that we cannot solve it individually as earlier Feminist generations attempted to do. We women must organize so that for man there can be no "other woman" when we begin expressing ourselves and acting politically, when we insist to men that they share the housework and childcare, fully and equally, so that we can have independent lives as well.

Human qualities will make us attractive then, not servile qualities. We will want to have daughters as much as we want to have sons. Our children will not become victims of our unconscious resentments and our displaced ambitions. And both our daughters and sons will be free to develop themselves in just the directions they want to go as human beings.

Sisters: men need us, too, after all. And if we just get together and tell our men that we want our freedom as full human beings, that we don't want to live just through our man and his achievements and our mutual offspring, that we want human power in our own right, not just "power behind the throne," that we want neither dominance or submission for anybody, anyplace, in Vietnam or in our own homes, and that when we all have our freedom we can truly love each other.

If men fail to see that love, justice and equality are the solution, that domination and exploitation hurt everybody, then our species is truly doomed; for if domination and exploitation and aggression are inherent biological characteristics which cannot be overcome, then nuclear war is inevitable and we will have reached our evolutionary deadend by annihilating ourselves.

And that is why we must bury this lady in Arlington Cemetery tonight, why we must bury Submission alongside Aggression. And that is why we ask you to join us. It is only a symbolic happening, of course, and we have a lot of real work to do. We have new men as well as a new society to build.

Kathie Amatniek Sarachild, Speech given in Washington D.C. to the main assembly of the Jeannette Rankin Brigade, January 15, 1968.

76 Truisms (excerpt)

1978–1987

Jenny Holzer

a little knowledge can go a long way
a lot of professionals are crackpots
a man can't know what it is to be a mother
a name means a lot just by itself
a positive attitude makes all the difference in the world
a relaxed man is not necessarily a better man
a sense of timing is the mark of genius
a sincere effort is all you can ask
a single event can have infinitely many interpretations
a solid home base builds a sense of self
a strong sense of duty imprisons you
absolute submission can be a form of freedom
abstraction is a type of decadence
abuse of power comes as no surprise
action causes more trouble than thought
alienation produces eccentrics or revolutionaries
all things are delicately interconnected
ambition is just as dangerous as complacency
ambivalence can ruin your life
an elite is inevitable
anger or hate can be a useful motivating force
animalism is perfectly healthy
any surplus is immoral
anything is a legitimate area of investigation
artificial desires are despoiling the earth

at times inactivity is preferable to mindless functioning
at times your unconscious is truer than your conscious mind
automation is deadly
awful punishment awaits really bad people
bad intentions can yield good results
being alone with yourself is increasingly unpopular
being happy is more important than anything else
being judgmental is a sign of life
being sure of yourself means you're a fool
believing in rebirth is the same as admitting defeat
boredom makes you do crazy things
calm is more conducive to creativity than is anxiety
categorizing fear is calming
change is valuable because it lets the oppressed be tyrants
chasing the new is dangerous to society
children are the most cruel of all
children are the hope of the future
class action is a nice idea with no substance
class structure is as artificial as plastic
confusing yourself is a way to stay honest
crime against property is relatively unimportant
decadence can be an end in itself
decency is a relative thing
dependence can be a meal ticket
description is more valuable than metaphor
deviants are sacrificed to increase group solidarity
disgust is the appropriate response to most situations
disorganization is a kind of anesthesia
don't place too much trust in experts
don't run people's lives for them
drama often obscures the real issues
dreaming while awake is a frightening contradiction
dying and coming back gives you considerable perspective
dying should be as easy as falling off a log
eating too much is criminal
elaboration is a form of pollution
emotional responses are as valuable as intellectual responses
enjoy yourself because you can't change anything anyway
ensure that your life stays in flux

even your family can betray you
every achievement requires a sacrifice
everyone's work is equally important
everything that's interesting is new
exceptional people deserve special concessions
expiring for love is beautiful but stupid
expressing anger is necessary
extreme behavior has its basis in pathological psychology
extreme self-consciousness leads to perversion
faithfulness is a social not a biological law
fake or real indifference is a powerful personal weapon
fathers often use too much force
fear is the greatest incapacitator
freedom is a luxury not a necessity
giving free rein to your emotions is an honest way to live
go all out in romance and let the chips fall where they may
going with the flow is soothing but risky
good deeds eventually are rewarded
government is a burden on the people
grass roots agitation is the only hope
guilt and self-laceration are indulgences
habitual contempt doesn't reflect a finer sensibility
hiding your emotions is despicable
holding back protects your vital energies
humanism is obsolete
humor is a release
ideals are replaced by conventional goals at a certain age
if you aren't political your personal life should be exemplary
if you can't leave your mark give up
if you have many desires your life will be interesting
if you live simply there is nothing to worry about
ignoring enemies is the best way to fight
illness is a state of mind
imposing order is man's vocation for chaos is hell
in some instances it's better to die than to continue
inheritance must be abolished
it can be helpful to keep going no matter what
it is heroic to try to stop time
it is man's fate to outsmart himself

it is a gift to the world not to have babies
it's better to be a good person than a famous person
it's better to be lonely than to be with inferior people
it's better to be naive than jaded
it's better to study the living fact than to analyze history
it's crucial to have an active fantasy life
it's good to give extra money to charity
it's important to stay clean on all levels
it's just an accident that your parents are your parents
it's not good to hold too many absolutes
it's not good to operate on credit
it's vital to live in harmony with nature
just believing something can make it happen
keep something in reserve for emergencies
killing is unavoidable but nothing to be proud of
knowing yourself lets you understand others
knowledge should be advanced at all costs
labor is a life-destroying activity
lack of charisma can be fatal
leisure time is a gigantic smoke screen
listen when your body talks
looking back is the first sign of aging and decay
loving animals is a substitute activity
low expectations are good protection
manual labor can be refreshing and wholesome
men are not monogamous by nature
moderation kills the spirit
money creates taste
monomania is a prerequisite of success
morals are for little people
most people are not fit to rule themselves
mostly you should mind your own business
mothers shouldn't make too many sacrifices
much was decided before you were born
murder has its sexual side
myth can make reality more intelligible
noise can be hostile
nothing upsets the balance of good and evil
occasionally principles are more valuable than people

offer very little information about yourself
often you should act like you are sexless
old friends are better left in the past
opacity is an irresistible challenge
pain can be a very positive thing
people are boring unless they are extremists
people are nuts if they think they are important
people are responsible for what they do unless they are insane
people who don't work with their hands are parasites
people who go crazy are too sensitive
people won't behave if they have nothing to lose
physical culture is second best
planning for the future is escapism
playing it safe can cause a lot of damage in the long run
politics is used for personal gain
potential counts for nothing until it's realized
private property created crime
pursuing pleasure for the sake of pleasure will ruin you
push yourself to the limit as often as possible
raise boys and girls the same way
random mating is good for debunking sex myths
rechanneling destructive impulses is a sign of maturity
recluses always get weak
redistributing wealth is imperative
relativity is no boon to mankind
religion causes as many problems as it solves
remember you always have freedom of choice
repetition is the best way to learn
resolutions serve to ease our conscience
revolution begins with changes in the individual
romantic love was invented to manipulate women
routine is a link with the past
routine small excesses are worse than the occasional debauch
sacrificing yourself for a bad cause is not a moral act
salvation can't be bought and sold
self-awareness can be crippling
self-contempt can do more harm than good
selfishness is the most basic motivation
selflessness is the highest achievement

separatism is the way to a new beginning
sex differences are here to stay
sin is a means of social control
slipping into madness is good for the sake of comparison
sloppy thinking gets worse over time
solitude is enriching
sometimes science advances faster than it should
sometimes things seem to happen of their own accord
spending too much time on self-improvement is antisocial
starvation is nature's way
stasis is a dream state
sterilization is a weapon of the rulers
strong emotional attachment stems from basic insecurity
stupid people shouldn't breed
survival of the fittest applies to men and animals
symbols are more meaningful than things themselves
taking a strong stand publicizes the opposite position
talking is used to hide one's inability to act
teasing people sexually can have ugly consequences
technology will make or break us
the cruelest disappointment is when you let yourself down
the desire to reproduce is a death wish
the family is living on borrowed time
the idea of revolution is an adolescent fantasy
the idea of transcendence is used to obscure oppression
the idiosyncratic has lost its authority
the most profound things are inexpressible
the mundane is to be cherished
the new is nothing but a restatement of the old
the only way to be pure is to stay by yourself
the sum of your actions determines what you are
the unattainable is invariably attractive
the world operates according to discoverable laws
there are too few immutable truths today
there's nothing except what you sense
there's nothing redeeming in toil
thinking too much can only cause problems
threatening someone sexually is a horrible act
timidity is laughable

to disagree presupposes moral integrity
to volunteer is reactionary
torture is barbaric
trading a life for a life is fair enough
true freedom is frightful
unique things must be the most valuable
unquestioning love demonstrates largesse of spirit
using force to stop force is absurd
violence is permissible even desirable occasionally
war is a purification rite
we must make sacrifices to maintain our quality of life
when something terrible happens people wake up
wishing things away is not effective
with perseverance you can discover any truth
words tend to be inadequate
worrying can help you prepare
you are a victim of the rules you live by
you are guileless in your dreams
you are responsible for constituting the meaning of things
you are the past present and future
you can live on through your descendants
you can't expect people to be something they're not
you can't fool others if you're fooling yourself
you don't know what's what until you support yourself
you have to hurt others to be extraordinary
you must be intimate with a token few
you must disagree with authority figures
you must have one grand passion
you must know where you stop and the world begins
you can understand someone of your sex only
you owe the world not the other way around
you should study as much as possible
your actions are pointless if no one notices
your oldest fears are the worst ones

A Manifesto

1970

Agnes Denes

Acknowledgments

A book like this leaves me with a mighty tab I may never be able to properly repay. This kind of book relies on an enormous amount of support from writers, thinkers, assistants, colleagues, friends, and family. I owe a great debt to the women who have taught me to understand the value of anger and rage, particularly the radical feminists I have had the pleasure to listen to and learn from. In particular, I thank Ti-Grace Atkinson, Roxanne Dunbar-Ortiz, Kathie Sarachild, Dana Densmore, Jane Caputi, Carol Giardina, Alice Echols, Eileen Boris, and Phyllis Chesler. Nearly everyone who had a hand in my earlier book on Valerie Solanas has influenced this book as well—thanks especially to Mary Harron and Amy Scholder for their support over the years.

I feel eternal gratitude for the palpable generosity and goodwill I receive from like-minded feminist scholars and thinkers, particularly Virginia Braun, Marlene Tromp, Abby Stewart, Leonore Tiefer, Jessa Crispin, Rebecca Plante, Larin McLaughlin, Deborah Tolman, Carla Golden, Sandy Caron, Patrick Grzanka, Jill Wood, Diana Álvarez, and the entire "menstrual mafia" (Chris, Joan, Ingrid, Liz, Maureen, David, Mindy, Heather, Jerilynn, Tomi-Ann, Peggy, and Jane). And extra love to the extraordinary Ela Przybylo, the epitome of a creative, smart, and generous scholar.

I humbly thank the Feminist Research on Gender and Sexuality Group—"the FROGS"—for your commitment to this project, your solidarity with difficult/angry writings, and all the affection and spiritedness you have shown to each other and to me. Decker Dunlop—who inspires and amazes me at every turn—did some serious heavy lifting and embodies radical politics, true generosity, and kindness. The most recent FROGS have pitched in beyond measure—thanks to Jakob Salazar, Ayanna Shambe, Claire Halling, Carolyn Anh Thu Dang, Atlas Pillar, Laisa Schweigert, John Payton, Mam Marie Sanyang, Mika Collins, and Ashley Gohr. You have all exceeded every expectation I could ever have. Thanks also to the rest of the gang, thriving out in the world: Madison Carlyle, Emma DiFrancesco, Crystal Zaragoza, Laura Martinez, Natali Blazevic, Michael Karger, Adrielle Munger, Jax Gonzalez, Stephanie Robinson, Rose Coursey, Kimberly Koerth, Chelsea Pixler Charbonneau, Corie Cisco, Elizabeth Wallace, Marisa Loiacono, Eva Sisko, Carissa Cunningham, Jennifer Bertagni, Alexis Starks, and Tatiana Crespo. You are simply the best.

For getting this book off the ground, I thank Arizona State University's New College for a summer's worth of research support. Thanks also to my colleagues, both close and far, who have shown such warmth for this project: Louis Mendoza, Todd Sandrin, Sharon Kirsch, Barry Moon, Miriam Mara, Arthur Sabatini, Gloria Cuadraz, Eduardo Pagan, Alejandra Elenes, and Majia Nadesan. And, for supporting this book from start to finish—and being the best possible feminist ally in the process—I thank my editor, Jessie Kindig, at Verso. To the rest of the Verso crew, especially Mark Martin, Julia Judge, Maya Osborne, and Anne Rumberger, this project would not exist without you!

Thank you to my dearest friends, the sturdy souls who fill me with joy and remind me that creating books like these matters—at least to them. To Lori Errico-Seaman, Sean Seaman, Chris Bobel, Sara McClelland, Clare Croft, Elizabeth Brake, Mary Dudy, Jennifer Tamir, Annika Mann, Denise Delgado, Garyn Tsuru, Jan Habarth, Marcy Winokur, Steve DuBois, Connie Hardesty, Katie Goldey, Pat Hart, Karen Swank-Fitch, Lanie Saunders, and Sadie Mohler—I love you all. To Elmer Griffin, every book—but especially this book—starts with you. And to my mom, my sister, and the three little ones—Simon, Ryan, and Fiona—you all have my heart. To Eric Swank, my partner on the front lines of the revolution, I'm with you 'til the wheels fall off. So much of what I do—especially my incessant efforts to destroy capitalism and patriarchy—would be impossible without your abundant love and the million little ways you make space for me to think and write. Finally, I dedicate this book to my dear friend Sarah Stage, who reminds me that friendships between women might be the only lifelong buffer between despair and joy. This one's for you.

About the Contributors

ACT UP, otherwise known as AIDS Coalition to Unleash Power, is a New York City–based group founded in 1987 that identifies as a "diverse, non-partisan group of individuals united in anger and committed to direct action to end the AIDS crisis." The original text of "Queers Read This" (the Queer Nation Manifesto) was published anonymously by queer activists in June 1990 and distributed at gay pride parades in New York and Chicago during summer 1990.

Aldebaran, also known as Sara Fishman, was one of the founding members of the Fat Underground in 1972, which built upon the strengths and weaknesses of Fat Power and Radical Therapy. The radical collective formed coalitions with other feminist groups and pushed back on institutions advocating for dieting and weight loss, biases in healthcare, and fat stereotypes. Throughout the 1970s, Aldebaran distributed Fat Liberator writings, including the *Fat Liberation Manifesto*. Aldebaran later taught science and Jewish spirituality.

Anarchafeminist International began in 1982 and is an offshoot of the Norway-based organization Anarchist International (founded 1968) known for its publication *IJ@*, or the *International Journal of Anarchism*, as well as its contributions to the anarcho-syndicalist *International Workers of the World* and the eco-anarchist *GAIA* publications. The *Anarchafeminist Manifesto* is the summary of the feminist political program decided upon by the 1982 third congress of Anarchist International's Norwegian affiliate, the Anarchist Federation of

Norway (founded in 1977). Anarchafeminist International circulates widely, publishing in several languages; the *Anarchafeminist Manifesto* was referenced by writers as diverse as Noam Chomsky and Marsha Hewitt.

Ti-Grace Atkinson (1938–), author of *Amazon Odyssey* (1974), was an early founder of the radical feminist movement in the late 1960s. After working as a writer for *Art News*, Atkinson became the chapter president of New York's National Organization for Women (N.O.W.) in 1967 and later founded The Feminists, a radical feminist group active from 1968 to 1973. Known for her militant activism and controversial public speeches, she was once slapped in the middle of one of her talks at a prominent Catholic University for discussing the Virgin Mary's sexuality. She has also crusaded against marriage as a form of spiritual and physical oppression, advocated political lesbianism as a response to patriarchy, and famously argued that vaginal orgasm was a "mass hysterical survival response." She protested anti-woman policies of the *Ladies' Home Journal*, battled the New York City marriage bureau, fought to reconfigure abortion politics, publicly defended Valerie Solanas after the Andy Warhol shooting, and was recognized by the *New York Times* as feminism's "haute thinker."

Frances M. Beal (1940–) is a black feminist, anti-war activist, and journalist. During the civil rights movement she co-founded the Black Women's Liberation Committee of the Student Nonviolent Coordinating Committee, which later transformed into the intersectional socialist organization Third World Women's Alliance. She wrote a weekly column for the *San Francisco Bay View* and was associate editor of *The Black Scholar*, in addition to editing and contributing to numerous other publications. She has worked for the National Anti-Racist Organizing Committee and the Racial Justice Project of the ACLU of Northern California. Beal continues to write in Oakland, California.

Simone de Beauvoir (1908–86) was a French writer, intellectual, existentialist philosopher, political activist, feminist, and social theorist. She studied mathematics at Institut Catholique de Paris in 1925; a year later, she attended the Sorbonne University where she studied philosophy. She met Jean-Paul Sartre in 1929 and famously worked and lived alongside him for decades prior to his death in 1980. Her influential philosophical writings impacted generations of feminists, particularly *The Second Sex* (1949).

Bikini Kill was a feminist punk band active from 1990 to 1997 that helped start the Riot Grrrl movement of the 1990s. Founded by Kathleen Hanna (vocals), Tobi Vail (drums), Billy Karren (guitar), and Kathi Wilcox (bass), the group saw bands as an avenue for cultural resistance and sought to encourage women and girls to get involved in punk and build a feminist punk scene. They recorded and released a demo tape, two EPs, two LPs, and three singles.

Bitch and Animal is a rock duo consisting of musicians Bitch and Animal Prufrock, a queercore band that performed from 1995 to 2004. Incorporating elements of rap, funk, pop, folk, and spoken word, their music is defiant of gender stereotypes and musical subgenres. They started performing as an opening act for Ani DiFranco and later launched their own tours. Their albums include *What's That Smell, Sour Juice and Rhyme*, and *Eternally Hard*.

Black Lives Matter is a collective of black activists that was started in 2013 by Alicia Garza, Patrisse Cullors, and Opal Tometi in response to the acquittal of Trayvon Martin's murderer, George Zimmerman. The movement today is a member-based organization with over 40 chapters worldwide. Black Lives Matter identifies itself as "an ideological and political intervention where Black lives are systematically and intentionally targeted for demise. It is an affirmation of Black folks' humanity, our contributions to this society, and our resilience in the face of deadly oppression."

The Bloodsisters is a Montreal-based organization dedicated to combatting the stigma attached to menstruation. Founded in 1996 by Courtney Dailey and adee at Concordia University in Montreal, Bloodsisters has worked to fight against the corporate appropriation of menstrual care products using writings such as "Ax Tampax" and workshops like "Be Rad, Make a Pad." They also created their own zine, "Red Alert," before they disbanded in 2007.

Boyfunk is an anonymous writer who writes "for all queer boys who don't feel tied to the titanic waste that is the mainstream gay male community."

Bread and Puppet is a politically radical puppet theater based in Glover, Vermont. The theater was famous for its anti-Vietnam demonstrations, which employed huge puppets that became its calling card. Active since the 1960s and founded by Peter Schumann, the name comes from the theater's practice of sharing its own fresh bread with the audience in order to create community.

Elizabeth Broeder (1993–) is a Phoenix, AZ-based interdisciplinary artist, choreographer, and actor inspired by the working class, small-town drug trends, and Christian cowboy culture she grew up around. Her writing highlights the toxic channels people siphon their desires through and what coping looks like in the truck stop towns of Arizona.

The Combahee River Collective was a collective of Black American feminist women from Boston, MA, founded in 1974 by Demita Frazier, Beverly Smith, and Barbara Smith. The name comes from honoring the actions of Harriet Tubman, who led a campaign that freed more than 750 slaves at the Combahee River in South Carolina. The collective focused on criticizing the exclusion of black women from the mainstream feminist movement while also laying out how feminist politics should have the goal of liberating black women.

Jessa Crispin (1978–) is a feminist critic and writer, and was editor-in-chief of *Bookslut*, a literary blog and webzine founded in 2002. Her books include *The Dead Ladies Project* (2015), *Creative Tarot* (2016), and *Why I Am Not a Feminist: A Feminist Manifesto* (2017). She is a regular contributor to *The Baffler*, the *New York Times*, NPR, *The Guardian*, and the *Boston Review*.

Cybertwee is an American artist collective co-founded in 2014 by artists Gabriella Hillman, Violet Forest, and May Waver that explores the intersections of femininities, feelings, and technology with a focus on community and education. Some of their projects include the cybertwee manifesto, the cybertwee dark web handbook, and the shared memory emotional infiltration project.

Steven F. Dansky (1944–) is a Williamstown, MA-based writer, activist, documentarian, and photographer who was a member of the Gay Liberation Front (GLF) in New York City in 1969 after the Stonewall

Rebellion. He is the director of Outspoken Films, which released two full-length films, *From Trauma to Activism* (2017) and *Bookish: Reading the Queer Subject* (2019). He co-founded the project Outspoken: Oral Histories from LGBTQ Pioneers—an extensive collection of video-taped interviews accessible at the website, www.outspokenlgbtq. org, and at ONE: National Gay and Lesbian Archives. His photography has been exhibited in galleries and other venues and has been published in anthologies. He is a frequent essayist for the *Gay and Lesbian Review*, writing on subjects from camp to Malcolm X and Robert Mapplethorpe.

Agnes Denes (1931–) is a Hungarian-born conceptual artist now based in New York City who began exhibiting works in the 1960s and has since had over 400 exhibitions. Working with diverse mediums, from poetry and philosophy to lithograph photography and sculpture, her work explores sociopolitical issues. She is a pioneer of environmental art and a founder of conceptual art; her most well-known piece, *Wheatfield—A Confrontation* (1982), featured a two-acre wheat field in downtown Manhattan.

Ani DiFranco (1970–) was born in Buffalo, NY and is a poet, musician, songwriter, and activist. She founded Righteous Babe Records and supports many social and political movements through the Righteous Babe Foundation including abortion rights, LGBT visibility, anti-war movements, and progressive US political candidates who support these issues. She also performs benefit concerts for communities devastated by natural disasters and environmental catastrophes. She has won a Grammy award for her music in 2004 and has received the Woman of Courage Award at the National Organization for Women conference in New York in 2006. She was also a Woody Guthrie Award recipient as a voice of positive social change in 2009.

D.M.D. (1994–) is a Phoenix, AZ-based activist born in Seattle, WA. They received their B.A. in Women and Gender Studies at Arizona State University and was radicalized by experiences working in restaurants, particularly after being fired for encouraging fellow employees to discuss their wages. They travel the western United States exploring sustainable communities.

Betty Dodson (1929–) is a New York City–based writer and sex educator most famous for her publications on women's masturbation. She wrote *A Meditation on Selflove* in 1974 and *Sex for One* in 1987. She later wrote *Orgasms for Two* in 2002. She helped to pioneer the feminist pro-sex movement and has encouraged women to embrace masturbation, often in groups. In 2011 she received both the Public Service award from the Society for the Scientific Study of Sexuality and the Masters and Johnson Award from the Society for Sex Therapy and Research.

Andrea Dworkin (1946–2005) was an American radical feminist and writer, best known for her sharp criticism of pornography as a form of violence against women. Her books include *Woman Hating* (1974), *Pornography: Men Possessing Women* (1981), and *Intercourse* (1987). She worked with Catharine MacKinnon to develop a legal precedent for outlawing pornography.

Marie Edwards (1920–2009) was a psychologist who pioneered the concept of "singles pride" in the 1970s through writing and workshops. *The Challenge of Being Single*, written in 1974 and including the "Singles Manifesto," is her best-known work.

Eskalera Karakola is a performance collective based in Madrid, Spain, where feminists gather to organize for LGBT rights and against racism and domestic violence. The collective is now in Calle Embajador. The feminists of Eskalera Karakola publish the *Mujeres Preokupando* review and formerly published a zine called *It's Raining Dykes*.

VALIE EXPORT (1940–), born Waltraud Lehner, is an Austrian artist who began her career in the late 1960s in Vienna, Austria, after living in a convent until age 14. Working in film, photography, performance, sculpture, and computer animation, VALIE EXPORT is known for participating in Actionism. Her most famous feminist art pieces include *Action Pants: Genital Panic*, *Body Sign Action*, and *Touch Cinema* where she worked to incorporate the body and to reverse the male gaze.

Silvia Federici (1942–) is an Italian-American scholar, teacher, and activist from the radical Marxist tradition. She co-founded the

International Feminist Collective in 1972. She is a Professor Emerita and Teaching Fellow at Hofstra University and also worked as a teacher in Nigeria for many years. She co-founded the Committee for Academic Freedom in Africa and is a member of the Midnight Notes Collective. Her books include *Caliban and the Witch* (2004), *Revolution at Point Zero* (2012), *Witches, Witch Hunting, and Women* (2018), and *Reenchanting the World* (2018).

Feminists for Sex Workers is an international group that formed in honor of International Women's Day (March 8). The group is a collaboration between sex workers, feminists, and sex worker advocates that began in Europe and has now expanded throughout the world.

Shulamith Firestone (1945–2012) was born in Ontario, Canada, and grew up in St. Louis, MO. She was an activist in civil rights and anti-war movements as well as a well-known radical feminist who cofounded New York Radical Women, Redstockings, and New York Radical Feminists. She worked to understand the subordination of women and articulate strategies to overcome it by drawing on the insights of Marx and Freud to develop an analysis of women's oppression that included race and class.

Grimes (1988–) is the stage name of Claire Boucher, a Canadian musician and visual artist. As of 2019, Grimes has released four musical albums: *Halfaxa*, *Geidi Prime*, *Visions*, and *Art Angels*. Her music incorporates influences from various musical antecedents and contemporaries, notably drawing upon dream pop, electronic, R&B, and hip-hop.

E. Jane (1990–), is a conceptual artist and writer based in Philadelphia. Inspired by black liberation and womanist praxis, their work incorporates digital images, video, text, performance, sculpture, installation, and sound design. They have displayed performance, art, and soundworks in venues throughout North America and Europe. In 2015 they wrote the widely-circulated NOPE manifesto. In 2017, their performance persona MHYSA released her debut album *fantasii*. E. Jane's work explores safety, futurity, and how marginalized bodies maneuver popular media on and off the internet.

Joreen (aka Jo Freeman) (1945–) is an American feminist, political scientist, writer, and attorney. She first became active in organizations working for civil liberties as a student at the University of California, Berkeley, in the 1960s. An early organizer of the women's liberation movement, she founded the Westside group in 1967 and went on to earn a Ph.D. in political science from the University of Chicago in 1973. She taught at the State University of New York for four years and worked as a Brookings Institute Fellow. She continues to write about politics and the public sphere today.

Judy Freespirit (1963–2010), a lesbian feminist activist and an early architect of the fat liberation movement, joined the women's liberation movement in Los Angeles in 1970 and later published *Daddy's Girl* in 1982. She helped to form the Fat Underground with Sara Fishman, Lynn McAfee, and others.

The Gay Liberation Front was a group founded by Bob Mellors and Aubrey Walter, students at the London School of Economics, in October 1970. The group disbanded in 1973 but gave root to many subsequent gay rights groups and organizations in the 1980s and 1990s.

Lindsey German (1951–) is a British left-wing political activist, formerly a member of the Socialist Workers Party. Previously, she was an editor for the *Socialist Review*, and later founded the antiwar Stop the War Coalition for which she is now vice-president.

Emma Goldman (1869–1940) was an American anarchist writer, activist, and feminist. A Russian-Jewish immigrant to the United States, her writings and lectures advocating anticapitalism, free love, freedom of speech, and women's rights attracted wide audiences in North America and Europe. Goldman founded the anarchist journal *Mother Earth* and remained active throughout her lifetime in opposing the draft, supporting birth control, and promoting atheism. During her lifetime she was often described as "the most dangerous woman in America."

Peter Grey (1971–) is a writer and the co-founder of Scarlet Imprint. His books include *The Red Goddess* (2011), *Apocalyptic Witchcraft* (2016), and *Lucifer* (2016). His work seeks to place witchcraft in conversation with the context of a landscape suffering climate and ecological collapse.

Hacktivismo is an international group of artists, lawyers, human rights workers, and hackers that evolved out of the publishing and computer security group, THE CULT OF THE DEAD COW (cDc). The group endorses the view that privacy and access to information are basic human rights and backs the ethical positions of the Universal Declaration of Human Rights and the International Convention on Civil and Political Rights. The group supports the Free Software and open-source movements. Founded by Oxblood Ruffin in 1999, Hacktivismo's projects include Camera/Shy, The Six/Four System, ScatterChat, and XeroBank Browser.

Donna Haraway (1944–) is a feminist scholar focusing on science and technology studies. Haraway is a Distinguished Professor Emerita in the History of Consciousness and Feminist Studies departments at the University of California, Santa Cruz. In 2000, Haraway was awarded the highest honor given by the Society for Social Studies of Science for lifetime contributions to the field. She graduated from Yale University in 1970 with a Ph.D. in Biology and published "A Cyborg Manifesto" in 1985. She has written numerous books, including *Primate Visions* (1989), *Simians, Cyborgs, and Women* (1991), and *The Companion Species Manifesto* (2003).

Stefano Harney (1962–) is Professor of Strategic Management Education at Singapore Management University and co-founder of the School for Study, an ensemble teaching project. He employs autonomist and postcolonial theory in looking into issues associated with race, work, and social organization. Together with Tonika Sealy Thompson, he runs the curatorial project *Ground Provisions*. Recent books include: *The Undercommons: Fugitive Planning and Black Study* (co-authored with Fred Moten, 2013), *The Ends of Management* (co-authored with Tim Edkins, 2013); and *State Work: Public Administration and Mass Intellectuality* (2002). Harney lives and works in Singapore and Barbados.

Susan Hawthorne (1951–) is an Australian writer, poet, and publisher. She co-founded, along with Renate Klein, the independent feminist publishing company Spinifex Press. She has written extensively about ecology, radical feminism, economics, war, and international relations. This has led to numerous accolades, including the Audre Lorde Lesbian Poetry Prize and her work *Wild Politics*, which was included in the Australian Book Review's list of Best Books for 2002.

HAVOQ: Horizontal Alliance of Very (or Vaguely or Voraciously) Organized Queers is a collective that formed in 2007 as a contingent to the US/Mexico No Borders Camp in Calexico/Mexicali. They are a collective of queer people organizing together in the San Francisco Bay Area to resist the violence created by the border both in the Bay Area and in the borderlands.

Jenny Holzer (1950–) is an American neoconceptual artist based in Hoosick Falls, NY. Her work primarily focuses on the delivery of words and ideas in public spaces as well as large-scale installations such as advertising billboards, projections on buildings, and illuminated electronic displays. Working among other feminist artists like Barbara Kruger, Cindy Sherman, Sarah Charlesworth, and Louise Lawler, her work seeks to find explicitly feminist ways of imagining visual objects.

Lisa Hymas is the director of the climate and energy program at Media Matters for America. She previously worked as a senior editor for Grist.org, a website focused on environmental activism and climate change. Her articles have been featured in *The Guardian*, *Slate*, and *EcoWatch* among other publications. Her primary focuses are encouraging environmental activism, childfree living for the benefit of the environment, and climate change.

Mette Ingvartsen (1980–) is a Swedish choreographer and dancer who holds a Ph.D. in choreography from UNIARTS/Lunds University in Sweden. Her major works include Manual Focus, The Artificial Nature Series, and The Red Pieces. She established her company in 2003 and has shown her work throughout Europe, Australia, the United States, and Canada. Yes Manifesto is part of 50/50, which premiered in 2004 in Frankfurt, Germany.

Jill Johnston (1929–2010) was an American feminist author and cultural critic who wrote *Lesbian Nation* in 1973 and was a longtime writer for New York City's *Village Voice*. She was one of the first countercultural lesbian writers at *Ms.* magazine and a leader of the lesbian separatist movement of the 1970s. She made a career as a dance critic, a freelance artist, and a literary critic and was known for flamboyant and in-your-face lesbian feminist activism.

John Knoebel (1947–) was an active member of the Gay Liberation Front (GLF) beginning in November 1969 and participated in many demonstrations as well as the first Gay Pride March in June 1970. He co-founded the Effeminists, a group of gay men who opposed sexism. His writings have appeared in the GLF newspaper, *Come Out!*, and in numerous early gay liberation anthologies.

Emi Koyama (1975–) is a multi-issue social justice activist and writer synthesizing feminist, Asian, survivor, dyke, queer, sex worker, intersex, genderqueer, and crip politics, as these factors, while not a complete descriptor of who she is, have all impacted her life. Emi's work can be found at eminism.org.

Laboria Cuboniks is a xenofeminist collective established in 2014 that spread across five countries. It seeks to dismantle gender, destroy "the family," and do away with nature as a guarantor of inegalitarian political positions.

Linda La Rue was a black feminist writer and essayist best known for "The Black Movement and Women's Liberation," published in 1970.

Zoe Leonard (1961–) is a New York City–based artist who has based much of her work on the built environment of New York City. She became well-known internationally following her installation at Documenta IX in 1992. Over the past three decades, Leonard has produced work in photography and sculpture that has been celebrated for its lyrical observations of daily life. She has exhibited widely since the late 1980s, including exhibitions in 1993, 1994, and 2014 at the Whitney biennials. She has also recently had solo exhibitions at the Museum of Contemporary Art, Los Angeles (2018) and the Whitney Museum of American Art (2018).

The Lesbian Avengers began in New York City in 1992 as a direct action group focused on issues connected to lesbian survival and visibility. They refined media-savvy tactics, often visually arresting public actions, and touched a nerve with the Lesbian Avenger Manifesto. The group quickly spread worldwide after the Avengers organized a Dyke March for lesbian visibility on the eve of the Lesbian and Gay March on Washington in 1993 that mobilized 20,000 lesbians. Founded by Ana Simo, Sarah Schulman, Maxine Wolfe, Anne-Christine d'Adesky, Marie Honan, and Anne Maguire, the group has championed "out" grassroots activism and the training of new activists.

The Lesbian Mafia is an online collective that includes a website, podcast, and manifesto, all initiated by Sandi T., a lesbian writer based in New York City. They describe themselves as "a secret society of sexual terrorists and a very violent gang of fun native New Yorkers" who like "rants, fun, foul language, hijinks, political incorrectness, chaos, seriousness, special guests … This isn't NPR, bitches!"

Mina Loy (1882–1966) was born in London and later studied art in England and Germany. She enjoyed success as a painter in Paris before moving to Florence, Italy, where she began publishing poetry in magazines. She served as a volunteer nurse during World War I before moving to the United States in 1916 and joining the avant-garde movement as a feminist poet.

Fred Moten (1962–) is Professor of Performance Studies at New York University, where he teaches courses and conducts research in black studies, performance studies, poetics and literary theory. His books include *In the Break* (2003), *Hughson's Tavern* (2009), *B. Jenkins* (2010), *The Feel Trio* (2014), *The Little Edges* (2015), *The Service Porch* (2016), and *A Poetics of the Undercommons* (2016).

Ni Una Menos is a collective of Argentinian feminists agitating to end sexist violence and patriarchy. They first became active in 2015, protesting the practice of femicide and gendered violence, and situate themselves within a rich Argentinian legacy of resistance, drawing upon the example of the Mothers of the Plaza Mayo and indigenous, Afro-Latinx, and LGBTQ struggles. Ni Una Menos see themselves as part of a loose and multifaceted social movement, acting in solidarity with various social movements in Argentina. They agitate from the local to the international level, participating in direct actions such as strikes, protests, and marches.

Lucy E. Parsons (1853–1942) was a key figure in the radical labor movement of the United States. Seen as intensely radical, she advocated for anarchy, an eight-hour workday, the dismantling of capitalism, women's suffrage, the rights of homeless individuals, free speech, and violence as a means to combat growing class struggles and demand worker's rights. Parsons's parents were slaves with Native American, African American, and Mexican heritage. In 1871, she married Albert Parsons, a white ex-Confederate soldier turned political activist, and together they fled from Texas to Chicago due to threats of violence because of their interracial marriage and political involvement. She helped to found the International Working People's Association (IWPA) in 1883 and wrote for its journals *The Alarm* and *The Socialist*. She also gave public speeches and participated in numerous protests for which she was jailed. On November 11, 1887, her husband was executed for his involvement in the Haymarket Riot, which was largely considered to be a conspiracy. Following his death, Parsons went on to found the Industrial Workers of the World ("The Wobblies") in 1905, which quickly became one of the most powerful international labor unions in the world. She died in a house fire in 1942; upon her death, her writings were seized by the FBI and have yet to be released.

Kenneth Pitchford (1940–) was a founding member of the male feminist Effeminist Movement and a self-described gay husband of radical feminist Robin Morgan.

Nina Power (1978–) is a British cultural critic, social theorist, philosopher, and translator. She teaches philosophy at Roehampton University and is the author of *One-Dimensional Woman*. She contributes writing to a variety of journals and publications including *Radical Philosophy*, *Wire*, *The Guardian*, and *The Philosopher's Magazine*.

Paul B. Preciado (1970–) is a writer, philosopher, and curator whose work focuses on identity, gender, pornography, architecture, and sexuality, originally from Burgos, Spain. A mentee of Jacques Derrida, he received his M.A. in Philosophy and Gender Theory at the New

School for Social Research, and his Ph.D. in Philosophy and Theory of Architecture from Princeton University. He has worked as professor of Political History of the Body, Gender Theory, and History of Performance at Université Paris VIII and is currently Curator of Public Programs of documenta 14, Kassel and Athens. He wrote *Testo Junkie* in 2008 which documented his "slow transition" from female to male.

Radicalesbians was formed by a group of New York City women participating in the Gay Liberation Front (GLF) in reaction to the National Organization for Women's anti-lesbian comments. They first called themselves the "Lavender Menace" and took over the second Congress to United Women in New York City on May 1, 1970. The group originally included Martha Shelley (1943–), a feminist activist also active with the Daughters of Bilitis, Artemis March (aka March Hoffman), and Karla Jay (1947–), a distinguished professor emerita at Pace University. The group dissolved in 1971.

Radical Women is a socialist feminist activist organization that was founded in 1967 in Seattle, WA. Its past activism included antiwar demonstrations, anti-poverty programs, abortion rights efforts, and worker strikes. Radical Women is formally affiliated with the Freedom Socialist Party. Visit their website at www.radicalwomen.org.

Redstockings is a radical feminist group founded in 1969 in New York City by Ellen Willis and Shulamith Firestone after the dissolution of the New York Radical Women group. The Redstockings Manifesto, included in the 1970 *Sisterhood is Powerful* anthology, contained seven sections advocating for Consciousness Raising and "The Pro-Woman Line," the idea that women's submission to male supremacy was a conscious adaptation to their lack of power under patriarchy, and not the internalized brainwashing on the part of women. The Redstockings Manifesto was issued in New York City on July 7, 1969. It first appeared as a mimeographed flyer, designed for distribution at women's liberation events. The organization also holds the view that all men oppress women as a class and it is each individual man's responsibility to give up male supremacy, rather than women's responsibility to change themselves. The modern-day Redstockings organization is a grassroots activist think tank dedicated to defending and advancing the women's liberation agenda through the development of new understandings and improved strategies. Further information and other materials from the 1960s rebirth years of feminism is available from the Redstockings Women's Liberation Archives for Action at www.redstockings.org, or PO Box 744 Stuyvesant Station, New York, NY 10009.

Sara Roebuck (1992–) is a London-based writer and a graduate of the London School of Economics. Her interests include politics, feminism, and social justice.

Valentine de Saint-Point (1875–1953) was a prominent French artist and futurist, whose diverse writings addressed such varied topics as dance, theater, poetry, gender, philosophy, and politics. Saint-Point challenged the prevailing disdain for women that characterized much of the futurist movement and sought to define the role of new futurist woman. She rejected feminism but espoused a view of the total equality of the sexes. Saint-Point's futurist stance influenced her performance as a dancer as well as her radical philosophies, which were characterized by an emphasis on order, geometry, and logic. Much of Saint-Point's personal life remains obscure; Saint-Point used multiple names during her career and claimed various kinship ties.

Kathie Sarachild (formerly Amatniek) (1943–) is an American writer, activist, and radical feminist who led the Redstockings in 1969 in their disruption of the New York State Abortion Reform Hearing. She coined the phrase "Sisterhood is Powerful" and was one of four women who held the Women's Liberation banner at the Miss America Protest in 1968. A member of New York Radical Women, she played a leading role in the consciousness raising movement of the 1960s and 1970s and contributed as an author to *Feminist Revolution* (1975). She currently manages the Redstockings Women's Liberation Archive for Action and lives in both Gainesville, FL, and New York City.

Leanne Betasamosake Simpson (1971–) is an Indigenous Canadian writer, scholar, and musician. Simpson is known as a Michi Saagig Nishmaabeg scholar and musician whose work focuses on Indigenous issues in Canada. Simpson approaches her work from the intersections of politics, story, and song while using Nishmaabeg praxis and indigenous land based education, in order to examine Indigenous Canadian issues. Simpson is well known for her involvement in the 2012 Idle No More protests.

Sisters Reply was a black feminist collective comprised of Patricia Haden, Sue Rudolph, Joyce Hoyt, Rita Van Lew, Catherine Hoyt, and Patricia Robinson. Scholar Beverly Guy-Sheftall described these women as a "radical group of mostly poor black women from Mt. Vernon and New Rochelle, New York, whose writings appeared (without description of the authors) in early treatises on women's liberation."

Valerie Solanas (1936–88) was a radical thinker and writer best known for writing and self-publishing the *SCUM Manifesto,* which urged women to overthrow the government, eliminate the money system, institute complete automation, and eliminate the male sex. She also wrote a play, *Up Your Ass,* which has recently received attention for its wild gender-bending characters. In 1968, Solanas famously shot (but did not kill) artist and film director Andy Warhol, with whom she had worked on the film *I, a Man* in the years prior. Solanas was well-known among radical feminists and countercultural activists during her years in New York City in the 1960s and 1970s.

Claude Steiner (1935–2017) was a prominent psychiatrist who was born in France but relocated during World War II to Spain and then to Mexico. He came to the United States in 1952 and earned a Ph.D. in clinical psychology from the University of Michigan, Ann Arbor. He later founded the practice of Radical Psychiatry after he became disillusioned with the abuses of power in traditional psychiatric practice and in the framing of Vietnam veterans as individually "ill." He wrote for *The Radical Therapist* from 1970 to 1972 and later published numerous books including *Scripts People Live* (1974), *Emotional Literacy* (2003), and *Readings in Radical Psychiatry* (1975).

Susan Stenson (1960–) is a Canadian poet from Vancouver Island, where she teaches English and creative writing to high school students. She co-publishes the literary magazine *The Claremont Review* and taught previously at the Waterford Kamhlaba's United World College in Swaziland. She has published numerous books of poetry and several anthologies. Recent books include *Nobody Move* (2010) and *My Mother Agrees with the Dead* (2007).

subRosa is a self-described "reproducible cyberfeminist cell of cultural researchers who combine art, activism, and radical politics to explore and critique the intersections of digital information and biotechnologies in women's bodies, lives, and work." First founded in Pennsylvania in 1998, the collective is active internationally and has since created myriad pamphlets, articles, performance pieces and exhibitions.

Valerie Tarico (1960–) is a Seattle-based writer and private practice psychologist who focuses on religious fundamentalism, gender roles, and reproductive empowerment. She has written two books, *Trusting Doubt* (2010) and *Deas ... and Other Imaginings* (2011) and is a founding member of Resilient Generation and Progress Alliance of Washington.

Katie Tastrom (1981–) is a freelance writer-lawyer-crisis line worker-consultant-hyphenate enthusiast who lives in Syracuse, NY, with her four kids. She is a self-described "queer disabled fat femme mama" who has written about a number of subjects including feminism, bodies, and fatness.

Sojourner Truth (1797–1883) was born Isabella Baumfree, a former slave who became an outspoken advocate for abolition, temperance, and civil and women's rights in the 1800s. In 1826, she escaped from slavery to the home of an abolitionist family who bought her freedom, after which she moved to New York City and worked as a preacher. She joined other abolitionists and women's rights activists and began a lecture tour where she delivered her famous "Ain't I a Woman" speech (which appears here as "I Am as Strong as Any Man"), in which she challenged prevailing notions of racial and gender inferiority and inequality.

VNS Matrix is an Australian cyberfeminist media art collective formed in Adelaide in 1991 that is made up of Virginia Barrett, Julianne Pearce, Francesca da Rimini, and Josephine Starrs. From 1991 to 1997 the group presented installations and public art works in Australia and overseas, working with new media, photography, sound, and video to explore the relationship between women and technology. Inspired by Donna Haraway's "Cyborg Manifesto," they created a billboard with the text of "A Cyberfeminist Manifesto for the 21st Century" on it.

Elizabeth Wallace (1992–) is a Portland, Oregon–based writer who graduated from Arizona State University in May 2018 with a Master of Arts in Interdisciplinary Studies and a Bachelor of Arts in Women and Gender Studies. Her work focuses on everyday forms of women's resistance in relation to the body, the environment, and mental health; storytelling and poetry as a means of political action; and the power/ value system that measures women's labor.

McKenzie Wark (1961–) is a Professor of Culture and Media at the New School for Social Research. They are the author, among other things, of *A Hacker Manifesto*, *Gamer Theory*, *The Beach Beneath the Street*, and *Molecular Red*, as well as co-author, with Kathy Acker, of *I'm Very Into You: Correspondence 1995–1996*. They teach at Eugene Lang College and The New School in New York City.

W.I.T.C.H. (Women's International Terrorist Conspiracy from Hell) is a New York City–based radical feminist group founded in October 1968 by socialist feminists or "politicos" Robin Morgan, Peggy Dobbins, Judy Duffett, Cynthia Funk, Naomi Jaffe, and Florika. The group opposed the idea that radical feminists should only campaign against patriarchy alone. Instead, they argued that feminists should fight for a range of left-wing causes to bring about wider social change. The group was known for theatrical public actions such as hexing Wall Street in 1968 and protesting a bridal fair in 1969.

Zapatista Army of National Liberation (Zapatistas) is a guerrilla group in Mexico that was founded in 1983 in the Lancandon jungle in Chiapas, Mexico, initially as a self-defense unit defending Chiapas's Mayan people from eviction and encroachment on their land. At least one-third of all Zapatistas are women, and the group is largely auton-omous for government, justice, security, healthcare, and education. On January 1, 1994, the Zapatistas declared war on the Mexican gov-ernment by demanding work, land, housing, food, health, education, independence, liberty, democracy, justice, and peace.

Crystal Zaragoza (1993–) is a Phoenix-based activist and a queer first generation woman who grew up in a small agricultural town in North-ern California. Her parents migrated to the United States from Mexico to give their children opportunities they did not have. As a child, she saw her parents' health impacted negatively by sixteen-hour work-days in fields and their lack of medical care. She now organizes with LGBTQ+ undocumented communities of color to transform oppressive health systems and is currently the Health Justice Coordinator at Trans Queer Pueblo, a local organization in Phoenix, AZ, that works to empower trans and queer migrant/undocumented communities of color.

He-Yin Zhen (c. 1884–1920) was a pioneering Chinese anarcho-feminist and theorist. She founded the Women's Rights Recovery Association that criticized the traditional, capitalist, male social order in China and advocated for the liberation of women. She contributed prolifically to Chinese anarchist publications *Tianyee* and *Xin Shiji* and later in life taught at Peking University.

Sources

Bibliography

ACT UP. "Queers Read This." Queer Resources Directory. Accessed October 13, 2018. qrd.org.

adee (The Bloodsisters Project). "Ax Tampax Poem Feministo." In Chris Bobel, "Introduction." *New Blood: Third Wave Feminism and the Politics of Menstruation.* New Brunswick, NJ: Rutgers University Press, 2010. (Originally published in *Red Alert* 3, self-published zine, n.d.)

Amatniek, Kathie. "Funeral Oration for the Burial of Traditional Womanhood." In *Notes from the First Year*, 20–22. New York: New York Radical Women, 1968. (Speech given in Washington D.C. to the main assembly of the Jeannette Rankin Brigade, January 15, 1968.)

Anarchafeminist International. "Anarchafeminist Manifesto." Unpublished manuscript, 1982.

Anonymous. "#AltWoke Manifesto." *&&& Journal.* Published February 5, 2017. tripleampersand.org.

Atkinson, Ti-Grace. "Vaginal Orgasm as a Mass Hysterical Survival Response." Paper presented at the National Conference of the Medical Committee for Human Rights, Philadelphia, PA, April 5, 1968.

Beal, Frances M. "Double Jeopardy: To Be Black and Female." In *Black Woman's Manifesto*, 19–33. New York: Third World Women's Alliance, 1970.

de Beauvoir, Simone. "Manifesto of the 343." Translated by Rachel C. Accessed January 16, 2019. 343sluts.wordpress.com/.

Bikini Kill. "Riot Grrrl Manifesto." *Bikini Kill: Girl Power,* no. 2, 1991.

Black Lives Matter. "Black Lives Matter Platform." 2016. Accessed October 20, 2018. policy.m4bl.org.

Boyfunk. "Boyfunk Manifesto." 2002. QZAP Zine Archive. Accessed January 14, 2019. archive.qzap.org

Broeder, Elizabeth. "TRASHGiRRRRLLLZZZ: A Manifesto for Misfit ToYZ." Unpublished manuscript, 2016.

Combahee River Collective. "A Black Feminist Statement." In *Capitalist Patriarchy and the Case for Social Feminism,* ed. Zillah Eisenstein. New York: Monthly Review Press, 1979.

Crispin, Jessa. *Why I Am Not a Feminist: A Feminist Manifesto.* Brooklyn: Melville House, 2017.

Cuboniks, Laboria. "Xenofeminism: A Politics for Alienation." 2015. laboriacuboniks.net.

Dansky, Steven F., John Knoebel, and Kenneth Pitchford. "The Effeminist Manifesto." *The Expropriationist* (blog). 1973. theexpropriationist .wordpress.com.

Denes, Agnes. "A Manifesto." 1970. Accessed October 20, 2018. evo1.org.

D.M.D. "American Beasts." Unpublished manuscript, 2017.

Dodson, Betty. "Masturbation Manifesto." *POZ.* July 1, 1997. poz.com.

Dworkin, Andrea. *Intercourse.* New York: Free Press, 1987.

Edwards, Marie. *The Challenge of Being Single: For Divorced, Widowed, Separated and Never Married Men and Women.* New York: Signet, 1974.

Eskalera Karakola. "Manifesto for a New Feminist Presence." *It's Raining Dykes,* 8. November 2007.

EXPORT, VALIE. "Women's Art: A Manifesto." *Neues Forum,* no. 228, 1973: 47. Translation by Resina Haslinger.

EZLN. "Zapatista Women's Revolutionary Laws." *The Mexican Awakener (El Despertador Mexicano),* 1994.

Federici, Silvia. *Wages Against Housework.* Bristol: Power of Women Collective and the Falling Wall Press, 1974.

Feminists for Sex Workers. "Feminist Manifesto to Support the Rights of Sex Workers." Accessed January 14, 2019. feministsforsexworkers .com.

Firestone, Shulamith. *The Dialectic of Sex: The Case for Feminist Revolution.* New York: Morrow, 1970.

Freespirit, Judy, and Aldebaran. *Fat Liberation Manifesto.* Self-published, 1973.

Gay Liberation Front. "Gay Liberation Front Manifesto." Nottingham: Russell Press Ltd., 1971.

German, Lindsey, and Nina Power. "A Feminist Manifesto for the 21st Century." *Counterfire*. March 8, 2010. counterfire.org.

Goldman, Emma. "Anarchy and the Sex Question." 1896. In *Anarchy and the Sex Question: Essays on Women and Emancipation 1896–1926*, ed. Shawn P. Wilbur. Oakland, CA: PM Press, 2016.

Grey, Peter. "The Manifesto of Apocalyptic Witchcraft." In *Apocalyptic Witchcraft*. London: Scarlet Imprint, 2013.

Grimes. "I don't want to compromise my morals in order to make a living." April 23, 2013. *grimes-claireboucher* (blog). Accessed October 21, 2018. grimes-claireboucher.tumblr.com

Haden, Patricia, Sue Rudolph, Joyce Hoyt, Rita Van Lew, Catherine Hoyt, and Patricia Robinson. "The Sisters Reply." *Poor Black Women*. Boston: New England Free Press, 1968.

Haraway, Donna J. "A Cyborg Manifesto: Science, Technology and Socialist-Feminism in the Late Twentieth Century." New York: Routledge, 1991. Reprinted in Donna Haraway, *Manifestly Haraway*. Minneapolis: University of Minnesota Press, 2016.

Harney, Stefano, and Fred Moten. "The University and the Undercommons." In *The Undercommons: Fugitive Planning & Black Study*. Wivenhoe: Minor Compositions, 2013.

HAVOQ. "Undoing Borders: A Queer Manifesto." *undoingborders* (blog). April 2011. undoingborders.wordpress.com.

Hawthorne, Susan. "The Wild Poet's Manifesto." *Hecate* 38: 1&2, 2013, 42–46. (Originally published 2012.)

Hileman, Gabriella, Violet Forest, and May Waver. "the cybertwee manifesto." Cybertwee. 2014. cybertwee.net

Holzer, Jenny. *Truisms*. 1978–1987. Photostat. Museum of Modern Art. New York. moma.org.

Hymas, Lisa. "Say It Loud—I'm Childfree and I'm Proud." *Grist*. March 31, 2010. grist.org.

Ingvartsen, Mette. "Yes Manifesto". Mette Ingvartsen (website). 2004. metteingvartsen.net/.

E. Jane. "Nope." Self-published, 2016.

Johnston, Jill. "Do Approach." In *Town Bloody Hall*. Directed by D.A. Pennebaker. New York: Pennebaker Hegedus Films, 1979.

Joreen. "Bitch Manifesto." 1968. jofreeman.com.

Koyama, Emi. "The Transfeminist Manifesto." In *Catching a Wave: Reclaiming Feminism for the Twenty-First Century*, eds. Rory Dicker and Alison Piepmeier. Boston: Northeastern University Press, 2003. (Originally published 2001.)

La Rue, Linda. "The Black Movement and Women's Liberation." *The Black Scholar* 1: 7, 1970, 36–42.

Leonard, Zoe. "I Want a President." *LTTR*, no. 5, 1992. lttr.org.

Lesbian Avengers. "Dyke Manifesto." Queer Zine Archive Project. Accessed January 9, 2019. qzap.org.

Lesbian Mafia. "Manifesto." Lesbian Mafia (website). Accessed January 16, 2019. thelesbianmafia.com.

Loy, Mina. "The Feminist Manifesto." November 15, 1914. Mabel Dodge Luhan Papers. Box 62, folder 1658. Yale University, Beinecke Library Collection.

Ni Una Menos (Not One Less). "Call to Women's International Strike." Self-published, 2017.

Parsons, Lucy. "To Tramps, the Unemployed, the Disinherited, and Miserable." 1884. Internet Archive. archive.org/details/lucyparsonstotramps.

Preciado, Paul B. *Countersexual Manifesto*. New York: Columbia University Press, 2018.

Radicalesbians. *The Woman-Identified Woman*. Pittsburgh: Know, 1970.

Radical Women. *The Radical Women Manifesto: Socialist Feminist Theory, Program and Organizational Structure*. Seattle: Red Letter Press, 2001.

Redstockings. "Redstockings Manifesto." New York, July 7, 1969. redstockings.org.

Roebuck, Sara. "A Letter to the Man Who Tried to Rape Me." *Human Development Project* (blog). December 13, 2016. medium.com.

Ruffin, Oxblood. "Waging Peace on the Internet." *The Register—Biting the Hand That Feeds IT*. April 19, 2002. theregister.co.uk.

de Saint-Point, Valentine. "Futurist Manifesto of Lust." 1913. *E-Flux Conversations* (blog). Accessed January 16, 2019. conversations.e-flux.com.

Simpson, Leanne Betasamosake. "Not Murdered, Not Missing: Rebelling Against Colonial Gender Violence." *Leanne Betasamosake Simpson* (blog). 2014. leannesimpson.ca.

Solanas, Valerie. *SCUM Manifesto*. Self-published zine, 1977.

Steiner, Claude M. "Radical Psychiatry." In *Handbook of Innovative Psychotherapies*, ed. Raymond J. Corsini. New York: Wiley, 1985.

Stenson, Susan. "Occupy Menstruation." In *Gush: Menstrual Manifestos for*

Our Times, eds. Ariel Gordon, Rosanna Deerchild, and Tanis MacDonald. Calgary: Frontenac House, 2018.

subRosa. "Refugia: Manifesto for Becoming Autonomous Zones." In *Feminist Art Manifestos: An Anthology*, ed. Katy Deepwell. London: KT Press, 2014.

Tarico, Valerie. "Why I Am Pro-Abortion, Not Just Pro-Choice." *Valerie Tarico: Psychologist & Author* (blog). April 26, 2015. valerietarico.com.

Tastrom, Katie. "Pajama Femme Manifesto." *Medium*. November 18, 2018. medium.com.

Bread and Puppet Theater. "The WHY CHEAP ART? Manifesto." Accessed October 15, 2018. breadandpuppet.org.

Truth, Sojourner. "I Am as Strong as Any Man" Speech, Akron, OH, December 1851.

VNS Matrix. *Cyberfeminist Manifesto for the 21st Century*. 1991. *Net Art Anthology*. anthology.rhizome.org.

Wallace, Elizabeth. "The People Behind the Mop Buckets." Unpublished manuscript, 2015.

Wark, McKenzie. "A Hacker Manifesto (Version 4.0). subsol. 2004. subsol .c3.hu/subsol_2/contributors0/warktext.html.

W.I.T.C.H. "W.I.T.C.H. Manifesto." In *Sisterhood is Powerful: An Anthology of Writings from the Women's Liberation Movement*, ed. Robin Morgan. New York: Random House, 1970.

Zaragoza, Crystal. "Manifesto of the Erased: Mujeres, Decolonize El Dios Americano." Unpublished manuscript, 2015.

Zhen, He-Yin. "The Feminist Manifesto." Originally published in *Tianyi*, no. 1, June 10, 1907, 1–7. Signed He-Yin Zhen. Reprinted in Wan Shiguo, pp. 654–56. Translated by Meng Fan and Cynthia M. Roe; edited by Dorothy Ko from the Chinese original.

Discography

Bitch and Animal. "Pussy Manifesto." 1999. Track 10 on *What's That Smell?* Dive Deep Records. Compact disc.

DiFranco, Ani. "Grand Canyon." Performed by Ani DiFranco. MP3 audio track. Righteous Babe Records. Recorded Chicago, IL, January 17, 2004. anidifranco.bandcamp.com.